The Accountant's Guide to Professional Communication

Writing and Speaking the Language of Business

Melanie McKay / Elizabeth Rosa

CENGAGE
Learning

Australia • Brazil • Japan • Korea • Mexico • Singapore • Spain • United Kingdom • United States

CENGAGE
Learning™

The Accountant's Guide to Professional Communication: Writing and Speaking the Language of Business

Melanie McKay / Elizabeth Rosa

Executive Editor:
Michele Baird

Maureen Staudt

Michael Stranz

Project Development Editor:
Linda de Stefano

Senior Marketing Coordinators:
Sara Mercurio

Lindsay Shapiro

Production/Manufacturing Manager:
Donna M. Brown

PreMedia Services Supervisor:
Rebecca A. Walker

Rights & Permissions Specialist:
Kalina Hintz

Cover Image:
Getty Images*

ISBN-13: 978-0-324-53301-9

ISBN-10: 0-324-53301-2

Cengage Learning
5191 Natorp Boulevard
Mason, Ohio 45040
USA

Cengage Learning is a leading provider of customized learning solutions with office locations around the globe, including Singapore, the United Kingdom, Australia, Mexico, Brazil, and Japan. Locate your local office at:
international.cengage.com/region

Cengage Learning products are represented in Canada by Nelson Education, Ltd.

For your lifelong learning solutions, visit **custom.cengage.com**

Visit our corporate website at **cengage.com**

Printed in the United States of America

AU PARFAIT MAGICIEN

GEORGE M. ROSA

ABOUT THE AUTHORS

Melanie McKay is Director of Writing Across the Curriculum at Loyola University New Orleans, where she teaches in the English Department and leads workshops in business writing, legal writing, résumé writing, grammar, and writing from sources using the World Wide Web. She received her Ph.D. in English from Tulane University in 1982. Since the early 1980s, Professor McKay has had a practice as a training consultant in professional writing, working with accounting firms, financial institutions, corporations, government agencies, and other clients. She has published articles and made numerous presentations at academic conferences on the subject of professional writing. Professor McKay received Loyola's Student Alumni Association Award for Teaching in 1992; she was selected for Who's Who Among American Teachers in 1998.

Elizabeth Rosa is Associate Professor of Business in the field of accounting at Allentown College of St. Francis de Sales and has professional experience in public accounting and retail art gallery management. She holds an MBA from Lehigh University and the professional credentials of Certified Public Accountant and Certified Management Accountant. She teaches courses in financial, managerial, tax, and cost accounting, auditing, and communication skills for accountants. She has published a case study in *Accounting Information Systems,* Second Edition, by James A. Hall and authored the corresponding *Instructor's Manual* for the textbook. Professor Rosa has delivered several papers on the subject of professional communication in accountancy at academic and professional conferences.

PREFACE
ABOUT THE BOOK

The Accountant's Guide to Professional Communication gives a comprehensive, real-world look at the major forms of communication used by accounting professionals. In accordance with the AECC guidelines for enhancing accounting students' communication skills, the text teaches students to write and speak more effectively as preparation for entering the accounting profession. It tailors communication instruction specifically to the writing and speaking that accountants commonly do in the first five years on the job. Moreover, virtually all the examples and scenarios in the book are adapted from the actual communications of practicing accountants. The text, which was designed to teach itself, can be used independently in an accounting communication course or as a supplement to enhance any course covering financial reporting, managerial accounting, auditing, or tax accounting topics.

The book prepares students for actual communications as practicing accountants. This instruction can make students attractive job candidates, can reduce the training time and expense companies and firms routinely invest in new hires, and can help new accountants advance more quickly than others with weaker communication skills.

The text shows students that any communication event—a business letter, an oral presentation, a client proposal, a phone call—is grounded in the relationships linking the communicator, the audience, the reason for the communication, and the goal of the communication. By sensitizing students to these relationships, the text helps them develop a habit of thinking critically about their communications, reminding them to shape communications around what the audience needs to know and what specific purpose the communicator wants/needs to achieve. Thinking about audience and purpose helps students understand how to adopt a proper tone in their communications, when to define technical terms, how to organize communications for easy understanding, and more.

Objectives of the Book
- To make students aware of the kinds of communication that take place in the accounting profession.

- To help students improve their writing skills and begin to master the style of writing required in business and in the accounting profession in particular.

- To help students improve their oral communication skills and begin to master the style of oral communication required in business and in the accounting profession in particular.

- To teach accounting students to communicate with the wide variety of audiences they will encounter in their professional lives.

Key Features of the Book
The Accountant's Guide to Professional Communication is the only text in its field that is genuinely comprehensive. This text gives detailed attention to such important accounting topics as communication through annual reports, new product planning in a managerial accounting setting, financial statement auditing, and the conduct of corporate and individual tax engagements.

The book . . .

- Exposes students to the types of communication that take place in the real world because virtually every situation and example has been modeled on actual samples obtained from working accountants in all areas of the profession.

- Treats communication holistically, focusing on the rhetorical situation (communicator, audience, purpose, context) as the basis for *all* communications.

- Devotes two full chapters to written communication, using models drawn from accountants' correspondence (letters, memos, e-mail), reports, and proposals.

- Devotes two full chapters to the various types of oral communication, providing strategies for meetings, client interviews, and oral presentations.

- Includes detailed instruction in creating high-quality visual aids such as graphs and charts for presentations and reports and explains how to choose appropriate visual aids for presentations and documents.

- Presents "bad-to-good" samples and explanations of memos, letters, reports, proposals, visual aids, and speaking scenarios that show students what is wrong with a faulty communication and precisely how to correct it.

- Devotes a full chapter to collaborative communications (documents and oral presentations produced by groups); includes extensive worksheets and samples to walk students through each step of the collaborative writing process.

Chapter Features

Chapter One prepares students for the job search with instructions for researching the job market, writing résumés and cover letters, and handling themselves on job interviews.

Chapters Two and Three encourage a process approach to writing. The process approach teaches students that any writing task (and this can include preparation for oral communications as well) should be broken down into four steps: prewriting, drafting, revising, and editing. The four-step process approach can lessen resistance to writing because it breaks the writing task into manageable segments and helps writers identify where their problems are.

Chapters Four and Five provide detailed instruction in the basics of the written communications accountants use: letters, memos, e-mail, proposals, reports. The chapters show students how to adapt the general writing instruction they have already received to the audiences for whom accountants commonly write: corporate and individual clients, other accounting experts within firms and companies, non-accounting co-workers, and others.

Chapter Six provides detailed instruction in interviewing and conducting meetings. The chapter teaches students how to plan and conduct fact-finding interviews, an essential skill for most staff and senior accountants (particularly those working in audit and tax). It also teaches students how to prepare for, participate in, and lead the most common types of meetings in the accounting workplace.

Chapter Seven instructs students in the skills required to deliver effective oral presentations; extensive instruction is given in preparing visual aids. The chapter shows students how to represent financial information via tables, graphs, charts, and other visual support; it also explains how to plan, draft, and deliver oral presentations in small and large meetings.

Chapter Eight provides detailed instruction on collaborative communication projects. The chapter teaches students the basics of group process as well as strategies for producing documents and oral presentations with others. The chapter's step-by-step guidelines prepare students to work as part of a team, an essential skill in the "real-world" workplace where collaboration on important projects is the norm.

Chapter Nine shows students how companies combine accountants' work (financial statements) with that of other areas (legal, management, marketing), to communicate through the annual report.

Chapter Ten teaches students how managerial accountants can most effectively communicate when involved in cross-functional team projects, which are an increasingly important aspect of managerial accounting.

Chapter Eleven focuses on the communication involved in auditing and teaches students to write effective workpapers, interview documentation, and management comments.

Chapter Twelve introduces typical communications in tax practice and sensitizes students to liability issues in documents associated with tax engagements.

The Reference Guides on grammar, usage, punctuation, and formats for correspondence at the end of the book provide the most important rules in each of these areas and give students practical tips on how to communicate successfully on the job. The guides (marked by screened tabs for easy access) tell students everything they need to know about the rules of correctness. Cross-referencing in the text directs students to the reference guide material.

End-of-Chapter Material
The end-of-chapter exercises are grounded in actual scenarios that staff and senior accountants regularly encounter on the job. The chapters' exercises encourage students to think critically and rhetorically by requiring students to explain how revision techniques have improved a writing sample. Furthermore, the exercises ask students to put their analyses into practice by requiring them to revise weak writing and give students a start on the writing they will do as professionals by requiring them to write and revise on their own. Exercises throughout the reference guides give students a chance to practice skill-building in grammar, usage, punctuation, and document formatting.

Instructor's Manual
The *Instructor's Manual,* prepared by Professor Paula Irwin of Muhlenberg College, provides teaching tips and lecture outlines, suggested solutions for end-of-chapter exercises, and answers for grammar, usage, and punctuation exercises. The manual provides instructors with the tools they need to teach the material in class and to correct work assigned outside of class.

Accounting Web Site

The Dryden Press has collaborated with Eric Sandburg and Crystal Barkley Corporation to develop a Web site especially for accounting. The Web site contains a wealth of accounting resources and student exercises designed to aid instructors and students in obtaining company information and annual reports, current news, and links to SEC filings and stock quotes. These resources can be located at www.dryden.com/account.

ACKNOWLEDGMENTS

We wish to extend our special thanks to Professor Paula Irwin of Muhlenberg College for providing helpful insights on the manuscript, for writing end-of chapter exercises for chapters 1, 4-7, and 9-12, and for writing the *Instructor's Manual* that accompanies *The Accountant's Guide to Professional Communication.*

We also would like to thank the following accounting and finance professionals who were most generous of their time in contributing information about communication in accounting practice:

Major Contributors

Todd Crouthamel, *Kreischer Miller & Co.*

Francis Dougherty, *PricewaterhouseCoopers LLP*

Ryan Fox, *Deloitte & Touche LLP,* who also authored the end-of-chapter-11 *Wilco* case

Virginia Hamilton, *Deloitte & Touche LLP*

Peter Roland, *Bergey, Yoder, Sweeney, Witter, & Roland, P.C.*

Contributors

Bradley Albertson, *Bergey, Yoder, Sweeney, Witter, & Roland, P.C.*

Philip Barreca, *The Goldman Sachs Group, L.P.*

Kari Barton, *John Nuveen & Co., Inc.*

Wendy Bayley, *Lehigh Portland Cement Company*

Eric Bloesch, *PricewaterhouseCoopers LLP*

Keith Bloesch, *PricewaterhouseCoopers LLP*

William Burg, *Quantum Epitaxial Designs, Inc.*

Frank Chou, *Dean Witter Reynolds, Inc.*

James Ciminelli, *Bankers Trust Global Lending*

M. Scott Crocco, *Air Products and Chemicals, Inc.*

Edward Cunnally, *Aramark Corporation*

Charles Cunningham, *Penn Mutual Life Insurance*

Paul Dressler, *Dun & Bradstreet*

William Dwyer, *Allentown College of St. Francis de Sales*

Wayne Evans, *Air Products and Chemicals, Inc.*

Maggie Frantz, *Lehigh Portland Cement Company*

Mark Guerin, *Kreischer Miller & Co.*

Gayle Guzzardo, *John Nuveen & Co., Inc.*

Linda Hess, *Bergey, Yoder, Sweeney, Witter, & Roland, P.C.*

William Hicks, *Arthur Andersen LLP*

Julie Hines, *Pittsburgh Plate Glass*

Peg Hungerman, *Dun & Bradstreet*

Bonnie Sue Hunsicker, *E Squared Corporation*

Cynthia Hutton, *Hershey Foods Corporation*

Jeanina Jacobs, *Arthur Andersen LLP*

Marty Kanefsky, *Deloitte & Touche LLP*

Colleen Kraelich, *Quantum Epitaxial Designs, Inc.*

Paul La Rosa, *Entergy Corporation*

Joseph Leary, *J.P. Morgan*

Jerry Manbeck, *Just Born, Inc.*

Jared Markowicz, *Air Products and Chemicals, Inc.*

Amelia Maurizio, *SAP America*

Peter Mercer, *Coors Brewing Company*

Montine Moore, *Dun & Bradstreet*

Kathleen Mroz, *Bergey, Yoder, Sweeney, Witter, & Roland, P.C.*

Steven Robbins, *Lucent Technologies*

Ann Roy, *Entergy Corporation*
Peter Ruggiero, *Binney and Smith*
Deborah Shinn, *CoreStates Bank*
Richard Siderman, *Standard & Poor's Corporation*
Amy Smyth, *First Fidelity Bank, N.A.*

William Strehle, *Campbell Soup Company*
Mario Vicari, *Kreischer Miller & Co.*
Terry Waldersen, *Keebler Corporation*
Paula Williston, *McGinley Mills, Inc.*
Jean Wyer, *PricewaterhouseCoopers LLP*

We are indebted to the following colleagues, students, administrators, and communication professionals for their generous input and assistance throughout the project:

Julie Boone, *Loyola University New Orleans*
Ana Buitrago, *Loyola University New Orleans*
Dennis Dougherty, *Allentown College of St. Francis de Sales*
Jason Frederick, *Allentown College of St. Francis de Sales*
Janelle Ganci, *Allentown College of St. Francis de Sales*
Michael Keene, *University of Tennessee*
Kate Livingston, *University of New Mexico*
Catherine Long McDonald, *Air Products and Chemicals, Inc.*
Kevin McGovern, *Allentown College of St. Francis de Sales*

Vicki Nicklas, *Allentown College of St. Francis de Sales*
Lolita Paff, *Lehigh University*
Heather Plank, *Loyola University New Orleans*
Joyce Rhoads, *Allentown College of St. Francis de Sales*
Kasey Riley, *Lafayette College*
Philip Salamone, *Allentown College of St. Francis de Sales*
Jaime Sharrock, *Allentown College of St. Francis de Sales*
Lois Weber, *Spectrum Communications*

The following reviewers read parts of the manuscript of the book and made helpful suggestions for its improvement:

Jane Baird, *Mankato State University*
Sarah Ruth Brown, *University of North Alabama*
Lynette Chapman, *Southwest Texas State University*
Al Chen, *North Carolina State University*
Mickey Cowan, *East Central College*

Joseph Donalon, *University of Northern Colorado*
Tim Eaton, *Marquette University*
Anita Feller, *University of Illinois*
David Stout, *Villanova University*
George Violette, *University of Southern Maine*

We are grateful to the following members of our book team at Dryden Press, who worked ably and effectively to see the manuscript through the process of development, revision, and production.

Linda Blundell
Biatriz Chapa
Jessica Fiorillo
Christy Goldfinch
Jennifer Sheetz Langer
Anne Lesser
Mike Nichols

Mike Reynolds
Kimberly Samuels
Bill Schoof
Sara Tenney
Charles Watson
Lois West

And thank you to the Dryden sales people for their observations, suggestions, and future efforts.

Finally, a special word of thanks to Avia Morgan, whose support for our work on this book was invaluable, to Meredith and Jane Rosa for their laughter, to Keith and Nicole Wood for their on-going encouragement, and to Jason Berry for his unfailing patience, understanding, and moral support.

Melanie McKay
Elizabeth Rosa

July 1999

CONTENTS

Chapter 1 **Communication: Launching Your Accounting Career** 1

Introduction 1
Communication and the Job Search 3
Researching the Market 3
    College Placement Office 3
    Job Fairs 4
    Internships and Cooperative Education Programs 4
    Your Professors 4
    The World Wide Web 5
Preparing a Résumé 8
    Assessing Your Qualifications 8
    Drafting Your Résumé 12
    Adapting Your Résumé for Electronic Application and Storage 18
Writing Cover Letters 19
    Preparing to Write Cover Letters 20
    Drafting Your Cover Letter 24
Preparing for the Interview 25
Doing the Interview 27
Following Up After the Interview 28
Conclusion 30
Notes 31
Exercises 31

Chapter 2 **Communication and the Writing Process** 37

The Rhetorical Situation 37
    Speakers and Listeners 38
    Writers and Readers 38
The Four Steps of the Writing Process 40
    Prewriting 40
    Drafting 46
    Revising 48
    Editing 57
Conclusion 57
Notes 57
Exercises 57

Chapter 3 **Developing a Professional Communication Style** 67

Learning by Imitation 67
Formal versus Informal Style 67
Effective Communication Is Clear and Concise 69
Effective Communication Is Clear and Direct 73
Effective Communication Is Clear and Correct 78
    Vague Pronoun Reference 79
    Unclear Modifiers 79
    Mixed Sentence Constructions 80

Translating the Official Style   81
Putting It into Practice   84
Conclusion   85
Editing Checklist   86
Notes   86
Exercises   87

Chapter 4 **Written Communications: Letters and Memos**   **95**

Letters and Memos: Print Transmission and Electronic Mail   96
Principles of Business Correspondence   99
Organizing Memos, Letters, and E-Mail   107
    Create Context   107
    State Your Purpose   108
    Organize Information from Most to Least Important   109
    Develop One Idea per Paragraph   109
    Close by Summarizing/Asking for Action   113
    Special Cases   116
Conclusion   119
Notes   119
Exercises   119

Chapter 5 **Written Communications: Proposals and Reports**   **127**

Proposals   127
    Characteristic Features of Proposals   128
Reports   131
    Characteristic Features of Reports   135
Conclusion   149
Notes   149
Exercises   149

Chapter 6 **Oral Communications: Interviews and Meetings**   **163**

Speaking and Listening   164
    Feedback in Oral Communications   164
    Interpreting Nonverbal Feedback   165
    Cross-Cultural Factors   166
    Active Listening   167
Speaking and Listening in Interviews   168
    Planning the Interview   169
    Preparing Questions   170
    Conducting the Interview   173
Speaking and Listening in Meetings   179
    Types of Meetings   179
    Preparing to Participate in Meetings   181
    Preparing to Present Information in Meetings   182
    Preparing to Lead a Meeting   182
    Closing and Following Up Your Group Meeting   189
Notes   190
Exercises   191

Chapter 7 **Oral Communications: Presentations and Visual Support**   **197**

Oral Presentations in Meetings   197
    A Word About Stage Fright   199
Planning Your Presentation   199
    Analyzing Your Audience and Purpose   199
    Organizing Your Information   200
Drafting Your Presentation   200
    Introduction   200
    Preparing Visual Aids and Presentation Graphics   205
Creating Your Slide Show   230
    Rehearsing Your Presentation   235
    Delivering Your Presentation   237
Conclusion   238
Notes   238
Exercises   239

Chapter 8 **Collaborative Communication**   **245**

Technologies of Group Communication   245
Advantages of Collaborative Communication   247
Types of Collaborative Communication at Work   248
    Primary-Author Collaboration   248
    Multiauthor Collaboration   249
Effective Collaboration: Putting It into Practice   252
    The Structure of Groups   252
    Generating Ideas   253
    The Value of Conflict   253
    Planning the Project   255
Conclusion   273
Notes   273
Exercises   274

Chapter 9 **Communicating Financial Information:**
         Annual Reports and 10-Ks   **279**

Communicating Financial Information Through the 10-K Report   280
    Contents of the 10-K Report   280
    Disclaimer About "Forward-Looking Statements"   281
    Plain English Guidelines   285
The Relationship Between the 10-K Report and the Annual Report to Shareholders   285
    Contents of the Annual Report to Shareholders   285
Sample Annual Report to Shareholders: Gap Inc., 1997   286
    Introductory Overview   286
    Financial Review Section   291
    Financial Statements and Notes   299
    The Auditors' Reports   303
Preparation of the 10-K and the Annual Report   303
Conclusion   305
Notes   306
Exercises   307

Chapter 10 **Communication and Managerial Accounting**   **313**

The Accountant's Role in Corporate Planning and Control   314
    Strategic Planning   315
    Capital Expenditure Planning   315
    Budgeting   315
    Controlling: Variance Analysis   316
    Controlling: Capital Expenditure Postaudits   316
Management Accountants and Capital Expenditure Planning   316
New Product Development at Millenium Nutritional Supplements, Inc.   317
    The Cross-Functional Project Team   318
    The Initial Project Team Meeting   318
    The Managerial Accountant's Role on the Team   319
    Presentation of the Team's Recommendation to Management   324
    The Capital Expenditure Proposal   329
Conclusion   336
Notes   336
Exercises   337

Chapter 11 **Communication and Auditing**   **345**

Communication Events in the Audit Engagement   346
The Audit Engagement   350
The Audit Engagement Letter   350
The Audit Planning Meeting   350
The Audit Planning Memo   354
The Audit Program   357
Interviews with the Client   358
Writing for the Audit Workpapers   366
    Types of Workpaper Writing   367
    The Audit Workpaper Review Process   379
Management Comments and the Management Comment Letter   379
The Audit Report   384
Conclusion   385
Notes   386
Exercises   386

Chapter 12 **Communication and the Tax Engagement**   **399**

Communication Events in the Tax Engagement   401
A Corporate Tax Engagement   403
    Requests for Information   406
    Tax Research Memorandum   409
    Opinion Letter   415
    Transmitting the Completed Tax Returns   417
An Individual Tax Engagement   421
    Initial Meeting with the Client   424
    The Engagement Letter   428
    Transmitting the Completed Tax Returns   431
Conclusion   436
Notes   437
Exercises   437

Reference Guides

A. Grammar Reference Guide   A-1

Sentence Problems   A-1
    Clauses   A-1
    Summary: Sentence Structure   A-7
Grammar Problems   A-8
    Sentence Fragments   A-8
    Run-On Sentences and Comma Splices   A-10
    Mixed Constructions   A-10
    Incomplete Constructions   A-12
Exercises   A-12
Subject-Verb Agreement Problems   A-13
Pronoun Problems   A-15
    Errors in Case   A-16
    Shifts in Person   A-18
    Errors in Gender   A-19
    Errors in Number   A-19
    Broad Reference   A-20
    Ambiguous Reference   A-20
Exercises   A-20
Modifier Problems   A-21
Exercises   A-22

B. Usage Reference Guide   B-1

Word-Choice Problems   B-1
Capitalization   B-6
Gender Bias   B-7
Numerals versus Words   B-8
Exercises   B-8

C. Punctuation Reference Guide   C-1

The Comma   C-1
The Semicolon   C-3
The Colon   C-4
The Period   C-4
The Apostrophe   C-4
The Dash   C-5
The Hyphen   C-6
Parentheses   C-7
Quotation Marks   C-7
    Punctuation with Quotation Marks   C-7
The Ellipsis   C-8
Italics   C-8
Exercises   C-9

D. Formats Reference Guide   D-1

Memos   D-1
      Parts of the Heading   D-1
      Memo Text   D-2
Letters   D-3
      Elements of a Business Letter   D-4
      Business Letter Formats   D-7

Index   I-1

CHAPTER 1

Communication: Launching Your Accounting Career

INTRODUCTION

Accounting is the language of business, and one of the professional accountant's most important challenges is to interpret this language for others. In public and private accounting alike, accountants serve as key business advisers and problem solvers, helping clients in industry, government, the professions, and the nonprofit sector to understand financial information. Although they spend much of their time creating accounting systems, maintaining company records, analyzing financial data, preparing tax returns, and conducting audits, experienced accountants know that their work only begins with these activities. They know that accounting is an information business, in which the product is, to a certain extent, sold and success measured through effective communication skills.[1]

Research confirms the importance of communication skills in the accounting profession and in a successful practice. In a survey of recently promoted accounting partners in top firms, for example, communication skills were considered essential for promotion. In promotions from senior to manager, communication skills were rated second only to technical competence; in promotions from manager to partner, all partners surveyed considered communication skills the most decisive factor.[2]

The central position of communication skills in today's accounting workplace is underscored by the prominence of emerging communication technologies. In the 1998 list of top ten technologies, published annually by the American Institute of Certified Public Accountants (AICPA), communications-related technologies, such as intranets, electronic data processing, telecommunications, and virtual offices, filled most of the top ten spots.[3]

Communication skills are so important in accountancy, in fact, that the Accounting Education Change Commission (AECC) has mandated that students in that field "must possess [effective] communication skills to become successful professionals."[4] In a similar move, the AICPA has begun testing for writing skills on the CPA exam. Candidates for CPA licensure must now not only demonstrate subject knowledge but also show that they can organize ideas, express themselves concisely, choose words precisely, write clear sentences, use correct grammar and standard English, and write appropriately for intended readers.[5] And more and more employers, including some Big Five

> **N**ew communications technologies are truly making our business part of the global marketplace. Developing technologies make communications easier between two or more individuals anywhere in the world, seamlessly packaging and transmitting data, text, voice, and video messages. . . . A big part of tomorrow's CPA's job is communication. We will need to take advantage of every opportunity and every technology to communicate more effectively to maintain our importance to clients and employers.
>
> **Source:** Gregory H. Toman
> "Technology Trends and You"
> *The Ohio CPA Journal*
> December 1996

firms, have begun requiring writing samples as part of their interview and hiring processes.

This textbook will help you develop the communication skills you need to become a successful accounting professional. It will give you the tools to become a skilled professional writer, and it will provide guidelines for effective oral communications in daily speaking and listening, informal meetings, and formal presentations. You will learn how to do the following:

- Create a professional résumé and prepare for a job interview.
- Break down the writing process into a series of steps and master the skills appropriate to each step.
- Articulate your purpose and target your audience effectively in written and oral communications.
- Create an effective professional style that is correct, clear, concise, and coherent.
- Gather information through skillful interviewing and well-planned meetings.
- Make successful oral presentations, supported by professional-quality visual aids.
- Collaborate productively on writing projects and presentations.

Most importantly, this text will help you master the communications common to the major areas of accountancy, especially those associated with entry-level practice in public and private accounting.

To give you a foundation on which to build oral and written communication skills, Chapters 2 through 5 focus specifically on writing. Writing skills create a foundation for all communication because effective writing requires a keen understanding of the audience, purpose, and content of the messages you want to transmit. Learning to write well requires you to think critically about your options for expressing ideas and information, plan what you have to say, and present it in a way readers can easily understand. Mastering the principles of effective writing thus gives you a set of tools you can use whenever you are communicating with others, whether you are drafting a document, speaking on the phone, or delivering a formal presentation.

COMMUNICATION AND THE JOB SEARCH

The job search is a major turning point in the lives of most students. It marks the transition between student life and the so-called real world, between studying and training on the one hand and practicing a profession on the other. Although this transition can be intimidating, the writing and speaking skills you will learn from this text can help make it successful.

Job prospects for accounting graduates are bright. The U.S. Bureau of Labor Statistics predicts that accounting will be one of the ten fastest-growing industries in this decade and projects a 34% increase in job openings by 2005.[6] With growth comes increased competition, however. Landing the job you want will depend on your ability to distinguish yourself from others whose credentials may be as strong as your own.

Getting a job in a competitive environment depends on your ability to communicate to an employer your talents, accomplishments, knowledge, and potential. It requires persuasive, polished writing; effective listening; and poised, confident speaking. No matter how strong your technical knowledge, you are unlikely to impress those who make hiring decisions if you cannot communicate your competence. Although communication skills cannot compensate for poor academic performance or weak accounting skills, of course, they can give a qualified applicant an edge over others vying for the job.

The job search consists of these six steps:

1. Researching the market
2. Preparing a résumé
3. Writing cover letters
4. Preparing for the interview
5. Doing the interview
6. Following up after the interview

RESEARCHING THE MARKET

As an accounting student, you have many sources of job information. Investigate each one thoroughly.

College Placement Office

The placement office at your college or university is a rich source of information on career options, employment trends, internships, and jobs. Most placement offices maintain libraries with reference materials on local, national, and international career opportunities, salary scales in various industries, guidelines for writing résumés and cover letters, tips for effective interviewing, and other topics. Many employers send announcements of job openings to college placement offices; some arrange recruiting efforts through these offices as well. At large institutions, the School of Business, or even the Department of Accounting, may have a separate placement office.

Get to know your placement director and counselors. Ask them for advice on researching the job market. Make an appointment to have them review your résumé. Schedule time for mock job interviews. The reason colleges pay placement officers is to help you launch your career. Take advantage of this free service.

Job Fairs

Many universities and local chapters of professional accounting associations, such as state CPA institutes, the Institute of Management Accountants (IMA), the Institute of Internal Auditors (IIA), and others, sponsor job fairs to help students find employment. These fairs are one- or two-day events that bring in recruiters from corporations, firms, banks, nonprofits, government agencies, and other places to advertise available jobs and to recruit students. In large urban areas, job fairs often draw hundreds of recruiters. Smaller colleges and chapters of accounting associations occasionally sponsor job fairs in consortium with one another to draw large numbers as well.

Job fairs give you the chance to talk informally with potential employers, to present your résumé for possible openings, and to learn more about firms and companies. A job fair may be your first contact with your employer-to-be. If you plan to attend one of these events, dress in business attire, bring a number of résumés, and be prepared to ask intelligent questions about the employer and to answer questions about yourself (see later in this chapter for suggestions in these areas).

Internships and Cooperative Education Programs

Internships allow students to gain part-time experience while they are in school. Cooperative education programs generally require students to take time off from school to work for a quarter or a semester. Both types of programs offer students excellent opportunities to gain career-related experience before they enter the job market.

These programs give you the chance to meet working professionals who can help you in your job search. They also give you contacts at firms and companies where you may later want to work. For these reasons, consider internships and coop programs very seriously.

Your Professors

Professors of accounting often have wide networks of contacts. Many professors had successful careers as accountants themselves before they turned to teaching and remain in close touch with former colleagues. Others, who have gone straight from PhD programs into the classroom, are active in professional associations such as the AICPA and in state and local CPA societies and institutes, where they work on committees with practitioners. Make appointments with several of your professors and interview them about possible contacts at the firms or companies that interest you.

The World Wide Web

In addition to postings in placement offices, contacts through job fairs and internships, and referrals from your professors, you can find a wealth of employment information via the World Wide Web. Indeed, electronic media has revolutionized the job search process, making jobs easier to find and applications easier to submit than ever before. Most large employers now use the Web to recruit applicants, posting job openings through their own sites or through job advertisements in commercial employment sites. These Web sites not only provide information on employment opportunities but also allow applicants to submit résumés online. In addition, electronic applicant tracking systems are becoming more and more common, especially among Fortune 500 companies.[7] These systems scan job seekers' résumés into computer databanks and keep them active electronically for extended periods of time.

Information on electronic and scannable résumés is provided later in this chapter. For now, let us focus on the ways the Web can help you find job opportunities in accounting.

General Searches   If you are just beginning your job search or if you want a broad overview of opportunities in accounting, general search engines such as Yahoo!, Excite, Infoseek, and others are excellent sources of information. Each of these engines has a Jobs or Careers category, which links to one of many commercial employment sites on the Web. Employers pay the costs associated with advertising and recruiting through these sites, which are an excellent source of information about openings in various accounting specialties and geographical locations. Some sites, such as www.nationjob.com and www.monster.com, offer job seekers e-mail notification options, collecting information on all jobs that match an applicant's search criteria and sending announcements of those jobs to the applicant's e-mail address. (See Figure 1.1.) Remember, however, that each employment site you consult has different subscribers. To get a broad overview of opportunities, visit as many sites as you can.

Web Sites of Accounting Firms   If you have a more specific idea of what jobs you are seeking, you can find information through firm and company Web sites. For job openings in public accounting, use the Rutgers University accounting gateway at http://www.rutgers.edu/Accounting/raw/internet/prof.htm (see Figure 1.2). This megasite is a clearinghouse for much of the accounting information on the Web. It offers links to the Web sites of the Big Five, each of which recruits new employees electronically, and to sites of hundreds of other public accounting firms, many of which post job opportunities as well. The Big Five Web sites offer job seekers valuable help, explaining what qualities the firms are looking for in job applicants, offering advice on preparing résumés and providing templates for submitting them, and giving tips on preparing for interviews.

Web Sites of Companies   For jobs in private accounting, the Web search engines can help you locate job openings quickly and easily. If you know you

Figure 1.1

Monster.com's Job Search Web Site

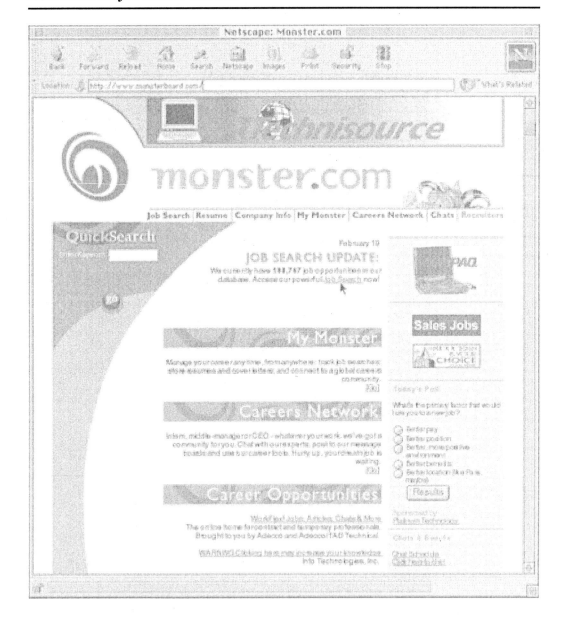

want to work for a certain company, use the Web to locate current openings in that company. Assume, for example, you are interested in conducting a Yahoo! search for accounting jobs at Dell Computer Corporation. Begin your search on the Yahoo! home page by category (Business and Economy). Yahoo! links you to a commercial employment site called CareerMosaic, which

Figure 1.2

Rutgers University's Gateway Web Site

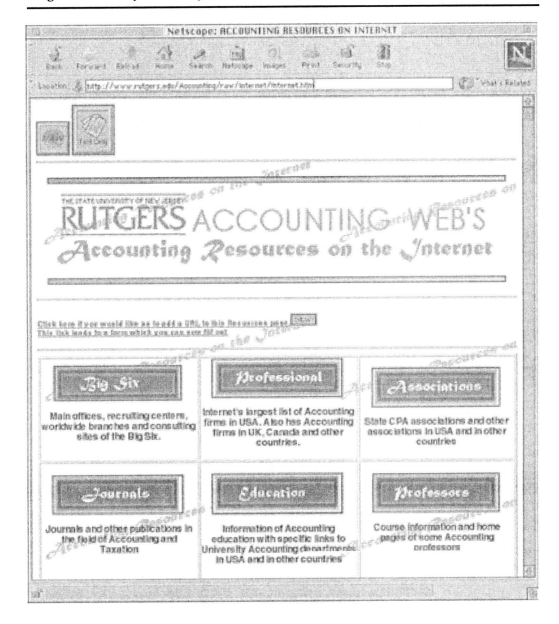

offers various ways of searching for openings (by company, by region, by field, etc.). The search choice "Employers" leads to an alphabetical listing of companies. A search of accounting openings at any company you choose can yield numerous options and job descriptions. Each search concludes in the opportunity to apply for the position online.

PREPARING A RÉSUMÉ

If you are seeking summer jobs or internships in accounting during your college years, you may need to prepare a résumé as early as your sophomore year. Definitely have a résumé ready by the end of your junior year; many firms and companies begin identifying job candidates in the spring of their junior year through calls to university accounting departments and placement offices. Most organizations begin actively recruiting at universities promptly at the beginning of students' senior year. If you have your résumé in hand at that point, you can concentrate on preparing for recruiting interviews that take place in the early fall.

Many people assume incorrectly that a résumé is a summary of qualifications which should lead to a job offer. On the contrary, a résumé is a sales instrument designed to get you an interview with a prospective employer. A good résumé sells the employer on the idea that you are worth talking to. Your communication skills, poise, interviewing savvy, knowledge, and experience do the rest.

Advice on résumé writing is widely available. Bookstores are full of how-to books on constructing winning résumés; college placement offices have guidebooks, samples, and, often, step-by-step instructions; numerous sites on the World Wide Web offer instructions, samples, and guidelines as well. In fact, so much information is available that it is easy to feel overwhelmed and confused.

There is no need to run to a professional résumé service, however. By using the suggestions in this chapter and consulting the samples here, you can produce a first-rate résumé.

Before you begin, remember: Your résumé is your first self-presentation to a prospective employer, and its purpose is to persuade. That is, the résumé should persuade the reader that you are the kind of person who will succeed at his or her firm or company. The résumé must do this persuading quickly: Experienced recruiters say that you have between 5 and 10 seconds to communicate these things during the initial screening of your résumé!

Assessing Your Qualifications

Whether you are planning to apply for a job online using an electronic résumé template, to prepare a scannable résumé for a job application, or to produce a traditional résumé to take to a job interview, begin by thinking carefully about those attributes employers want, about how your accomplishments and experience match them, and about how you can present these accomplishments and experience in the most persuasive way possible. Before you begin drafting, therefore, conduct a thorough self-assessment to ensure that your résumé presents all possible evidence of the attributes described here.

Employers look for certain characteristics in job applicants:

- Technical knowledge
- Communication skills

- Team spirit
- Motivation and work ethic
- Leadership
- Flexibility

Your résumé should show prospective employers that you are competent, hard-working, accomplished, and knowledgeable in your field; that you can communicate effectively; that you can handle several tasks at once and work well under pressure; and that you can work well with others when you need to and take charge when appropriate. If you are planning to take the CPA exam, your résumé should also indicate how close you are to completing your state's education requirements and when you plan to take the exam.

To prepare a résumé that highlights these attributes and facts, perform a careful and formal self-assessment of your strengths, your experience, and your accomplishments. Your self-assessment should be a review of all experience, education, and extracurricular activities that could demonstrate your suitability for a responsible job in accounting. Include nonaccounting experience as well as jobs and internships in the accounting field.

To begin your self-assessment, create a three-column worksheet like the one in Figure 1.3. This three-column structure will help you focus on what you have done, what it involved, and what desirable attributes it demonstrates.

Left column: List information about your education and academic achievements including the date of your graduation or anticipated graduation; the title and location of each paid job, internship, or volunteer position you have held along with dates (month, year); and any special skills you have acquired.

Center column: Elaborate on each item, describing it in more detail and explaining what duties were involved. For all work experience, try to describe what you did in terms of the skills you developed, and focus on the skills listed earlier—those that you know accounting employers are seeking. Be as specific as you can: If you handled a large number of accounts or worked for several people, list the numbers. Specific numbers help your reader visualize the workload. If your class rank compared favorably with that of others, say so; if your job performance was recognized as outstanding, make a note of that fact as well. In fact, if you made special contributions to any organization or distinguished yourself in any way, be sure to say so and explain in detail.

Third column: Explain how each item and description offers evidence of attributes that accounting firms or corporations value in their employees: technical knowledge, communication skills, team spirit, motivation, work ethic, leadership, and flexibility.

Fill in your worksheet as completely as you can. Brainstorm until you are satisfied that you have listed everything relevant to your professional goals: educational accomplishments, awards, honors, special recognitions; paid jobs, internships, volunteer work, offices in campus organizations, civic organizations, community groups. The information in each column will go on the résumé. You will use the information in column 3 again in your cover letter and later in your job interview. Therefore, thorough prewriting is worth the time it takes.

Figure 1.3

Sample Self-Assessment Worksheet for Résumé and Cover Letter

Brian T. Randolph

Experience	Description	Evidence Of . . .
Accounting major, Big Sky University. Grad May 2000 BBA and MACC (150-hour program).	Dean's List, 7 out of 10 semesters. 3.35 GPA in major.	Discipline, hard work, superior technical knowledge, communication skills.
Cum Laude grad.	Honor for GPA.	Ability to distinguish myself in competitive environment.
Financed 45% of college education through summer and part-time work.	Worked offshore Texas on oil rig (summers 96, 97); delivered pizzas part-time, school year 96, 97; waiter, school year 98; paid internship, Texas Instruments, June–September 1999.	Motivation, work ethic, teamwork, determination to achieve goals, initiative and flexibility; ability to juggle multiple responsibilities and perform at optimum level.
Internship, Texas Instruments, Dallas. June–September 1999 (paid, full-time).	Assisted in internal control audits; prepared financial analysis reports; processed three-month rolling forecasts; created spreadsheets for sales managers' performance analyses; examined revenue accounts in detail to detect troubled product areas. After summer internship, invited to work part-time during school year.	Experience in major responsibilities of corporate accounting. Ability to work as member of a professional team. Analytical skills; communication skills; efficiency in handling and managing information. Invitation to continue part-time shows outstanding performance of duties.
Internship, Brigsten & Lomax, Richmond, VA, a public accounting firm. June–August 1998.	Prepared federal, state, and local taxes for individuals and small businesses for supervisor review; developed spreadsheets to accumulate client information; prepared payroll taxes and monthly bank reconciliations; maintained depreciation schedules for assets for federal form 4562.	Experience in responsibilities of tax practice in public firm; communication skills with clients; flexibility in working with others.

Figure 1.3

Sample Self-Assessment Worksheet for Résumé and Cover Letter—*continued*

Certified Income Tax Assistant, January–April 1998. Volunteer Income Tax Assistance Program, Albany, TX.	Provided tax assistance to elderly and less fortunate by preparing their federal income tax returns under the VITA program sponsored by the IRS.	Community involvement, motivation to help others and to gain experience; interpersonal and communications skills; ability to juggle multiple responsibilities and maintain top academic performance.
Treasurer, Big Brothers of America, Albany, TX, 1996–present.	Prepare payroll schedules utilizing spreadsheet software, analyze expense accounts, pay monthly invoices, prepare nonprofit tax information returns, prepare quarterly budgets, and perform monthly cash flow analyses.	Community involvement, motivation to help others and to gain experience; ability to juggle multiple responsibilities and maintain top academic performance.
Student Affiliate, TX Society of Certified Public Accountants.	Attended monthly meetings and annual conferences; assisted with annual College Student Night events.	Commitment to involvement in professional activities.
Junior Achievement 1998–00. Albany, TX, area.	Volunteered to teach local elementary school students about the U.S. economic system through workshops. Taught state economics, management, production, marketing, advertising, and sales.	Team spirit. Ability to impart knowledge to others.
Junior Achievement Elementary School Program Volunteer of the Year, 1999.	Demonstrated ability to work well with others and to teach Junior Achievement subjects.	Team spirit. Ability to work well with others; communication skills.
Software: Microsoft Office Suite (Word, Excel, PowerPoint); Lotus; Harvard Graphics; Netscape Navigator.	Worked with integrated software (MS Office) to produce reports incorporating spread-sheets and graphics; with PowerPoint, produced support for business presentations. Used PageMill to create Web page for Brigsten and Lomax. Netscape WebBrowser for Net searches.	Competence with industry-standard applications.

Drafting Your Résumé

The method of application you choose should determine how your résumé looks. If you apply online from an electronic job posting, you will complete an electronic form (template) provided by the employer. The form structures your information, requiring you to place certain information in specified spaces. If you apply using a scannable résumé from which a computer will extract information, you will use techniques (discussed later) to maximize the number of computer hits your résumé will receive.

Even if you plan to apply via an electronic form or a scannable résumé, however, begin the drafting process by creating a traditional résumé, one that is concise, persuasive, and formatted on a single sheet of standard-sized paper. If your electronic application is successful, you will present a traditional résumé at the job interview; therefore, it should be the master document from which you generate all other types. And in many cases, employers still want traditional résumés as the first step in the application process.

Your résumé should have six components: a **heading,** a **career objective,** and sections on **education, experience, activities/awards,** and **skills.** The sample résumé in Figure 1.4 illustrates these components.

Let us consider each component in detail.

Heading   To draft your résumé, begin with a heading containing your personal information. This section, positioned at the top of the résumé, lets employers know how to get in touch with you. It lists your name (first, middle initial, last), your address(es) (home and campus, if different), and your phone number(s). Include your e-mail address if you check your e-mail regularly. Never put the word *résumé* in your heading.

Career Objective Statement   Career professionals disagree over the need for a job or career objective statement on a traditional résumé. Because traditional résumés are most often presented at the job interview, the position in question is already specified and a career objective statement is redundant. If you send a traditional résumé as part of a solicited job application—one for which a single, specific position has been advertised—an objective statement may be unnecessary.

A well-focused objective statement is important on electronic applications and scannable résumés, however. Online job postings often advertise a broad range of opportunities and frequently result in thousands of applications. Readers must be able to assign your application to the proper category when it is received. Whether you apply for such positions via an electronic application form or a scannable résumé, your stated job objective allows readers to categorize your application appropriately.

As you draft your master résumé, therefore, include a career objective statement at the beginning. Take care, however, to write an objective statement that serves the purpose. Many applicants' objective statements are so general that they waste the reader's time: "An interesting position in the accounting field" tells the reader nothing and identifies the writer as an applicant who has

Figure 1.4

Sample Résumé

Brian T. Randolph
btrando@aol.com

Home: 8412 Oak Hollow Drive   Campus: 131 Laguna Way
Richmond, VA 23173   Albany, TX 76430
(804) 282-7536   (254) 756-3901

OBJECTIVE
An entry-level position in corporate accounting requiring strong technical and communication skills.

EDUCATION
Big Sky University, Bachelor of Business Administration in Accounting and Master of Accountancy, May 2000. Overall GPA 3.35; Accounting GPA 3.6
Achievements: Cum Laude Graduate
Dean's List (7 out of 10 semesters)
Completed 150-hour requirement
Financed 45% of my education through summer and part-time work

EXPERIENCE
Accounting Intern
Texas Instruments, Inc., Dallas, TX, June–September 1999
Worked as member of internal control team; developed communication skills by interviewing clients and participating in meetings; prepared financial analysis reports; processed three-month rolling forecasts; assisted sales managers with performance analysis by creating spreadsheets; developed analytic skills in reviewing revenue accounts to detect troubled product areas.
Accounting Intern
Brigsten & Lomax, Richmond, VA, June–August 1998
Refined technical and communication skills by preparing federal, state, and local taxes for individual and small business clients; learned to manage client information on spreadsheets; developed flexible approach in working with small business payroll services; prepared monthly bank reconciliations; prepared asset depreciation schedules for federal Form 4562.
Certified Volunteer Income Tax Assistant
Volunteer Income Tax Assistance Program, Albany, TX, January–April 1998
Assisted elderly and less fortunate by preparing their federal income tax returns under the VITA program sponsored by the IRS. Developed client-service abilities.
Treasurer
Big Brothers of America, Albany, TX, 1996–present
Use accounting skills to serve community as member of volunteer team; prepare payroll schedules; analyze expense accounts; pay monthly invoices; prepare budgets; perform monthly cash flow analyses.

ACTIVITIES
Student Affiliate, Texas Society of Certified Public Accountants
Junior Achievement, 1998–00
   Elementary School Program Volunteer of the Year, 1999

SKILLS
Software: Microsoft Office Suite (Word, Excel, PowerPoint); Lotus; Harvard Graphics
Language: Competence in Spanish (reading, writing, speaking)

not thought carefully about personal career goals. To craft an effective job objective statement, use what some career counselors call the "three-statement/one-breath" rule: Identify (1) the position you are seeking in (2) the field you have targeted (3) making use of the skills you have to offer.

> **Example:** An entry-level position in international taxation that will utilize bilingual Spanish-English skills.

> **Example:** An entry-level audit position in a midsized firm needing individuals with strong communication skills.

Education   The first major section of the résumé should present your strongest qualifications—that is, your area of greatest accomplishment and achievement. If you consult résumé writing guides, you may see samples that place experience or even skills first, immediately beneath the objective statement. And some online application forms require job seekers to place experience information in this first position. This organization is fine for people who have been out of college for five years or more and have considerable work experience. For students just graduating from college, however, "education" should be the first category on the résumé (unless, of course, otherwise specified by a template). Even students like Brian, who have had solid internships and volunteer experience, do not have enough real-world work history to position the "experience" category first.

In the "education" section, list the college you attended or are attending and its location (unless the name makes that clear), the degree(s) you earned or will earn, the date or expected date of your graduation, and information on progress toward the 150-hour requirement (if required by the state in which you are applying). If you have attended more than one college, include only the school from which you received or will receive your degree. If you have attended a summer-, semester-, or year-long program abroad, however, include that information because it indicates experience of other cultures and may be of interest to employers with global practices. Similarly, if you have attended graduate school but did not complete a degree, include that information as well because it gives evidence of educational advancement. Do not include high school information.

Also list your major(s) and minor (if any), your grade-point averages (overall and in your major) if over 3.0, and any special recognitions or achievements you have earned while in school. In the sample résumé (Figure 1.4, p. 13), Brian lists under Achievements his graduation honor (cum laude) and his recognition on the Dean's List. He also includes here the facts that he has completed 150 hours and that he financed 45% of his education through summer and part-time work. Students whose awards or honors are associated with extracurricular rather than academic activities should list them in the last section of the résumé (Activities/Awards).

Experience   List all experience in reverse chronological order (starting with the most recent experience and working backward). The "experience" section shows prospective employers at a glance how you have prepared beyond the classroom for your career. The scope and variety of your experience will demonstrate the effort you put into career preparation while you were in school: A résumé with relevant summer work, internships, volunteer experience, relevant positions in service organizations, and the like creates a picture of a person with initiative and motivation to get ahead. Do not hesitate to list nonaccounting experience in this section, however. Many nonaccounting jobs provide valuable experience in communicating with others, working in teams, assuming leadership, managing time effectively, juggling multiple projects, and many other skills that employers seek in job candidates. The résumé in Figure 1.5 shows how to present such experience.

As we noted earlier, describe both accounting and nonaccounting work experience in terms of the skills employers seek. Instead of saying, "Worked in the controller's office at AT&T," describe what you did in terms of communication skills, teamwork, and other relevant skills: "Developed skills in cross-functional teamwork as an assistant to the budget development group at AT&T." For nonaccounting jobs, remember that many of the skills you developed are transferrable to the accounting workplace. If you were assistant manager at TGIFridays, say, "Learned to manage time, handle multiple responsibilities, and communicate effectively with co-workers and customers as assistant manager at TGIFriday's; supervised a wait staff of seven; was responsible for daily revenues of $3,000 to $6,000." By describing your experience in this way, you show potential employers not only what you did but also what you learned on the job.

Brian's résumé not only shows initiative in securing accounting employment but it also presents his experience in terms of skills. He has held two accounting internships (one in his hometown and one near his university). These internships have given him broad exposure to the profession because one was with a CPA firm and one with a large corporation. His certification from the IRS and volunteer work as a tax preparer reflect commitment to learning and to helping others. This volunteer work also demonstrates Brian's effort to develop communication skills by interviewing clients and discussing their taxes with them. Brian's service to the Big Brothers of America has given him experience with routine accounting duties, and, on top of all of his other activities, it demonstrates his willingness to make an extra effort for his community. Moreover, Brian has described his experience in terms of the skills he acquired in these positions to help prospective employers see the breadth of his abilities.

Activities This section of the résumé shows employers how you spend your free time. Here you should list extracurricular activities that are relevant to your career goals. Student memberships in business clubs or professional associations (such as Brian's affiliation with the Big Brothers and his work with Junior Achievement) should be included here. Include relevant offices held in service organizations (treasurer of social fraternities or sororities, for example) as well as any tutoring you have done while in college (in accounting or other business courses, computer technology, or writing, for example).

Opinion is divided on the inclusion of hobbies and sports activities. Some employers are put off by listings of such information. Others believe that

Figure 1.5

Sample Résumé—Traditional—Palatino Type

Allison K. Beckle
532 Holly Oak Drive
Bethlehem, PA 18015
(610) 555-3761
akbeck@hotmail.com

OBJECTIVE
An entry-level position in public accounting requiring strong technical and computer skills.

EDUCATION
Keystone State University, Bachelor of Science in Accounting. May 2000
Overall GPA 3.0
Accounting GPA 3.25
Achievements: Dean's List (5 semesters)

EXPERIENCE
Accounting Intern, Oglesby & Nash, P.C., Easton, PA, June–September 1999
Worked with audit team in audits of local high schools; interviewed clients about internal control testing; conducted cut-off and cash procedures for various bank accounts; tested employees in the payroll fund for proper coding, valuation, and Act 72 clearance; prepared reconciliations of bank statements and other accounts.
Accounting Intern, Ingersoll-Rand, Bethlehem, PA, Spring semester, 1999
Developed skills in accounting information systems by working on accounts payable processes in computerized control system. Enhanced technical skills by preparing bank, inventory, and vendor reconciliations and by compiling expense reports.
Front Desk Clerk, Comfort Inn, Bethlehem, PA, June–August 1998
Developed time management, customer service, and communication skills by working as night desk clerk at busy motel. Processed check-ins, wake-up calls, special requests, reservations, early-bird computer check-outs for an average of 75 guests an evening.

ACTIVITIES
Peer Tutor for computer science and economics courses
Member of the Business Club

SKILLS
Software: WordPerfect, Lotus, Quicken, Asset Keeper, Pro Series, Quattro Pro, Turbo Tax, Excel, PowerPoint, MS Word.

participation in fitness activities and team sports shows that you have experience with teamwork and know how to balance work and play. As you tailor each résumé for a specific employer, consult with your professors and your college placement office on this question. They may have experience with specific employers that can help you make this judgment call.

Skills   This final section lets an employer know your level of competence with basic workplace tools. The most frequent skills listed are computer applications skills. Knowing whether you are proficient with industry-standard software helps an employer predict how much training you will need if you are hired. In today's increasingly global workplace, foreign language skills are also highly desirable in job applicants. If you have such skills, be sure to list them. Do so in such a way that accurately describes your proficiency level, however. If you are fluent in a foreign language, say so. If you can get around in a foreign country, read the newspaper without much help, and write a letter in the language, say you are competent. If you can read fairly well but cannot speak well enough to be confident in the language, say you possess a "reading knowledge" of the language. Do not exaggerate your linguistic skills. Not only would exaggeration be dishonest, but you never know when your interviewer will be fluent in the language you have listed!

Revising Your Résumé   When you have completed drafting, you may need to revise to fit all of your information on one page or to format your material for easy reading. Remember: Career professionals almost unanimously advise entry-level job seekers to limit résumés to a single page. If you have a lot of information, choose a compact font such as Times or Times New Roman. If your résumé is a bit sketchy, choose a larger font such as Palatino or New Century Schoolbook. You can get away with 11-point type rather than the standard 12 point if you need to shrink your résumé a bit, but any font smaller than 11 point will be hard to read and is not recommended. (The résumés in Figures 1.4 and 1.5 were reduced to fit on their pages.) Another way to adapt your material effectively to the one-page requirement is to make use of the full width of the page to lay out your material. Your résumé should be laser printed on 100% rag bond, white or ivory only. It should be error free.

The sample résumé in Figure 1.5 contains less information than the résumé in Figure 1.4, but it fills a page nicely. This résumé is set in Palatino type, which is large and readable. (The one in Figure 1.4 is set in Times New Roman type.) The section headings begin flush left, but the entries are indented throughout. This format creates a good deal of white space, which makes for easy reading and stretches the information to fill a page completely. Notice that this résumé contains information about nonaccounting employment, described in terms of transferable business skills.

Proofreading and Editing Your Résumé   When you have revised your résumé to your satisfaction, proofread it diligently, ask others to proofread it too, and edit to correct all errors. Typos and grammar errors in a résumé are a sign of carelessness and suggest that other work you produce might be careless as well. Check your style: Is it concise, clear, and direct? Then check for parallel structure and usage. (Consult Chapter 3 for assistance with these checks.) Your descriptions should consistently use the simple past tense of the verb *(performed, provided)* unless you are listing present or continuing employment. In that case you should use the present tense (note that in Figure 1.4, Brian's ongoing work as treasurer for his church is described in the present tense). If you have separated items with commas in your lists detailing experience, activities, and skills, make sure your use is consistent. If you have used semicolons, make sure you have used semicolons throughout. Make sure you have used proper postal codes for the names of any states you have abbreviated, and double-check the phone numbers you have listed for transposed numbers or other errors.

Reference Sheet After you have completed your résumé, prepare a reference sheet that you can send to a prospective employer on request. The reference sheet lists those people who know your work and are willing to answer inquiries about you. Listings should include names of your references with their titles, their organizations, their addresses, and current office phone numbers. Be sure to ask all references for permission to use their names before including them on your list. Also, send each reference person a copy of your résumé.

Plan to take a copy of your traditional résumé and your reference sheet to the job interview. Figure 1.6 illustrates Brian's reference sheet.

Adapting Your Résumé for Electronic Application and Storage

As we noted earlier, many employers who advertise jobs on the Web request that you apply online using electronic résumé templates. To modify your traditional résumé for electronic application, simply copy and paste information from your master résumé into the spaces provided on the form. If the form contains blanks that do not apply to you, skip them and go to the next category. Be sure to place information about your activities, awards, and skills in the final box. When you have finished filling in the form, check the information carefully. Then click on "Submit" to send your résumé.

Other employers request scannable résumés—résumés that can be read by computers equipped with Optical Character Recognition (OCR) software and maintained in résumé tracking systems. These systems help employers sort through large numbers of applications because the computer searches for applicants whose skills and experience match employers' needs. The computer searches are based on key words (usually nouns) that the software recognizes; therefore, modify the language of your résumé to ensure as many computer hits as possible. Where possible, convert verbs to nouns (change "responsible for *writing*" to "worked as *writer*"; change "*reconciled* balances" to "performed *reconcilations*") even though this conversion may complicate your style.

The Web site of Resumix, a leading résumé software system, offers useful guidelines for producing scannable résumés (see Figure 1.7).

Resumix suggests preparing one résumé for the computer (to send by fax or e-mail) and another, with attractive layout, typography, and style, to take to the job interview.

Figure 1.6

Sample Reference Sheet

References

Brian T. Randolph
131 Laguna Way
Albany, TX 76430
btrando@aol.com

Dr. Margaret Langston
Professor of Accounting
Big Sky University
Dept. of Accounting and
Business Law
P.O. Box 98002
Albany, TX 76430-8002
(972) 995-6000

Mr. Armin Barraclough
Assistant Controller
Texas Instruments, Inc.
P.O. Box 655474
Dallas, TX 75265
(254) 755-1111, Ext. 1234

Mr. Daniel Linley
Partner
Brigsten & Lomax, PC
74282 Forest Hill Avenue
Richmond, VA 23225
(804) 560-6927

Mr. Byron Foreman
Big Brothers of Albany
P.O. Box 34398
Albany, TX 76430
(254) 776-8244

WRITING COVER LETTERS

Traditional résumés are always sent to employers with cover letters that highlight the applicant's unique qualifications for the job. In a 1996 survey, 60% of the executives surveyed considered cover letters as important as résumés in the job search.[8] As electronic résumé tracking systems become more common, however, the importance of cover letters may diminish. In one study of employers using electronic résumé tracking systems, a majority did not retain cover letters in their databases.[9] Some online applications include a field for a "cover letter" or "brief message" to accompany the electronic résumé; others do not. Use your judgment, but wherever possible, send a cover letter with your résumé. It offers you one more opportunity to promote yourself.

Cover letters should be brief and follow standard formats for professional correspondence. They should be printed on the same 100% rag bond as your résumé, if you are submitting a traditional application. The guidelines in the next section will help you draft cover letters that do the job well.

Figure 1.7

Resumix's Online Résumé Tips

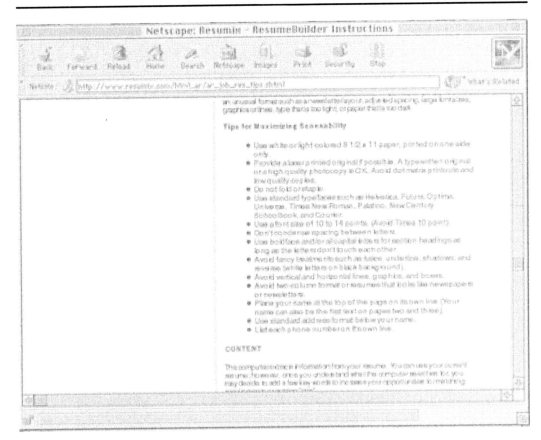

Preparing to Write Cover Letters

Prepare to write your cover letter by gathering information about the position and about the firm or company to which you are applying. Always make every effort to determine who is in charge of hiring at the firm or company, and address your cover letter to that person by name and title. If you cannot find out the individual's name, use the appropriate title ("Dear Human Resources Director") or address the letter to the appropriate committee ("Dear Personnel Committee"). Do *not* write "To Whom It May Concern" salutations.

Cover letters should not rehash your résumé. Instead they should achieve these three purposes (plan to devote a paragraph to each one):

1. Identify whether your application is solicited or unsolicited;
2. Explain how your qualifications fit the position for which you are applying; and
3. Ask for an interview.

Figure 1.7

Resumix's Online Résumé Tips—*continued*

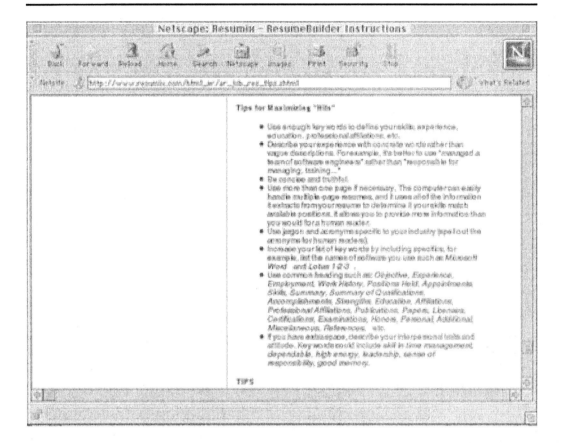

Paragraph 1: Solicited vs. unsolicited applications. When employers open letters of application, the first thing they want to know is whether you are responding to a solicitation they have made for applicants or writing to inquire about job possibilities.

As we noted earlier in this chapter, most employers solicit applications for entry-level jobs through word of mouth, position announcements in newspapers, and job postings on university campuses. Many firms and corporations also recruit entry-level applicants at job fairs and recruiting sessions on campuses. Still others, including the Big Five firms, invite applications through their home pages on the World Wide Web.

Explaining the source of your application is the way you provide context and purpose in a cover letter. Along with the career objective statement on your résumé, the explanation helps your reader categorize your inquiry. The first paragraph of your cover letter should indicate the position for which you are applying and where you learned of the position (if solicited).

Example:

Dear Ms. Walshok:

Please consider my application for one of the entry-level staff positions your firm recently advertised at the Central Valley Job Fair.

If someone with whom the reader is acquainted (a professor, a colleague, a business connection) has suggested that you apply, be sure to say so in the first or second sentence. If you have had an internship at the firm or company and have been invited to apply for a full-time position, make this fact clear in the first paragraph as well.

Example:

Dear Mr. Villani:

Please accept this application for the position of staff accountant at Texas Instruments. After my summer internship in the controller's office last year, Mr. Armin Barraclough, assistant controller, suggested I seek full-time employment with the company.

If your application is unsolicited, explain that you are interested in a position should one be available:

Example:

Dear Mr. Honeywell:

I am writing to apply for an entry-level audit position with your firm should such an opening exist.

Paragraph 2: Your qualifications for the position. The body of the cover letter should show the reader what you can bring to the job that will make you an asset to the organization. Achieving this purpose can be a bit tricky for students just entering the job market. Whereas experienced professionals seeking new jobs can point to their accomplishments in similar positions, few accounting students have a professional track record when they graduate from college. In preparing cover letters for entry-level positions, therefore, you need to show that despite limited experience, you have the attributes that will make you a valuable employee. To do so, think about the attributes employers seek in new accountants and provide evidence—from concrete experience—that you possess them.

Remember: Most employers look for the following qualities in applicants:

- Technical knowledge
- Communication skills
- Team spirit
- Motivation and work ethic
- Leadership
- Flexibility

Many applicants assume that the experience listed on their résumés provides sufficient evidence of the attributes just listed. These people make the mistake of simply restating information from the résumé in the cover letter. Such repetition wastes the reader's time and renders the résumé redundant. Instead of restating experience from the résumé, use the cover letter to explain what positive qualities your experience exemplifies.

> **Wrong:** I worked as an accounting intern last summer at Del Rios Engineering in Madrid, Spain.

> **Corrected:** My internship at Del Rios Engineering in Madrid, Spain, gave me valuable experience in cross-cultural business practices as well as a grounding in international corporate accounting.

Whereas the first sentence in this example merely repeats a fact from the résumé, the revised sentence refers to that fact as an example of the job applicant's technical knowledge.

To draft the body of the cover letter, review the self-assessment worksheet you used to create your résumé. Select the two or three items that best exemplify the qualities you want to emphasize and condense each entry into a sentence or two. The worksheet in Figure 1.3 (pp. 10–11) might yield the following paragraphs:

> **Example:**

> At Big Sky University, I maintained a strong academic record while working 20 hours per week or more; this record illustrates my commitment to the work ethic, my determination to achieve my goals, and my ability to handle multiple tasks effectively.

> My strong academic performance also attests to my professional communication skills because the accounting program at Big Sky is communications-intensive throughout the curriculum.

> I was able to build on this academic foundation through an internship that gave me valuable practical experience in corporate accounting.

These sentences will form the backbone of your second paragraph.

Paragraph 3: Asking for an interview. Conclude your cover letter by politely asking for an interview and explaining how you can be reached to set one up. Although you have listed your address(es), phone number(s) and, perhaps, your e-mail address on your résumé, use your cover letter to explain any unusual circumstances or details the reader may need to be able to contact you. If you are applying for a job in another city, for example, and plan to be there on a certain date, your cover letter should communicate that information. If you are frequently away from your phone and want prospective employers to leave voice mail messages for you, say so in closing. Do not forget, of course, to close with thanks.

> **Example:** I will be in the Chicago area during the week of June 10 and would welcome the chance to talk with you about the position at that time. If you

would like to arrange an interview, please call me at (209) 432-8967. Thank you for your consideration.

Example: I would like to present my qualifications to you in person. I will call you in a week or two to see if an interview is possible. In the meantime, I can be reached at (254) 756-3901. Thank you for considering my application.

Drafting Your Cover Letter

Assemble the elements you have generated in your prewriting, adding transitions and details as necessary (see Figure 1.8).

When you are satisfied with your cover letter, sign it, attach it to your résumé with a paper clip, and mail the application in a No. 10 (standard size)

Figure 1.8

Sample Cover Letter

LETTER

Dear Mr. Villani:

Please accept this application for the position of staff accountant at Texas Instruments. After my summer internship in the controller's office last year, Mr. Armin Barraclough, assistant controller, suggested that I seek full-time employment with the company.

As a fifth-year accounting major at Big Sky University, I have consistently maintained a superior academic record while working 20 hours per week or more. This record illustrates my commitment to the work ethic, my determination to achieve my goals, and my ability to handle multiple tasks effectively. Big Sky, whose accounting major is communications-intensive, has afforded me the chance to develop strong communication skills as well as solid technical expertise in the fundamentals of accounting. The internship last summer allowed me to build on this academic foundation while gaining valuable practical experience in corporate accounting.

I would like to present my qualifications to you in person and will call your office in a week or two to see if an interview is possible. In the meantime, I can be reached by phone at (254) 756-3901. Thank you for considering my application.

Sincerely,

Brian T. Randolph

envelope. If you are applying online, copy and paste your letter into the designated field.

An important reminder: During the job search, employers will be calling you at the phone numbers you have provided. You must plan to accept these calls in a businesslike manner. If you have a creative, humorous, or otherwise unconventional message on your answering machine or voice mail, change it. If you live with roommates or family members, explain to them how you want them to handle calls from potential employers. Always return calls promptly.

If you have not heard from an employer within four weeks after submitting an application, it is appropriate to call and inquire about the status of your application.

PREPARING FOR THE INTERVIEW

Employers hire people who can show they have done their homework, so prepare thoroughly for your interview. Here are some suggestions:

- Gather information about the firm or company and study it carefully. You will want to show in your interview that you understand the organization's priorities, its strategic direction, its main practice areas, its client base, its emerging markets, its positioning among the competition, and so forth. The organization's annual report can provide this information. Check the World Wide Web to see whether the firm or company maintains a Web site. If no annual report or Web site exists, consult the organization's brochures and any other literature you can acquire.
- Research the company and its industry by reading articles in business publications, professional journals, magazines, and newspapers.
- Talk with faculty and placement counselors about the firm or company. Ask about the organization's strengths, about practice trends, and about alumni who have been hired in the last few years.
- If possible, attend presentations sponsored by the firm or company where you hope to interview. Talk to the organization's representatives at recruiting sessions and/or professional meetings.
- If possible, talk with people who work for the organization. Ask for their opinions of the company and their advice on interviewing for the job.
- Expand the self-assessment you conducted for your résumé. Take an inventory of your skills and strengths, and think of concrete examples that you can use in the interview to illustrate them. Think about your career goals and describe them to yourself. Ask yourself why you want to work for this organization (the one where you are interviewing), and be able to explain the answer clearly.
- Consult the organization's Web site, if one exists, for advice on preparing for interviews. Some firms post sample questions to help interviewees prepare. Or check one of the Big Five accounting firms' Web sites even if you are not interviewing there. Each of the Big Five offers tips on interview preparation, and these suggestions may be helpful in the interview you are planning. The

KPMG Web site, for example, suggests that applicants prepare answers to a number of questions before reporting for an interview (see box).

- Prepare several questions of your own. You can demonstrate that you have done your homework by asking the interviewer intelligent questions about the company. Use the information you have gathered about the company and the industry to frame questions about the company's competitive strategies, emerging markets, and so forth. Anchor each question in specific information to show the interviewer that you are knowledgeable about the organization:

Examples: Has your company's recent restructuring yielded the kinds of positive changes that it was expecting?

How has the company adjusted to its new CEO after the retirement of Andrew Adams last year?

Your market entry efforts in Japan have been impressive. Do you foresee continued growth in the Asian sector?

- Practice. Practice. Practice. Make an appointment with your college placement office for a mock interview. Placement counselors can give you

---

Sample Questions for Interview Preparation

How effectively do you balance your course load at school with any jobs or extracurricular activities that you may have?

Can you describe the most challenging situation you've ever had to deal with and how you dealt with it?

What is your greatest accomplishment to date, and why?

While you are on an engagement and auditing cash, you come across a possible error. You have become very good friends with the client and the error could result in his termination. What do you do?

What would someone you've worked for describe as your strengths . . . as well as areas that need improvement?

Describe a situation in which someone was unhappy with your performance . . . and how you responded.

Describe a situation in which you've shown a great deal of initiative.

If you had to choose a different major, what would it be, and why?

How do you define success?

What are your goals for the next 4–5 years?

What do you consider to be an auditor's most important skills?

Source: From Interviewing with KPMG
Interviewing Tips
http://www.kpmgcampus.com
July 7, 1998

expert feedback on your performance and suggest ways to improve. If this option is not available, have a friend ask you questions about yourself, listen to your answers, and offer feedback. The important thing is to practice talking about yourself so that you seem natural and relaxed in your interview.

DOING THE INTERVIEW

If you are interviewing at a large firm or company, the initial interview may be part of a screening process involving a large number of job candidates. In these circumstances, the interviewer's purpose is to determine which applicants to invite back for more in-depth interviews. At smaller organizations, hiring decisions may be made on the basis of a single interview. Interviews may be highly structured, following a series of specific questions, or may have little structure at all, with the interviewer simply asking the applicant, "Tell me about yourself." Although no two interviews are alike, the following guidelines are applicable in most interviewing situations:

- Dress appropriately, in conservative business attire.
- Arrive on time.
- Offer your interviewer a smile and a firm handshake.
- Maintain eye contact with your interviewer.
- Pay attention to your body language (not too tense, not too relaxed).
- Express yourself in complete thoughts; use proper grammar; answer questions as logically and clearly as you can.
- Remember that you are promoting yourself to the interviewee; frame your answers where possible to demonstrate your knowledge, team spirit, leadership ability, and motivation to succeed.
- Give concrete evidence to support general statements (if you describe yourself as a team player, for example, support that assertion by describing a situation in which your teamwork had productive results).
- Demonstrate in your answers your understanding of the employer's business, goals, corporate culture, and the like.
- Never blame anyone or anything else for a less-than-outstanding grade or other deficiency on your résumé. Address the subject directly, emphasize your strong points, and speak about yourself in a positive way.
- Listen carefully to everything the interviewer says, whether it is a question or an answer to a question you have asked. Use the active listening techniques described in Chapter 6. Showing that you are a good listener is an important part of promoting yourself in the interview.
- If you do not understand a question, ask the interviewer to clarify. Trying to respond to an unclear question will probably result in an unsatisfactory answer.
- Ask the questions you have prepared and any others that you have formulated during the course of the interview.
- You should have an idea of how much entry-level accountants earn at the firm or company where you are interviewing. Do not ask about

salary. A salary offer will be made when (or after) an offer of employment is made. Feel free to ask, however, about employee training and career paths within the company. If the interviewer asks you about your salary requirements, explain that you are more interested in the "job fit," the opportunities for advancement, and other matters at this stage than you are in a specific target salary.

■ At the conclusion of the interview, thank the interviewer and offer another smile and firm handshake. Ask for a business card if the interviewer has not given you one. You will use it for the follow-up note.

FOLLOWING UP AFTER THE INTERVIEW

Send the interviewer a thank-you note within 48 hours of the interview. Although some career professionals suggest handwritten notes, you are always safe with a clean word-processed letter. You can adopt a more personal tone in the thank-you note than you did in the cover letter because you are now acquainted with your reader. In addition to thanking the interviewer for his or her time, you may want to comment on something you learned during the interview or refer to a key point that arose in the conversation. You should reiterate your interest in the position and comment briefly on your qualifications to fill it. The thank-you note in Figure 1.9 offers a model.

If the interviewer has requested any materials—additional references, work samples—send them along with the thank-you note—that is, within 48 hours. If the employer has requested transcripts, ask your college registrar's office to send them out immediately, and let the employer know that they are on the way.

If you have a reference or contact who has influence with the company, you may want to ask that person to call the interviewer and put in a good word for you. Use your judgment before making such a request, however. If the interviewer seemed very interested in your application, he or she will probably be receptive to an extra push. If, however, the interviewer was hard to read, firm about the screening procedures, or explicit about the method of checking references, you should simply leave matters in the interviewer's hands.

If two weeks or more have elapsed since the interview and you have not heard from the employer, it is appropriate to call and ask about the status of your application. Simply do so politely, and express your continued interest in the job.

If you have received another job offer but want this one, call the interviewer and explain that you need to make a decision. If the screening process is still under way, the interviewer may at least be able to tell you when offers will be made.

If you are offered the position for which you interviewed and you accept it verbally, it is a courtesy to send a brief letter of acceptance as well (see Figure 1.10).

If you are offered the position for which you interviewed and want to decline it, you should do so in a brief letter as well (see Figure 1.11). The

Sample Interview Thank-You Letter

> ### LETTER
>
> Dear Mr. Higgins:
>
> Thank you for the opportunity to meet with you yesterday to discuss the staff accountant position at Global Oil Exploration, Inc.
>
> It was interesting to see the similarities between the accounting operations of Global Oil and AT&T, where I have worked as an intern for the past nine months. I was quite impressed to hear of the efficiency and speed with which Global recently implemented the new SAP software system. Successful implementation of such a complex system speaks well for the people who work for your company. Our conversation affirmed my belief that I can bring valuable accounting, computer, and communication skills and experience to the job.
>
> I am enclosing the article we discussed about the CPA WebTrust program for company Web sites. I think you will find it interesting.
>
> Thanks once again for the interview. I look forward to discussing the position further.
>
> Sincerely,
>
> Brian T. Randolph

Sample Acceptance Letter

> ### LETTER
>
> Dear Mr. Higgins:
>
> I am happy to accept the position of staff accountant in your controller's office. As you know, Global Oil has been my first choice throughout the job search process.
>
> I have completed the forms you enclosed in your letter of offer, and I look forward to seeing you on Monday, June 13.
>
> Sincerely,
>
> Brian T. Randolph

Figure 1.11

Sample Letter Declining Job Offer

LETTER

Dear Mr. Higgins:

Thank you for your offer of an accounting position at Global Oil. Global is one of the most dynamic companies in the oil business today, and it would be a privilege to be a part of your team.

I have also received an offer, however, from Texas Instruments, where I worked as an intern last year. The relationships I have already begun to build there, coupled with a very attractive financial package, have led me to accept Texas Instruments' offer.

I appreciate your interest in me and regret that I cannot accept your generous offer.

Sincerely,

Brian T. Randolph

---

purpose of this letter is to maintain goodwill with the employer because you may wish to reapply for a position at some future time or you may find yourself coming in business contact with employees of the company. Therefore, take care to reject the offer politely and to offer a plausible reason for declining.

CONCLUSION

Now, more than ever before, job seekers have access to valuable, up-to-date information on career opportunities worldwide. The guidelines in this chapter will help you take advantage of the wealth of resources available to accounting graduates and will put you on the track to the accounting career you want. Now you are ready to learn the communication skills that will make your career successful.

NOTES

[1] Jeffrey A. Porter, "Writing Skills of New Accountant Hires," *The Tax Adviser* 28, no. 8 (August 1997): 518.

[2] Sak Bhamornsiri and Robert E. Guinn, "The Road to Partnership in the Big Six Firms: Implications for Accounting Education," *Issues in Accounting Education* 6 (Spring 1991): 9–24.

[3] AICPA, "Top Ten Technologies Stress Communications," *Journal of Accountancy* 185, no. 2 (February 1998): 22.

[4] Accounting Education Change Commission (1994).

[5] Neal R. VanZante and Samuel Person, "The New CPA Examination," *The CPA Journal* 64, no. 4 (April 1994): 42–49.

[6] National Association of Colleges and Employers, "Getting into Accounting by the Numbers," *Job Choices in Business: 1998,* 41st ed., p. E7.

[7] By one estimate, at least two-thirds of Fortune 500 companies will be using electronic résumé management systems by the beginning of the 21st century. William H. Baker, Kristen DeTienne, and Karl L. Smart, "How Fortune 500 Companies Are Using Electronic Résumé Management Systems," *Business Communications Quarterly* 61, no. 3 (September 1998): 8–19.

[8] Baker, DeTienne, and Smart, p. 16.

[9] Ibid.

EXERCISES

1. **Communication task:** Prepare a database of ten or more contacts in a field related to your career goal. Include in your database your contact's full name, title, firm, address, and phone number, as well as any other information or comments you think would be helpful.

   If you do not have access to database software, you can prepare a simple database using spreadsheet software such as Excel, which includes some data manipulation features. Follow the on-screen help for organizing data in a list; you will soon have a simple database that can be sorted and filtered as you like. If you do not have access to spreadsheet software, you can create a database using word processing software, although you will not be able to sort and filter data.

2. **Communication task:** Interview your contacts. Follow up on Exercise 1 by calling one or two people on your list. Ask if you can talk with them by phone or in person about careers in accounting. Alternatively, plan to speak to one or two accountants at a job or career fair that you attend.

   Keep the interview brief—15 minutes at most. Before your interview, outline the types of information you would like to obtain from your contact and the issues you would like to discuss. Depending on how far along you are in the job search process, you will probably want to discuss different types of concerns.

If you are just beginning to think about accounting as a career, you might want to discuss the different types of positions available for accountants. How are careers in public accounting, government, corporate accounting, and not-for-profit organizations different? How are they the same? What skills or strengths does each type of firm look for in its employees? What types of professional certifications are required or desirable for each type of position?

At a later point in your education, you might be more interested in learning specific information about a particular industry or position. What type of work does a health care auditor do? Does a CPA tax consultant spend more time working with clients or researching and writing about issues? Does a corporate accountant need a CPA or CMA credential to be promoted? At this time you might also want to get advice on résumés, application letters, and interviews.

3. **Communication task:** After your interview, update your database with brief comments and other information you do not want to forget. Prepare a more detailed (one- to two-paragraph) summary of the information obtained from each of your contacts, and keep a copy on file for future reference. Interview two accountants, preferably in different types of positions, about the ways that oral and written communications skills affect their jobs. As in Exercise 2, call to request and schedule an interview (or approach participants at a job or career fair), prepare your questions before you begin, and add this information to your database. Then, write a one- or two-paragraph summary of the answers to these questions. Be prepared to hand these in to your instructor or to discuss in class.

    Here are questions you might consider:

    - What percentage of their time is spent writing?
    - What types of documents do they prepare?
    - Who reads these documents? How do they write differently depending on the needs of their reader?
    - How are documents reviewed at their firm or company?
    - What characteristics do they feel are essential for good writing?
    - What are the rewards for good writing? What are the consequences of poor writing?
    - What types of oral presentations do they make?
    - How much time do they spend talking, meeting, and interacting with co-workers?
    - How much time do they spend talking, meeting, and interacting with clients? How are their interactions with clients different from those with co-workers?

4. **Scenario:** You are a recruiter for a large firm and have received the following résumé and cover letter from a student applying for a position as staff accountant.

Christine R. Michaels
1234 Rand Way
Normantown, PA 19999
(215) 555-8888

OBJECTIVE
To obtain a well-paying entry-level position in accounting.

EDUCATION
Delta University, Philadelphia, PA
MBA May 2000
Marks College, Harrisburg, PA
BA in Accounting; Japanese Minor May 1998

EXPERIENCE
Alpha Beta Kappa Service Fraternity, Harrisburg, PA
Treasurer, September 1996–May 1998
Prepared annual budget
Maintained all cash receipt and cash disbursement records
Utilized computerized small business accounting software

Pennsylvania Electric Co., Philadelphia, PA
Accounting Intern, May–August 1998
Prepared spreadsheets
Prepared bank reconciliations
Prepared analyses for management
Recorded daily revenue activity

Baker, Baker and Baker, LLP, Philadelphia, PA
Accounting Intern, January–May 2000
Developed business plans
Helped prepare documents for IPO
Prepared tax returns
Audited several clients

ACTIVITIES
Habitat for Humanity
Student Affiliate—AICPA
Student Affiliate—Institute of Management Accountants
Marks College Academic Support Services Tutor for accounting courses

SKILLS
Fluent in Japanese
Microsoft Office, Quicken, Quickbooks

LETTER

Christine R. Michaels
1234 Rand Way
Normantown, PA 19999
(215) 555-8888

Ms. Valerie Andrews
Baker, Baker and Baker, LLP
Philadelphia, PA 19999

Dear Ms. Andrews:

I would like to apply for a job as a staff accountant at your firm. In May I graduated from Delta University with an MBA and so I believe I am qualified for this job. Please refer to my résumé, which is enclosed, for details about all the important information you need to know about me and my experience.

You will see from my résumé that I worked for your firm as an Accounting Intern for the past few months. I also worked as an intern for Philadelphia Electric and served as Treasurer for a service fraternity while I attended Marks College in Harrisburg.

Please let me know when I can stop by for an interview.

Sincerely,

Christine R. Michaels

Communication task: Prepare a written critique of both the résumé and the cover letter. Be sure to answer the following questions in your critique: Do the documents follow acceptable formats? What are their strengths? What are their weaknesses? Do these documents clearly show evidence of the following?

- technical knowledge (competent, hard-working, accomplished, and knowledgeable in your field)
- communication skills (effective written and oral communication skills)
- team spirit (can work well with others to accomplish a goal)
- motivation and work ethic (have a commitment to the firm; can handle several tasks at once; work well under pressure)
- leadership (can take charge when necessary and motivate others to complete tasks effectively)

- flexibility (can adapt to changing work conditions, different work teams, and varying tasks)

5. Revise the cover letter and résumé in Exercise 4 to highlight more effectively the attributes and facts that need to be communicated. If necessary, make up additional details.

6. Communication task: Prepare a self-assessment using the three-column worksheet format illustrated in Figure 1.3, pp. 10–11. After you have completed your worksheet, review the characteristics that employers look for in job applicants. Have you included evidence of each of them? If not, prepare a list of personal goals for activities and internships that could be used to fill in the gaps in your qualifications. Work toward accomplishing these goals within the next year.

As you fill out your self-assessment, remember to include nonaccounting as well as accounting experience. A position as a restaurant server may have provided you with excellent opportunities to work as part of a team to provide customer satisfaction. Working as a salesclerk may have enhanced your interpersonal skills as you tactfully handled difficult situations and people. Tutoring other students in accounting may have provided you the opportunity to communicate clearly and precisely by explaining difficult concepts to others. Babysitting may have helped you develop patience and a strong work ethic. Consider all the jobs, accomplishments, honors, and projects you have experienced to develop your self-assessment as thoroughly as possible.

7 a. Communication task: Acquire a selection of sample résumés and cover letters from various sources; select two or three of them and write a brief critique of their strengths and weaknesses, using the criteria in Exercise 4. Bring your samples and your critique to class. Be prepared to hand these in to your instructor or to discuss in class.

b. Based on your self-assessment and the samples you have collected, prepare your own résumé and cover letter. Have it critiqued by your career development office, professors, and/or other accounting professionals, including one or two of your networking contacts. Revise your résumé and cover letter as appropriate.

8. Communication task: Using the World Wide Web, research each of the Big Five firms and prepare a worksheet summarizing the results of your research. Format your worksheet as shown here, but be sure to add differentiating characteristics based on the information you are able to obtain. Whenever possible, obtain information about the firm as a whole and about the particular office location you are interested in applying to. You may find that a particular firm is well known for its expertise in health care, for example, but that the location you are interested in has no health care clients.

```
┌─────────────────────────────────────────────────────────────────────┐
│                                                                       │
│  ┌─────────────────────────────────────────────────────────────┐    │
│  │                    WORKSHEET                                   │    │
│  └─────────────────────────────────────────────────────────────┘    │
│                                                                       │
```

Characteristics	AA	D&T	E&Y	KPMG	PWC
Size of firm					
Size of office					
Industries—overall					
Industries—office					
Opportunities in auditing? Tax?					
Consulting?					
Separate or combined					
consulting?					
Recent changes					
Strengths of firm					
Characteristics desired in staff					
Location of training					

If you or your instructor prefers, this exercise may be modified to focus on corporations within an industry of interest to you. For example, if you are interested in the automotive industry, you could investigate parts manufacturing firms using the same technique.

9. **Communication task:** Arrange for a mock interview. Many career development offices routinely schedule these for students; however, if your school does not, you have several alternatives. Check with your accounting club or society. Many Big Five firms are willing to send recruiting personnel to do mock interviews with interested students. Or ask a local chapter of a professional organization if they have members who would be willing to do one or more mock interviews. Local chapters of state societies of CPAs, the Institute of Management Accountants, the Institute of Internal Auditors, and the Financial Executive Institute usually have committees that work with local colleges and would welcome the opportunity to hold a mock interview session with students.

   After you have completed the mock interview, make a list of changes you need to make before your initial interview with a potential employer. These changes may include résumé or cover letter changes, changes in your dress or appearance, modifications to your handshake or body language, or improvements to the specific answers you gave during the interview.

10. **Scenario:** You have recently interviewed with Barbara Jones, the accounting manager at Current Technologies, Inc., for a position in their tax department. As part of the interview you toured their manufacturing facilities and had lunch with John Smith, who also works in the tax department.

    Communication task: Prepare a thank-you letter to Ms. Jones.

CHAPTER 2

Communication and the Writing Process

When you land your first job as a professional accountant, you will move into a world in which communications are the engine driving the conduct of business. In this world, you will find your communications have more serious and far-reaching consequences than those in which you engaged as a student. For example, at school, being unprepared for class discussion or submitting hastily written work might have incurred only minor penalties; on the job, however, making a remark at an audit planning meeting that reveals you did not read the advance materials about your new client could mean you will not advance through the ranks as quickly as more careful communicators. Similarly, giving your supervisor an industry analysis report that lacks important information and contains grammar, spelling, and punctuation mistakes could single you out as a problem employee.

To be successful in the professional workplace, you will need strong skills in both oral and written communications. This chapter helps you lay the groundwork for these skills by focusing on the writing process.

THE RHETORICAL SITUATION

Every communication task, from the simplest phone call or e-mail message to the most elaborate written report, exists in what is called a rhetorical situation. The term *rhetoric* originally referred to the art of public oratory in classical Greece.[1] In contemporary usage, the term describes the relationships between communicator and audience that determine all communications. As a communicator, you are constantly involved in rhetorical situations. Whether you are talking to someone on the phone, giving an oral presentation, or writing a memo for your internship supervisor, your communications are being shaped, to some extent at least, by your awareness of the purpose of your communication, of the various ways in which it could be expressed, and of any obstacles that might keep your audience from understanding it. The greater your understanding of these rhetorical elements, the more likely it is that your communication will be successful: that is, that the message you intended to send is in fact the one your audience receives.

Speakers and Listeners

If you are having a face-to-face conversation, it is relatively easy to ensure that you are understood because the physical presence of your listener helps you make your message clear. As you speak, your listener interacts with you through verbal and nonverbal signals, indicating whether he or she understands your message. Through signals such as questions and comments, body language, and facial expressions, your listener helps you see where you need to clarify an idea, repeat a key point, or take a different approach. If you use an unfamiliar word, for example, your listener may signal you with a direct question or an expression of puzzlement. If you are communicating clearly, your listener may signal comprehension by recapitulating what you have said, by elaborating on it, or by nodding assent. As a speaker in a face-to-face transaction, you are constantly gauging your listener's comprehension by picking up such replies and signals and, consciously or not, revising your delivery to make sure your message is understood.

Writers and Readers

As a writer, however, you do not have the advantage of this immediate feedback. You must shape your message without knowing whether your reader will have questions about what you are communicating. Without the signals that allow ongoing revision in one-on-one conversation—the verbal and nonverbal behaviors that help you test comprehension—you must rely on careful planning to ensure that your message gets through to the reader.

One reason writing is more difficult than speaking is that you must compensate for the absence of your listener when you sit down to compose. The quality of this compensation is the key to effective writing. Just as awareness of your listener helps you shape conversations as they occur, awareness of your reader must shape the choices you make as you write. If you are to communicate effectively as a writer, you must first of all be guided by a sense of what your reader needs to know.

Consider the poorly crafted memorandum in Figure 2.1, written by a manager to one of his company's accountants. The memo is hard to understand because the main information the reader needs is in the final paragraphs. The memo begins with a description of several confusing events, arranged in chronological order, and fails to state its purpose until the end. As a result, Sue Baker, the recipient, will have to move through the whole document before she understands how any of the comments are relevant to her work. She must read the entire message before she discovers what it is the writer wants her to do; then she must reread the document to see how the details relate to this main point.

The writer of the memo has wasted his reader's time because he has not asked himself in advance what the reader needs to know and organized his document accordingly. Asking that question and following through on the answer are essential to effective writing.

Organizing communications to meet the reader's needs means more than simply sitting down and writing what comes to mind. It requires you to

Figure 2.1

Poorly Organized Memo

> ### MEMO
>
> **To:** Sue Baker, Accounts Receivable
> **From:** Barry McKenna, Sales Manager
> **Subject:** John Hampton, Account 084-27-96
> **Date:** July 10, 1999
>
> On May 18, Mr. Hampton contacted his sales representative, Rob Monroe, about an invoice he received for $843.50. He claims the invoice was paid last fall. Rob contacted me in late May regarding this matter.
>
> Rob requested a list of payments made to us in the last year. The list of payments along with check copies were forwarded to you on June 1.
>
> On June 15, you informed Rob that copies of all invoices for the last year were being reviewed for this account. Since then, however, nothing has been communicated to Rob or the customer about the status of his account.
>
> This customer has placed another order for software, which cannot be shipped until the matter of the $843.50 invoice is resolved. On June 30, our national sales director, Barbara Greenacre, received a telephone call from Mr. Hampton complaining about the way his account was being handled.
>
> Barbara immediately contacted me. After researching the problem myself, I discovered that Hampton's account was not credited for a check in the amount of $843.50 that was received in September last year. The funds were credited to another account in error. Please credit account 084-27-96 for the $843.50 and debit account 063-13-96. The attached account records will supply you with the information you need to make the necessary corrections.

approach writing as a process. This process involves analyzing your reader, thinking about what you want to accomplish, and planning how best to do it before you compose your message. It also involves reviewing what you have written from the reader's point of view and reorganizing and making adjustments to ensure that the reader understands the message. This process is a series of four steps: prewriting, drafting, revising, and editing.

THE FOUR STEPS OF THE WRITING PROCESS

The first two steps in the writing process—prewriting and drafting—involve generating ideas and information. In prewriting, you get a picture of your reader, define your purpose (what you want the reader to learn or do), think about ways to achieve this purpose, gather needed information, and plan how to structure that information for your intended reader. Composing involves organizing and rendering your ideas on paper or computer screen in draft form.

The last two steps—revising and editing—involve judging and evaluating your draft. In the revision process, you reconsider your completed draft to evaluate whether you have done what you set out to do. Your goal is not to generate ideas but to judge how effectively you have organized information, whether your ideas flow logically from sentence to sentence, and whether each section of your draft seems adequately developed. Then you make the necessary changes in structure, tone, and syntax to improve your draft. In the last stage—editing—you polish grammar and style and correct any mistakes you may have made in spelling, punctuation, citation, and numbering.

The first two steps engage different mental faculties from the last two. Prewriting and drafting call on your abilities to get ideas flowing. Revising and editing require that you discriminate among these ideas and judge their presentation with distance and objectivity. As a result, it is important to follow the steps in order. People who begin writing tasks without adequate time for prewriting quickly find themselves struggling with vague ideas and undigested information. People who try to revise and edit as they compose often fall victim to writer's block because their desire to make every sentence perfect prevents them from generating a draft. Because prewriting and drafting engage different mental functions from those demanded by revising and editing, it is difficult to do these tasks at the same time. Taking the four steps in the proper sequence, however, gives you a blueprint for effective written communications. Let us examine these steps in detail.

Prewriting

Identify Your Reader   Because effective communication is grounded in what the reader needs to know, getting a clear picture of the reader is the first step in the writing process. Even before you gather your facts, background information, and numerical data, ask yourself questions that will bring the reader into clear focus.

Who is your reader? If you are writing to someone you know, visualize that person. If you are writing to a stranger, create a picture of that person. If you are writing to a larger group, consider what sets that group apart from any other. Thinking of your readers helps you remember that effective writing conveys specific messages to specific receivers.

What is your reader's relationship to you? Is the reader a peer? A subordinate? A superior? A supervisor on the job? A member of a professional accrediting association? A client?

What tone is appropriate for this reader? Awareness of your relationship to the reader helps you adopt the proper tone for your document or presentation. Think of tone as the attitude you convey toward your reader. Do you want to come across as friendly and personal? Respectful and reserved? Assertive? Conciliatory? Neutral?

Consider the letter in Figure 2.2 from James Weaver, a CPA, to a new and rather worried client who has sought professional help for the first time. The tone of James Weaver's letter is courteous, personal, reassuring, and conveys eagerness to please because he hopes Mr. Emerson will become a regular client. Furthermore, the letter is very easy to understand. It does not discuss any of the possible problems involved in preparing Mr. Emerson's tax returns because the CPA knows his job is to resolve those problems himself. The CPA also knows he will make the most efficient use of his time by answering any detailed questions Mr. Emerson may have either over the phone or during the appointment on March 18.

Contrast the tone of Mr. Weaver's letter with that in Figure 2.3, which also was written by a CPA, requesting an extended payment plan for a client's tax bill. In this letter, the tone, although courteous, is more assertive because the

---

Figure 2.2

Reassuring Letter

> **LETTER**
>
> Dear Mr. Emerson,
>
> It was a pleasure to meet you yesterday, and I look forward to being of service to you by preparing your 1999 income tax returns. Rest assured that all of your questions regarding your home office expenses and the sale of your residence will be answered.
>
> Your tax consultation is confirmed for Tuesday, March 18, at 1 P.M., at my Quakertown office. Please bring along your purchase receipts for home office supplies, which were not included among the documents you gave me, and the settlement sheet from the sale of your home last November.
>
> I look forward to seeing you next Tuesday. Please feel free to call with any questions you might have in the meantime.
>
> Sincerely,
>
> James Weaver, CPA

| Figure 2.3 | |

Assertive Letter to the IRS

> ### LETTER
>
> March 30, 2000
> Internal Revenue Service
> Philadelphia, PA 19000
> RE: Elliott Simon, SS# 222-44-5555
>
> Dear Mr. Smith,
>
> Enclosed please find Form 433B and a cash-basis version of Form 1120S for the taxpayer described above. I am also including a copy of my client's aged accounts receivable trial balance as of 12/31/99.
>
> Mr. Simon maintains his books using the accrual basis, but his Form 1120S information must be revised in this case to the cash basis because the cash basis best reflects my client's ability to pay his tax obligations. Although Mr. Simon's 1999 accrual-basis records reflect a loss of $9,025, $4,956 of this loss is due to depreciation. Therefore, Mr. Simon's cash-basis loss for the year is only $4,069.
>
> I have discussed a payment plan with my client to extinguish his debt to the IRS. Although my client suffered a loss in 1999, he believes his current cash position will permit him to pay $1,300 per month starting this month and that having reduced his company's payroll costs in the last quarter of 1999, he will be able to make these payments on a timely basis.
>
> Once you have reviewed this information, please call me to discuss the proposed payment plan. Thank you for your cooperation in this matter.
>
> Sincerely,
>
> Pyron & Seland, P.C.

firm of Pyron & Seland wishes to ensure that the Internal Revenue Service accommodate Mr. Simon. And the author does not hesitate to make use of technical terms and of a highly condensed, telegraphic style, knowing the IRS expects to receive a tersely businesslike communication from a CPA firm. Note that the letter carries the full authority of the firm in question, which is the actual signatory, no individual author being specified, to help counterbalance the authority of the IRS. The tone of the letter, in short, suggests that sender and receiver are on an equal professional footing.

Once you are clear on your relationship to your reader, ask yourself these questions: How much does the reader know about your profession? Is the reader another accountant in your office? A tax attorney? A stockbroker? A first-time client? What your reader knows about accounting should guide you in making decisions about vocabulary, technical terminology, and definitions of concepts.

As you take your place in the community of accounting professionals, you join an extensive group that shares specialized knowledge and vocabulary. Within this community, the common ground you share with others allows you to communicate via an insider language, using technical terms and concepts that you can assume your readers understand. When talking or writing to another accountant, you do not have to explain what you mean by aged accounts receivable trial balances, cash-basis records, or Forms 433B and 1120S. Other accountants use these terms regularly and know precisely what you mean when you use them. Communication is even easier with co-workers in your office. Not only do they speak the insider language, they also know the specific nature of your daily work. Such insider communication can be quick and easy, based on brief references and verbal cues.

Explaining any aspect of the work of accountancy to a reader outside this community is another matter. Without the common language of a shared profession, the burden is on you, the writer, to explain terms and define concepts. It is easy to forget that accounting vocabulary you use every day sounds like a foreign language to people outside your discourse group, so remember to put yourself in your reader's place to identify those items or concepts that will seem unfamiliar to him or her. Then clarify your meaning for that reader.

The best way to make your meaning clear to nonexpert readers is to define accounting terms explicitly, using the techniques of formal definition. In formal definition, a term is assigned to a class of similar items; then it is distinguished from the other items in that category:

Item	=	**Category**	+	**Distinguishing Characteristics**
Coffee	is a	beverage		that stimulates the central nervous system
An investment	is an	expenditure for property or other assets		that is expected to produce revenue
An extraordinary item	is a	material expense or revenue item		that is both unusual in nature and infrequent in occurrence

By supplying definitions of unfamiliar terms, you place the term in context and specify how it differs from other terms in that context. This method has the advantage of isolating the unfamiliar term and of comparing it to other terms with which the reader might confuse it.

Figure 2.4

Reader Profile Worksheet

WORKSHEET

1. Reader's Position:
Internal/external _____
Superior/subordinate/peer/mixed _____
Client/prospective client _____

2. Reader's Readiness:
Requested document _____
Expecting document _____
Not expecting document _____

3. Reader's Attitude:
Friendly/hostile/neutral/don't know _____
Interested/uninterested/neutral/don't know _____

4. Reader's Knowledge:
New business/old business _____
Familiar with terms/unfamiliar with terms _____

5. Other:
Age _____ Gender _____ Educational Level _____
Biases _____

To help define your reader, establish the reader's relationship to you, and estimate how much the reader knows about your field of expertise, use the worksheet in Figure 2.4.

Define Your Purpose   After you have clearly identified your reader, the next step in prewriting is to define your purpose. Ask yourself, What do I want my reader(s) to learn or do as a result of this communication?

Many writers plunge into writing tasks with only a general sense of their purpose for writing. Thinking about what you want your reader(s) to learn or do as a result of your letter, memo, report, or presentation helps make your purpose clear. Before you write, jot down in a single, complete sentence what you hope to achieve in your document. Do you want your reader to

- understand technical information?
- pay for your services?
- perform a task for you?

- accept your position on a question or issue?
- evaluate your suggested solution to a problem?
- send you information that you need?

Unless you know exactly what you want your readers to learn or do, you cannot be sure your document will achieve the desired results. Keep your purpose statement in front of you as you write. Check each paragraph against this statement to ensure that what you are writing contributes to achieving the result you want.

Gather Your Data   When accountants write, accounting data is almost always involved, whether the data themselves are the main subject of communication or whether they are provided as supporting information. An accountant's data-gathering process varies according to the end user's requirements. If a client has a complex tax question, the accountant consults reference guides or does a search in the tax code to gather the information needed. If a client's banker wants an idea of how well the client's company will handle an increase in its line of credit, the accountant reviews prior years' financial statements, analyzes the company and its industry's cash collection patterns, and obtains sales projections from the company's sales manager to prepare a set of forecasted financial statements. If the CEO has a question about last year's property, plant, and equipment acquisitions, the accountant produces a detailed schedule of long-term assets acquired over the previous 12 months, perhaps accompanied by related financing information.

Accountants are uniquely placed to have access to financial data they need to create or support the documents they write, and the data-gathering process often consists not so much in struggling to obtain enough data but rather in sifting through a superabundance of data to provide users with only the most pertinent and relevant information. *Data sifting* is a particularly important skill in the accounting workplace because clients and other users of financial data rely on accountants to organize and explain what sometimes can be overwhelming amounts of information.

As you gather your data, ask yourself these questions:

- Does this data answer the question I was asked?
- Is this bit of data redundant?
- Will my reader understand the information as it is presented here?
- Is there another body of data that might better explain what's going on?

Once you have gathered enough of the right data, you can begin to organize it.

Organize Your Data   Busy professionals want communications to be to the point, and they want to know from the start how information presented is relevant to their concerns. Their main question when confronted with a document that presents a confusing jumble of facts, such as the memo to Sue Baker (Figure 2.1 on page 39), is, "How does this information relate to my work?" To ensure that your reader does not have to ask this question, arrange your data in categories that articulate the main points of your message.

Before you begin to write, jot down the main points you want to make. Unless your message is unusually complex, plan to cover no more than three or four points. Then group each fact, each set of numbers, and each document under the point it supports, explains, proves, or clarifies. The worksheet here offers a model for organizing data. The message—suggesting potential tax savings—is from a CPA to a client. Although it is not necessary to make a formal outline, arranging your information in categories will facilitate drafting later.

Data Worksheet

Point 1
Convert Interest Income
$5,000 interest income to tax-exempt investments (Save $1,500/yr).

Point 2
Eliminate Vehicle Allowance Income
Reimbursed auto expenses not taxable $2,000 allowance income now (Save $600/yr).

Point 3
Create Charitable Contribution Deduction
Donate appreciated property—no capital gains. Deduction = fair market value of property.

Point 4
Create Other Deductions
Make December mortgage payment early to get deduction this year. Pay last quarterly estimate in December (Save $200).

Drafting

Once you have analyzed the nature and requirements of your reader, articulated your purpose, and arranged your data in categories, you are ready to draft your document. The time you have devoted to prewriting should make the drafting process easy, so move through this stage as quickly as possible to produce a draft.

Follow these steps to draft your document:

Organize Your Information From Most Important to Least Important   Whether you are drafting a letter, a memo, a report, or an oral presentation, you will find the order of descending importance is the easiest structure for readers to follow. Giving readers the most important information first helps them understand how the less important details relate to it.

The Order of Descending Importance

Data 1 (Most Important)
Data 2 (Less Important)
Data 3 (Less Important)
Data 4 (Least Important)

With only a few exceptions (discussed in later chapters), choose the order of descending importance to organize letters, memos, reports, oral presentations, and other documents.

Focus on One Idea per Paragraph and Develop That Idea Completely   Paragraphs are units of thought that state a point and provide enough relevant information to support that point adequately. Well-constructed paragraphs are among the most important devices for making messages clear because (a) they isolate the categories into which information is organized, (b) they show the relationship of detailed information to general categories, and (c) they express these relationships in logical structures.

To draft paragraphs that convey your message clearly, review the notes you made when you organized your data. Begin each paragraph with a topic sentence that articulates one of the points from your data worksheet. Then illustrate and support the idea expressed in your topic sentence with explanatory detail. (For sample paragraphs and topic sentences, see pp. 49–50.)

Here is a diagram of paragraphs, properly introduced and supported, arranged in descending order:

Paragraphing

Idea 1 (Most Important)
    Topic Sentence
    Support with an appropriate mix of data
    Idea 2 (Less Important)
        Topic Sentence
        Support with an appropriate mix of data
        Idea 3 (Less Important)
            Topic Sentence
            Support with an appropriate mix of data
            Idea 4 (Least Important)
                Topic Sentence
                Support with an appropriate mix of data

Remember: It is much easier for readers to pay attention to one idea at a time than to process a lot of different information at once. By making each of your points clearly and thoroughly before moving on to the next, you help your readers understand your message.

Conclude by Summarizing and/or Asking for Action   Effective communications not only begin with the reader's needs in mind; they end this way as well. Leave your reader with a clear sense of what you have tried to achieve in your document or presentation. If you have explained an issue or resolved a problem, conclude by summarizing your main points. If your letter was designed to get the reader to do something, make your request explicit in closing.

When you have finished drafting, your document normally should look like this:

Draft Document

1. Introduction
    Context/Statement of Purpose
2. Body/Argument
    Paragraph 1 (Most Important)
        Start with topic sentence
        Develop with explanatory details

<u>Paragraph 2 (Less Important)</u>
    Start with topic sentence
    Develop with explanatory details
<u>Paragraph 3 (Less Important)</u>
    Start with topic sentence
    Develop with explanatory details
<u>Paragraph 4 (Least Important)</u>
    Start with topic sentence
    Develop with explanatory details

3. Closing
    Summary or Request for Action

Revising

Revising literally means "seeing again"; in the revision process, you look again at your draft, as if through the eyes of your reader, to determine whether you have presented information in a way the reader can easily grasp.

As you consider what you have written, ask yourself, "Am I leading my reader through this document? Have I provided context and stated my purpose? Have I made it easy to see the connections among my ideas? Have I made clear what I want my reader to learn or do?"

Looking at your document this way—seeing it again—requires that you make an imaginative leap from the point of view of writer to the point of view of intended reader. Because you are close to the information and it makes sense to you, it may be difficult to achieve this detachment. Your ability to do so will increase with practice, but until it seems natural for you, ask a classmate or colleague to read what you have written and to tell you whether your purpose and reasoning are clear.

In Figure 2.1, page 39, we considered a document that needed substantial revision, the memo from Barry McKenna to Sue Baker, which seemed to be an unrevised catalog of the writer's thoughts, drafted without much concern for the reader's point of view. It was hard to follow and frustrating to read. Assume for a moment that you and McKenna are co-workers, and that he has asked you to read over this memo before he sends it. How do you offer suggestions for improvement? Fortunately, McKenna has a number of options for improving his communication to Baker, including eight techniques for leading readers through documents:

- Provide context and purpose in your introduction.
- Focus your paragraphs with topic sentences.
- Repeat key words and phrases.
- Link your ideas with transitions.
- Use parallel structure.
- Dovetail your sentences and paragraphs.
- Format for readability.
- Conclude with a summary or request for action.

You can use these techniques any time you revise.

Check Introduction for Context and Purpose   Your opening sentence should introduce the reader to your context by anchoring your communication in information the reader already has. Your next sentence should state your purpose—that is, it should summarize what you want your reader to learn or do. If the introduction fails to do either, it is probably inadequate.

Compare the following:

First paragraph of original draft:
To: Sue Baker, Accounts Receivable
From: Barry McKenna, Sales Manager
Subject: John Hampton, Account 084-27-96
On May 18, Mr. Hampton contacted his sales representative, Rob Monroe, about an invoice he received for $843.50. He claims the invoice was paid last fall. Rob contacted me in late May regarding this matter.

First paragraph of revised version:
A problem has arisen with Mr. Hampton's account as a result of our failure to credit a payment of $843.50 that he made last September. We need to credit his account in the amount of $843.50 and to debit account 063-13-96 to correct our mistake.

The original draft fails to introduce Sue Baker to the new information she needs. The revised version, however, links new information ("A problem has arisen . . . as a result of our failure to credit a payment . . .") with information Sue Baker already has (for she possesses a record of "Mr. Hampton's account"). In addition, the revised version explains clearly what the writer wants the reader to do ("to credit his [Mr. Hampton's] account in the amount of $843.50 and to debit account 063-13-96"). As for the references in the original draft to Rob Monroe, whose involvement in the case is of secondary importance, they will be relegated in the revised version to later paragraphs.

Check That You Used Topic Sentences to Focus Each Paragraph
Reread your text to verify that you have used a topic sentence to tell the reader what subject you are developing in each paragraph. Without one, a paragraph may well seem aimless, and without clearly focused paragraphs, a document is very difficult to follow.

Look again at the first five paragraphs of Figure 2.1, page 39. These five paragraphs jump from thought to thought without apparent focus. To revise them, find one or more common threads that link them together. Here is a possible revision that reduces the five paragraphs to two by rearranging the constituent parts (the topic sentences are in italics):

Paragraphs 2–3 of revised version:
A review of the account indicates that Mr. Hampton has made efforts to have the error corrected. In May, he called his sales representative, Rob Monroe, to point out the error, explaining that the invoice for $843.50 had already been paid. Shortly thereafter, Mr. Hampton placed another order for software but was told it could not be shipped until the matter of the $843.50 invoice was resolved. On June 30, Mr. Hampton telephoned our national sales director, Barbara Greenacre,

to complain about the way his account was being handled, and Barbara immediately contacted me to ask that I investigate the case.

Account records indicate that we have taken steps to correct the problem. Thus far, however, the problem has not been resolved. After hearing from Mr. Hampton in May, Rob Monroe requested a list of payments made to us in the last year. In addition, he requested that the list of payments be forwarded to you by June 1, along with copies of all checks. You informed Rob on June 15 that copies of all invoices were being reviewed for this account, but since that time, nothing has been communicated to Rob or to the customer about the status of his account.

By focusing on the steps Mr. Hampton has taken in one paragraph and on the steps the company has taken in the following paragraph, you impose an understandable order—in the form of two distinct subjects—on what previously had seemed a chaotic series of unrelated events. And by placing topic sentences that define those subjects at the beginning of the two revised paragraphs, you make their development easy to follow.

Remember: A good paragraph introduces the subject in a topic sentence, sticks to that subject, hangs together in a way that makes sense, and provides enough information, details, and illustrations to support the main point satisfactorily.

Repeat Key Words and Phrases in Similar Sentence Positions

Repetition is a way of anchoring information in memory, and a good way to keep readers focused on your subject throughout your paragraphs is to repeat important words and ideas in similar sentence positions. The paragraphs in Figure 2.1 are hard to follow, not only because they lack topic sentences, but because they introduce key ideas without repeating them. In the original draft the subject moves from "Mr. Hampton" to "Rob" to "list of payments" to "you" to "nothing" to "this customer" to "sales director" to "I" to "the funds." Below, the second paragraph of the revised version maintains a sharp focus on "Mr. Hampton" by using his name or the personal pronoun "he" as subject in each of the four sentences that the paragraph contains.

Paragraph 2 of revised version:

A review of the account indicates that *Mr. Hampton* has made efforts to have the error corrected. In May, *he* called his sales representative, Rob Monroe, to point out the error, explaining that the invoice for $843.50 had already been paid. Shortly thereafter, *Mr. Hampton* placed another order for software but was told it could not be shipped until the matter of the $843.50 invoice was resolved. On June 30, *Mr. Hampton* telephoned our national sales director, Barbara Greenacre, to complain about the way his account was being handled, and Barbara immediately contacted me to ask that I investigate the case.

Use the Right Transitions to Link Ideas

Transitions link ideas, sentences, and paragraphs by indicating relationships. Well-chosen transitions make it easier to follow a text by showing how the ideas it contains connect. Here is a list of useful transitions categorized according to their functions:

To Illustrate

for example	for instance
i.e. (similar ideas)	e.g. (subordinate example)
to illustrate	in particular
specifically	to exemplify

To Affirm

actually	certainly
in fact	indeed
surely	undoubtedly
indubitably	unquestionably
positively	precisely
of course	to be sure

To Negate

on the contrary	on the other hand
despite	notwithstanding
nonetheless	nevertheless
however	but
conversely	

To Add

and	also
additionally	another
moreover	or (nor)
furthermore	next
again	too
second (etc.)	in other words
that is	and then
and besides that	further
likewise	again
even more important	

To Concede

even though	although
granted that	no doubt
doubtless	certainly
whereas	

To Summarize

finally	thus
hence	to sum up
in brief	as has been noted
therefore	in conclusion
accordingly	in short
then	last
to finish	to terminate
to consummate	consequently

Use Parallel Grammatical Structure   We have seen that repetition helps the reader stay on track by anchoring key words and ideas in memory. Parallel grammatical structure is another form of repetition, one that involves expressing similar ideas in similar sentence patterns. By using similar patterns to express similar ideas, you help the reader understand and retain those ideas. Consider the following sentence:

> **Example:** By
> *creating accounting systems,*
> *maintaining records within businesses,*
> *analyzing financial data,*
> *preparing tax returns,*
> and *conducting audits,*
> accountants serve as key problem solvers in many areas of the workplace.

By structuring each of the five italicized phrases in a "verb + direct object" pattern, the writer links them together into a grammatically defined group. And, in doing so, the writer helps the reader see that the phrases also are linked conceptually, inasmuch as each of those phrases describes a task that accountants perform.

Casting closely related sentence elements in nonparallel structures can confuse the reader, as the following sentence illustrates.

> **Faulty parallel structure:** Accountants devote much of their time to creating accounting systems, to maintain records within businesses, analyze financial data, the preparation of tax returns, and conduct audits.

> **Corrected parallel structure:** Accountants devote much of their time to creating accounting systems, maintaining records within businesses, analyzing financial data, preparing tax returns, and conducting audits.

Parallel grammatical structure makes it relatively easy to draw together a number of ideas succinctly and to make points emphatically. Here is a paragraph using parallel grammatical structure that could usefully be added to our revision of Barry McKenna's memo to Sue Baker:

> **Paragraph 4 of revised version:** Three steps are necessary to resolve this matter. First, please credit account 084-27-96 for the $843.50 and debit account 063-13-96. Second, please draft a letter to Mr. Hampton for my signature apologizing for the

inconvenience our error has caused, explaining the resolution of the problem, and offering him a 10% discount on his next software order. Third, please send copies of the letter to our sales, customer service, and shipping departments.

This paragraph holds together tightly and makes its points forcefully as a result of its logical organization and of its use of parallel grammatical structure: It begins with a topic sentence specifying that three actions must be taken to rectify the mistakes the company made in handling Mr. Hampton's account; it assigns each of those actions an ordinal number ("first," "second," "third"); and it describes each of the three needed actions in three parallel sentences beginning with "please" + imperative verb: "please credit," "please draft," and "please send." After the imperative verb, the three sentences diverge grammatically, but each maintains parallel structure within itself: "please credit account . . . and debit account"; "please draft a letter . . . apologizing for the inconvenience . . . , explaining the resolution, and offering him a 10% discount"; "please send copies . . . to our sales, customer service, and shipping departments." Such patterning gives the paragraph a clear, coherent design that the reader can readily perceive and assimilate.

Dovetail Your Sentences and Paragraphs to Ensure the Logical Flow of Ideas   *Dovetail* is a carpenter's term describing a method of constructing a tightly fitting joint (see Figure 2.5). The joint is formed by two pieces of wood: One is a projecting wedge that looks like the tail of a dove, and the other contains an opening of the same size and shape.

The purpose of dovetailing is to ensure a smooth, strong fit between two pieces in a structure. You can ensure a similarly smooth, strong fit between sentences or paragraphs by placing a key idea from one sentence in a prominent position in the next. The important idea repeated in the second sentence

---

Figure 2.5 _____

Dovetail Illustrated

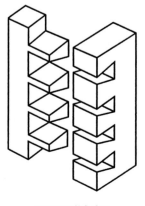

Dovetail joint

functions as the inner portion of the joint, surrounded and contained by the context that the first sentence provides.

The simplest way to dovetail sentences is to place the idea that you wish to develop at the end of one sentence and to repeat it at the beginning of the following sentence:

> **Example:** *Dovetail* is a carpenter's term describing a joint in which *one piece fits tightly inside another.* Just as the *pieces of the dovetail interlock,* so do sentences in *a coherent paragraph.* One way to achieve *paragraph coherence* is to link *the beginning of each sentence to the end of the sentence* before it. By *linking sentences beginning to end,* you make the *connections between ideas explicit. These explicit connections,* in turn, strengthen the logic of your paragraph, much as the *dovetail* strengthens the structure it supports.

As you can see, the words at the beginning of the second sentence fit neatly into the context provided by the words at the end of the first sentence. The same is true of each succeeding sentence. In other words, the sentences dovetail.

You can do the same thing with paragraphs:

> **Example:** *Dovetail* is a carpenter's term describing a method of constructing a tightly fitting joint. The joint is formed by two pieces of wood: One is a projecting wedge that look like the tail of a dove, and the other contains an opening of the same size and shape. *The purpose of dovetailing is to ensure a smooth, strong fit between two pieces in a structure.*
>
> *You can ensure a similarly smooth, strong fit between sentences or paragraphs* by placing a key idea from one sentence in a prominent position in the next. The important idea repeated in the second sentence functions as the inner portion of the joint, surrounded and contained by the context that the first sentence provides.

Remember: Dovetailing your sentences and paragraphs makes the logical structure of your prose strong.

Format for Readability The sample passage below appears in two different formats: first as a block of text, and second as a schematized list. Which one does your eye naturally move to read? Probably the second. It is much easier to read than the first because of its arrangement on the page.

> **Version A:** Formatting is another technique you may use to make your documents reader friendly. Formatting information allows you to use the space on the page to emphasize points, to subordinate ideas to one another, to summarize, to list, and to lead the reader through your logic. Use formatting to break up text blocks with white space, headings, and subheadings; to isolate elements in bulleted hierarchies; to set off text elements with graphics; and to indicate relationships with diagrams.
>
> **Version B:** *Why use formatting?*
> Formatting information allows you to
>
> - emphasize points,
> - subordinate ideas to one another,

- summarize,
- list,
- lead the reader through your logic.

How do I format?

- break up text blocks with white space, headings, and subheadings,
- isolate elements in bulleted hierarchies,
- set off text elements with graphics,
- indicate relationships with diagrams.

Formatting is particularly useful in leading the reader through information presented in parallel grammatical structure. Recasting such information from a straight text block format into a list format allows the reader to process it quickly.

> **Text block format:** Three steps are necessary to resolve this matter. First, please credit account 084-27-96 for the $843.50 and debit account 063-13-96. Second, please draft a letter to Mr. Hampton for my signature apologizing for the inconvenience our error has caused, explaining the resolution of the problem, and offering him a 10% discount on his next software order. Third, please send copies of the letter to our sales, customer service, and shipping departments.

> **List format:** Three steps are necessary to resolve this matter:

> 1. Credit account 084-27-96 for the $843.50 and debit account 063-13-96.
> 2. Draft a letter to Mr. Hampton for my signature
>   - apologizing for the inconvenience our error has caused,
>   - explaining the resolution of the problem, and
>   - offering him a 10% discount on his next software order.
> 3. Send copies of the letter to our sales, customer service, and shipping departments.

Check That Your Conclusion Summarizes What You Have Said and/or Asks for Action   Let us look now at the final paragraph of Barry McKenna's memo to Sue Baker.

> **Last paragraph of original version:** Please credit account 084-27-96 for the $843.50 and debit account 063-13-96. The attached account records will supply you with the information you need to make the necessary corrections.

This paragraph clearly is the best written part of McKenna's original letter, and it would indeed provide a good conclusion in a number of possible revisions, reminding Sue Baker that she should take immediate action. In our revision, however, only its second sentence need be retained, along with a word of thanks to Baker for her expected cooperation.

Remember: Whenever you revise a draft—your own or someone else's—check it against these eight ways of leading the reader: provide context and purpose in your introduction; focus your paragraphs with topic sentences; repeat key words and phrases; link your ideas with transitions; use parallel

Figure 2.6

Revised Memo

MEMO

To: Sue Baker, Accounts Receivable
From: Barry McKenna, Sales Manager
Subject: John Hampton, Account 084-27-96
Date: July 10, 1999

A problem has arisen with Mr. Hampton's account as a result of our failure to credit a payment of $843.50 that he made last September. We need to credit his account in the amount of $843.50 and debit account 063-13-96 to correct our mistake.

A review of the account indicates that Mr. Hampton has made efforts to have the error corrected. In May, he called his sales representative, Rob Monroe, to point out the error, explaining that the invoice for $843.50 had already been paid. Shortly thereafter, Mr. Hampton placed another order for software but was told it could not be shipped until the matter of the $843.50 invoice was resolved. On June 30, Mr. Hampton telephoned our national sales director, Barbara Greenacre, to complain about the way his account was being handled, and Barbara immediately contacted me to ask that I investigate the case.

Account records indicate that we have taken steps to correct the problem as well. Thus far, however, the problem has not been resolved. After hearing from Mr. Hampton in May, Rob Monroe requested a list of payments made to us in the last year. In addition, he requested that the list of payments be forwarded to you by June 1, along with copies of all checks. You informed Rob on June 15 that copies of all invoices were being reviewed for this account, but since that time, nothing has been communicated to Rob or to the customer about the status of his account.

Three steps are necessary to resolve this matter:

1. Credit account 084-27-96 for the $843.50 and debit account 063-13-96.
2. Draft a letter to Mr. Hampton for my signature
   - apologizing for the inconvenience our error has caused,
   - explaining the resolution of the problem, and
   - offering him a 10% discount on his next software order.
3. Send copies of the letter to our sales, customer service, and shipping departments.

The attached account records will supply you with the information you need to make the necessary corrections. Thank you for your help in straightening out this account.

structure; dovetail your sentences and paragraphs; format for readability; and conclude with a summary or request for action.

To see how useful these tools are, compare Barry McKenna's original memo, on page 39, with the completed revised version, Figure 2.6.

Editing

The final step in the writing process is to check your text for clarity, concision, and correctness. Whereas revising focuses primarily on logical organization, editing focuses primarily on grammar, style, and mechanics. In practice, these processes often overlap: As you revise, you may wish to make the portions of your document that you restructure grammatically sound; as you edit, you may discover problems of organization that previously had escaped your notice. Revising and editing are very important steps of the writing process. Each should be given your full and separate attention.

Chapter 3 focuses on stylistic editing and introduces you to techniques for improving your sentence structure. The Reference Guides at the end of the book provide comprehensive rules on proper grammar, usage, and punctuation.

CONCLUSION

In the chapters that follow, you will learn more about techniques for oral and written communication, and you will be introduced to the specific communications that accountants produce within different places of work and various fields of specialization. In the last three chapters, you will find models of well-written documents and descriptions of effective oral communications representing typical samples of accountants' communications. In the exercises at the end of each chapter, you will be asked to draft documents and describe scenarios of your own; you will also encounter sample documents that require revision. As you work on these communication tasks, remember the lesson of this chapter: A process approach to writing—prewriting, drafting, revising, and editing—is the key to successful workplace communications.

NOTES

[1]For an excellent discussion of historical rhetoric, see Edward P. J. Corbett, *Classical Rhetoric for the Modern Student* (3rd ed.) (New York: Oxford University Press, 1990).

EXERCISES

1. **Writing task:** Read the two versions of the memorandum provided. Then write a memo to your teacher explaining why the second version is more reader friendly in terms of tone, organization, and focus than the first version. Explain specifically why version 2 is easier to follow than version 1, and use the principles of reader-based writing to compose your memo.

MEMO

To: Angela Romero, Controller
From: Sam Waterson, Accounts Payable
Date: November 17, 1999

A lot of questions that come up in accounts payable cannot be answered as quickly as they should be. We spend considerable time manually looking up information that should be available on computer. Much research is involved in retrieving vendor history, check information, and customer payment history. We are losing time and money, especially since our recent expansion. This research affects the timeliness with which reports are completed. It slows down the entire process so that it takes days instead of hours. This information should be available at our fingertips.

After working with several different systems, I believe we are lacking various functions that could speed up the process. When we need to look up an invoice, we can only do so by the invoice number. Other systems can search by PO number, invoice date, and dollar amount. With our system, we cannot view the general ledger account codes through accounts payable.

I recommend that we upgrade our accounts payable computer system to one that is more specialized and versatile. Searching for invoices in such a limited way is causing errors and wasting valuable time. Also, if we could view account codes while keying invoices, we would save time and eliminate errors.

MEMO

To: Angela Romero, Controller
From: Sam Waterson, Accounts Payable
Date: November 17, 1999
Re: Problems with Accounts Payable Computer System

Since our recent expansion, it has become clear that the computer system in accounts payable is inadequate. We need to upgrade to a more specialized and versatile system to prevent ongoing waste of time and money.

Our existing system limits our ability to retrieve information quickly. When management calls to ask about vendor history, customer payment history, or check information, for example, we spend considerable time in manual research to find the answer. Producing the report takes days rather than hours.

We need a system that will allow us to look up invoices not only by invoice number (as our present system does) but also by PO number, invoice date, and dollar amount. In addition, we need one that allows us to view general ledger account codes through accounts payable so that, when necessary, expenditures may be traced.

With your approval, I will begin investigating alternatives to our present system. I am confident that we can find one to meet our needs and make information more easily accessible.

---

2. The following is a poorly written memo from Bill Simpson, staff accountant at Omega Technologies, to Erica Schwartz, assistant production manager. Erica, who was working on a budget development team, had called to ask Bill about the past three years' allocations for #16 steel rods used in constructing robotic arms for auto assembly plants. She will use this information to help the team estimate costs for expanding output of this product.

MEMO

To: Erica Schwartz, Assistant Production Manager
From: Bill Simpson, Staff Accountant
Date: August 12, 1999
Re: Allocation for #16 Rods, 1997–1999

The allocation in 1999 was $2,378,430 based on production's estimate of a 17% increase in demand. In 1998 and 1997, the allocation was $1,974,100 and $1,792,260, respectively. We won't know for a couple of months how close we're coming to projections.

So far this year, however, sales have failed to live up to that increase. If we're lucky, we'll net a 6–7% increase for the fiscal year. That kind of increase would bring us back to the levels we saw in 1998.

If I can provide further information, please call me.

Revise the memo to improve its clarity.

Revising

a. Consider the first paragraph. Put yourself in Erica's shoes and revise the paragraph so that it opens by stating context and purpose. Assume it has taken Bill ten days to reply to Erica's phone call.

b. Reorganize the elements of the memo so that the logic is easier to follow.

c. Rewrite the memo, creating paragraphs with clear topic sentences.

d. Link ideas using appropriate transitions.

Editing

a. Run your word processor's spell check on your document.

b. Double-check the letter yourself for spelling, grammar, and mechanical errors.

3. **Writing task:** For each of the following scenarios, write a paragraph describing how you might address these rhetorical issues: (1) tone, (2) vocabulary, (3) technical terminology, and (4) definition of terms and concepts.

a. While another accountant in your office took two weeks' vacation, you were assigned to oversee a key project with one of her long-term clients. You need to write a memo summarizing your interactions with the client over the past two weeks so the accountant can be quickly "brought back into the loop" upon her return to the office.

b. You need to write an introductory letter to the owner of Johan's Café, Johan Bertsin, a new client with whom you first spoke last week. The letter should cite your willingness to work closely with Mr. Bertsin to prepare his tax returns.

c. As an accounting intern, you need to write your supervisor a memo that synthesizes the information you have gathered for her on a new client.

d. You are a CPA working for a large multinational firm. You need to write a letter to your counterpart in the firm's U.K. branch office to update him on some changes in the specialized accounts.

e. You need to write a letter to the Internal Revenue Service on your client's behalf suggesting a quarterly payment plan to begin reducing significant tax debt his business incurred last year.

4. Your client is the owner of Clip N' Snip, a pet grooming business established last year. Using the information provided, write a letter to the client suggesting ways to increase net income for next year.

Clip N' Snip

Partial Trial Balance

For the year ended December 31, 2000

	Debit	Credit
Flea and Tick Dip Service Revenue		$80,000
Wash and Trim Service Revenue		60,000
Wage Expense (Receptionist and Part-Time Assistant)	40,000	
Shop Rent Expense	36,000	
Depreciation Expense (Clip N' Snip Minivan)	4,000	
Depreciation Expense (Furniture and Equipment)	2,500	
Utilities Expense	3,400	
Advertising Expense	1,000	
Auto Expense (Gas, etc.)	2,100	
Pet Wash Supplies	5,000	
Flea and Tick Dip Supplies	23,000	

Prewriting

a. Make brief notes about each line item. Jot down ideas about ways that revenues could be increased and expenses reduced.

b. Here is a reader profile worksheet on your client, Ms. Tammy Grimes, owner of Clip N' Snip. Write a brief statement, based on this worksheet, about Ms. Grimes's needs as a reader.

WORKSHEET

Reader Profile

1. Position: Existing Client

2. Readiness: Requested/Expecting Document

3. Attitude: Interested in the information. Needs help!

4. Knowledge: New business owner. Familiar with most basic terms (revenues, expense); no accounting knowledge.

5. Other: Age 29; Gender F

Educational Level: Two years, community college

Ms. Grimes learns fast and wants to do everything she can to increase the bottom line. She is a true animal lover, however, and will not cut corners where animal care and welfare are concerned.

---

    c. Write a one-sentence purpose statement that succinctly captures what you want the client to know/do.

Drafting

Quickly draft the letter, incorporating the ideas you generated in your prewriting.

Remember to focus on one idea per paragraph and to develop that idea completely.

Revising

    a. Put yourself in the client's shoes and reread your drafted letter. (Or exchange papers with a classmate and discuss your drafts.) Decide on the two most important steps the client can take to increase net income. Retain those two ideas and eliminate the rest.

    b. Revise the topic sentence for each paragraph, checking for context and purpose.

    c. Organize your content in descending order of importance.

    d. Check your format: Have you used lists and bullets to highlight important points? If not, revise to do so.

    e. Choose at least one other way of leading the reader and use it to improve the clarity of your letter.

Editing

    a. If you are writing on a computer, run the word processor's spell check.

    b. Double-check the letter yourself for spelling, grammar, and mechanical errors.

5. Scenario: You are the student assistant to an accounting professor who has asked you to collect information for a recruiting letter to high school seniors. The letter, which will be sent to students who have expressed an interest in a business career, will highlight the career advantages of an accounting degree. The professor has suggested you perform a search on the World Wide Web to locate information that would encourage prospective students to consider an accounting major.

    Writing task: Locate several Web sites that provide information on accounting careers and summarize your findings in a memo to your professor.

Prewriting

    a. Locate the Web site and jot down the points your professor would want to include in the letter to prospective accounting majors.

    b. Complete a reader profile on the high school seniors who will read the final letter. (Keep in mind that the information is for your professor to include in a letter to prospective accounting majors.)

    c. Write a one-sentence purpose statement for the memo.

    d. Organize the collected data in order of descending importance.

Drafting

    a. Begin the memo by summarizing your purpose so your professor will understand "where you are going."

    b. Flesh out the rest of the memo by incorporating the ideas you generated in your prewriting. Remember to conclude by summarizing your key points.

Revising

a. Put yourself in your professor's shoes and reread the memo. Decide on the three or four most important pieces of information your professor would want to include in a letter to prospective students. Retain these points and cut the rest.

b. Organize your points using the order of descending importance.

c. Check your format to ensure that you have used lists and/or bullets to highlight key points.

d. Use at least two transitional words or phrases from the list on pp. 51–52 to link your ideas more clearly.

Editing

a. Run your word processor's spell check on your document.

b. Double-check the letter yourself for spelling, grammar, and mechanical errors.

6. **Writing task:** Switch your focus. Assume your professor had asked you to gather the accounting information from the Web sites and then draft the letter to the prospective students yourself. How might that letter differ from the summary memo you've prepared for your professor? Jot down at least three differences you could foresee in the writing process and/or the written product. Now write the letter to the students.

7. **Scenario:** Listed here are the comparative income statements for Penelope's Loom, a weaving and needlepoint boutique:

	2000	1999
Sales	$100,000	$50,000
Cost of sales	50,000	30,000
Gross margin	50,000	20,000
Operating expenses	12,000	10,000
Operating income	38,000	10,000
Loss on sale of equipment	(40,000)	
Net income	(2,000)	10,000

Penelope Bidwell, the owner, believes the company performed better in 2000 than it did in 1999. She understands nothing about accounting, however, and has asked you to write a letter she can use to approach potential investors.

Writing task: Write the letter explaining why the company is financially sound and why the investor should not be alarmed by the $2,000 loss in a year when sales have doubled.

Prewriting

a. Make comparative notes about the line items. Compare and contrast the statements for 2000 and 1999 and summarize your analysis by jotting down key points.

b. Write a brief description of the tone this letter should adopt.

c. Consider your reader's needs. (*Remember:* The letter will be written on behalf of the owner to a potential investor.) Given your audience, write a few short notes to yourself about how you will address issues of vocabulary, technical terminology, and definitions of concepts.

d. Write a one-sentence purpose statement that clearly states the key message(s) Ms. Bidwell should convey to the investor.

Drafting

a. Quickly draft the letter and incorporate the ideas you generated in your prewriting. Limit each paragraph to one central point/idea.

Revising

a. Put yourself in the investor's shoes and reread the letter (or exchange papers with a classmate and discuss). Check to ensure that your opening sentence introduces the reader to your context by anchoring your communication in information the reader already has. Make sure your second sentence clearly states your purpose by summarizing what you want your reader to learn or do. If your sentences do not reflect these points, revise them to make them do so.

b. Organize the points you wish to communicate using the order of descending importance.

c. Dovetail some of your sentences to ensure the logical flow of ideas.

d. Use parallel grammatical structure to keep your reader on track.

e. Check your format for readability.

Editing

a. Run your word processor's spell check on your document.

b. Double-check the letter yourself for spelling, grammar, and mechanical errors.

(Adapted from G. A. Porter and C. L. Norton, *Financial Accounting,* Dryden Press, 1998.)

8. Scenario: The memo here is from an investment firm research analyst who studies municipalities and other government entities that issue bonds. The analyst writes to her supervisor, the director of research, to update him on the work she has been doing.

Writing task: Revise the memo as necessary to improve its tone.

MEMO

To: Pete Rodriguez
From: Sally Higgins
Date: February 10, 2000

This memo is to let you know that although I haven't (as yet) added much to Sun Systems, I have been working on several projects:

I've been researching the New Mexico counties (I sent the spreadsheet and write-up to you already).

I recently finished a project for Jim on four municipalities in the Bay Area.

I am currently working on 17+ school districts in Arizona for Molly and have a working spreadsheet for her.

Anyway, I just wanted to provide you with an update on my activities. I know I'm probably the least of your concerns at this point, but I might forget to let you know about the projects I'm working on if I don't send you the information now.

9. **Scenario:** Here is a memo from an accounting intern to his supervisor.

   Writing task: Use some of the eight techniques for leading the reader outlined in the chapter to make it clearer and more coherent.

MEMO

To: Ms. Richardson
From: Scott Grover, accounting intern
Date: January 31, 1999
Subject: Report on Past Due Accounts

I have completed the Accounts Receivable analysis project. In working on the project, I found that our 456 past due accounts receivable pertain to just 61 customers. I have prepared a report on the company's past due accounts.

I compiled a list of all accounts that were over 60 days past due (according to the December 31 Aging Schedule). They are categorized by customer. Since the number of delinquent customers is so small, our credit department should be able to handle the collections with no additional personnel or overtime.

I recommend that we conduct our own collection effort rather than turn our accounts over to an outside agency.

If you have questions about my report or recommendation, you may contact me at extension 233.

10. **Scenario:** The letter here, from an investment counselor to a client, contains terms and concepts that require definition. Identify the items that should be defined and substitute simpler language that will be easy for the client to understand.

LETTER

Dear Mrs. Miller,

It was a pleasure to meet with you and your daughter last week, and I look forward to working with you and to helping you refine your investment strategy. I have been researching the stocks in which you expressed an interest and have some recommendations on how you should invest the proceeds of your late husband's life insurance.

Given your other sources of income, including Social Security, I would advise you to invest in revenue securities so that you may maintain your comfortable lifestyle. The stocks that you specifically requested are growth stocks, so I must advise against them for the time being. In a year or so, when your husband's estate is settled, you may have some extra funds that you could put into growth stocks to enhance the long-term value of your estate for your children.

I understand you may have questions at this point, so please feel free to call me or to stop by my office, and I will be happy to explain further.

Sincerely,

Michele Foster, CFP

Developing a Professional Communication Style

Becoming a professional accountant demands more than simply passing the CPA exam. It also requires you to learn to speak and write the language of accountancy—in other words, you must develop an appropriate professional communication style. A professional style identifies you as a colleague to other accountants, builds your credibility with clients, and enhances the image you present in the workplace.

LEARNING BY IMITATION

You will learn the language of accountancy in the same way you learned language in childhood—by imitating others who speak and write it. By listening to professional accountants and reading what they write, you will gradually become familiar with the specialized vocabulary of accountancy and with many of the communications that define professional practice. While you are learning this new language, you must also learn to distinguish the levels of style used in different types of communications because language appropriate in some contexts is not appropriate in others.

FORMAL VERSUS INFORMAL STYLE

As an accounting student, you will be exposed constantly to language that is dense, formal, and abstract. In course after course, you will study the guidelines, regulations, and pronouncements that govern the practice of accounting. You will study Statements of Financial Accounting Standards (SFAS), Statements on Auditing Standards (SAS), the Internal Revenue Code (IRC), and other official documents that set professional standards and regulate professional conduct.

Here is a sample of such language from an SFAS on reporting payments of artist royalties in the music industry:

> The amount of royalties earned by artists, as adjusted for anticipated returns, shall be charged to expense of the period in which the sale of the record takes

place. An advance royalty paid to an artist shall be reported as an asset if the past performance and current popularity of the artist to whom the advance is made provide a sound basis for estimating that the amount of the advance will be recoverable from future royalties to be earned by the artist.[1]

Here is another, from the Internal Revenue Code, on deductions for entertainment expenses:

(a)(1) In general
No deduction otherwise allowable under this chapter shall be allowed for any item
(a)(1)(A) Activity
With respect to an activity which is of a type generally considered to constitute entertainment, amusement, or recreation, unless the taxpayer establishes that the item was directly related to, or, in the case of an item directly preceding or following a substantial and bona fide business discussion (including business meetings at a convention or otherwise), that such item was associated with, the active conduct of the taxpayer's trade or business. . . .[2]

These passages are typical of the official language of accountancy, characterized by highly complex syntax and consistently difficult style.[3] Because professional standards statements and regulatory documents must be as inclusive as possible in their coverage of complex issues, they rely on abstract language and resist specificity. And because they represent the voice of collective authority in the accounting profession, these documents maintain an impersonal distance from the individual reader.

While you are becoming familiar with this formal style, you will likely have less exposure as a student to the language accountants routinely use in daily practice with colleagues and clients, the language of phone conversations and meetings, of letters and memos, of written reports and oral presentations. In contrast to the language of the profession's governing documents, the language of day-to-day practice is, at its best, simple and direct, concise and clear, concrete, and, in many cases, informal.

Unfortunately, many entry-level accountants try to adopt in their writing the profession's most formal style for routine communications on the job. It is easy to understand why they make this mistake. The formal style predominates in the textbooks, academic journals, and professional and government publications that constitute much of the accounting student's reading. And because this style conveys a sense of authority and expertise, it *seems* to set a standard to which those entering the profession should aspire.

In ordinary workplace communications, however, this official style is usually inappropriate. It is hard to read, and it confuses clients, who lack the expertise to understand specialized vocabulary and need examples to understand abstract accounting principles. It tries the patience of co-workers, who are busy and want messages to come to the point. Therefore, although you must understand the formal, authoritative language of accountancy (and know when and how to incorporate it in your communications), you must also know how to communicate in a style that is simple, concise, and direct.

This chapter will help you develop such a style by identifying techniques for the following:

- eliminating wordiness
- avoiding clichés
- expressing yourself directly
- handling sentence structure
- avoiding common stylistic errors

We focus primarily on *written* style for three reasons:

- writing skills are harder to master than speaking skills
- written communications fall more easily into the so-called official style than oral communications do
- the writing process provides a foundation for both written documents and oral presentations

After you have mastered the writing techniques described here, you will find they are easy to apply in oral communications.

EFFECTIVE COMMUNICATION IS CLEAR AND CONCISE

In a recent survey of accountants' writing skills, nearly 60% of the CPAs responding rated new accountants below average on concise language usage.[4] Concise writing is important in day-to-day practice because it is easy for others to understand. Because concise writing is direct, specific, and to the point, it saves time for both the writer and the reader. Here are some rules you can use to ensure that your writing style is concise:

Use short, simple words instead of long, fancy ones. Many simple, one-syllable English words have longer, multisyllable synonyms. Because these longer words are common in formal prose, many writers use them in an effort to create a voice of authority. But too many of these multisyllable words make for stuffy writing. In most communications, rely on the straightforward, simple words listed here rather than their longer counterparts:

Long, Fancy	Short, Simple
accomplish, execute	do
facilitate	help
implement, commence	start
opportunity	chance
component	part
instruct	tell
request	ask
convey	give
identify	show
attempt	try
utilize	use

Compare these two sentences:

Long, fancy words: A budget facilitates communication by making each manager throughout the organization aware of the plans being implemented by other managers.

Short, simple words: A budget helps managers throughout the organization to communicate because it lets them know what other managers are planning to do.

Where possible, choose a single word instead of a phrase. Sometimes it is easier to express ideas in several words than to find the word that best conveys your meaning. But regularly using several words in place of the right one puffs up your prose and makes it imprecise. Such phrases as *due to the fact that, during the period of,* and *for the purpose of* are what writing experts call "deadwood" and need to be pruned away. Here are some other examples of deadwood, along with preferable alternatives:

Deadwood	Concise
by means of	by
by reason of	because of
by virtue of	by, under
for the reason that	because
in connection with	with, about
in order to	to
in terms of	in
in the event that	if
on the basis of	by
prior to	before
subsequent to	after
with regard to	about
have the capability of	can
have the capacity to	can
in conjunction with	with
at the present time	now

Phrases that substitute for single adjectives or adverbs are another common source of deadwood (see the Grammar Reference Guide at the end of the book for information on adjectives and adverbs).

Deadwood: The system allows auditors to prepare electronic workpapers *that are consistent and complete.*

Improved: The system allows auditors to prepare *consistent, complete* electronic workpapers.

Deadwood: In recent years, companies worldwide have been dealing with an issue *that has become increasingly significant.*

Improved: In recent years, companies worldwide have been dealing with an *increasingly significant* issue.

Redundant expressions, those that state the same thing twice, are a third source of deadwood. Edit them out.

Redundant	Simple
absolutely essential	essential
assembled together	assembled
filled to capacity	filled
small in size	small
close proximity	proximity
final outcome	outcome
future plans	plans
hidden pitfall	pitfall
past experience	experience
plan ahead	plan
postponed until later	postponed
refer back to	refer to
unforeseen disruptions	disruptions
unsolved problem	problem
very unique	unique

Redundant: Holmes, Co., Ltd., has not developed a *formal* disaster recovery plan *which would be implemented in the event of unexpected interruptions in* business and/or computer operations.

Improved: Holmes, Co., Ltd., has not developed a disaster recovery plan for business and computer operations.

Redundant: We believe that there are significant tax planning opportunities available to you. These opportunities, *which we believe could be significant, go beyond federal income taxes to* include state income taxes and estate and gift taxes.

Improved: We believe significant tax planning opportunities are available to you. These opportunities include potential savings on federal and state income taxes as well as on estate and gift taxes.

In the first set of sentences above, eliminating superfluous words and phrases reduced sentence length nearly 50% (from 27 words to 15) without a loss of content. Eliminating the redundant "which" phrase in the second set has a less dramatic effect on sentence length, but it gets rid of the glaring repetition of the word *significant*.

Avoid formulaic expressions and clichés. Busy accountants, writing under pressure, often resort to communication formulas and clichés, especially at the beginning and end of letters and memos. These formulaic expressions are not only empty and impersonal; they are wordy as well.

Instead of . . .	Say . . .
Pursuant to our conversation	When we talked; spoke yesterday; spoke on the phone; and so on.
We are in receipt of	We have received
Attached herewith	We/I have attached
Enclosed please find	We/I have enclosed
Per your request	As you asked; as you wanted
Please be advised that	(Omit)
Please rest assured	(Omit)
If you should have any questions, please do not hesitate to contact me.	If you have questions, please call me at at . . .

Limit prepositional phrases. Prepositional phrases help explain the relations between sentence elements. But sentences with too many prepositional phrases seem clogged and awkward.[5]

> **Awkward:** There will be an investigation *(of the problem) (by the planning team) (in order) (to arrive) (at alternative solutions.)*

> **Improved:** The planning team will investigate the problem and suggest alternative solutions.

> **Awkward:** *(In connection) (with the audit) (of Toys and Gadgets, Inc.) (for the period ended 12/31/99,)* Corporate Audit Services will provide assistance *(to Jones & Smith LLP).*

> **Improved:** Corporate Audit Services will assist Jones & Smith LLP *(with the Toys and Gadgets, Inc. audit) (for the period ended 12/31/99).*

Read these sentences aloud. You will be able to hear the clutter caused by excessive prepositions. When you encounter a sentence that seems unusually dense and wordy, put parentheses around all the prepositional phrases as we have done here. This technique will help you see instantly whether the density results from excessive prepositions.

Use *It is/There is/There are* constructions sparingly. These constructions make your writing wordy because they set up dummy subjects and verbs. Such subjects do not explain what the sentence is about, nor do such verbs express the sentence's action. For this reason, the *real* subject and verb must appear in an additional clause (for a review of clauses, see the Grammar Reference Guide):

>   **Dummy S-V**   **Real S**   **Real V**
> **Wordy:** *It is* the responsibility of each *organization* to *assess* its software.

>   **S**   **V**
> **Improved:** Each *organization should assess* its software.

>   **Dummy S-V**   **Real S**   **Real V**
> **Wordy:** *There is* no question that certain *assets might not be realized* at full value.

>   **S**   **V**
> **Improved:** Certain *assets might not be realized* at full value.

These constructions can be useful for creating sentence variety, but use them judiciously.

Break up long sentences into several shorter ones. Concise sentences should not exceed an average of 20 words. If your sentences consistently run longer than a line or line-and-a-half of 12-point type, they are too long. They are probably wordy as well. The grammar checker on your computer can help you check your sentence length at a glance (Grammar checkers cannot be relied upon to correct all grammatical mistakes, however.)

Consider the pairs of sentences here. The first sentence in each pair is almost incomprehensible. It contains more ideas than its sentence structure can handle, not to mention superfluous words. The revised versions are more concise because the sentences have been divided, long introductory phrases have been cut, and excess words have been eliminated.

Too long: Until Mr. Hawkins returns and instructs otherwise or expounds in more detail upon the relevant procedures, listed below are a few interdepartmental guidelines to be followed when an accident occurs.

Improved: Here are the procedures for handling accidents in your department. Please continue to follow them unless Mr. Hawkins changes them on his return.

Too long: By copy of this letter with attachments to the London office, we kindly request that they critique our analysis, give their approval if they agree to it, and copy Blackburg Shipyard to the attention of Mr. C.A. Gillis and ourselves on such approval.

Improved: We have sent the London office a copy of this letter (with attachments) and asked them to critique our analysis. We have asked them to let us know if they approve it and, if so, to notify Mr. C.A. Gillis at Blackburg Shipyard as well.

Our suggestion that sentences be 20 words *on average* does not mean that *every* sentence should be 20 words long. Once you have learned to deflate dense, wordy sentences, you can begin experimenting with sentences of varying lengths. The next section will help you learn principles for proper sentence construction, whether you are writing sentences of 10 words, 20 words, or even more.

EFFECTIVE COMMUNICATION IS CLEAR AND DIRECT

Experts on writing unanimously agree that strong verbs are the key to a strong, clear writing style.[6] And experts also agree that passive verbs do more to weaken business writing than any other single writing practice. We turn next to the problem of the passive voice and consider ways to handle it in your professional prose.

In most cases, choose the active voice over the passive. *Voice* is the flow of action in a sentence. The typical English sentence is structured in the *active voice.* In an active sentence, the subject does something and the verb tells what the subject did:

$$\overset{\text{S}}{\text{The taxpayer}} \overset{\text{V}}{\text{completed}} \text{ the 1999 } \overset{\text{O}}{\text{return.}}$$

The **passive voice** reverses the typical S-V-O word order. What was originally the direct object (the tax return) is moved into the subject position, a form of the verb "to be" is added to the original verb, and the subject (often called the *agent* of the action) is moved to the end in a prepositional phrase:

$$\overset{\text{S}}{\text{The 1999 return}} \overset{\text{V}}{\text{was completed}} \overset{\text{Prep Phrase}}{\text{by the taxpayer.}}$$

Because the passive sentence has a new subject and verb (and can stand on its own), the old subject may disappear altogether:

$$\overset{\text{S}}{\text{The 1999 return}} \overset{\text{V}}{\text{was completed}} \text{ on time.}$$

The active voice is generally preferable to the passive because it keeps sentences straightforward, direct, and consequently clear. Yet writers often adopt the passive without thinking and use it when it is unnecessary. Unnecessary or excessive use of the passive leads to *increased wordiness* (because we form the passive with a past participle of the verb plus a form of "to be") and *decreased concreteness* (because the passive voice obscures or eliminates the agent).

You may choose the passive voice in certain situations. When the object of the action is, in fact, more important than the agent, the passive voice is appropriate. Depending on the context, the previous example may illustrate such a case: If the writer wants to emphasize only the timely completion of the tax return, the agent of that completion is unimportant. If the writer wishes to emphasize, however, that it was the taxpayer and not an accountant who completed the return, the passive voice could obscure that distinction. Because the passive voice allows you to eliminate the agent of an action, it is a useful device for reporting bad news. If, for example, you are a member of an audit team that overlooked important information, which of these sentences would you rather use in a report to your supervisor?

> **Active voice:** We will have to repeat that portion of the audit because we did not get complete information.

> **Passive voice:** That portion of the audit must be repeated because the information obtained was not complete.

You would choose the second one, of course. The first (active) sentence implies that the audit team failed to collect all the facts. The second (passive) sentence suggests that the client failed to provide the information, but avoids directly blaming anyone.

Do not smother working verbs. The passive often goes hand in hand with another offense against clarity: the practice of smothering verbs, also called *nominalization.* Verbs drive sentences. They describe action and tell the reader what happened. Too often, however, writers under the sway of the official style drain the life out of their sentences by turning their verbs (needlessly) into nouns or adjectives. Not only does this practice mask the action of the sentence, it creates other stylistic problems as well.

> **Original/working verbs:** The committee *intends* to *decide* on the matter by June 1.

> **Smothered verbs:** *It is* the *intention* of the committee that a *decision will be made* on the matter by June 1.

Notice what happened when the verbs changed to nouns. The sentence became more wordy and less clear because smothering the verbs did the following:

- nearly doubled the length of the sentence, turning 11 words into 19
- added a prepositional phrase *(of the committee)*
- transformed two-syllable verbs *(intends, decide)* into three-syllable nouns *(intention, decision)*
- converted an active statement into a passive one
- shifted the agent subject *(The committee)* to a dummy subject *(It)*
- added two "to be" verbs (one to form the passive and one to form the dummy subject)

As you can see, the practice of smothering verbs can instantly clutter a sentence and obscure its meaning. Although we sometimes need derivative nouns and adjectives, overusing them is a surefire way to damage prose style. Smothered verbs are easy to spot by their endings: *-al, -ant, -ance, -ence, -ency, -en, -ery, -ion, -ure.*

Here is a list of common smothered verbs:

Smothered Verb	Working Verb
analysis	analyze
authorization	authorize
commencement	commence
determination	determine
failure	fail
formulation	formulate
performance	perform
reliance	rely
discover	discovery

Smothered verb: Melissa *conducted an analysis* of the financial statements.

Working verb: Melissa *analyzed* the financial statements.

Smothered verb: The CPA *made a determination* that his client owed $2,350 in penalties and interest.

Working verb: The CPA *determined* that his client owed $2,350 in penalties and interest.

Some verbs do not change their form when we smother them, but they act as nouns nevertheless:

report	report
change	change

Smothered verb: Julian *issued a report* of his findings to the SEC.

Working verb: Julian *reported* his findings to the SEC.

Smothered verb: Some verbs do not *undergo a change* when we smother them.

Working verb: Some verbs do not *change* when we smother them.

Here are some examples of the close connection between passive voice and smothered verbs:

Original: New procedures *are predicated* on the *assumption* that reporting delays *will not be tolerated* by management.

Revised: Because management will not tolerate reporting delays, we have developed new procedures.

Original: No formal procedures or approval processes exist in the *determination* of accounts receivable *to be written off.*

Revised: The company has no formal procedures or approval process to determine which accounts receivable to write off.

In both cases, converting the passive voice to the active helps eliminate smothered verbs *(assumption, determination)* and prepositional phrases *(on the assumption, by management, in the determination, of accounts receivable)*. And restoring an agent to the subject position *(we, The company)* makes the action of the sentence clear.

Put your subject near the beginning of your sentence. We noted earlier that the typical English sentence is structured **subject-verb-object.** This pattern is, in fact, so deeply ingrained in English speakers that we automatically expect sentences to begin by introducing their subjects. Sentences that delay the introduction of their subjects beyond a few brief words can be disorienting because they violate our expectations and make us wait for the main point.

Consider the following example:

Delayed subject: *Despite the protection afforded surviving spouses by the laws of community property, considering the size of the estate,* **the best choice** is to leave the trust intact.

The reader has to move through *18 words* before arriving at the subject of this sentence. These words support the recommendation that follows, but because they *precede* the recommendation rather than follow it, they lack an anchor to the subject. For this reason, the 18-word introductory phrases seem not to explain but merely to impede the business of the sentence.

> **Improved:** *Despite the protection of community property law,* **the surviving spouse** will benefit most from leaving the trust intact.

> **Improved:** *Considering the size of the estate,* **the best choice** is to leave the trust intact.

To make sure your sentences get to the point, apply these guidelines:

- Never use more than one introductory phrase or clause in a single sentence. The sample sentence has two, which make it particularly clumsy: *Despite the protection afforded surviving spouses by the laws of community property,* and *considering the size of the estate.*
- Keep your introductory elements under eight or ten words *(Despite the protection of community property law* = seven words; *considering the size of the estate* = six words).

Put your verb near your subject. The S-V structure that makes us seek subjects at the beginning of sentences also makes us expect a close connection between the subject and verb. The subject and verb are the key elements of any sentence, the basic grammatical unit. In this sense, they depend on each other: Once the subject appears, we expect to see the verb. Long interrupters between subject and verb frustrate readers because they split up a natural pair. Such is the case with the following sentence, where 16 words intervene between subject and verb:

> **Delayed verb:** Tolson International, *the management company for off-shore investment firms organized in Bermuda under UK tax-free laws,* was established on 1/1/98.

> **Improved:** Tolson International is the management company for several off-shore investment firms organized in Bermuda under UK tax-free laws. It was established on 1/1/98.

Sometimes, excessive prepositional phrases delay the verb:

> **Delayed verb:** Basic procedures *for the valuation of inventory* such as stock counts and review *of the provisions* made *for obsolescence* will be handled by Jackson and Samuels.

> **Improved:** Jackson and Samuels will handle basic procedures for inventory valuation. These procedures will include stock counts and a review of provisions for obsolescence.

If a sentence seems long and unclear, underline the subject, double underline the verb, and see how closely they are placed to one another. If they are separated by more than three or four words, revise.

Recast negative statements as positive ones. Negative statements are harder to understand than positive ones. Furthermore, multiple negatives in a single sentence can almost completely obscure meaning.

Some verbs and conjunctions are implicitly negative. Using them with other negatives creates confusion:

Implicitly negative verbs: *avoid, deny, refuse, exclude, contradict, preclude, prevent, lack, fail, doubt, reject, prohibit*

Implicitly negative conjunctions: *except, unless, provided, however, without, against, lacking, absent, but for*

When you combine negative words with the passive voice, smothered verbs, and complex sentence structure, you may leave your readers in the dark:

Negative: Disentangling this client's tax problems is not possible without release of the disputed records.

Financial statements should not be compiled if there has not been authorization by this office.

The failure of the controller's office to notify the department should not have precluded timely filing of the reports.

To straighten out such sentences:

Turn the Obvious Negatives Around

is not possible	is possible
should not be compiled	should be compiled
has not been authorized	has been authorized

Change Implicitly Negative Words and Phrases to Affirmative Ones

disentangling this client's problems	straightening out the client's problems
without the release	when . . . are released
precluded timely filing	could have been filed on time

Improved: We will need to obtain the disputed records to straighten out this client's tax problems.

Please get authorization from this office before compiling financial statements.

The reports could have been filed on time without controller notification.

EFFECTIVE COMMUNICATION IS CLEAR AND CORRECT

A professional communication style shows mastery of standard English. Errors in grammar and usage mark a communicator as professionally deficient, whether they occur in writing or in speaking. Such errors can also make your communications confusing because grammar governs the relationships among ideas in the sentence.

Certain grammatical errors common in professional writing create special problems with clarity. These errors include **vague pronoun reference, unclear modifiers,** and **mixed sentence constructions** (see the Grammar Reference Guide for detailed coverage of these and other errors).

Vague Pronoun Reference

In speech, we often use the pronouns *this* and *these* to refer in a general way to the idea expressed in a preceding clause or sentence. In writing, however, such loose pronoun reference may be ambiguous or confusing:

> **Vague:** Operating margins grew to 23% in 2000 from 22% in 1999. *This* is attributable to sales growth outpacing moderate growth in selling expenses.

To correct the problem, insert a noun after the pronouns *this* and *these:*

> **Improved:** Operating margins grew to 23% in 2000 from 22% in 1999. *This increase* occurred because sales growth outpaced moderate growth in selling expenses.

If you find that you cannot insert a single noun, rewrite:

> **Vague:** We will review the accrual for sales delivered but not paid. *This* was a problem in the past, where the company had old unpaid accounts on the books, but management should have collected *this.*

> **Improved:** We will review the accrual for sales delivered and not paid. The company had some problems with unpaid accounts in the past, but management should have collected on those accounts by now.

Unclear Modifiers

Many writers have trouble with introductory phrases using *-ing* and *-ed* forms of verbs (present and past participles). Sometimes the words these phrases modify are far away from the modifier or even absent from the sentence. When the words are far away from the introductory phrase, we say the modifier is **misplaced.** When no words appear in the sentence for the phrase to modify, we say the modifier is **dangling.**

> **Misplaced modifier:** *Once prepared and approved,* we will send *the documents* to the shareholders.

The introductory phrase here appears to modify the subject, *we,* which makes nonsense of the sentence. Here is one way to correct the problem:

> **Corrected:** Once prepared and approved, the documents will be sent to the shareholders.

In the following sentence, the introductory phrase modifies the subject, *reorganization,* creating nonsense:

> **Dangling modifier:** *Discouraged by low profits and high overhead,* reorganization was the only solution.

To correct a dangling modifier, add a subject that the phrase could properly modify:

> **Corrected:** *Discouraged* by low profits and high overhead, *the company* decided to reorganize.

> **Dangling modifier:** The engagement was given to another firm after *becoming frustrated* with the team's frequent delays.

> **Corrected:** The engagement was given to another firm after *management became* frustrated with the team's frequent delays.

Mixed Sentence Constructions

Sometimes during the editing process, you will find a sentence that seems particularly awkward. The first part does not fit properly with the second part so that the sentence seems to shift direction midway through. These mixed constructions are hard for readers to understand because they confuse the grammatical relationships among sentence elements. Here are some examples:

> **Mixed construction:** *By asking clients to schedule appointments before March* is one way to reduce the pressure during tax season.

The writer begins with an introductory phrase and then tries to make that phrase serve as the subject of the sentence, which it cannot do. A rewrite is needed:

> **Corrected:** One way to reduce the pressure during tax season is to ask clients to schedule appointments before March 1.
>
> *or*
>
> **Corrected:** Asking clients to schedule appointments before March 1 is one way to reduce the pressure during tax season.

> **Mixed construction:** *Although he has worked in an accounting firm* does not make him a CPA.

> **Corrected:** Although he has worked in an accounting firm, he is not a CPA.
>
> *or*
>
> **Corrected:** Working in an accounting firm does not necessarily qualify him as a CPA.

A related type of mixed sentence uses the "by . . . . this" construction:

> **Mixed construction:** *By* having Emily as sole shareholder of LifeZone, *this* will keep the IRS from asserting the "reincorporation-liquidation" doctrine.

The easiest way to correct this error is to eliminate "by" and "this":

> **Corrected:** Having Emily as sole shareholder of LifeZone will keep the IRS from asserting the "reincorporation-liquidation" doctrine.

TRANSLATING THE OFFICIAL STYLE

As we have noted, you must master the authoritative language of accountancy because it is used to convey much of the specialized knowledge of the profession. Your challenge as a practicing accountant, however, will most frequently be to explain accounting issues to others in simple language. As a CPA working on a tax problem, for example, you may have to consult federal and state tax codes and apply the complex language you find there to clients' financial information. Clients are paying for your ability to understand this technical language, use it in their behalf, and recommend a solution in language they can easily understand. As a corporate accountant working with your company's product management team, you would follow Generally Accepted Accounting Principles (GAAP) in setting up and maintaining an accounting system for inventories. But your report would not cite these principles in full; instead, it would focus on explaining your conclusions as clearly and simply as possible.

Keeping language clear for clients and other non-expert readers is so important, in fact, that the SEC issued guidelines in 1998 to help keep disclosure documents, such as Form 10K filings, simple. These guidelines are compiled in "A Plain English Handbook" available on the SEC Web site (www.sec.gov/news/handbook.htm) and in hard copy upon request. In the handbook, you will find further examples of the principles set forth in this chapter. Both of these sources can help you "translate" the official language of accountancy into language that communicates with a wide range of readers. To see how, let us return to the two passages cited at the beginning of this chapter.

Here is the sample from SFAS No. 50 on financial reporting in the music industry:

> The amount of royalties earned by artists, as adjusted for anticipated returns, shall be charged to expense of the period in which the sale of the record takes place. An advance royalty paid to an artist shall be reported as an asset if the past performance and current popularity of the artist to whom the advance is made provide a sound basis for estimating that the amount of the advance will be recoverable from future royalties to be earned by the artist.

This 82-word passage consists of two sentences, one of 29 words and one of 53 words. The average sentence length in this passage is 41 words. To shorten and simplify these sentences, follow these steps in order:

1. *Locate the subjects.* Whenever you tackle a problematic sentence, look for the subject first. Check to see whether that subject is delayed or otherwise buried in wordiness. The subjects here are easy to locate because they appear at the beginning of each sentence: *The amount,* and *An advance royalty.*

2. *Locate the verbs.* Always look for the verb next because the verb explains the action of the sentence. The verbs in the main clauses here—*shall be charged,* and *shall be reported*—are both in the passive voice, although they are reasonably close to the subjects with which they are paired (for review on clauses, see the Grammar Reference Guide).

3. *Isolate the prepositional phrases.* Remember: Excessive prepositions are a notorious source of clutter. Good editing turns as many prepositional phrases as possible into single modifiers. The first sentence of this passage has 8 prepositional phrases totaling 19 words, or 66% of the sentence: *(of royalties), (by artists), (for anticipated returns), (to expense), (of the period), (in which the sale), (of the record).* The second sentence has 8 prepositional phrases totaling 26 words, 49% of the sentence: *(to an artist), (as an asset), (of the artist), (to whom the advance is made), (for estimating), (of the advance), (from future royalties), (by the artist).*

4. *Check for smothered verbs, redundancies, long fancy words, and other offenses against conciseness and clarity.* A quick check shows few problems with smothered verbs, although many of the prepositional phrases are redundant (see revision).

This passage is relatively easy to revise because its wordiness is a result of two major problems: passive verbs and excessive prepositions. Here is a possible revision:

> Charge an artist's royalties to expense in the period of the sale. Report an artist's advance royalty as an asset if you estimate that future royalties will recover the advance. Base your estimate on the artist's past performance and current popularity.

By shifting from the legalistic voice of authority *(shall be charged, shall be reported)* to a more conversational voice *(Charge, report, base),* the revision eliminates awkward passive verbs. Judicious pruning converts numerous prepositional phrases to adjectives *(by artists > the artist's)* and simply eliminates others *(The amount of royalties > royalties) (period in which the sale of the record > of the sale) (An advance royalty paid to an artist > an artist's advance royalty).* The result is a passage exactly half as long as the original (41 words instead of 82) and much easier to read.

The passage from the Internal Revenue Code is even more difficult to read than the SFAS sample, partly because of its formatting. Eliminating that formatting leaves us with the following sentence of 83 words:

> No deduction otherwise allowable under this chapter shall be allowed for any item with respect to an activity which is of a type generally considered to constitute entertainment, amusement, or recreation, unless the taxpayer establishes that the item was directly related to, or, in the case of an item directly preceding or following a substantial and bona fide business discussion (including business meetings at a convention or otherwise), that such item was associated with, the active conduct of the taxpayer's trade or business. . . .

To revise this one, follow these steps:

1. *Locate the subject.* The subject here, *No deduction,* is the first phrase in the sentence.
2. *Locate the verb.* The verb here, *shall be allowed,* is in the passive voice; it is separated from the subject by only five words.
3. *Untangle the negatives.* This passage is so difficult because it consists of an unusually long sentence cast in the negative. The negative in the main clause, *No deduction,* is complicated by the negative cast of the long subordinate clause (beginning with the implicitly negative conjunction *unless*). Recast the sentence: *Deductions shall be allowed . . . if.*
4. *Eliminate wordy phrases.* Regulatory writing is often wordy because it must be so inclusive; that is, it must be broad enough to cover every instance that might fall under a given rule. Wordy sentences result, in part, from this need for inclusiveness.

    Look, for example, at the first 30 words of the sentence we are considering; *No deduction otherwise allowable under this chapter shall be allowed for any item with respect to an activity which is of a type generally considered to constitute entertainment, amusement, or recreation, . . .* . The phrase *otherwise allowable under this chapter* seems redundant, if not in the strictest legal sense, certainly in most practical contexts. The phrase *with respect to* is vague; the "which" clause, *which is of a type generally considered to constitute,* is simply deadwood. Together, these elements total 18 words, and cutting them away reduces the sentence considerably.
5. *Break the long sentence into several shorter ones.* Isolate the points and subpoints; then write a separate sentence for each.

Here is a revision:

Deductions shall be allowed for expenses associated with entertainment, amusement, or recreation if those activities meet certain requirements. The taxpayer must show that the expense was directly related to the active conduct of the taxpayer's trade or business. Such activities may include those directly preceding or following a substantial and bona fide business discussion (including business meetings at conventions).

To make the sentence even more direct, you could address the reader directly:

You can deduct expenses associated with entertainment, amusement, or recreation if those activities meet certain requirements. *You* must show that the expense was directly related to the active conduct of *your* trade or business. Such activities may include those directly preceding or following a substantial and bona fide business discussion (including business meetings at conventions).

PUTTING IT INTO PRACTICE

As we have stressed, it is important to treat editing as a separate step in the writing process. *Do not try to edit as you write,* especially while you are working to develop your style. Even though computers make changes easy to accomplish,

---

Figure 3.1

Draft of an Internal Memo (with Handwritten Notations)

> ## MEMO
>
> ### Watson, McManus, Barron & Wood
>
> TO: Franklin Thomas
>
> FROM: Mary Ellen Adams
>
> DATE: August 18, 1998
>
> RE: To liquidate or not to liquidate Jemson Foods, Inc.
>
> *smothered verb*
> Since the (completion) (of the asset purchase) (between Orion, Inc. and Jemson
> *"dummy" subj.*   *wordy*
> Foods, Inc.) (JMI), there has been a good deal (of discussion) (on the possible)
> *smothered verb*
> (liquidation) (of JMI.)   Although (from a non-tax standpoint) the continuation (of the
> *"dummy" subj.   smothered verb*
> corporation) seems advisable since there is an (affiliation) (with a union) that supplies
> *"dummy" subj.   smothered verb*
> workers (to JMI,) there are no advantages (from a tax standpoint) to (continuing) its
> existence.
>
> All (of the assets) (of JMI) have been sold, (with only cash remaining.)   If JMI is
> *passive v.   passive v.   smoth. v.*
> liquidated and the cash distributed (to the shareholders,) a gain (on the (redemption) (of
> *passive v.*
> the stock) will be recognized (by the shareholders) (at the capital gains tax rate) (of
> *smoth. v.   passive v.*
> 28%.)   If (liquidation) does not take place and the cash is distributed to the
> *smoth. v.   passive v.*
> shareholders, the (distribution) will be deemed a dividend if the corporation has
> *redundant   dangling modifier*
> earnings and profits, which for our discussion purposes, JMI has.   As a dividend, the
> *passive v.*
> shareholders will recognize ordinary income and be taxed at rates as high as 39.6%.
>
> *"dummy" subj.*
> If is obvious that a tax rate savings (of approximately 11.6%) (39.6% – 28%) can
> *passive v.   smoth. v.*
> be had (by the shareholders) if the corporation is (liquidated.)   Based (upon the
> *"dummy" subj.*
> disparate tax rates) that apply (to the two scenarios) discussed above, it makes sense
> *smoth. v.*
> to liquidate the corporation and tax the cash distributions at 28%.

Figure 3.2

Internal Memo—Revised

> ## MEMO
>
> *Watson, McManus, Barron & Wood*
>
> TO: Franklin Thomas
> FROM: Mary Ellen Adams
> DATE: August 18, 1998
>
> RE: To Liquidate or Not to Liquidate Jemson Foods, Inc.
>
> Since Orion, Inc. purchased the assets of Jemson Foods, Inc. (JMI), Joyce and I have been discussing whether to recommend liquidating JMI. From a non-tax standpoint, continuing the corporation makes sense; it has a strong affiliation with the union, which supplies it with workers. However, there are no tax advantages to continuing its existence.
>
> With all of JMI's assets sold, only cash remains. If JMI is liquidated and the cash distributed, the shareholders will realize a gain on the stock redemption at the capital gains tax rate of 28%. If JMI continues in existence and the cash is distributed, the shareholders will receive it as a dividend (since the corporation has earnings and profits). As a dividend, the cash will be considered ordinary income and will be taxed at rates as high as 39.6%.
>
> The shareholders will recognize a tax rate savings of approximately 11.6% (39.6%–28%) if the corporation is liquidated. Based on these disparate tax rates, we recommend liquidating JMI.

trying to edit while you write usually produces poorly drafted and edited documents. Instead, draft your ideas, revise them for organization, and print a double-spaced copy of your document. Then go through it carefully with a pen or pencil and mark the problems you see. Figure 3.1 offers you a model.

After you have marked your draft with your editorial changes, you are ready to produce a final draft (see Figure 3.2).

CONCLUSION

If you conscientiously apply the guidelines in this chapter, you will develop and maintain a clear, concise, and correct communication style. By editing your work to eliminate deadwood, passives, smothered verbs, and other stylistic problems, you will soon improve your communications. In the meantime, use the following checklist to ensure that you communicate like a pro.

EDITING CHECKLIST

1. Have I consistently used short, simple words instead of long, fancy ones?
2. Have I consistently replaced wordy phrases with single words?
3. Have I edited out all deadwood?
4. Have I eliminated all formulas and clichés?
5. Have I eliminated excess prepositional phrases throughout?
6. Have I kept my sentences under 20 words on average?
7. Are most of my verbs in the active voice?
8. Have I eliminated most smothered verbs?
9. Have I placed my subjects near the beginning of my sentences?
10. Have I placed my verbs close to my subjects?
11. Have I placed my modifiers close to what they modify?
12. Have I made my points in positive statements rather than negative ones?
13. Have I inserted a noun after every instance of *this* or *these?*
14. Have I checked for mixed constructions?
15. Are my sentences correctly punctuated? (See Punctuation Reference Guide.)
16. Have I used gender-neutral language? (See Usage Reference Guide.)
17. Is my word choice appropriate and precise? (See Usage Reference Guide.)
18. Have I proofread carefully for typographical errors and numerical inaccuracies?

NOTES

[1] Financial Accounting Standards Board, *Financial Reporting in the Record and Music Industry,* Statement of Financial Accounting Standards No. 50 (Stamford, CT: Financial Accounting Standards Board, 1981), para. 10.

[2] Internal Revenue Code, Sec. 274(a).

[3] In *Revising Prose,* 3rd ed. (New York: Macmillan, 1992), Richard Lanham uses the term *official style* to describe business writing that is dense, overblown, and hard to understand.

[4] Sandra J. Nelson, Susan Moncada, and Douglas C. Smith, "Written Language Skills of Entry-Level Accountants as Assessed by Experienced CPAs," *Business Communications Quarterly* 59, no. 4 (December 1996): 122-128.

[5] Lanham, in *Revising Prose,* suggests that writers begin the revision process by circling prepositional phrases in a document, counting them, and considering whether too many appear in a single sentence.

[6]Joseph Williams stresses that verbs are the foundation of effective writing in *Style: Ten Lessons in Clarity and Grace,* 5th ed. (New York: Addison Wesley Longman, 1997), as does Richard Lanham in *Revising Business Prose* (New York: Macmillan, 1992).

EXERCISES

1. **Editing task:** In the following sentences, circle the smothered verbs and double underline passives. Then rewrite the sentences, unsmothering verbs, changing passives to actives, and improving conciseness using the techniques described in this chapter.
   a. A management letter comment was generated in prior periods regarding the collection of these types of accounts.
   b. It was suggested that the audit program be revised by the engagement manager.
   c. Compilation of the financial data should be completed by branch managers no later than July 1.
   d. Software should be purchased for the tracking of additions, disposals, and depreciation.
   e. Management must be provided with information to assist in the evaluation of operating results and the facilitation of appropriate decision making.
   f. Measures should be taken to ensure that returns are recorded in the appropriate period in order to properly reflect accurate sales and accounts receivable balances at the end of the accounting period.
   g. Questions were raised concerning certain operations of the company and whether its not-for-profit status could be put in jeopardy by them.
   h. In response to changes in the tax law, new investment products have been added to provide clients with superior rates of return.

2. **Editing task:** Mark the sentences provided, labeling the problems that you see.
   a. We solicit any recommendations you wish to make, and you may be assured that any such recommendations will be given careful consideration.
   b. In an effort to ensure that the self-retention insurance program is working in the manner in which we intended, Carl Dugan has requested that we establish and implement procedures within the technical department.
   c. Further to our previous discussions, attached please find Guilford and Johnson's letter of November 1, 1999, showing that the resistance of our system to security violations is much better than the industry standard's.

    d. Effective planning, increased communication, and senior management support will lead to the more cost-effective utilization of information technology and ensure that the implementation of technology is consistent with corporate strategic goals.

    e. In the event that the resolution of any technical questions requires significant research or the issuance of a formal report, we will consider this as a billable project outside the scope of our audit fees set forth below and provide you with a fee estimate for your approval before the work starts in order to avoid surprises.

3. Writing task: Now revise the sentences from exercise 2 to improve conciseness and clarity.

4. Writing task: For each passage that follows, write a few sentences explaining the sources of wordiness and lack of clarity. Then rewrite the passages to improve conciseness and clarity.

    a. We discussed the development of a computer-based test for inventory obsolescence to provide further comfort that the obsolescence provisions were adequate. While not required based on other procedures being performed, it was suggested that this would be an option worth pursuing since this location has had significant problems with obsolete product.

    b. It is critical for your accounting and information management systems to provide information needed by management to evaluate operating results and facilitate appropriate management decisions.

    c. The major focus in this area is on collectability of receivables resulting from advertising revenue. Our procedures will be limited to obtaining an understanding of the materiality associated with these types of accounts and inquiry of management regarding action taken to address a prior management letter comment on the subject.

    d. It is my understanding that you are using this information in connection with your evaluation of the company's operations. The use of these documents is therefore intended for your evaluation and not for the use of any other person who is not familiar with or is uninformed about the operations of the company.

    e. In order to liquidate a corporation there are certain documents which must be prepared and submitted in conjunction with the corporation's final federal income tax return.

    f. Pursuant to your letter dated 3/6/99 (herewith attached), enclosed please find two schedules which summarize on a monthly basis the beginning and ending balances of those assets generating interest income of $37,296 for the above mentioned tax year.

5. Scenario: A colleague has asked you to look over this draft.
   Writing task:
   a. Mark the document to indicate editorial changes that should be made (use the edited sample on p. 84 as a model).
   b. Rewrite it, incorporating your editorial changes.

LETTER

August 27, 2000

Dear Mr. Selby,

In conjunction with our 1999 financial statement audit we will conduct an assessment of the information technology and application controls related to the financial systems for Barkerding Transport, Inc. Our review of the sustaining accounts payable systems control environment represents a significant part of our annual audit. The audit approach used to assess the control environment of the payable cycle includes:

- Updating our understanding of the flow of transactions through the payable systems, including the main payable system and the various ancillary systems.
- Updating our understanding of the control procedures, both automated and manual, over these systems. This includes program change control, program and data security, authorization of transactions, completeness and accuracy of transaction processing, and reconciliation of the subledger to the general ledger and bank statements.
- Testing the key control procedures identified in the process above through inquiry of personnel, observation of the control procedures, reperformance of certain procedures, and examination of documentation.

Our audit work for the payable systems control assessment is scheduled to be completed during the months of September and October. Limited test procedures will also be performed in November for year-end updates.

Eric Jackne will be contacting you to further discuss our audit approach and the coordination of our work. If you have any questions regarding this year's audit, please do not hesitate to contact me.

Sincerely,

Catherine Shelbourne

6. Scenario: A colleague has asked you to look over this draft.
Writing task:
  a. Indicate editorial changes that should be made.
  b. Rewrite the letter, incorporating your editorial changes.

LETTER

May 31, 1999

Dear Frank:

Per your request, we have designed and drafted an expense report format for use by your employees to request reimbursement for their business-related expenses. I don't think I need to stress the critical importance of its use in the present environment of IRS scrutiny.

As a general background to the format used or perhaps to refresh your memory, the IRS is very stringent regarding the treatment of reimbursed expenses whereby an employee has income to the extent that he is reimbursed for expenses he has incurred in connection with his duties on behalf of the employer. The expenses are only deductible if reimbursed under an "accountable plan," the definition of which I have attached herewith.

To establish with certainty that reimbursement of employee expenses are deemed to have been made under an accountable plan, you should forthwith require your employees to utilize the enclosed format for any and all reimbursement requests. Employees who are granted advances should be required to complete the bottom portion of the format so as to reconcile any overages and to control any such excess reimbursements by requesting their prompt return, deduction from the next advance, or inclusion in the employee's gross income (and therefore subject to withholding and payment of employment taxes). These forms should be regularly completed on a monthly basis, but expenses must be substantiated within 10 days of the date paid or incurred. This is necessary in order to meet the rigorous substantiation requirements of the regulations, and it is particularly important for those individuals to whom you grant advances, so that any overages are cleared by the end of any applicable reporting periods (e.g., employment tax and financial reporting periods).

Please do not hesitate to contact me if you have any questions.

Sincerely,

Bernie Klassen

7. **Scenario:** The passages that follow are taken from the conclusion of an operational efficiency report performed on a client's new accounting software system by the computer systems advisory division of a public accounting firm.

   Writing task: Use the techniques described in Chapters 2 and 3 to simplify the prose and make it more readable.

After routines are established and implementation of the new accounts receivable system is closer, the routine work flow responsibilities should be passed from the department supervisors to the accounting department staff. This will free the supervisors to be more involved in the implementation of the new system.

Before any changes are made to the existing accounts receivable system, the cost of making those changes should be contrasted to the business benefit of making those changes. Changes to the existing systems should only be made if the cost of making the changes to the system is exceeded by the business benefits.

This will be a long implementation as it requires the coordination of all the team leaders and the commitment to act by management. All the resources are within local control and there is little need for systems development (reprogramming) to enable our recommendations. In addition, our consulting team's collective impression is that these changes will be well received by the department staff.

Office performance in the areas of productivity and quality will be dramatically improved by these modifications. During the review of these recommendations, several accounting department staff members started to generate suggestions for improvement that were stimulated only by the communication of the goals.

8. **Scenario:** The following paragraphs are from a public accountant's report to a client on options for upgrading a computer system.

   Writing task:
   a. Use the techniques described in Chapter 2 to organize these paragraphs more effectively. You may break existing paragraphs into smaller units and add details if you think doing so will improve them.
   b. Use the techniques described in this chapter to make the language more clear and concise.
   c. Use the rules and guidelines in the reference sections (at the end of the book) to correct errors in grammar, usage, or punctuation.

Backup Systems

Most people think of catastrophic situations when they think of the use of backups. Although this is one of the primary uses of backups, we use that term to mean a couple of different things. In our servers, we normally install "mirrored drives." In this situation, when something is written to the server, it is written to both drives simultaneously, the benefit of this is that there is practically no downtime for the server. If a drive fails, it automatically switches over to the other drive and the user is informed that it has made the switch. Tape backups in our scenario are used for archival purposes. If something has been deleted, we can go back and retrieve something for last Monday's tape. A minimum of five tapes are recommended. Some clients have one tape for each day of the month. More tapes gives you greater flexibility with how far back you can go to retrieve files. We also recommend taking tapes out of the rotation at certain milestones (year-end especially).

Telephone Issues

There are many options to choose from with how to use your telephones in conjunction with your computer. The more commonly used options includes a Digi board, which is a device that allows for all computers on the network to access multiple phone lines. With the appropriate software, they can be used for calling, faxing, and "surfing the net" from any workstation. This will normally serve the majority of your clients and their needs. With the addition of a "post office" on your network, you can have incoming faxes routed to individuals. The post office, with Microsoft Outlook as the backbone, adds many other functions. You can use it for e-mail, schedule monitoring, and other group functions. If you have other telephone needs that we have not yet discussed, we can investigate them further. A T_1 line can be installed that would allow for everyone (up to 250 people) to be on the Internet all the time. However, it costs significantly more than the other option described and it only allows for Internet use. You would still need the Digi board for faxing.

9. Writing task: Paraphrase this excerpt from a FASB statement to simplify the language:

Financial Accounting Standards Board, Accounting for Certain Investments in Debt and Equity Securities, Statement of Financial Accounting Standards No. 115, paragraphs 11 and 22, describe special circumstances under which a debt security may be classified as "held-to-maturity" upon its sale and the related disclosure requirements for such sales.

Sales of debt securities that meet either of the following two conditions may be considered as maturities ["held-to-maturity"] for purposes of the classification . . . [if] (a) The sale of a security occurs near enough to its maturity date that interest rate risk is substantially eliminated as a pricing factor. That is, the date of sale is so near the maturity or call date (for example, within three months) that changes in market interest rates would not have a significant effect on the security's fair value. (b) The sale of a security occurs after the enterprise has already collected a substantial portion (at least 85 percent) of the principal outstanding at acquisition. . . .

For any sales of or transfers from securities classified as held-to-maturity, the amortized cost amount of the sold or transferred security, the related realized or unrealized gain or loss, and the circumstances leading to the decision to sell or transfer the security shall be disclosed in the notes to the financial statements for each period for which the results of operations are presented.

10. Writing task: Translate the following passage from the Internal Revenue Code into language that a client could easily understand:

Section 6001
Notice on regulations requiring records, statements, and special returns
Every person liable for any tax imposed by this title, or for the collection thereof, shall keep such records, render such statements, make such returns, and

comply with such rules and regulations as the Secretary may from time to time prescribe. Whenever in the judgment of the Secretary it is necessary, he may require any person, by notice served upon such person or by regulations, to make such returns, render such statements, or keep such records, as the Secretary deems sufficient to show whether or not such person is liable for tax under this title. The only records which an employer shall be required to keep under this section in connection with charged tips shall be charge receipts, records necessary to comply with section 6053(c), and copies of statements furnished by employees under section 6053(a).

Section 6053

Reporting of tips

(a) Reports by employees

Every employee who, in the course of his employment by an employer, receives in any calendar month tips which are wages (as defined in section 3121(a) or section 3401(a)) or which are compensation (as defined in section 3231(e)) shall report all such tips in one or more written statements furnished to his employer on or before the 10th day following such month. Such statements shall be furnished by the employee under such regulations, at such other times before such 10th day, and in such form and manner, as may be prescribed by the Secretary.

CHAPTER 4

Written Communications:
Letters and Memos

Accountants spend a large part of every day communicating in writing because the very nature of the work they do demands written expression. Writing is the necessary medium for recording and documenting information, whether the written product exists on paper or in a permanent computer file. Writing is also the ideal medium for much of the other work accountants do, such as explaining numerical data, discussing complex management issues, and describing business processes, because written texts allow readers to move through material at their own pace, to return to important points for clarification, and to see connections among ideas in a tangible structure. For these reasons, writing is also an excellent medium for persuading others, for analyzing systems, for solving problems, and for laying out business plans. Because so much of their work involves these activities, accountants must know how to employ the techniques of business writing effectively and to adapt them appropriately to their communications on the job.

The writing that accountants do varies according to the firm or company and practice or functional area in which they work. CPAs in public accounting firms generate business through written proposals. They maintain relationships with clients through letters in which they request information, transmit materials, explain technical issues, and solve problems. They communicate with the Internal Revenue Service and other taxing authorities through letters on behalf of their clients. They document work and meet the requirements of state and federal government agencies, such as state business regulatory boards and the SEC, through reports. Internally, they share information with co-workers through memos, status reports, write-ups of research on Financial Accounting Standards Board (FASB) pronouncements, tax memoranda, and other documents. They record the work they perform on audit, tax, and other engagements in workpapers to engagement files.

Corporate accountants engage in a variety of communications as well, writing letters to customers, public accounting firms, and government agencies and sending e-mail memos to those within the company to convey details of day-to-day operations, to request and provide information, to answer technical questions, to confirm agreements, and to make recommendations. Corporate accountants also write numerous periodic reports analyzing their companies' financial position, quarterly performance, quarterly and annual forecasts, and other information. Because corporate accountants usually play a key role in product development and strategic planning for the companies in which they work, they frequently prepare agendas and write up notes for meetings, write progress reports, and contribute to business plans.

Chapters 10, 11, and 12 provide numerous examples of the documents specific to each major practice area. Although the documents and their mode of transmission appear to be quite diverse, they all fall into one of these four basic categories:

- letters
- memos
- proposals
- reports

To prepare you to write the types of documents you will encounter in later chapters, this chapter teaches you the basics about letters and memos, including

- guidelines for transmitting correspondence
- principles of effective correspondence
- strategies for organizing letters and memos.

(For instructions on formatting letters and memos, see the Formats Reference Guide at the end of the book.) The next chapter focuses on principles of proposal and report writing.

When you have mastered the principles in these two chapters, you will be ready to apply them to more specialized writing situations in later chapters and on the job. Whether you find yourself drafting a tax opinion letter, documenting accounts receivable procedures in an audit workpaper, or preparing forecasted financial statements for a corporate executive committee meeting, you will benefit from the techniques described in this chapter and the next.

LETTERS AND MEMOS: PRINT TRANSMISSION AND ELECTRONIC MAIL

Letters, the major form of external correspondence, are among the most important documents accountants produce. Through letters, accountants forge and maintain client relationships, transmit and explain information, and initiate and formalize engagements. But letters are important for another reason. As the primary means of communicating outside the company, letters extend the company's identity into the professional workplace. Every message sent out on letterhead is an official representation of the organization's identity, credibility, and professionalism. It is easy to understand why top management places such importance on the quality of employees' letters.

Memos are the primary means of internal correspondence in firms and companies. Accountants write memos to co-workers to convey information, describe findings, make recommendations, and introduce larger documents. In some organizations, memos are primarily printed documents, sent on paper and stored in file folders; in others, memos are more often electronic documents, transmitted and stored on computers. Whether on paper or on computer disk, memos are routinely used to provide written records of decisions, actions, and events. In fact, in many workplace settings, the creation of permanent records is the primary purpose of memos.

Although strictly speaking, memos are short and informal types of internal correspondence, the term *memo* is commonly used in the accounting workplace to apply to many different types of internal communication. On the job, therefore, you will find that various types of written communication are presented in memo format and referred to as memos. Internal reports of all kinds, proposals, research analyses, and planning documents routinely are labeled with the heading *Memorandum*. In addition, the workpapers accountants write to document tasks performed on audits, tax, and business advisory engagements are often prepared as memos to engagement files. Although the content of these workpapers may in fact be structured more like that of reports (discussed in Chapter 5) than of correspondence, they are called memos nevertheless.

In this chapter, we have followed the conventional practice of treating memos, along with letters, as types of business *correspondence*. Accordingly, our discussion focuses on techniques associated with writing brief messages that are intended to achieve specific purposes for specific readers. For guidelines on composing other internal communications referred to as memos—workpapers, tax memoranda, and internal proposals—use the techniques for report and proposal writing described in the next chapter.

For the most part, the products accounting firms deliver to their clients are written ones: audit reports, review engagement reports, management letters, and the like. These products indicate the quality of a firm's service in a variety of ways:

- Documents with too much information suggest that wasted time has been charged to the client.
- Products that clients cannot understand because of poor organization or unfamiliar technical terms suggest the firm does not understand its clients or their businesses.
- Grammatical or typographical errors, analogous to carelessness on an engagement, suggest a lack of professionalism and attention to detail. . . .

Source: Gale Ruby Cohen
"Author! Author!"
CA Magazine, March 1993

Electronic mail (e-mail) has become the primary means of internal document transmission at firms and companies. In more and more organizations, internal communications are conducted almost exclusively by e-mail—either over the Internet or over private electronic internal communications systems called *intranets*—using software such as Lotus Notes, Groupwise, and Microsoft Exchange. A survey in the late 1990s estimated that the average Fortune 1000 employee was at that time sending and receiving 178 e-mail messages and documents every day. Intranet communications have become so popular that the market for intranet hardware and software is expected to soar from the $5.8 billion it represented in 1995 to over $20.1 billion by the end of 2000.[1] Because e-mail allows people to share information quickly and inexpensively—often replacing long-distance phone calls, large mailings, and even face-to-face meetings—some companies have seen a 1000% return on their investment in electronic communications technologies.[2]

E-mail messages are usually shorter and more casual than printed letters and memos. Because readers must scroll to read long messages, it is a courtesy to limit e-mail communications to the space of the computer screen. Writers often compose e-mail messages spontaneously, with less attention to organization and sentence structure than they devote to more formal means of communication. This spontaneity gives e-mail some of the immediacy of speech and encourages quick interaction between sender and receiver.

By attaching computer files to e-mail messages, it is easy to transmit lengthy documents electronically as well. This means of document transmission, which has become commonplace in large firms and companies, allows for dramatically reduced turnaround time on shared work.

Advantages of E-Mail

- Because messages are transmitted and accessed electronically, e-mail saves the expense and clutter of paper.
- E-mail offers recipients the chance to reply immediately without composing a formal letter or memo and without using the phone.
- E-mail can be simultaneously distributed to multiple receivers on project teams, in departments, and in other groups.
- E-mail messages are faster than those sent through postal and courier services.
- Unlike phone calls and voice mail, e-mail leaves a written record for an absent receiver.
- Most e-mail systems allow users to transmit computer files quickly, cheaply, and easily.

Disadvantages of E-Mail

- E-mail does not afford the same privacy as print. Although the Electronic Communications Privacy Act of 1986 (ECPA) protects individuals' rights to e-mail privacy, courts have held that employers and system operators may monitor employees' e-mail.[3] At many organizations, employers routinely monitor e-mail to ensure that employees are not wasting time with personal correspondence or using the system inappropriately. Unless your organization has an explicit policy against the monitoring of e-mail, you should assume that your messages may be reviewed at any time. Therefore, do not use e-mail for sensitive or confidential communications.

- Computer problems and system breakdowns can delay transmission of messages. Although e-mail operates as an instantaneous communication medium, problems with internal systems, servers, and individual workstations can result in considerable lag time between transmission and receipt of a message. If your message needs immediate action, pick up the phone.

- E-mail addresses must be accurate, down to the last letter of the person's name. If you misspell the recipient's name on the "To" line, the message will either come back to you or be transmitted to the wrong receiver. In the event of the latter, confusion and even embarrassment can result.

- E-mail does not simply land on your desk like regular mail does. It is stored in an electronic in box that must be checked at least once a day. Neglecting to check regularly for messages can result in backlogs, missed deadlines, and other communication mix-ups.

PRINCIPLES OF BUSINESS CORRESPONDENCE

A few principles apply to most client correspondence that accountants write and to much internal correspondence as well. These principles help keep your correspondence *reader based* rather than *writer based*.[4] Whether you are writing a memo to your supervisor, a letter to an important client, or an e-mail to a co-worker on the next floor, apply these principles consistently:

Focus on your reader. As we saw in Chapter 2, effective correspondence is constructed around the reader's need to know, not the writer's need to tell. By keeping the focus of your document on the reader, you will maintain a "*you* attitude."

Think for a moment about conversations. Have you ever been in a conversation with someone who talked exclusively about himself, who told you about what he thought, felt, and believed without listening to you? How much did you enjoy that conversation? Wouldn't you rather have talked with someone who seemed interested in your opinions and experiences, who showed he had thought about your point of view? A person who shows regard for you in these ways conveys the "*you* attitude."

In professional correspondence, the "*you* attitude" anticipates the reader's need for information, explains information in terms of the benefits to the reader, and shifts the point of view from the first person to the second person (from "I" or "we" to "you"). The "*you* attitude" conveys to the reader a sense of being valued, appreciated, and understood.

The two versions of the letter reproduced in Figures 4.1 and 4.2 exemplify the difference between the "*we* attitude" and the "*you* attitude."

The letter in Figure 4.1 may at first appear appropriate for a competitive marketplace. After all, the writer is trying to "sell" the firm to the potential

Figure 4.1

Sample Letter Illustrating Lack of "*You* Attitude"

LETTER

January 3, 1999

Mr. Clarence Bastia
Blue Ash Capital Management, Inc.
354 West Roosevelt Avenue, Suite 123
Blue Ash, OH 45242

Dear Mr. Bastia:

Michelle, Tom, and I enjoyed meeting with you, Jim, and Carol to discuss the accounting and tax needs of Blue Ash Capital Management, Inc.

We recognize your need to engage an accounting firm that can meet your growing and varied needs while providing efficient and cost-effective service. As we described in our proposal, our firm will utilize individuals who understand the investment industry and have the knowledge to provide you with that service.

We pride ourselves on doing much more for our clients than just "adding up the numbers." We work hard at being a proactive adviser to our clients, providing a strong return for the fees invested.

We are pleased at the possibility of providing services to your organization, and we thank you for the opportunity to present the attached proposal. We encourage you to communicate continually to us your needs and expectations, since clients receive an outstanding return from our services when we clearly understand their objectives.

I trust we've been responsive to your needs. I look forward to responding to any questions you may have or providing any other information you may need regarding this proposal.

Sincerely,

John C. Henderson

Figure 4.2

Sample Letter Illustrating Improved "*You* Attitude"

LETTER

January 3, 1999

Mr. Clarence Bastia
Blue Ash Capital Management, Inc.
354 West Roosevelt Avenue, Suite 123
Blue Ash, OH 45242

Dear Clarence:

Thank you for the opportunity to meet with you, Tom, and Carol last Thursday to discuss the accounting and tax needs of Blue Ash Capital Management, Inc.

With the dynamic growth of your company over the past year, you need to engage an accounting firm that can provide responsive, efficient, and cost-effective services. Moreover, you need an accounting team with expert knowledge of the investment industry to handle the scope and variety of your business.

Hoffman McCormack is that firm.

As a Hoffman McCormack client, you will realize a strong return on the fees invested. You will benefit from services that go far beyond merely "adding up the numbers," services grounded in an aggressive, proactive stance to client advising and tax planning.

The attached proposal outlines the services we can offer Blue Ash Capital Management. If there are additional needs you would like to see addressed, please let us know. We will be happy to amend the proposal to bring it more closely in line with your objectives.

If you have any questions or need more information, give me a call. Thank you for the opportunity to present this proposal.

Sincerely,

John C. Henderson

client; he stresses how hard he and his colleagues will work; he talks about the firm's strengths, its track record, and its client-service philosophy.

What the letter fails to do, however, is to convey an awareness of the reader's unique needs. The letter does not show that the writer understands the reader's business, much less the reader's particular accounting issues. It is, instead, an expression of the writer's feelings (*Michelle, Tom, and I enjoyed* meeting with you . . . *We are pleased* at the possibility of providing service . . .); perceptions (*We recognize* your need to engage an accounting firm . . .); expertise (*We pride ourselves on doing more* . . . *We work hard* at being a proactive adviser . . .); and assumptions (*I trust we've been responsive* to your needs. . .). Notice that the subject of every sentence (and most clauses) is the writer:

Michelle, Tom, and I enjoyed meeting . . .

We recognize your need to engage an accounting firm . . .

As *we* described in *our* proposal, *our firm* will utilize . . .

We pride ourselves . . .

We work hard at being a proactive adviser . . .

We are pleased . . . and *we* thank you for the opportunity . . .

We encourage you continually to communicate . . . when *we* clearly understand their objectives.

I trust *we've* been responsive to your needs.

I look forward to responding to any questions . . .

This letter sends the message, "We want to talk about what we do, not what you need."

The version illustrated in Figure 4.2 does a much better job of conveying the "*you* attitude." Although the content remains largely unchanged, the focus of the second letter—and thus the attitude—shifts from *what the writer does* to *what the reader needs.*

The writer has accomplished a shift to the "*you* attitude" with only the slightest changes to the content. The real change results from a recasting of the sentences. Now the subject (or main idea) of each sentence is the reader:

Thank *you* for the opportunity . . .

With the dynamic growth of your company . . . *you* need to engage an accounting firm . . .

Moreover, *you* need an accounting team with expert knowledge . . .

As a Hoffman McCormack client, *you* will realize . . .

You will benefit from services . . .

If there are additional needs *you* would like to see addressed, . . .

If *you* have any questions . . .

Thank *you* for the opportunity to present this proposal.

The second version refers specifically to the reader's company, indicating the writer's familiarity with its particular requirements: *With the dynamic growth of your company over the past year . . . you need an accounting team . . . to handle the scope and variety of your business.* Rather than focusing only on what the writer has to offer, the revised version emphasizes that the reader will benefit from the services of the writer's firm: *you will receive a strong return on the fees invested . . . You will benefit from services . . .*

These changes are simple to implement, but their results are far reaching. They tell the reader, "You are the most important party in this discussion. You run the show." In doing so, these changes increase the writer's chance that the reader will accept the proposal that this letter introduces.

Just as important as the "*you* attitude" is the second general principle of business correspondence:

Adopt a positive tone. Like the "*you* attitude," a positive tone helps maintain a good relationship with the reader. As we noted in Chapter 2, the tone of your communications is largely responsible for the reactions of your readers. A positive tone conveys courtesy, cordiality, and respect. Correspondence written in a positive tone conveys the writer's sense of the reader's competence and professionalism. A negative tone conveys hostility. Negative tone is often responsible for correspondence that is condescending, authoritarian, or mistrustful of the reader.

Sometimes, unfortunate word choice or abrupt phrasing can turn a neutral message into one with an unintentionally hostile tone. Unlike the words in the first list here ("positive" words), those in the second ("negative" words) can convey hostility and provoke resistance in a reader.

Positive Words and Phrases

appreciate	outstanding
benefit	pleased
can	recommend
careful	service
commend	solution
congratulate	success
efficient	thank you
excellent	timely
glad	thoughtful
grateful	together
great	trust
happy	"As soon as . . . we'll be happy to . . ."
help	"Thank you for . . ."

Negative Words and Phrases

allege	late
blame	liable
careless	must
cannot	neglect
complain	problem

Negative Words and Phrases

decline	unfair
deny	vague
disappointed	worried
doubtful	wrong
fail/failure	"If you do not . . . we cannot . . ."
impossible	"You need to . . ."

Figures 4.3 and 4.4 show two versions of a letter from an auditor to a client requesting information necessary to conclude an audit. The tone of the first version (Figure 4.3) is unintentionally hostile, partially as a result of the use of words and phrases such as those in the negative word list.

Several factors create the hostile tone in Figure 4.3.

Finger-pointing phrases such as *you failed to* and *I haven't received from you* accuse readers and may put them on the defensive.

Emphatics suggest an escalation of the writer's emotions, creating a tone that demands rather than requests. For example:

- underlining *(your, we),* which is the textual equivalent of shouting
- block capitals *(ASAP),* also suggestive of shouting
- negative words *(must, failed)*
- intensifiers *(definitely, in fact)*

Abrupt phrasing indicates a lack of respect *(The following is a list of items I haven't received from you. See what you can do to expedite this request.)*

The second version (Figure 4.4) represents a shift from negative to positive tone. The writer addresses the client appropriately, with courtesy and respect. The revision uses phrases that emphasize the positive aspects of the situation (the audit is *nearly complete,* [these are] *the last things I need from you*) and assume a satisfactory outcome *(as soon as I receive . . . we can wrap up the audit).*

Words and phrases that minimize problems (*just* provide, *a few* variances) help reduce reader anxiety. The revision also employs words and phrases with positive connotations (I'm *happy* to report, *Thanks* for *your help*).

The positive tone of the revision assumes the reader's cooperation and prompt response. It is far more likely than the original to elicit this response.

Remember: A positive tone is a result of empathy—the ability to understand the reader's feelings and anticipate how a communication will make the reader feel. Empathy not only helps build good relationships with readers; it also helps writers achieve the responses they want. Most people respond positively to courteous and friendly communications, and most people react with resistance to harsh ones.

Positive tone is important with all messages, not just positive ones. Indeed, even negative messages should be expressed with a positive tone, that is, with an attitude of friendliness and concern toward the reader. See the bad-news letter in Figure 4.9, p. 117, for an example of a negative message expressed with a positive tone.

Figure 4.3

Sample Letter Illustrating Hostile Tone

LETTER

April 10, 2000

Marcus Avedon
Western Communications, Inc.
398 Independence Road, Suite 286
Los Angeles, CA 90025

Dear Marcus:

Enclosed is a copy of the management representation letter that needs to be copied onto your letterhead, signed by Ralph Kelly, and returned to us. The following is a list of items I haven't received from you. I must have them ASAP to complete the audit.

1. Copies of the notes receivable confirmations to you and Ralph Kelly. Attached are copies of last year's if you need them. The confirms must be prepared on your letterhead and returned to us so we can mail them out.

2. Copies of the minutes or written indications from you that you failed to keep them.

3. An explanation of why the check to ABCO in the amount of $14,750.83, written in May 1999, is still outstanding.

4. Documentation supporting the Line of Credit balance of $390,000 at 12/31/99. The initial confirmation received from ABCO is at variance with your report, showing $320,000.

5. Documentation that $179,000 in debt was in fact paid off in January 2000.

This is our second request for the notes receivable confirmations. Some of the accounts receivable confirmations you sent us have variances, so we will definitely need to come back in a week to perform additional procedures.

See what you can do to expedite this request. Thank you.

Sincerely,

Christina Madison

Figure 4.4

Sample Letter Illustrating Improved Tone

LETTER

April 10, 2000

Marcus Avedon
Western Communications, Inc.
398 Independence Road, Suite 286
Los Angeles, CA 90025

Dear Marcus:

I'm happy to report that the audit is nearly complete. Here is a list of the last things I need from you.

1. A copy of the management representation letter on your letterhead, signed by Ralph Kelly. I've enclosed a copy that you can reproduce.

2. Copies of the notes receivable confirmations to you and Ralph Kelly. These copies should also be on your letterhead (see attached copies of last year's).

3. Copies of the minutes. (If you don't have them, just provide a written indication of that fact.)

4. An explanation of the outstanding check payable to ABCO in the amount of $14,750.83, written May 1999.

5. Documentation supporting the line of credit balance of $390,000 at 12/31/99. ABCO's initial confirmation shows $320,000.

6. Documentation that $179,000 debt was paid off, January 2000.

We will need to visit your office one more time to reconcile a few variances in accounts receivable confirmations. As soon as I receive the documents listed above and complete that visit, we can wrap up the audit.

Thanks for your help.

Sincerely,

Christina Madison

ORGANIZING MEMOS, LETTERS, AND E-MAIL

As we mentioned in Chapter 2, well-written business documents are organized in descending order of importance (from most to least important). This structure allows readers to grasp immediately the main point that a writer wishes to make. In memos, letters, and e-mail, this structure is supported by a larger pattern of organization consisting of an opening statement that orients the reader to the context, a summary statement of the document's purpose, a body paragraph or paragraphs that develop one idea at a time, and a closing that lets the reader know what action or response the writer expects. With a few exceptions (discussed later), this pattern should be used to organize any correspondence you write. Here is the pattern, summarized for you:

1. Create context.
2. State your purpose.
3. Organize information from most to least important.
4. Develop one idea per paragraph.
5. Close by summarizing/asking for action.

If you follow this five-step pattern in your memos, letters, and e-mail, you will create messages that are easy to follow.

Create Context

As we discussed in Chapter 2, show readers from the start how the information you are presenting relates to information they already have. Even if your readers are other accountants, who understand your terminology and know your business, they will not know how your correspondence relates to them unless you tell them.

A context statement links new information (the document at hand) with information the reader already has. In other words, context establishes common ground between writer and reader.

On the job, you will frequently receive correspondence that begins with formulas such as *Per your instructions, Enclosed please find,* and so on. Writers use these expressions in the hopes of providing context quickly. But such expressions are ineffective because they do not establish specific connections between the document at hand and earlier communications on the subject.

Making your context clear means that your message can stand alone; that is, your reader will not need to consult other documents, to phone you, e-mail you, or send you a return memo for clarification of your message. Remember that written correspondence creates historical records; in some cases, readers will consider your document months or even years after you have written it. Therefore, make the subject and occasion of your correspondence clear even if you think your immediate reader is familiar with the context.

How do you ensure that your context is clear? First, put yourself in the shoes of your immediate reader. Imagine how much background your reader needs to understand what follows.

- Have you specified the name of the client/engagement/subject to which this message relates?
- Have you indicated where this document falls in relation to other communications on the subject?
- Have you referred at the beginning to other communication you have had on this subject with your reader? To meetings in which you have discussed this client or topic with the reader? Have you referred to recent phone conversations about the client or topic? To other letters, memos, or e-mail messages on the topic (referenced by date and a brief summary of content)?

Next, put yourself in the position of more remote readers, those who may read your document later or who are less familiar with the situation at hand. Ask yourself what other information these readers will need to understand your document by itself.

- Will they need a brief summary of the client's position?
- Will they need definitions for certain technical terms?
- Will they need an explanation of the correspondence you have had with your immediate reader about the topic?

Use your judgment to balance the needs of remote readers with those of your immediate audience.

State Your Purpose

We also noted in Chapter 2 that readers want to know the purpose of your correspondence from the start. Why are you writing? What do you want the reader to do or to know? Your context statement should make your purpose clear.

Ways to State Context and Purpose

1. Refer to an event or conversation familiar to both writer and reader:

Reference to event: This memo summarizes my assessment of the financial statement software package NumberCrunch, Inc. presented to us on September 10, 2000.

2. Refer specifically to a request by the reader:

Reference to request: As you requested by phone on 11/21/00, I am sending you balance sheets, income statements, and statements of cash flows for American Tire Company for the fiscal years 1998 and 1999.

3. Make a request of your own:

Request: I am writing to request the schedule of aged accounts receivable on the Westfall engagement.

4. On other occasions, you may want to state your purpose after introducing context:

Context statement: Thank you for engaging Johansen, Smythe, and Taggart to assist with your business start-up plan. As we agreed at our recent meeting, the firm will conduct the appropriate financial analyses and provide a report by March 30.

Purpose statement: To begin the process, we need to obtain several documents from you.

Organize Information from Most to Least Important

By stating your purpose at the beginning, you are indicating to the reader your most important reason for writing. The rest of your message should consist of information that explains or supports that main point. Place your most important explanation immediately after your purpose statement and organize other information in descending order of importance.

The memo in Figure 4.5 illustrates this structure. The memo is a cover page to an audit file being given by the audit senior to the supervising partner for review. The memo highlights for the partner the most significant issues that have come to light during the audit and leaves a record of those issues for next year's auditor.

Develop One Idea per Paragraph

To ensure that your explanation is clear, isolate the points you want to make and develop each one in a single paragraph. Begin each paragraph with a topic sentence summarizing your point, and develop that point by giving details, examples, or other supporting information.

Simple Message/Single Point   In a brief memo, letter, or e-mail addressing a single point, your organization and paragraph development will take care of themselves:
Opening Paragraph
    Context
    Purpose
Body Paragraph
    Single Point
       Introduced with Topic Sentence
       Developed with Details, Examples, Other
Closing Paragraph
    Summary or Request for Action
The example in Figure 4.6 illustrates this structure.

Figure 4.5

Well-Structured Memo

<table>
<tr><td colspan="2" align="center">MEMO</td></tr>
</table>

> TO: Bagel Emporium, Inc., audit file
> FROM: Josh Adams, audit senior
> SUBJECT: Highlights of issues from the 1999 audit
> DATE: February 10, 2000
>
> This audit file memo summarizes the most important business issues that were discovered during our 1999 audit of Bagel Emporium, Inc.
>
> **[most important]** Although 1999 sales were double that of 1998, and the percentage of sales for COGS stayed in line, income dropped by more than half. The company had sales of $3,500,000 and net income of $140,000 for the year ended 12/31/99. For the 1998 year, sales were $2,000,000 and net income was $300,000.
>
> The main reason for the decrease in net income is that operating expenses for 1999 have increased over those for 1998. Part of this increase is due to fees paid to an executive headhunter firm for recruiting Haley Holliday, the new CFO. In addition, the company wrote off $25,000 of bad debts in 1999, whereas in 1998, there were no bad debt write-offs. Other 1999 expenses include a legal settlement against Bagel Emporium, Inc., for $175,000 paid to Wheatberry Flour Mills, Inc.
>
> **[less important]** The company's long-term growth plans expect sales to double in 2000 to approximately $7 million and to increase to approximately $20 million by 2003. (See the client-prepared strategic plan, which can be found in the permanent file.)
>
> **[less important]** The company made significant purchases of fixed assets during 1999 in the amount of $200,000. Most of these additions were for leasehold improvements made to various bagel shops and for computer equipment.
>
> **[least important]** By February 2001, the company's owner, Bud Bergen, plans to give 30% of the company's S-corporation stock to four key employees: Haley Holliday, 10%, Alice Pettit, 10%, Bob Esposito, 5%, and Tom Schmidt, 5%.

Figure 4.6

Effective E-Mail Message (Single Point)

> ## MEMO
>
> FROM: smith@autoworld.com
> DATE: Mon May 12 1999
> SUBJECT: Accounts Receivable Training Session
> TO: roberts@autoworld.com
> endicott@autoworld.com
> michaels@autoworld.com
> hummel@autoworld.com
> booth@autoworld.com
>
> Hello Everybody,
>
> This message is to remind you that I will be conducting the accounts receivable training session on Tuesday, May 13, at the Headquarters building (conference room 2B, second floor). We'll start at 8:30 a.m. (Coffee and bagels at 8.)
>
> The training is designed to familiarize you with the accounts receivable function of the SAP system and to provide an orientation to processing nonsales invoices and credit memos.
>
> Looking forward to seeing you there.
>
> Yours,
>
> Randy Smith

Complex Message/Multiple Points   In longer messages it is a courtesy to your reader to explain in a *forecasting statement* how you will organize your message and to map out your organization using bulleted lists, headings, and subheadings.

A forecasting statement gives the reader an overview of what to expect in each section of your document and makes complex messages easier to follow.

> **Forecasting statement:** Section 1 explains the benefits of the package to corporate accounting; section 2 analyzes costs; section 3 discusses future considerations and needs.

> **Forecasting statement:** After providing you with an analysis of these financial statements and an overview of my client's financial position, I will summarize for you American Tire Company's strengths as a potential borrower.

Here is a diagram of a multipoint message properly introduced and supported, organized in descending order of importance:

Opening Paragraph
 Context/Purpose Statement
 Forecasting Statement
Body Paragraph 1 (Most Important Point)
 Topic Sentence
 Data, Examples, Details
Body Paragraph 2 (Less Important Point)
 Topic Sentence
 Data, Examples, Details
Body Paragraph 3 (Least Important Point)
 Topic Sentence
 Data, Examples, Details

The letter in Figure 4.7 exemplifies this structure. Notice how it isolates the main points, develops a single idea per paragraph, forecasts the organization, and formats information for easy readability.

Remember: It is much easier for readers to pay attention to one idea at a time than to process a lot of different information at once. By making each of your points clearly and thoroughly before moving on to the next, you help your readers understand your message.

Figure 4.7

Effective Client Letter (Multiple Points)

LETTER

Robert Richardson
378 Colorado Blvd.
Tallahassee, FL 32301

Dear Robert:

I have reviewed your income tax returns for 1999 and want to suggest some ideas to help you reduce your taxes. Here is a summary of those ideas. The first two items focus on ways of handling income; the second two, on strategies for deductions:

1. *Interest income:* You can reduce your taxable income, which is taxed at a rate of approximately 30%, by converting some of your taxable interest-bearing bank bonds to tax-exempt state and local bonds. By converting, for example, $5,000 of taxable interest income to tax-exempt interest income, you would enjoy a tax savings of $1,500 per year.

Figure 4.7

Effective Client Letter (Multiple Points)—*continued*

---

2. *Auto expenses:* Arrange to have your employer reimburse you dollar for dollar for the business use of your auto rather than give you a "vehicle allowance" of $2,000 at the end of the year. Because the deduction you take against the $2,000 is reduced by 2% of your adjusted gross income, you usually cannot deduct your expenses, and so you are being taxed on that $2,000. None of the $2,000 will be taxed, however, if it can be considered as a direct reimbursement of your expenses, and as a result, you will save approximately $600 per year.

3. *Charitable contributions:* Consider giving away appreciated property held for more than one year to a charitable organization. This contribution will not result in capital gains tax and will generate a charitable tax deduction equal to the fair market value of the appreciated property.

4. *Flexible spending plan:* Join your employer's flexible spending payroll deduction plan and use it to remove from your taxable income your payments for health insurance premiums and other medical expenses. Currently, your income level prevents you from taking any deductions for medical expense.

If you implement them, these suggestions will help you take advantage of tax breaks for next year. Let me know if I can answer any questions for you.

Sincerely,

Charles Porter Allen, CPA

Close by Summarizing/Asking for Action

At the end, leave your reader with a clear sense of what you have tried to achieve in your letter or memo. People expect closure at the end of a written message; for this reason, the closing line is a power position in any letter or memo. Use the closing to drive home your main point (that is, what you want to the reader to do, know, agree to, or take away from your message).

Depending on the purpose of your message, you can conclude either by summarizing content or by asking for action.

Summarizing content: In summary, you will be able to save approximately $5,000 on next year's tax bill by keeping track of your home office and employee expenses, by investing in municipal bonds, and by claiming your elderly mother as a dependent.

Summarizing content: Based on the foregoing, we recommend purchasing this package. It should improve both work flow and file management.

Asking for action: Please copy the documents onto company letterhead, sign them, and return them to me by August 12.

Asking for action: I hope everything is going well. If you have any questions, give me a call at extension 8431.

Figure 4.8 displays an original draft of a poorly organized memo written by an audit senior to another member of the audit team. The memo describes a

---

Figure 4.8

Poorly Organized Memo

MEMO

TO: Joshua Crenshaw
FROM: Helen Miller
DATE: 4/17/99
SUBJECT: ABC, Inc.—Insurance Risk Management Questionnaire

I am the senior associate on the ABC, Inc. engagement. The following information represents ABC's IRMQ as completed by the controller and risk management director at ABC. I have also included the loss runs and prior year accrual amounts that were provided to us by the controller at ABC. Further, the prior year memos from Tom Jones and yourself have also been included for reference purposes.

In the prior year, Tom was not comfortable with the pension plan reserve of ABC. After much time and effort by both the audit team and ABC, we coordinated a meeting between us and ABC to resolve the matter. At the meeting, the matter was resolved with no additional accrual being necessary.

I am hoping that this year we can resolve any problems that might exist before spending a great amount of time and effort that is wasted on both sides, as was the case in the prior year. Please let me know if I can assist in any matters. I can be reached at ext. 8041.

We plan to begin fieldwork during the week of May 5. Thanks!

problem that had occurred with the previous year's audit. Its purpose is to open discussion on the issue before this year's audit begins.

The original draft is difficult to follow because the writer fails to state her purpose, to map out her organization, or to close with her point. In addition, the writer tries to cover too many ideas in each paragraph.

The revision in Figure 4.9 is much easier to follow than the original because the writer provides context in paragraph 1 *(background on the audit in which the reader participated last year);* states her purpose explicitly in paragraph 2 *(I would like to resolve . . .);* uses a forecasting statement to introduce her

---

Figure 4.9

Well-Organized Memo

MEMO

TO: Joshua Crenshaw
FROM: Helen Miller
DATE: 4/17/99
SUBJECT: ABC, Inc.—Insurance Risk Management Questionnaire

In last year's audit of ABC Inc. our team spent unnecessary time and effort on a disagreement over the pension plan reserve on ABC's balance sheet. The disagreement was eventually resolved, without the need for additional accrual, in a meeting between our audit team and ABC.

As the senior associate on this year's ABC, Inc. engagement, I would like to resolve any such disagreements in advance.

May I ask you to review the attached documents and let me know if you foresee problems such as those that arose last year:

- ABC's Insurance Risk Management Questionnaire (IRMQ) as completed by the controller and risk management director at ABC
- the loss runs and prior year accrual amounts, provided by ABC's controller
- copies of the memos you and Tom Jones exchanged last year on the pension plan reserve question

I will call you in a day or two to get your feedback. In the meantime, please give me a call at ext. 8041 if you have questions or need more information.

We plan to begin fieldwork during the week of May 5. Thanks!

attachments *(May I ask that you read. . .)*; and isolates key elements *(references to the documents)*, formatting them in a bulleted list. In addition, the writer closes with action, offering to call for the reader's feedback.

Special Cases

Bad-News Messages   When you have to send a message that represents bad news for your reader, do not begin with an explicit purpose statement. Why not? Because a reader confronted with bad news in an opening paragraph may discard your correspondence after reading the first few sentences. Any efforts you make in the remainder of the letter to soften the disappointment or build goodwill may be wasted. Such messages are more effective when constructed using an indirect approach.

Structure for Bad-News Messages

1. *Open with a "buffer" statement.* Start by establishing rapport with your reader, creating a positive atmosphere, and conveying goodwill.
2. *Explain your reasoning.* Your reader is more likely to accept the bad news if you explain your reasoning in a way that makes sense.
3. *State your news clearly.* State the bad news in terms that cannot be misunderstood.
4. *Close with a goodwill message.* As in any correspondence, use the last lines to promote good relations with your reader.

The letter in Figure 4.10 from a CPA who is "firing" a client illustrates how to apply this formula.

Requests to Skeptical or Hostile Readers   When you need to persuade an unsympathetic reader to grant a request or accept your point of view, the indirect approach is also preferred. With such a reader, an explicit purpose statement at the beginning will most likely result in immediate rejection of your request. To achieve results in these circumstances, begin by laying out the facts and reasoning that led up to your request. Only after you have shown that your facts are compelling and your reasoning sound will you convince the reader that what you are requesting is necessary.

Structure for Requests to Skeptical Readers

1. *Open with a statement of the problem.* Establish that a problem exists, preferably one that both you and your reader share.
2. *Document the problem with facts.* Point out specifically how the problem is costing the company money, wasting employees' time, or having other negative effects.
3. *Explain your reasoning.* Share with your reader the logical process by which you concluded that your solution to the problem is the best one.

Figure 4.10

Bad-News Letter

LETTER

May 12, 2000
Mr. Gerald Finnegan
2760 Commonwealth Avenue
West Hartford, CN 06107

Dear Mr. Finnegan:

You have been a valued client to my tax practice over the past three years, and I would like to thank you for your business.

As one of our clients who returns each year during tax season, you deserve the highest quality of service. But as you know, our firm recently has been experiencing rapid growth, so much so that we have become concerned about our ability to serve you and our other tax season clients properly. To serve my year-round business clients adequately, I now find it necessary to restrict my tax practice to those clients. I regret, therefore, that I can no longer serve as your accountant.

Please let me know if you would like me to refer you to another qualified CPA who can assist you with your 1999 tax returns. Once again, thank you for your past business.

---

4. *Make your request/point clearly.* As with a bad-news message, state your request in terms that cannot be misunderstood.
5. *Close with a goodwill message.* Use the end of the message to promote good relations. Show that you assume your request will be approved.

Figure 4.11 shows an example of such a request. Notice that the *real* subject of the memo (a $10,000 equipment request) is not introduced until the fourth paragraph.

Figure 4.11

Request Memo to Skeptical Reader

MEMO

TO: Martin Wilson, Managing Partner
FROM: Tracy Dougherty, Senior Accountant
DATE: February 20, 2000
SUBJECT: Procedures for Document Production

In an effort to improve productivity, I have recently reviewed the document production procedures in our section. This memo summarizes these procedures, identifies problem areas, and recommends solutions.

At present, each accountant in our group drafts documents on a desktop PC and prints on the department laser printer in Sherry's office. When people are working individually, this system is reasonably efficient, although the printer queue sometimes results in wasted time as people wait for documents.

When people need to work together, however, problems inevitably arise. Three of our people use WordPerfect 6.1 and Lotus; one uses Word 6.0 and Excel. The others all use MS Office 97. File transfer among these workstations is complicated and time consuming. Last week, for example, Jonah, Alex, and Kim spent more than *two days* manually exchanging disks to revise the final report to Spectra, a task that should have taken two or three hours. The costs to the firm of such practices can be multiplied across the 15 people in our section.

To solve the problem and use staff time more productively, we should purchase new machines and software for Jonah, Alex, Roland, and Meredith to give them access to MS Office 97, which is the standard in our section. Then we should network the workstations to cut file transfer time to a minimum.

We can acquire the necessary hardware and software for under $10,000. With your approval of this request, I will begin investigating the options.

Thank you. I look forward to working with you on this project.

CONCLUSION

When writing letters, memos, and e-mail, remember:

- Use the "*you* attitude"
- Adopt a positive tone, even when sending negative messages
- Organize correspondence using the five-step formula (except with bad-news messages and requests to skeptical readers)

  1. Create context.
  2. State purpose.
  3. Organize information from most to least important.
  4. Develop one idea per paragraph.
  5. Close by summarizing/asking for action.

- Use the indirect approach with bad-news messages and requests to skeptical readers.

NOTES

[1]Sarah J. F. Braley, "Internal Affairs: Planners Tapping into Corporate Intranets to Reach Out to Meeting-Goers Online," *Meetings and Conventions* 32, no. 2 (August 1997): 74–79.

[2]AICPA, "Top 10 Technologies Stress Communications," *Journal of Accountancy* 185, no. 2 (February 1998): 22.

[3]Marian M. Extejt, "Teaching Students to Correspond Electronically," *Business Communications Quarterly* 61, no. 2 (June 1998): 57–67.

[4]Linda S. Fowler uses the term *reader-based prose* to describe writing crafted to meet the reader's need to know rather than the writer's desire to tell, in "Writer-Based Prose: A Cognitive Basis for Problems in Writing," *College English* 41, no. 1 (September 1979): 19–37.

EXERCISES

1. **Writing task:** For each of the following situations, choose the best form of communication (letter, memo, e-mail message, personal meeting, or phone call) and give a brief explanation for your choice.
   a. Information to a client about a technical tax issue.
   b. Date and time of next week's meeting to co-worker.
   c. Detailed follow-up information to your supervisor about an accounting issue she asked you to research.
   d. Communication accompanying a report on alternative information systems, prepared for a client.
   e. Suggestions to a client about possible improvements to internal controls.

 f. Criticism of the sloppy grammar and typographical errors in letters and memos written by an intern whom you supervise.

 g. Information to employees describing a change in your company's employee benefit package.

 h. Request to a client for answers to several simple questions that need to be obtained immediately.

 i. Complaints to a co-worker about your supervisor.

 j. Schedule of activities for a special event affecting everyone in your department.

2. **Writing task:** The following paragraphs are part of a letter from an accounting firm to a prospective client, Black & Black Paper Products, Inc. Rewrite them to reflect a "*you* attitude."

We have carefully considered your professional needs and have included our response to those needs in our proposal. We have also set forth detailed information that we believe you should consider in making your decision to select our firm to service your needs. We can provide the finest professional auditing, accounting, and tax services that you require and also go one step further in being a valuable business consultant and adviser to Black & Black Paper Products, Inc.

Our proposed engagement team, which has significant experience in serving manufacturers, will be available to meet with you to discuss any issues or concerns as needs arise. The proximity of our Cedar Rapids office to your headquarters and the dedication of our professionals ensure a high level of responsiveness. We have no better way of guaranteeing the quality that this proposal describes than to be personally involved with and accessible to Black & Black Paper Products, Inc.

3. **Scenario:** You are a CPA, working as a manager in the Small Business Group of Kern & Kline, CPAs. Recently, you were a speaker at a conference for small business owners and you made a presentation on accounting systems. This presentation gave you the opportunity to share some of your expertise with small business owners who probably have limited knowledge of accounting. It also provided you with an opportunity to market the services of your firm as the conference attendees could see your accounting system expertise and learn about your firm's auditing, tax, and consulting services.

 Writing task: Write a follow-up letter to the people who attended your presentation. Be sure to thank them for attending and remind them of the professional services provided by Kern & Kline. Focus on writing with a "*you attitude*," a *positive tone,* and *good organization.*

4. A "*you* attitude" is particularly important when writing to prospective employers, whether for a summer internship or for a permanent position. Recruiters are interested in whether you can focus on their firm's position and needs. Writing a good cover letter, with a "*you* attitude," shows you can relate to being a part of their team.

Writing task: Write a cover letter to a potential employer, requesting that you be considered for either a summer internship or a permanent position. As an alternative, if you wrote a personal cover letter for the Exercises in Chapter 1, revise it to improve its tone, organization, and "*you* attitude."

5. **Scenario:** Assume you are an accounting supervisor for a major corporation. You have noticed that many of your employees' letters and memos are badly written. This correspondence reflects poorly on your department and your firm.

   Writing task: Write a memo to the employees in your department suggesting ways they can improve their written communication. Be sure to explain why good communication is important and outline some of the basic points they need to keep in mind when writing. Organize your memo following the suggestions given in the chapter.

6. **Scenario:** Doug Benton is the new finance director for *The Daily Reporter,* a San Diego newspaper. The company's vice president of operations, David Samuels, made an unexpected visit to *The Reporter* in June. The VP requested a review of all upcoming capital project proposals related to production.

   Doug had just reviewed a capital project proposal sponsored by the production director, Pete Stadori. Doug had been impressed by the proposal, which he believed would streamline operations in production. Although Pete was out of town, Doug presented the pro-

---

MEMO

TO: Doug Benton
FROM: Pete Stadori
SUBJECT: Production Press Upgrade Proposal
DATE: March 6, 1999

I have just learned that you presented my project proposal to Samuels last week and had it turned down. My source at the presentation has told me that you neglected to mention my role in the proposal development and that you failed to provide any real supporting evidence for the project. I am sure you realize what a problem this will cause for the production staff.

It was careless and unfair of you to make the presentation, regardless of the circumstances. I am worried that the small window of opportunity for approval of such a major capital project has passed for this year. Needless to say I am extremely disappointed.

---

posal to the VP. Doug's lack of production expertise made him unable to defend the proposal effectively, however, and it was turned down.

Pete found out about the failed presentation when he returned to his post a week later. Pete immediately wrote the memo on p. 121, which is hostile and unprofessional.

Writing task:

   a. Rewrite the memo to reflect Pete's frustrations without the personal attack on Doug.

   b. Assume instead that Doug has to be the one to break the news to Pete about the project's defeat. Write an appropriate bad-news message memo from Doug to Pete informing him of the outcome.

7. **Writing task:** The memo below, to Jonathan Van Dorn from Melissa Hadley, is unintentionally hostile. Revise the memo to improve its tone.

8. **Scenario:** Marie Newman, the office manager for HM Landscaping, wrote the memo opposite to the business's sales manager, Hank Mar-

---

MEMO

TO: Jonathan Van Dorn
FROM: Melissa Hadley
DATE: April 23, 2000
SUBJECT: Computer Malfunctions

Since you upgraded my computer to Windows 97, I have had constant problems with it:

- It now takes anywhere from 30 seconds to 60 seconds to process information. Often, the e-mail times out before I can send the message. The machine has never run this slowly before.
- I can't have more than two programs open at one time. If I try, the system locks up.
- When I send a print command to the color printer, I always get an error message ("spooling problem"). The thing tells me to close all open programs, shut down, and restart Windows after a ten-second wait. Having to reboot every time I try to print in color is a major hassle. I never get a print job completed.
- I can no longer access Javelin or Quattro. That means I can't update the division's forecasts.
- It is critical that these problems be fixed immediately. As it stands, I can't answer inquiries or update reports. With each day that passes, I fall further and further behind.

MEMO

TO: Hank Martin, Jr.
FROM: Marie Newman
DATE: March 1, 1999
SUBJECT: New Procedures Needed

We need to make some changes in how the paperwork flows through the office before the busy season starts this year and client "surprises" start occurring. To implement these changes, I need to order prenumbered work orders, a date stamp, and several in/out baskets.

Prenumbered work orders will allow us to track jobs better than we have in the past. By prenumbering the work orders, we will know exactly how many jobs have occurred, what services were performed, and for whom. The date stamp will provide formal evidence of the timing of paper flow through the office. Such evidence will help us keep track of work orders as well as requests for supplies. The in/out baskets will be labeled to facilitate the smooth flow of documents and eventual filing of records.

During last year's busy season, the sales staff frequently took on new clients without receiving office approval. In addition, the team leaders placed orders for supplies with various unauthorized suppliers. Finally, several of the team leaders accepted direct cash payments without adequate paperwork.

These events created real control problems for the office. Although new clients are good for the business, we risk taking on more than we can handle if we accept them ad hoc. If we stretch our resources, the quality of our service will suffer. Also, this practice might result in extra costs: If we don't know about the new clients in advance, we can't schedule their appointments in the most efficient manner.

All purchases should be made through this office. Inadequate purchasing controls can result in our buying more supplies than we need because rarely have the team leaders investigated competitors' costs before placing an order. In addition, waste and pilferage may occur if we do not have good controls over supplies.

Customers need to be reminded to pay by check—in the mail or through the team leader—with proper accompanying paperwork. Under no circumstances should cash be accepted. You can imagine the problems we might encounter if a dispute boils down to a "he said, she said" situation.

Thank you for your time and attention to this matter.

tin, Jr., requesting his cooperation in putting some new office procedures in place. Hank's responsibility is to develop new clients for the firm. He is an aggressive salesman who has little patience with paperwork. He is also the son of the owner.

Writing task: Revise the memo to increase the chance of Marie's request being granted. Use the format suggested for persuading skeptical readers.

9. **Writing task:** Read the following memo and describe in a paragraph how it violates the five-step pattern for a well-organized memo described in this chapter. Then rewrite the memo to improve

---

MEMO

TO: Steve Rush, Accounting Manager
FROM: Rob Jensen, Staff Accountant
SUBJECT: Note Payable Confirmation Process, BMC Audit
DATE: January 12, 1999

Some of the confirmations we have received for the BMC Management Corp. conflict with the client's books and the notes payable schedule originally prepared by the client. For instance, although the client's schedule total agrees with the general ledger total, the classifications by category show some discrepancies. In one case, a note is collateralized with fixed equipment but is categorized as an unsecured debt. This error could cause problems with proper balance sheet presentation in the financial statements.

During the confirmation process of the notes payable, there seemed to be some confusion as to the maturity dates of notes issued on the first day of the year (i.e., 1/1/96). Some people thought the maturity date of notes in this case was 12/31/97; others thought it was 1/1/98. A five-year note dated 1/1/94 will mature on 12/31/98. A three-year note dated 12/31/96 will mature on 12/31/99, and so on.

Although a one-day difference in maturity dates is immaterial as far as accrued interest, it was important to create a five-year maturity schedule and for the client to establish some type of policy.

To rectify this difference in opinion, management has agreed that the notes will mature as described above.

its organization. As you rewrite, apply the following techniques from Chapter 2 for leading the reader:

- State your main point up front.
- Dovetail your sentences to ensure the logical flow of ideas.
- Format for readability.

10. **Writing task:** The intranet e-mail message below is unnecessarily complicated and poorly organized. Revise it to improve its organization and simplify the message by removing non-essential information.

MEMO

To: Accounting Department Group
From: Mark Burns
Date: February 15, 2000
Re: This afternoon's meeting

As you know, I had scheduled a department meeting for 3:00 PM today in the conference room. Sally and Bob have contacted me explaining that many schools are dismissing early due to the bad weather. Human Resources have said we may leave at 3:00 today if all critical work has been completed. The meeting was going to cover the proposed changes to our accounting information systems reports, as suggested by our auditors, Harkins and Smith. As a result of these things, I have decided to reschedule today's meeting for Monday at 3:00. In the meantime, if you have any comments related to the proposed changes, please send them to me by e-mail, so I can compile them prior to next Monday's meeting. If you need to, you may also leave early—just be sure to tell Maria when you go.

CHAPTER 5

Written Communications: Proposals and Reports

PROPOSALS

In public accounting, firms use proposals to obtain new clients and to create opportunities to perform accounting services. The proposals written by public accountants are usually addressed to professional firms, small businesses, corporations, and nonprofits who have been identified as potential clients for audit, tax, and consulting engagements. In private accounting, proposals are used to win approval for new projects, to initiate cost-cutting measures, and, in some cases, to shut down areas of operation. The proposals written by accountants in private companies are most often addressed to internal audiences, primarily to the financial decision makers in upper management.

As a key source of business development in public accounting, engagement proposals are usually written by those in the firm with the most experience and technical knowledge and prepared by marketing specialists. Proposals are frequently the end product of months of work, including numerous needs assessment meetings with the prospective client, extensive industry research, and careful planning and drafting by marketing staff and partners. These proposals are often delivered to the prospective client both in writing and in carefully prepared oral presentations. Although staff accountants and seniors in public firms rarely write engagement proposals, they may be asked to contribute to the research and preliminary drafting.

Accountants in private companies can frequently play a key role in proposal development as well. Internal proposals written to obtain funding for resources (equipment, systems, personnel) rely on the financial analyses that accountants provide to establish why the resources are needed or how they will save the company money. Proposals written to launch new ventures, open new markets, or initiate organizational changes depend on accountants' input as well.

The length, scope, and appearance of proposals can vary considerably. Simple internal proposals are often written in memo format with few headings or textual divisions. In larger companies, internal proposals may resemble long reports. Engagement proposals for audit, tax, and consulting services can vary from simple letters to elaborate publications with tables of contents, section divisions, and professional binding. Those addressed to government agencies follow prescribed formats outlined in the "Request for Proposals"

(RFP) issued by the agency. (RFPs specify the services that the agency needs, the criteria it will use for evaluating the proposals, and the structure proposers must use in presenting material.) In government proposals, numerical heading systems are frequently used to mark sections and subsections.

Characteristic Features of Proposals

Regardless of surface differences, however, proposals can be identified (and distinguished from other types of written communication) by their function and structure: What all proposals have in common is that they are all written *to persuade* an audience through the development of a unified argument. Like an attorney building a case, a proposal writer uses facts and logic to convince readers that they have a need which can best be filled by the proposer. This argument is built on the following components:

- **Background:** You have a problem to be solved or need to be filled
- **Proposal:** Here is how to solve your problem/fill your need
- **Benefits:** These are the specific ways in which you will benefit by accepting this proposal
- **Rationale/Description of Methods:** Here is how and why this proposal will work
- **Costs:** These are our fees for achieving the objectives

In individual proposals, these components may be structured in different sequences, and other components may be added. The components are usually indicated by divisions in the text, which can be described by various headings. Some proposals may combine major components; others may not indicate divisions at all.[1] But the common denominator of all proposals is the underlying argument.

Figure 5.1 illustrates the typical structure of an internal proposal. This proposal creates a persuasive argument by showing that the current situation presents a problem ($25,000 a year wasted), by proposing a change to solve the problem, by explaining the benefits of the change in terms of cost and time savings per job, and by explaining the potential for total annual savings. Because the writer and reader of the proposal work for the same company, they can be presumed to understand the context of the communication. The writer does not need to present extensive background or elaborate justifications, because she can assume the reader shares her concerns for the company.

Those preparing external proposals, however, do not usually enjoy this advantage. External proposals in accounting are often prepared by public accounting firms to secure business engagements with other companies. Those preparing external proposals cannot assume that prospective readers will share knowledge of their firm or understanding of their expertise and values. To establish common ground with the reader, engagement proposals often go into great detail in presenting background information, outlining benefits, and explaining the proposer's unique qualifications for the job. Because competition among firms for tax, audit, and business advisory engagements is fierce,

Figure 5.1

Sample Internal Proposal

PROPOSAL

TO: John Ibitson, Corporate Headquarters Office Manager
FROM: Polly Harrington, Assistant to the Controller
SUBJECT: Proposal to outsource printing services
DATE: June 4, 2001

Background

Our company currently maintains a printery, which processes photocopying and binding jobs that exceed 100 printed pages. To handle existing volume, the printery requires two full-time employees who run photocopies, produce bound copies of reports and proposals, and assist customers (company employees such as secretaries and executive assistants). The printery houses five large photocopiers, two binding machines, and a large inventory of paper and other supplies. Printing jobs are billed at established rates to the various company departments, and costs run approximately $150,000 per year. Turnaround time on an average printing job (1,000 printed pages) is 1 1/2 days.

We have been approached by Coleman's Copying (Park Boulevard location), who has proposed to take over the company's printing jobs. According to their analysis, our present system is wasting approximately $25,000 per year, an amount that they claim they can save us.

Proposal

We should close the company printery and outsource all printing jobs of over 100 printed pages to Coleman's. Individual departments can continue to use their own copy machines for jobs under 100 printed pages.

Benefits

By using Coleman's service, our cost per page printed would be lowered by half a cent per page (see cost section), and Coleman's will guarantee a 24-hour turnaround on our average-sized printing jobs. Coleman's is well known for producing a high-quality product, and because they are located just two doors down from us on Park

Figure 5.1

Sample Internal Proposal—*continued*

Boulevard, they will pick up and deliver the printing jobs at no extra charge.

Rationale

As you can see from the cost data provided, outsourcing our printing jobs would eliminate the costs we currently incur for material, overhead, salaries of two employees, and depreciation of equipment (which would be sold at book value). These costs, which amount to 3 cents per page, would be replaced by the Coleman's charge of 2½ cents per page. This savings of half a cent per page would amount to $25,000 over the course of one year (assuming average volume of 5 million pages).

	Costs Per Page	Estimated Annual Total*
Variable costs:		
Material	$.01	$50,000
Variable overhead	.005	25,000
Fixed costs allocated to print jobs:		
Employee salaries	.01	50,000
Depreciation of equipment	.005	25,000
Total cost	$.03	150,000
Cost of Coleman's Copying:	$.025	125,000
Cost saved per page:	$.005	25,000

*Assumes average annual volume of 5 million pages.

As soon as I get your approval, I will arrange for a contract with Coleman's Copying. Thank you for considering my proposal.

---

engagement proposals must establish a firm's *unique* qualifications and must find ways to distinguish it from other proposers.

Thus a typical engagement proposal includes more information designed to sell the proposed idea than an internal proposal does. And the most effective way for firms to sell, or promote, themselves in a competitive marketplace is to focus on how their services will help clients achieve specific business objectives. According to one expert, many firms make the mistake of focusing their proposals on *what they do* and leaving it to the prospective client to determine how those services will be useful. Instead, a proposal should be written so specifically to the needs of the prospective client that it could not be used for any other business prospect.[2]

In addition to the sections outlined earlier (Background, Proposal, Benefits, Rationale/Methods, and Costs), an engagement proposal includes sections that demonstrate the proposer's understanding of the client's needs and goals and highlight the special expertise of the engagement team in these business areas. These additional sections make the engagement proposal more sales oriented than an internal proposal because they repeatedly emphasize client benefits.

Typical Structure and Content, Engagement Proposal

1. Firm Background
   - defines the scope and location of the proposer's firm
   - highlights the proposer's reputation and credibility
   - describes the proposer's competitive positioning
2. Firm Qualifications
   - shows the proposer's understanding of the client's company
   - shows the proposer's understanding of the client's industry
   - summarizes the proposer's experience in that industry, including a list of similar clients
3. Proposed Services and Methods/Procedures
   - articulates what the accounting firm will do for the client
   - describes the methods to be used, including the proposer's strategic approach to integrating services (tax and management consulting, audit and tax)
4. Benefits (Including Client Service Team)
   - details the major outcomes to be expected from the engagement
   - describes the services to be rendered as an investment
   - introduces key engagement team members and highlights their expertise (biographical sketches or résumés)
5. Summary of Fees
   - describes how fees are assessed
   - itemizes proposed fees

Figure 5.2, a sample proposal by a large regional accounting firm to an expanding telecommunications company, illustrates the typical organization of an engagement proposal. As you read and write proposals on the job, you will no doubt encounter other arrangements of the elements you see here.

REPORTS

After a proposal is accepted and the services are performed, a report is almost always produced to document the work. In this respect, the relationship between proposals and reports is one of cause and effect because reports represent the necessary follow-up to successful proposals. An engagement for audit services, for example, culminates in an audit report, which presents the independent auditor's opinion on its client's financial statements along with the statements and notes to the statements. After completing a client's annual tax returns, the public accountant may write a report informing his or her client of future tax savings strategies. Upon completing a business advisory engagement, an accountant may write a report to the client recommending ways of

Figure 5.2

Sample Engagement Proposal

PROPOSAL

A Proposal to Provide Professional Services to Triton Technologies

Background

Randall & Sokowski was founded in 1953 and has grown, through its outstanding reputation for quality and service, to the 375-person firm it is today. This growth has been accomplished through careful recruitment and development of qualified personnel to meet the needs of our growing client base, represented by a cross section of regional, national, and multinational businesses and not-for-profit organizations.

Strategic leadership at Randall and Sokowski is provided by directors experienced in corporate financial management, computer information systems, and international accounting. The diverse expertise of our directors has allowed us to expand our services beyond traditional auditing and tax planning to broad-based business consulting and information management support services.

Our engagement team is exceptionally well qualified to assist management in Latin American start-up ventures and in profit enhancement opportunities for established businesses there.

Firm Qualifications

One of the most important resources available to Triton Technologies as a growing telecommunications company is the professional services firm you select to provide auditing, accounting, tax, and business consulting services. Our experience in serving high-tech companies offers Triton an excellent opportunity to benefit from the knowledge and insight our professionals can provide.

With the recent infusion of capital from Optima Venture Group, you are now in a position to expand operations to new markets, including Latin America. Randall and Sokowski is prepared to assist you during this challenging time.

Choosing this strategic area in which to concentrate our expertise, we have for the last decade specialized in offering innovative, yet practical solutions to the challenges confronting middle-market businesses, start-up companies, and entrepreneurs. Among our numer-

Figure 5.2

Sample Engagement Proposal—*continued*

ous technology clients, we have recently provided audit, tax, and consulting services to several highly successful companies whose growth has extended to Latin America:

Sunbelt Telecom
The Woodward Group
InfoTech, Inc.
AudioTel
RBC Technologies

Proposed Services

Coordinating the Latin American expansion will be complex and time consuming for Triton's management. Randall and Sokowski can reduce the difficulties inherent in this process by making recommendations on site selection and offering advice on international tax implications. The goal is to free Triton's management so you can focus on financing and expansion of operations.

You will receive a comprehensive study that will compare potential sites in terms of their legal, economic, demographic, and technological environments. We will also prepare and analyze projections of financial outlook for expansion in each site.

Under the leadership of Rod Skinner, our Latin American tax group will prepare for you a detailed analysis of Triton's international tax structure. This study will be integrated with the site selection study.

Concurrently, the Latin American tax group will analyze alternative foreign organization structures. The final recommended structure will encompass your Latin American operations and provide for future growth in other areas.

Benefits (Including Client Service Team)

You will receive comprehensive site information researched with the most up-to-the-minute techniques in the industry. This information will allow you to make the best business decisions possible about your foray into Latin America. You will feel confident about your investment in the site and in the organizational structure you adopt.

You will be served by professionals skilled in the specific areas in which you confront immediate challenges—site selection and international taxation.

Figure 5.2

Sample Engagement Proposal—*continued*

Our team will work under the guidance of engagement director **Tom Bonnura,** managing partner, who brings more than 15 years' experience in working with both private and public clients in the telecommunications industry. Tom's understanding of the Latin American business environment, earned over 8 years of work with the Venezuelan subsidiaries of RBC Technologies, will be a valuable asset in all phases of your project.

Ryan Comiskey, managing partner at our Houston office, has international tax expertise with such clients as Sunbelt Telecom, RBC Technologies, Cayman Airways, CaribGas, and many others. As project partner, Ryan offers Triton more than two decades of experience in international tax law.

Elizabeth Martinez is responsible for serving the international tax needs of our multinational clients in the southeastern United States. Elizabeth is particularly well versed in international tax restructuring.

Summary of Fees

Our fees are based on the time expended by the professionals assigned to the engagement, plus reimbursement for expenses. You will find that our billing rates are well in line with those of firms that have similar professional capabilities.

Fees for the Services Described Above:	
Site Selection Study	$60,000
International Tax Study	
Phase I	$21,000–$35,000
Phase II	To be determined after Phase I

improving accounting systems, expanding product lines, or otherwise enhancing profitability.

These final reports are almost always supported by written workpapers produced during the course of the engagement to document procedures performed, issues analyzed, research conducted, and other activities. Although these workpapers are often formatted as memos, they are in fact reports in terms of their rhetorical structure and content. In addition, many of the letters accountants write during engagements to clients and regulatory agencies are structured like reports as well.

Other reports in the practice of accountancy are generated without the impetus of proposals, however. A cost accountant in a manufacturing company might produce for the engineering sector a regular monthly report summarizing variances between expected and actual costs on a project. An accountant in the controller's office of an international trading company might prepare a report on the financial performance of its Italian affiliate for review by the U.S. management team. An internal auditor for a private bank might prepare a report recommending solutions to a problem with records management in the commercial lending division. A senior accountant at a publicly traded company might work with other accountants, corporate attorneys, and communications staff to prepare the company's annual report.

For government and nonprofit accountants, reports are often very specialized and in many cases must adhere to reporting requirements set by outside authorities. An accountant at a university might prepare a federal grant compliance report using forms and guidelines provided by the grantor agency. An accountant for an airport authority might prepare an operational report for the local government to which it is responsible using standards set by the FAA, and a local government accountant might prepare the city's Comprehensive Annual Financial Report (CAFR).

This great diversity makes it difficult to offer formulas for report writing in accountancy. As with proposals, however, we can identify certain common features among the reports accountants write.

Characteristic Features of Reports

Reports are informative documents. Whether a report is verifying that procedures were performed correctly, explaining how an accounting system works, outlining for stockholders the annual performance of a company, or analyzing an individual's tax liability in the light of altered tax law, its primary purpose is to make readers understand the subject under discussion.

Report writing draws on these common techniques: narration, summary, analysis and evaluation, and visual support. We discuss these in turn.

Narration   Narration, the recounting of events in coherent, usually chronological order, is a simple and frequently used technique in report writing. Accountants use narration to describe sequential events and accounting procedures. Sections of reports documenting procedures performed rely heavily on narration because these sections document the care with which the accountant carried out the task under discussion.

Figure 5.3 illustrates two sample narrations. Figure 5.3a is a narrative excerpt from an audit workpaper reporting on cash disbursement procedures. Notice that the writer explains step by step how accounts payable checks are paid. Figure 5.3b is a narrative excerpted from the annual capital expenditure report of a chemical company. This section of the report describes the steps involved in adopting a new software system.

The level of detail in the first narrative offers an important foundation for later work: for the tests the audit team will perform, the analyses they will conduct, and the conclusions they will ultimately draw about the company's systems of control. Although the second narration is less detailed, it effectively places events in sequence for the reader.

Figure 5.3 a and b

Sample Narrations

---

a. Accounts payable checks are paid twice a week based on the detail previously entered into the system and the invoice due dates. The checks are prepared by the accounts payable clerk, who compares the total of checks written to the check register and individual checks to the invoices. The voucher copy of the check is attached to the vendor invoice, which is then stamped "paid." The checks are then signed by the check signing machine with the signature plate of the vice president for administration.

The check signer and plate, along with both keys required for its operation, are kept in the safe in the Business Office. Ralph Franks, Mary Ann Jacobson, and Cindy Cummings have the combination to the safe.

Susan Hendricks operates the check signer after she has run the checks. She then totals the checks run and compares that total to the amount of checks written according to the accounts payable check register. After checks have been signed, they are mailed out to respective vendors.

---

b. The ERP project will deliver new business systems for sales, purchasing, inventory, operations, accounting, and plant maintenance. We have begun implementation, and that process has run on schedule. The rapid prototype milestone was achieved on target on March 6. The second milestone—the completion of the conceptual design— was reached on May 5. The third milestone—completion of preproduction configuration and testing—was reached November 1. On January 5, the Fort Worth office went on line as scheduled.

Summary   Because most readers do not need or have time to deal with large amounts of raw data, narration usually goes hand in hand with summary in accounting reports. Indeed, the bulk of accountants' report writing involves summarizing information. Summaries condense material by highlighting what is most important and eliminating incidental information. Thus, summarizing requires the ability to distinguish between what is essential information and what is supporting detail, what has top priority in a given situation and what has less.

Most reports are introduced by summaries that further condense the material they present. Sometimes labeled "executive summary" and sometimes presented as cover letters, these initial summaries—usually a paragraph or two—allow the reader to grasp at a glance the content and purpose of the report.

Figure 5.4 presents two sample summaries. Figure 5.4a is an executive summary from the corporate operating plan of a company that manufactures industrial laundry equipment. This summary serves as the report's cover page; in the body of the report, a section is devoted to each point bulleted in the summary. Figure 5.4b illustrates a summary found in the notes to the financial statements from an annual report. The summary highlights information about the company's pension benefits.

Figure 5.4 a and b

Sample Summaries

---

a. Highlights

- The economic environment in North America is generally buoyant. The economies of the eastern and southern states continue at healthy levels, although upstate New York has high unemployment and will remain generally slow. Economic conditions are strong in the midwest and north central states, with employment at an all-time high.
- The 1999 operating income is forecast to be slightly ahead of plan, as increases in revenues have been only partially offset by increased maintenance and other costs. Operating income is expected to increase steadily in 1999 and 2000 and to flatten out in 2001.
- Specialty products operating income will decline significantly in 1999, mainly as a result of our plan to stop producing model 24056 dryers. We will phase in production of a new model (24368), and, as a result, expect operating income to rebound in 2000.

---

b. Pension Benefits

The Company sponsors and/or contributes to pension plans covering substantially all U.S. employees and certain employees in international locations. The benefits are primarily based on years of service and the employees' compensation for certain periods during the last years of employment. Pension costs are generally funded currently, subject to regulatory funding limitations. The Company also sponsors nonqualified, unfunded defined benefit plans for certain officers and other employees. In addition, the Company and its subsidiaries have various pension plans and other forms of postretirement arrangements outside the United States.

Total pension expense for all benefit plans, including defined benefit plans, amounted to approximately $73 million in 1998, $57 million in 1997, and $49 million in 1996.

Analysis and Evaluation   Reports prepared by accountants frequently provide opinions based on an analysis of issues or evaluation of facts in the light of the accountant's expert knowledge. These opinions may take the form of conclusions, recommendations, or attestations.

In rendering opinions, accountants apply professional rules—GAAP, FASB pronouncements, regulations from the tax code—to the case in question and draw conclusions based on that application. When a CPA advises an individual on tax liability, for example, she applies the relevant tax code regulation to the client's financial information; when an auditor recommends changes in a company's procedures for reporting marketable securities, he applies GAAP to his observations of that company's accounting practices.

What these scenarios have in common is that each one involves isolating information and interpreting it to draw a conclusion. Unlike narration, which describes events, and summary, which highlights information, analysis breaks information down and examines it in the light of principles, guidelines, or rules that govern professional practice. Because the validity of the conclusion drawn depends on how well the principle was applied to the facts, readers of analyses want to see how that application was handled. Well-written analyses, therefore, do not ask readers to accept conclusions on faith. Instead, they take readers step by step through the logical process by which the facts were interpreted. They clearly articulate the following:

- the *facts* under discussion
- the *issues* that arise from these facts
- the *accounting principle, guideline, rule,* or *technique* that applies to the case
- the *reasoning* by which the principle was applied to the specific facts
- the *conclusion* reached

When you are writing analyses, remember not to ask your reader to take your word for the conclusions you draw. Instead, show the reader exactly how you arrived there.

Figure 5.5 illustrates a short report written by an accountant in charge of the inventory accounts for a manufacturer of vinyl, ceramic, linoleum, and other floor covering products. After a brief introduction that summarizes the purpose and context of the report, the accountant provides the sales manager with his analysis of one aspect of vinyl flooring sales.

Notice how the introduction presents the facts *(that the inventory turnover ratio has declined)* and the issues *(the decline will cost the company more money and may point to more serious underlying problems).* The fourth paragraph introduces the analytical technique *(the inventory turnover ratio),* and the fifth paragraph lays out the reasoning by which the writer came to his conclusions. In the final paragraph, the writer states his conclusion: He and the sales manager should meet to discuss the problem.

Visual Support   The adage that "one picture is worth a thousand words" is especially true in the case of accountants' written reports because pictorial representations make numbers and complex concepts easy to grasp. Because

Figure 5.5

Sample Analysis

REPORT

TO: Elaine Mitchell, Sales Manager
FROM: Steve Roberts, Inventory Accountant and Analyst
DATE: October 10, 2000
SUBJECT: Inventory turnover slowdown in vinyl flooring

Now that the books have closed on fiscal year-end 9/30/00, I have run some analyses of our various floor covering inventories. One of my findings possibly concerns you and the Sales Department: Our inventory turnover ratio for vinyl flooring has declined significantly this year.

The industry's average inventory turnover ratio for similar product lines, for example, is 4.5 times in a year. Last year, our turnover ratio was 4.6, a bit better than the industry average. This year, however, it has dropped to 3.8. (Over the past five years, our turnover ratio has held steady at around 4.4.)

Not only does a slower-moving inventory cost the company more in storage and other carrying costs, but it may also be an indication of more serious problems. We may be holding on to a larger amount of obsolete inventory; we may have priced some of our lines too high; or there may be reasons that are linked to the Sales Department.

The inventory turnover ratio is calculated by dividing our cost of goods sold by the average dollar amount of inventory on hand during the year. The resulting number tells us how many times during the year we moved out our average inventory on hand. For FY 1999, it cost us $10,350,000 to manufacture the vinyl flooring we sold that year. Dividing that by our average inventory on hand of $2,250,000 gives us an inventory turnover ratio of 4.6. In FY 2000, however, on $13,300,000 in cost of goods sold we kept an inventory of $3,500,000—an inventory turnover ratio of only 3.8. These numbers, although not very meaningful when each stands alone, do take on meaning when we compare them to how we did in previous years and to what is happening across the industry.

We in the Accounting Department are committed to assisting all departments plantwide in investigating and finding solutions to problems. I would like to get together to discuss your insights into possible reasons for the slowdown in vinyl flooring turnover. Please give me a call at ext. 333 as soon as you can.

many of the reports accountants write are directed to nonfinancial audiences—external clients, internal management—visual aids such as tables, graphs, and charts are commonly used to make numerical content accessible to readers.

Chapter 7 provides detailed information on preparing tables, graphs, and charts along with a discussion of which visual aids are best to convey certain types of data. The section that follows here offers a brief overview of that information.

Tables quickly convey large amounts of numerical data at once. Although tables are not as visually appealing as other graphics that represent numerical data, they are the best way to present a great deal of information in a compact format. When item-by-item details are needed, a table often best suits that purpose. The table in Figure 5.6 provides numerical data about a company's asset acquisition and depreciation plan for the next five years.

Graphs are the best way to illustrate quantitative relationships quickly and easily. The two most common types of graphs, line graphs and bar graphs, both help illustrate comparative information. Line graphs show a relationship between two variables over time, and bar graphs measure several different indicators against a common standard of measurement (dollar amounts, percentages, etc.).

The line graph in Figure 5.7, for example, shows readers two things at a glance: how the company's actual direct labor costs rose and fell over a six-month period and how those costs compared to those that had been predicted (budgeted). The bar graph in Figure 5.8, in contrast, shows readers the comparative importance of *several* factors in problems arising from software implementation.

To observe how visual support can make a text easier to understand, let us look once again at Steve Roberts's report to Elaine Mitchell about inventory turnover that we analyzed earlier. This time, shown in Figure 5.9, Steve has illustrated key numerical concepts by means of graphs. Although Elaine might

---

Figure 5.6

Table

Planned Asset Purchases and Depreciation

Assets Purchased	Life	2001	2002	2003	2004	2005
Building	30 years	$1,250,000				
Plant equipment	7 years	800,000		35,000	25,000	80,000
Office equipment	5 years	45,000			3,500	3,500
Furniture	8 years	30,000				
Totals		$2,125,000		35,000	28,500	83,500
Depreciation						
Building		$41,667	$41,667	$41,667	$41,667	$41,667
Plant equipment		114,286	114,286	119,286	122,857	134,286
Office equipment		9,000	9,000	9,000	9,700	10,400
Furniture		3,750	3,750	3,750	3,750	3,750
Total depreciation		168,703	168,703	173,703	177,974	190,103

well have understood the original version, visual aids will make her comprehension more certain.

Reports include a large variety of elements, dictated by their differing purposes and contents. These elements can generally be categorized, however, into the following components:

- An *introduction,* or *summary,* explaining the subject, purpose, and occasion of the report as well as significant conclusions reached. In longer reports, the introduction may include an explanation of how the report is organized. This section allows readers to know at a glance the main questions raised in the report and the answers provided.
- A *background section* summarizing the problem the accountant studied, the situation the accountant investigated, or the subject's relevant financial history. If the report involves analysis, the background section should include a statement of accounting principles, tax laws, or government regulations relevant to the case.

Figure 5.7

Line Graph

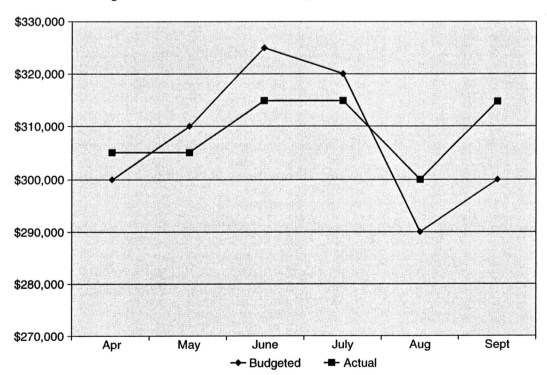

Budgeted vs. Actual Direct Labor Cost, 2nd and 3rd Quarters 2001

Figure 5.8

Bar Graph

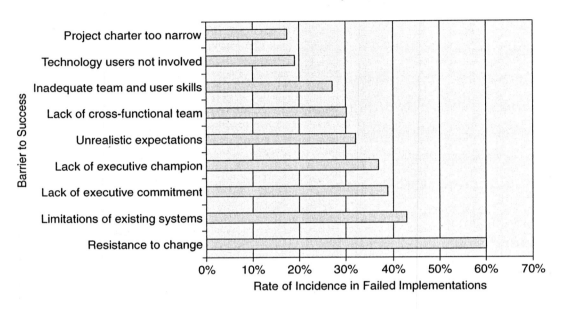

Barriers to Successful Software Implementation

- A *body of the report* narrating procedures performed or analyzing the information in question. This section may include various visual aids to support textual content; it may be a few paragraphs or several pages long. The heading of this section and subheadings within it vary greatly, depending on the audience, purpose, and content of the report.
- A *conclusion* summarizing the information, rendering an opinion, and/or recommending improvements or solutions. Although the general conclusions are stated in the summary section, this final section details specific recommendations, solutions, and action plans.

Whether the report is presented in a brief letter, a workpaper in memo format, or a formal document running hundreds of pages, these four elements should form the skeleton of its structure.

These components are illustrated in the sample operational efficiency report in Figure 5.10, pp. 145–148. The report is the final product of an engagement in which a business information systems consulting firm reviewed a client's accounting systems and cash application processes.

In place of a long textual narrative, the consulting team's report uses tables and a flowchart to represent the interviewing and testing processes conducted at Comtech. These visual representations are much more compact and easy to follow than a narrative would be because of the number of people and functions involved.

Figure 5.9

Analytical Report

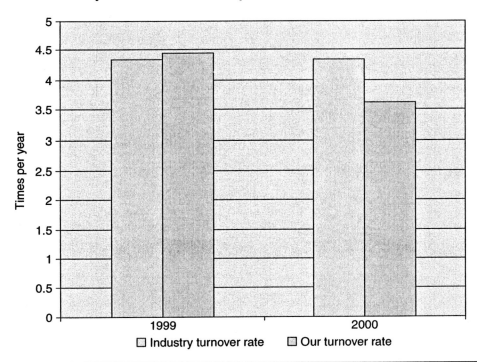

REPORT

TO: Elaine Mitchell, Sales Manager
FROM: Steve Roberts, Inventory Accountant and Analyst
DATE: October 10, 2000
SUBJECT: Inventory turnover slowdown in vinyl flooring

Now that the books have closed on fiscal year-end 9/30/00, I have run some analyses of our various floor covering inventories. One of my findings possibly concerns you and the Sales Department: Our inventory turnover ratio for vinyl flooring has declined significantly this year.

The industry's average inventory turnover ratio for similar product lines, for example, is 4.5 times in a year. Last year, our turnover ratio was 4.6, a bit better than the industry average. This year, however, it has dropped to 3.8. This bar graph illustrates the magnitude of our drop-off (this year and last year) compared to industry norms:

Inventory Turnover Ratio: Industry vs. Our Performance

Figure 5.9

Analytical Report—*continued*

Over the past five years, our turnover ratio has held steady at around 4.4. As the line graph shows, our recent turnover represents a significant drop-off from our own five-year performance norms as well:

Inventory Turnover Ratio: Past Years' Performance

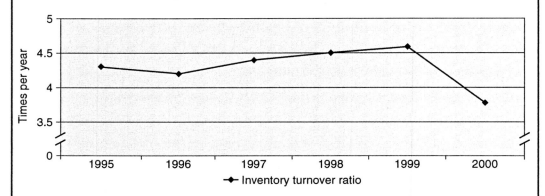

Not only does a slower moving inventory cost the company more in storage and other carrying costs, but it may also be an indication of more serious problems. We may be holding on to a larger amount of obsolete inventory; we may have priced some of our lines too high; or there may be reasons that are linked to the Sales Department.

The inventory turnover ratio is calculated by dividing our cost of goods sold by the average dollar amount of inventory on hand during the year. The resulting number tells us how many times during the year we moved out our average inventory on hand. These numbers, although not very meaningful when each stands alone, do take on meaning when we compare them to how we did in previous years and to what is happening across the industry.

We in the Accounting Department are committed to assisting all departments plantwide in investigating and finding solutions to problems. I would like to get together to discuss your insights into possible reasons for the slowdown in vinyl flooring. Please give me a call at ext. 333 as soon as you can.

Figure 5.10

Sample Report

> ## REPORT
>
> **A Report to Comtech, Inc.**
> **Los Gatos, CA**
> **Cash Application Analysis**
> **May 1999**
> **Prepared by**
> **Rawson Consulting, Inc.**
> **San Jose, CA**
>
> **Summary:** After reviewing the cash application process at Comtech, the consulting team agreed that the current process *does work* and that no critical steps are missing. The process can be improved on, however. The recommendations contained in this report suggest ways to do so.
>
> **Background:** Comtech is a leading national distributor of educational software. Its credit department is made up of more than 30 associates involved in all facets of accounts receivable management, including the cash application process.
>
> Comtech uses an out-of-date TAS A/R system for its cash application, but the company is in the final stages of selecting a new system to replace it. To ensure that the new system is optimally effective, Comtech's corporate credit manager retained Rawson Consulting to document the current cash application process.
>
> This report explains the procedures that the Rawson team followed to collect the data, describes the scope of the investigation, and documents critical processes with diagrams and summaries. The report also offers recommendations for improvement and suggests key requirements for the new system.
>
> **Methodology:** The consulting team reviewed the cash application process during a two-day site visit (Monday, May 8, and Tuesday, May 9). The following table lists the Comtech associates whom the team interviewed during those days:

Figure 5.10

Sample Report—*continued*

Name	Title
Scott Johansen	Corporate Credit Manager
Joe Avalon	Director, Receipts/Disbursements
Delia Nelson	Manager, Receipts/Disbursements
Sarah Fulton	Financial Processing Specialist
Mavis Drake	Input Clerk
Hank La Rue	Input Clerk
Joel Berry	Input Clerk
Holly Livingston	Input Clerk
Pam Alford	Input Clerk

The following table lists the tasks covered, the associates interviewed, and the time spent with each:

Cash Applications

Task	Interviewed	Time
Lockbox batch	Mavis Drake	30 minutes
ID/verification	Joe Avalon	30 minutes
Unapplied/unidentified inventory	Joel Berry, Holly Livingston	45 minutes
Distribution of cash batches	Hank La Rue	30 minutes
Cash application—retail	Hank La Rue	30 minutes
Cash application—wholesale	Joe Avalon	1 hour
Cash application—credit card	Pam Alford, Mavis Drake	30 minutes
Cash application—wire transfers	Pam Alford	30 minutes
Cash application—data input	Mavis Drake, Pam Alford	15 minutes
Live check processing		

Accounts Receivable

Task	Interviewed	Time
Letters of open credit	Joel Berry	15 minutes
Refund processing	Mavis Drake	1 hour
Manual invoice processing	Delia Nelson	15 minutes
Account maintenance	Hank La Rue	15 minutes
Notification of customer address changes	None	0
Monthly reporting/Lockbox activity	Joe Avalon	15 minutes
Other monthly reporting	Joe Avalon, Holly Livingston	1 hour
Training	Scott Johansen	30 minutes
Transfer from RAGI	Hank La Rue	30 minutes
Transfer to RAGI	Hank La Rue	30 minutes

Figure 5.10

Sample Report—*continued*

Reconciliations

Task	Interviewed	Time
ATB reconciliation	Mavis Drake	30 minutes
Sales reconciliation to A/R	Mavis Drake	30 minutes
A/R reconciliation to G/R	Joe Avalon	15 minutes
Bank reconciliation	Mavis Drake	30 minutes

Documentation of Key Work Flows: The attached Cash Application Process Flowchart depicts Comtech's cash application process as the consulting team understood it. This flowchart is not designed to account for every activity but to show the primary inputs and outputs of the process.

Observations and Recommendations: All Comtech systems close on Friday of every week, which allows for completion of processing over the weekend. Only basic accounts receivable reports are produced at the end of the week. Because the input from accounts receivable to the general ledger is manual, however, much time is required to complete the weekly close, and the department staffing levels are affected accordingly.

Recommendation: Build an automated interface between accounts receivable and the general ledger. Creating such an interface will be a minor change that can be handled with an export utility program. It will take about a day to develop.

Benefit: The automated interface will speed the production of reports, cutting completion time from 5 days to 2 days from week's end. According to Joe Avalon, the change will save about 20 staff hours per week.

Implementation: Exact requirements for the export must be defined for Mark Larson, director of development, who will implement the change. Then the project must be sized and prioritized. Although Mark believes the change will be simple, Scott Johansen will have to put it on his priority development list. Once that is done, implementation and testing should take no more than six weeks.

Figure 5.10

Sample Report—*continued*

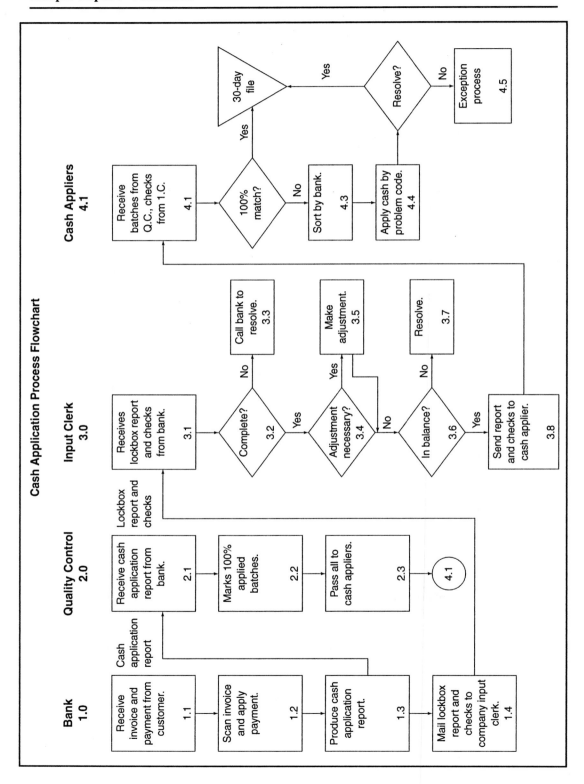

Cash Application Process Flowchart

CONCLUSION

In practice, you will find that the types of written communications discussed in this chapter overlap with those in Chapter 4. Your audience, the occasions for your writing, the content of your documents, and the purposes you seek to achieve may require you to combine various techniques for written communication. In a letter to the IRS, for example, you may employ the techniques of summary and analysis that characterize report writing. In a report to a client, you may pay special attention to tone and the "*you* attitude." In a proposal to management, you may want to narrate the events that will occur as your proposal is implemented. However you combine the techniques for effective written communication, the guidelines in this chapter, along with those in Chapter 4, will help you do so effectively.

NOTES

[1]Richard C. Freed and David D. Roberts, "The Nature, Classification, and Generic Structure of Proposals," *Journal of Technical Writing and Communication* 19, no. 4 (1989): 317–351.

[2]Colette Nassutti, "Art and Science of Proposals," *Outlook* 61, no. 3 (Fall 1993): 18–22.

EXERCISES

1. **Scenario:** Your corporate accounting manager has been approached by a credit card company that has offered to take over your firm's accounts payable function, thereby allowing you to employ fewer people in the accounting department. The credit card company will process all the vendors' invoices, issue vendors' payments through the credit card system, and provide monthly reports of expenditures that tie into your general ledger accounts. Most of the cost of this system would be absorbed by the vendors, who pay a fee to accept credit card payments; thus, your firm could be expected to save a significant amount of money each year.

   Writing task: Make a list of information you would need to prepare an internal proposal for your company to switch to this type of an accounts payable system. (Do not actually prepare the proposal.)

2. **Scenario:** You are a staff accountant for the Phoenix, Arizona, office of a large CPA firm. Your office prepares numerous presentations, proposals, and reports that are copied and sent out to clients and other professionals. Because the appearance of documents often has a significant impact on others' opinions about your firm, many of your competitors routinely distribute documents in color.

   Your office has a high-speed black and white copier. For color copies, the original must be sent to the firm's Atlanta office. Because of the distance and backlog of work at the Atlanta office, which makes color copies for all of the southern offices of your firm, turn-around time for the copies frequently is 7 to 10 days. Thus, color documents often cannot be distributed on a timely basis. Your managing partner thinks your firm should purchase its own color copier so that top-quality, competitive documents can be distributed quickly. The color copier will cost $30,000.

Writing task: Prepare an internal proposal to your firm's Budget Committee requesting a color copier for your office. Follow the structure of a proposal given in the chapter. Make up any additional facts you believe are necessary.

3. **Scenario:** Tom Bielski is the general manager for Doughnuts N' More, Inc.'s Illinois facility. He has received the following report from the internal audit staff:

REPORT

Illinois Region
Internal Audit Report
March 31, 1999

Exception Noted

The corporate fixed asset disposal policy is not being enforced. Currently, the corporate policy states: "Operating personnel must notify accounting personnel at corporate headquarters when disposing of fixed assets." Unrecorded disposals can result in overstating fixed assets and depreciation expense.

Recommendation

The corporate policy should be clarified and enforced. A new policy statement should be written requiring that a member of the corporate accounting staff authorize all disposals of fixed assets. Disposal forms should be created for such authorizations. Operating personnel should complete a disposal form, which should list the disposal date, asset description, operating area, and tag number, and should submit the form to corporate accounting for approval. Adherence to the corporate policy will ensure better control over fixed asset disposals and improved operating area accountability and financial record keeping.

Tom agrees in theory with the internal auditor's recommendation, but he has made the following list of points that he feels should be considered in the creation of the new policy:

■ Not all dispositions are material. Filling out a form for every transaction is a waste of resources—paper, processing, and filing costs. Suggest minimum threshold of $1,000/transaction.

■ Some opportunities to sell off old assets are short lived, and excessive red tape can mean lost opportunities. (Remember the recent transaction when Hoffman's Bakery needed to purchase a used bakery oven? If we had had to wait for corporate approval, we would have lost the chance to sell our outmoded bakery oven for $3,000.)

■ Staffing cost to process each transaction will increase substantially. Current staff is already working to capacity, and an additional clerk will probably cost between $8 and $10 per hour.

Writing task: Using Tom's notes, write an internal proposal to the corporate accounting leadership at headquarters, supporting a modification of the current policy. (Refer to the characteristic features of a proposal as discussed in the chapter.)

4. **Scenario:** You are a CPA who recently attended a party where you were introduced to a prospective client, Sarah Miller. Ms. Miller opened a nail and tanning salon last month. She commented that she dislikes preparing her own tax return, and doesn't know how to handle many of the business' tax issues, but was unsure whether she wants to incur the cost of paying a CPA to prepare the return for her.

   Writing task: Prepare an engagement proposal to Sarah Miller, to "sell" the idea of having you prepare her Form 1040, Individual Tax Return taxes, including a Schedule C, Profit or Loss from Business. Emphasize the ways you can benefit her in the long run. From the background information Sarah provided, you estimate your fee for preparation of the tax return to be approximately $300. Create any additional details you believe are needed.

5. **Scenario:** Bob Hart is the new systems director for a medium-sized advertising firm, Anderson & Smith. The former director was fired on January 31, 2000, because of her inadequate response to the Y2K problem. The firm is now experiencing various technical difficulties associated with Y2K, and Bob's job is to solve these problems. Bob's first step is to write an internal proposal to the firm's president suggesting a solution to the problems. Bob knows his proposal must convince the president—who is not highly computer literate—to loosen the purse strings to fund the necessary programming changes.

   Here are Bob's notes:

   ■ Anything computerized must be evaluated for possible Y2K problems, including embedded systems in the building, computing and telecommunications equipment.

- There are currently so many problems that we must start with each area and assess its need.
- Another primary concern is the Y2K status of the periodicals that publish our advertising.
- Electronic data interchange (EDI) is experiencing significant disruption.
- We are currently unable to communicate directly with several periodicals: *Time, Newsweek, People.*
- Limited communication is available with *New York Times, Washington Post.*
- Lost revenue to date: $14,000 in January.
- Projected revenue loss for February: $24,000.
- The current trend is increasing and could reach $100,000 of lost revenue per month.

Steps to be taken:

- Educate our firm's members and clients; coordinate efforts with our largest business partners.
- Hire a programming consultant: I have all I can handle with my duties at present (estimated cost: $100 per hour; estimated time needed: minimum 240 hours).
- Gather estimates for necessary software upgrades/replacements.

In addition, the firm must consider the legal ramifications of client advertising being mishandled because of systems glitches. Three major accounts have already threatened legal action if service is not improved.

Writing task: Use the techniques described in this chapter to write the proposal from Bob to the president of A&S. Remember to define the problems clearly before proposing solutions to solve them.

6. **Scenario:** Period Collectibles, Inc., a large antique dealer, has experienced a recent change in the collectibility of its receivables. A summary of Period Collectibles' aging of accounts receivable for the past two years is shown opposite.

   Writing task: As the accounting analyst for Period Collectibles, you have been asked to write a report, in memo format, for the treasurer of the company. In the report you should analyze the change in collectibility of receivables, explain the implications of the change, and make recommendations for measures that the company could take to improve the situation. Include any visual aids you feel would make your report easier to understand.

7. **Scenario:** In April 2000, Frances Ryan, a securities analyst for Brady, Light & Co., wrote the memo opposite for her quarterly file on TTT Industries. Shortly thereafter, she left the company to take a job with the SEC. It is now May 2000. You have just taken over Frances's position.

REPORT

Period Collectibles, Inc.
Summary of Aging of Accounts Receivable
For the Years Ended December 31, 2000 and 1999

Year Ended	Total A/Rec.	0-30 Days	31-60 Days	61-90 Days	91-120 Days	Over 120 Days
12/31/00	$256,600	$125,400	$55,200	$35,600	$15,900	$24,500
12/31/99	$205,000	$140,800	$35,100	$20,400	$6,500	$2,200

Sales for the year ended 12/31/00 were $2,813,000, while sales for the year ended 12/31/99 were $2,654,000. Although many of Period Collectibles' larger sales to other businesses are on account, most smaller sales to individual customers are paid in cash at the time of the sale.

MEMO

DATE: April 12, 2000
SUBJECT: First Quarter Summary, TTT Industries

The following significant debt and equity activities occurred:

- No early extinguishment of debt occurred, despite management's press release dated 10/15/99.
- No new financing occurred during the first quarter.
- No new common stock or treasury stock transactions were initiated.
- $200 to $300 million of new corporate debt is to be issued sometime late this year.
- Pass-through certificates approximating $200 million are expected to be issued sometime this summer.

This information was primarily obtained from press conferences and releases. In addition, I met with TTT's treasury personnel, K. Beal and R. Barken, to discuss the significant changes in debt and the company's reasoning for initiating those changes. TTT plans to expand its Southeast Asian manufacturing facilities to take advantage of declining costs in that area.

Your boss has asked you to summarize TTT's first quarter activities for his May report to the senior portfolio managers. The TTT file contains only this memo and the supporting first quarter financial statements.

Writing task:

a. Make a list of the questions you need answered and of the additional information you need to gather before you can write the requested report.

b. Using the information provided by the memo, write an outline for the report. Then indicate where you would place the additional information you requested in (a).

8. **Scenario:** Phillip Smith is the new office manager for Treble Manufacturing, a manufacturer of hearing aids. Phillip needs to prepare a report to the president, Samantha Lawson, on ways of upgrading the company's computer system. Philip wants to integrate all users into one network, but Samantha is not convinced a network arrangement is necessary. Phillip sees this challenge as a good career enhancement opportunity; therefore, his report must be well-written and organized to impress the president on this first major assignment. He has asked you to research the issue and to draft the report.

Company background: Treble has been in business for fifteen years and has changed dramatically over the last five. The company has moved from a purely manual record-keeping environment to one in which nearly every person uses a computer. However, systems development has been sporadic and uncoordinated. The production staff are all computer literate, but the skills of the office staff range from beginner level to those of advanced user.

A variety of hardware is in use:

Production

25 Macintosh users
10 Power PCs Model 6100
10 Power PCs Model 7200
5 Power PCs Model 8500

Office

10 IBMs
5 Model IBM 330-PC133
5 Model IBM 350 P466-DX2

Software Owned

5 copies of Microsoft Office
10 copies of AutoCAD

Unfortunately, several computers have bootleg copies of software on them. One of the goals of formalizing of systems will be to gain compliance with the manufacturers of software used.

Time is often wasted in the transfer of data from disk to disk and from computer to computer. The goal of the new system will be to save the company money by improving communication and data transfer. The president of this family-owned business wants to be sure that the system selected will minimize problems with lost or destroyed data. Given the current growth projections for Treble, the system must be one that upgrades easily and is able to accept additional users with minimal impact on processing speed.

After considerable research, Phillip has obtained the following information:

Estimated Cost

Two LAN servers will be needed:	
Mac compatible	$20,000–30,000
IBM compatible	$20,000–30,000
Maintenance agreements for each	$100/month
Communication lines needed:	
T1 line	$1,000
Required maintenance	$1,500/month
Or	
Frame-Relay Wiring	$5,000
Plus necessary additional phone lines	$200/workstation
Communication accessories:	
Ethernet, Switches and Hubs	$2,000
Software Licensing for LANs:	
Windows 98 and Office 97 for IBM users	$10,000 for 15-user maximum
Office 98 for Macintosh users	$10,000 for 25 users
OS8 operating system for Mac	$2,500 for 25 users
AutoCAD	$18,000 for 25 users
Training Costs	$2,000 per week

The company's key concern is cost. Management is concerned not only with the initial outlay but also with the costs of maintenance and training.

Writing task: Using the information provided, write a report detailing the company's current position and needs and recommending a specific set of options.

- Use *narration* to describe how the need for the new system has arisen.
- Use *summary* to describe Treble's current computing environment.

- Use *analysis* to discuss the relative merits of the alternatives available given the company's cost concerns.
- Be sure to justify your recommendations and conclusions.

9. **Scenario:** You are working in your university's small business advising center as one of the requirements for a course you are taking. The center provides advice to local small business owners when they are unable to, or prefer not to, hire professional consultants. Mr. Minkin, owner of Minkin Electric, a local electrical contractor, has come to you for advice about how to prevent fraud in a small business such as his. He had recently attended a conference where small business fraud was discussed. He found out that a significant amount of fraud occurs in small businesses where separation of duties is ignored. He learned that a company can have adequate internal controls with as few as three employees, as long as three major functions are performed by different people: (1) custody of assets, (2) recording of transactions, and (3) authorization or approval of transactions. Mr. Minkin has provided you with the following list of tasks that are now handled by him and his office staff:

   - Receipt of materials
   - Preparation of receiving report
   - Verifying correctness of vendor invoices
   - Preparing checks
   - Approval and signing of checks
   - Recording of cash disbursements
   - Receipt of customers' cash payments
   - Deposit of cash
   - Recording of cash receipts and updating accounts receivable ledger
   - Preparing estimates of work to be performed
   - Scheduling work to be performed by service team
   - Preparing customer invoices
   - Recording revenues
   - Preparation of bank reconciliations
   - Review of bank reconciliations

   Writing task: Prepare a report for Mr. Minkin explaining how he can assign these tasks to have adequate separation of duties with only three people working in the office. Your report should detail how and why the tasks listed above should be divided between him and his two office employees to maintain adequate internal controls. Remember that the handling of cash or other assets, the recording of transactions, and the authorization / approval functions must be kept separate in order to have good internal controls. As you write your report, keep in mind that Mr. Minkin has no formal education in accounting, and needs clear, simple explanations of accounting concepts.

10. The figures on the following pages are "before" and "after" versions of a brief report. Compare the two versions.

Writing task: In several paragraphs, explain what changes the writer made on revision and why the second version is better (more readable, easier to understand) than the first. Be specific; cite or quote passages from both versions to support your assertions. Consider principles from Chapters 2 and 3 as well as from Chapter 4 in your analysis.

REPORT

**General Hospital
Report on Tests of Internal Controls over Purchasing
Within the DataWiz Information System**

This report is a supplement to the auditor's study of internal controls for General Hospital's general accounting system. It evaluates the DataWiz System's internal controls that are designed to prevent individuals from making purchases that exceed their assigned dollar limits. Testing was performed to assure that controls are sufficient and that they work effectively within the system.

Ralph Smith, associate director of purchasing, and Debbie Jones, administrative assistant for the Purchasing Department, were questioned regarding the purchasing approval hierarchy and related controls. Purchase orders are created in the field by an individual in a department and once created, approval is based on the following:

Criterion	Action	Forward To
PO is under both the individual's $ limit and $5,000 and it contains no attachments	Approve and reserve for PO	Not necessary
PO is under both the individual's $ limit and $5,000 but it contains attachments (attachment would be some type of agreement or contract required to be reviewed by Purchasing Department)	Reserve for PO	Forward to Purchasing for review of the attachment and approval of the PO
PO is under the individual's $ limit but over $5,000	Reserve for PO	Forward to Purchasing for review and approval (all POs over $5,000 must be reviewed by Purchasing Department)
PO is over the individual's $ limit	Reserve for PO	System automatically forwards the PO to the Purchasing Department for approval since it exceeds the individual's $ limit

Based on the auditor's knowledge of the DataWiz information system, questioning management, and the members of the audit team, tests were developed and performed.

"Before" continued on p. 160

REPORT

**General Hospital
Report on Tests of Internal Controls over Purchasing
Within the DataWiz Information System**

Introduction

This report evaluates the quality of the DataWiz Information System's internal controls designed to prevent individuals from making
purchases that exceed their assigned dollar limits. The purpose of
the auditor's testing was to assure that sufficient controls are in
place and to verify that those controls are working effectively within
the hospital's system. This study supplements the auditor's study of
internal controls for General Hospital's general accounting system.

Background: The Purchasing Approval Hierarchy

The auditor questioned the Purchasing Department, particularly
Ralph Smith, associate director of purchasing, and Debbie Jones,
the administrative assistant for the Purchasing Department, regarding the purchasing approval hierarchy and related controls. Smith
and Jones provided the following background.

Purchase orders are created by individuals in a department. Once
the PO is created, approval is based on the following:

Criterion	Action	Forward To
PO is under both the individual's $ limit and $5,000, and it contains no attachments	Approve and reserve for PO	Not necessary
PO is under both the individual's $ limit and $5,000, but it contains attachments (attachment would be some type of agreement or contract required to be reviewed by Purchasing Department)	Reserve for PO	Forward to Purchasing for review of the attachment and approval of the PO
PO is under the individual's $ limit but over $5,000	Reserve for PO	Forward to Purchasing for review and approval. (All POs over $5,000 must be reviewed by Purchasing Department)

"After" continued on p. 161

"Before" Version—*continued*

- Reviewed and assessed the reasonableness of the purchasing approval hierarchy.
- Had to determine that individual dollar limits for purchases are not being exceeded by those making the purchases. This test was performed by selecting a sample of 10 purchases over $5,000 made by different individuals and verification by comparison to the Logon ID Request Form that the purchase amount did not exceed the individual's dollar limit. In addition we selected a sample of 5 purchases made below $5,000 and performed the same procedure.
- Verified if any approval by the department head was necessary for purchases over a certain dollar limit. If approval for purchases over certain dollar limits is necessary, we ascertained whether proper approval was obtained. This step was performed in conjunction with the previous step.

Tests Performed and Results

A sample of 15 purchases, 10 over $5,000 and 5 under $5,000, was selected, identifying who approved the PO and verifying that the approved amount did not exceed the individual's dollar limit established on their Purchasing Application Logon ID Request. The following grid identifies 15 PO's selected and indicates whether they were properly approved after being matched to the respective ID Requests:

Purchase Order Number	Vendor Name	Dollar Amount of PO	Proper Approval Obtained
10 Over $5,000			
1. 201050	Everclean Linen, Inc.	$25,000	Yes
2. 207858	Super Office Co.	$19,800	Yes
3. 200004	Medical Central, Inc.	$11,250	Yes
4. 245116	Main Pharmaceutical	$6,730	Yes
5. 233600	Comfort Supply, Inc.	$9,870	Yes
6. 220400	Acme Drug Co.	$35,450	Yes
7. 222555	Merck	$5,000	Yes
8. 213987	Institutional Food, Inc.	$8,975	Yes
9. 201369	Medical Associates, Inc.	$15,110	Yes
10. 238938	Computer Assist, Inc.	$6,500	Yes
5 Under $5,000			
1. 200452	Acme Plastic	$4,777	Yes
2. 202456	Abraham Marketing	$4,819	Yes
3. 205801	USA Tech	$3,770	Yes
4. 248598	Northwood Supply	$4,910	Yes
5. 226476	MedAid, Inc.	$4,530	Yes

"Before" continued on p. 162

"After" Version—*continued*

Criterion	Action	Forward To
PO is over the individual's $ limit	Reserve for PO	System automatically forwards the PO to the Purchasing Department for approval when it exceeds the individual's $ limit

Tests Performed and Results

The tests described here were developed based on the auditor's knowledge of the DataWiz Information System, conversations with management, and collaboration of the members of the audit team:

- Test to evaluate the reasonableness of the purchasing approval hierarchy
- Test to determine that dollar limits are not being exceeded by those making the purchases
- Test to verify that required department head approval for purchases over certain dollar limits is obtained

To perform these tests, the auditors selected a sample of 15 purchases (10 over $5,000 and 5 under $5,000). They identified who approved the PO and verified that the approved amount did not exceed the individual's dollar limit established on his or her Purchasing Application Logon ID Request. The team also verified that purchases were properly approved after they were matched to the respective ID Requests. The grid here displays the results of this testing:

Purchase Order Number	Vendor Name	Dollar Amount of PO	Proper Approval Obtained
10 Over $5,000			
1. 201050	Everclean Linen, Inc.	$25,000	Yes
2. 207858	Super Office Co.	$19,800	Yes
3. 200004	Medical Central, Inc.	$11,250	Yes
4. 245116	Main Pharmaceutical	$6,730	Yes
5. 233600	Comfort Supply, Inc.	$9,870	Yes
6. 220400	Acme Drug Co.	$35,450	Yes
7. 222555	Merck	$5,000	Yes
8. 213987	Institutional Food, Inc.	$8,975	Yes
9. 201369	Medical Associates, Inc.	$15,110	Yes
10. 238938	Computer Assist, Inc.	$6,500	Yes

"After" continued on p. 162

"Before" Version—*continued*

> Based on the testing performed, the auditor considers the client's purchasing approval hierarchy to be appropriate. Adequate approval control procedures appear to be in place regarding the approval process. The auditor's test for proper approval of 15 purchase orders resulted in no exceptions.

"After" Version—*continued*

Purchase Order Number	Vendor Name	Dollar Amount of PO	Proper Approval Obtained
5 Under $5,000			
1. 200452	Acme Plastic	$4,777	Yes
2. 202456	Abraham Marketing	$4,819	Yes
3. 205801	USA Tech	$3,770	Yes
4. 248598	Northwood Supply	$4,910	Yes
5. 226476	MedAid, Inc.	$4,530	Yes

Conclusions

1. The auditor's test for proper approval of 15 purchase orders resulted in no exceptions.
2. Adequate approval control procedures appear to be in place.

Based on the testing performed, the auditor considers the client's purchasing approval hierarchy to be appropriate.

CHAPTER 6

Oral Communications: Interviews and Meetings

As important as written communications are—for documenting information, for explaining complex issues clearly, for presenting numerical data—almost all accountants spend more time communicating orally than they do in writing. In fact, the written communications discussed in Chapters 2 through 5—memos, letters, workpapers, reports, and proposals—usually flow out of the oral communications that occur between accountants and their clients and co-workers.

Except for the most casual hallway conversations, accountants' oral communications primarily occur in meetings and interviews. The contexts for these communications vary widely, depending on the size of the organization, the practice area, and the accountant's duties and level of experience. A staff accountant at a small CPA firm, for example, might communicate with clients either at the office or over the phone, interviewing them about their tax situation and explaining accounting issues to them. A partner at a larger firm might set up informal lunch or dinner meetings to talk with prospective clients and to market the firm's services. An internal auditor might meet individually with members of the company's accounting staff to interview them about their handling of receivables or to review lists of documents that the internal auditor will need to be able to complete his audit. The CFO of the same company might communicate with the company's shareholders at a large annual meeting by delivering a formal presentation, complete with multimedia support, on the company's performance and plans. A business advisory consultant in a Big Five firm might use video conferencing to "meet" with co-workers in her Tokyo office on a multinational project. In addition, each of these people would spend considerable time communicating orally in meetings initiated and led by others.

Despite the great diversity of these communication scenarios, they require common skills. Mastering these skills will allow you to present yourself as a credible professional communicator, whether you are interviewing a client or answering a supervisor's questions, participating in a meeting or leading one, making a high-tech formal presentation or responding to a presentation made by someone else. This chapter introduces you to these common skills and teaches you the following:

- how to speak in an appropriate, professional manner
- how to listen, interpret nonverbal signals, and give feedback
- how to conduct fact-finding interviews
- how to participate in and lead meetings.

163

The first section of this chapter focuses on general speaking and listening skills, nonverbal messages, cross-cultural communications, and active listening techniques. The second section shows you how to apply these principles in interviews. The final section focuses on communications in meetings such as updates and briefings, problem-solving meetings, planning meetings, and business development meetings. Chapter 7 provides guidelines on planning and delivering oral presentations, choosing appropriate presentation technology, and preparing effective visual aids.

SPEAKING AND LISTENING

As a speaker in the professional workplace, you should present yourself appropriately in all communications by being pleasant and easygoing on the one hand and maintaining a serious, professional demeanor on the other. How you accomplish this self-presentation depends in large part on the way you speak to colleagues and clients. To be perceived by others as serious and professional, speak clearly and confidently, with a strong (but not too loud!) voice. Always be polite by observing the general rules of good manners and by using language that is appropriate to a workplace environment. To be perceived by others as pleasant and easygoing, remember to smile and to listen to others actively. Never show anger or hostility, and always be patient and open minded. By following this advice when you speak to colleagues and clients, you will project a likeable image and inspire others' respect. And if people like and respect you, they are more likely to accept you and your ideas.

Feedback in Oral Communications

As we noted in Chapter 2, communications involve the exchange of messages between speakers and listeners, writers and readers. Communication occurs when receivers (listeners and readers) understand the messages transmitted to them by senders (speakers and writers). In oral communication, speakers can evaluate their listeners' understanding by asking for feedback and attending to nonverbal cues. A speaker may pause, for example, in the middle of an explanation and ask, "Am I being clear? Does this make sense?" and wait for the listener's answer. The same speaker might also watch the expressions on the listener's face for signs of confusion (or be alert for bewildered silences on the other end of the phone).

These and other forms of feedback make oral communication a dynamic process, subject to on-the-spot revision. This ongoing revision can make oral communications easier than written ones, but it can also present challenges that writing does not. Unlike writing, which gives rise to a final, tangible *product* (the document), speaking always remains a *process* in which speakers use listeners' replies and nonverbal cues constantly to gauge the effect of their messages. From the most casual conversations to the most carefully orchestrated presentations, oral communications remain fluid, dependent on the feedback loop between speaker and listener. Given this fluidity, oral communications are never really fixed the way written texts—that emerge from a process of planning, drafting, revising, and editing—eventually come to be.

In one-on-one communications, speakers and listeners constantly switch roles, sending messages, giving feedback, receiving messages, and sending others. Whether meeting face to face or on the phone, those in a conversation can usually signal to one another with little difficulty whether they understand the messages the other is sending. In group meetings, conference calls, and other situations involving several speakers and listeners, however, feedback is more problematic. At best, participants take turns speaking; at worst, certain participants dominate while others remain silent, implying understanding or assent that is not in fact there.

Interpreting Nonverbal Feedback

Because of the variable nature of verbal feedback, it is important to learn to interpret the *nonverbal* feedback that listeners commonly offer. Indeed, nonverbal behaviors play an important role in interpersonal communications: Some researchers estimate that between 65% and 90% of the message that oral communications convey derives from nonverbal factors.[1] Some nonverbal behaviors are easy to interpret: smiling and nodding to indicate assent, frowning to register disagreement, folding the arms across the body to suggest resistance. Other behaviors, particularly those that mask evasive or deceptive responses, are subtler and require skill and experience to understand.

Communication experts often classify nonverbal behaviors as those involving body positions (kinesics), those involving distance (proxemics), and those involving voice pitch and rhythm (vocalics).[2] By learning to read the messages suggested by the behaviors in these categories, you will improve your ability to establish rapport with others, determine whether others are telling the truth, and build trust with clients and co-workers.

Kinesics   Kinesic behaviors, which include body movements and positions, send some of the strongest nonverbal messages between communicators conversing face to face. Body movements such as smiling and frowning, head nodding, hand gestures and arm positions, eye contact, and body postures are all easy to detect and often conveyed unconsciously. These behaviors can signal how involved your listener is in the conversation and how positively (or negatively) he or she is responding to your communications. Listeners who sit in a relaxed posture with an "open stance," who make steady eye contact with you, and who smile and nod while you are speaking send a definite message: "I am comfortable with our communication; I have nothing to hide; I agree with what you are saying." Conversely, listeners who avert their eyes before answering you, cross their arms, or cover their mouths with their fingers while speaking may be sending a clear message as well: "I'm not sure how to answer you. I'm threatened by your question. I know something that I don't want to tell you."[3]

In some contexts, you will find an ample display of positive cues and involvement behaviors. If you are talking with another staff accountant, for example, on a subject of mutual interest, you might exchange such cues to indicate mutual friendliness and cooperation. An open display of withdrawal behaviors and negative cues is less common, if only because codes of politeness inhibit them. Moreover, some listeners tend to remain impassive while others are speaking, regardless of their levels of involvement and receptivity to the message. Neutral facial expressions and cool nonverbal cues do not necessarily indicate communication problems. Be attuned to kinesic cues because they can convey crucial information in many communication contexts.

Proxemics Proxemic behaviors involve the distance maintained between speakers and listeners. In general, people move closer to those they like.[4] Firm and friendly handshakes communicate a positive attitude. Pats on the back (of same-sex colleagues) communicate affiliation.[5] A listener who leans back suddenly or shifts the position of his or her chair may be signaling an unwillingness to cooperate. If this movement is accompanied by negative kinesic cues or by an evasive answer, it may indicate an effort to hide information.[6]

As you can see, kinesic and proxemic cues are detectable only in face-to-face communications because they must be observed. Vocalic behaviors can be detected, however, whether your listener is physically present or not.

Vocalics We frequently make judgments about others' attitudes on the basis of vocal cues. In addition to verbal cues (*"Yes." "I see." "Right." "What do you mean, exactly?" "I don't think so." "OK." "Fine."*), vocal behaviors involving speech tempo, rhythms, volume, and pitch send an array of messages both in phone conversations and in face-to-face conversations. When people speak on the phone, vocalic cues are especially important because communicators cannot see one another.

Research has shown that rapid speech conveys an image of competence and honesty. People tend to hesitate when they are faced with difficult or threatening questions; therefore, significant pauses and slow answers may suggest reluctance or even deception.[7] (Remember, however, that hesitation and deliberate speech may simply mean the speaker is thinking deeply about what he or she is saying.) Speech marked by tempo variety also conveys a relaxed, open attitude, unless, of course, that variety becomes extreme, with stammering, mumbling, or alternating hesitance and very rapid tempo.[8] Deep or moderate vocal pitch usually suggests relaxation and openness as well. Studies have shown that vocal pitch rises considerably when people are tense or threatened.[9]

Cross-Cultural Factors

The descriptors just discussed are, at best, generalizations about nonverbal signals in American culture. The meanings attributed to the behaviors described may differ widely from person to person, and they certainly differ from culture to culture. In the global business climate of the twenty-first century, you must realize how differently a simple gesture may be interpreted across the cultures in which you may be working.

Experts advise professionals conducting business in foreign countries to read about customs of the countries they will visit so they can avoid using nonverbal behaviors that will offend their hosts.[10] In Buddhist cultures, for example, the head is sacred, and touching anyone's head is considered an insult. In Muslim cultures, pointing with or touching another with the left hand is insulting; in many cultures, pointing with the index finger is considered rude. Conversely, experts advise international businesspeople to be prepared for behaviors that might be offensive in American culture. In many Latin countries, it is customary for people to stand quite close to those with whom they are conversing and to touch them frequently. In Switzerland, as in America, it is rude to come late to a meeting; in Cameroon, however, a meeting scheduled for 9 A.M. may not begin until after noon.[11]

If your professional duties take you abroad, consult a guide to cross-cultural communication before you go.

Active Listening

Paying attention to nonverbal behavior is a way of listening to another's message. In the workplace, it is not enough to *hear* what others are saying; you must also *listen* effectively. Listening to another person means focusing your full attention on that speaker's message. Hearing is a physiological process in which sound waves register on your eardrum. Listening is deliberate behavior in which you use your cognitive faculties to understand a message.

Restate to Clarify Content   To test whether you are listening effectively (and therefore understanding a speaker's message), it is useful to respond at intervals by restating or summarizing what you have heard the speaker say. If you have misunderstood a concept or misheard a fact, the speaker can correct the error. If your summary of the information meets with the speaker's assent, you both can feel satisfied that the communication is working. Moreover, periodic restatements by the listener can encourage the speaker to open up more fully and to elaborate at greater length on the subject. The conversation excerpt below illustrates the principles of active listening.

Production Supervisor: I got the word from your office that my budget line item for #18 dye is too high. But what do the accountants know about how much dye we're going to need for Product AH456 next year? They just automatically expect us to not ever increase any costs from the prior year.

Cost Accountant: So costs have gone up on #18 dye this year?

Production Supervisor: Exactly. Look at all the overages we had each month that were due to having to use more #18 dye than budgeted.

Cost Accountant: Why do you think these overages are happening?

Production Supervisor: Well, for one thing, the usage estimates from engineering are way off base. But also, we're expecting to produce 3% more of AH456 next year, so we're obviously going to need more #18 dye.

Cost Accountant: So you're saying the #18 dye is budgeted too low for two reasons: The product is taking more dye than it was supposed to and production is expected to increase next year. Is that right?

Production Supervisor: That's right. Could you see what you can do to get this budget line item through for me? Thanks.

Reframe to Clarify Feelings   In addition to focusing on content, active listening requires awareness of the feelings behind the speaker's words. By showing sensitivity to a speaker's feelings—particularly if you sense these feelings are negative—you create a comfort zone in which the speaker may be willing to describe a problem more completely or explain the source of those feelings in more detail. You can show such sensitivity by reframing a speaker's statement to reflect the feelings you perceive behind it.

Assume, for example, that you are an accountant at GreenSpaces, a national nonprofit organization that assists communities in their efforts to contain and eliminate pollution by local industries. You are meeting with David Moran, the business manager, to review the organization's quarterly grant revenue report. At one point in your review of the report, David frowns, looks exasperated, and says, "We'd do a lot better at winning grants if we had enough staff to do research!" You sense David's frustration and want to learn more about the organization's budget plans for the grant writing department. Rather than restating the point David has just made ("You don't have enough help to find out about funding opportunities"), you reframe it to reflect the feelings it implies: "You're discouraged because you're so shorthanded?" In reframing the statement, you convey empathy, and the chances are good that David will tell you more about the staffing problem.

To hone your listening skills, remember these tips:

- Pay attention to nonverbal cues.
- Use restatements to clarify content.
- Use reframing to clarify feelings.

SPEAKING AND LISTENING IN INTERVIEWS

A particularly important type of communication for accountants is the fact-gathering interview. Because accountants' primary responsibility is to gather, analyze, and record facts about business transactions, many accountants spend considerable time interviewing others to obtain information. In an audit, the auditor interviews the client, asking questions that probe into the heart of the client's financial situation. In a tax engagement, the tax accountant interviews the client to obtain factual information about the client's tax year and to learn about the client's tax and other financial goals. In preparing a company's production budget for the approaching year, the cost accountant interviews production personnel to learn about reasons for increasing or decreasing estimated production costs from the prior year. By interviewing a client or a company colleague, accountants not only gather essential information; they also help create a positive working relationship with that person by demonstrating an awareness of the client's or colleague's needs and problems.

Conducting productive interviews requires well-developed speaking and listening skills. It also requires careful planning and documentation. Whether you are interviewing an individual for whom you will be preparing tax returns, a factory supervisor at the plant where you are a new cost accountant, or the chief financial officer of a Fortune 500 company that your firm is auditing, follow the procedures outlined here.

Planning the Interview

Your first step is to learn as much as you can about the interviewee.

Begin by Reviewing Relevant Documents   In public accounting, these documents might include your firm's workpapers from prior engagements, the client's organizational charts, annual reports and 10K reports, prior years' tax returns, promotional brochures, and any other documents you have collected from the client before the interview. In private accounting, documents might include your organization's mission statement, strategic planning documents and financial projections, financial statements of various business segments, vendor contracts, and project plans.

Familiarize Yourself with the Names of Key People Involved in the Engagement or Project   For example, if you are a cost accountant in charge of gathering budget information from various operational sectors, know the names of the production supervisors who prepare those pieces of the budget for their product areas. If you are an analyst for a bond rating agency and will be interviewing representatives from a company that is attempting to issue bonds with a favorable rating, know the names of the top executives from that company. If you are a staff auditor, know the names of the controller and other key accounting personnel at the company that you will be auditing.

Gather Information About the Person You Will Be Interviewing   What is her position relative to others on the engagement or project? What is her level of experience in the area you will be investigating? How long has she been with the company? How extensive are her responsibilities? How sophisticated is her understanding of accounting practices? Does she have a positive attitude about being interviewed by cost accountants/bond rating analysts/ auditors? *Remember:* Just as the writing process begins with analyzing your reader, so the speaking process begins with analyzing your audience.

Decide on Your Goals for the Interview   Are you trying to gather preliminary information that will lead to later interviews? Obtain specific information to complete a client's tax return? Identify sources of problems with a client's information system? Clarify capital requests on the proposed budget from a manufacturing segment? Understand the legal implications of an investment strategy you have recommended for your company? Unless you know precisely what you are trying to accomplish, you may waste the interviewee's time and your own. When you have decided on your goals, write them down in complete sentences. *Remember:* Just as a purpose statement shapes effective writing, so an explicit goals statement guides effective interviewing.

Preparing Questions

Prepare a detailed set of questions. Think about the kinds of questions that will elicit the information you want. If you want to find out how accounting information is communicated to managers, for example, you need a question that will get the interviewee to explain the whole process. If you want to determine whether the interviewee had any dependents for the previous tax year, you need a question that will elicit a specific response.

In the interviews that accountants conduct, three kinds of questions are typically used to gather information: open, closed, and probing.

Open questions get people talking. They offer respondents the chance to give both broad and in-depth answers. Open-ended questions often begin with the words *how, what, why,* and *where.*

Examples of Open Questions

Describe the accounting system you use to record raw material inventory purchases.

How do you process the invoices for those raw material purchases?

I understand that you've been having some quality problems in the cotton textile facility. The scrap and rework rates seem very high. What do you think is causing the problems? Do you think there's a solution?

You've expressed an interest in planning for your eventual estate. Can you tell me about your financial hopes for yourselves and your family?

The numbers all seem to be in line and adequate to support the bond issue you're planning. Can you tell me about the qualitative factors in your company's plans for the future that will help my firm determine a rating for the bonds?

As you can see, open questions are an excellent way to encourage description and explanation because they allow interviewees to go into as much detail as they want. Open questions can, however, result in overly long answers and in answers that wander off the topic. For this reason, plan to combine them with closed questions.

Closed questions narrow the focus of the interview. Questions that force respondents to choose among two or more possible answers (*yes* or *no,* method *a, b,* or *c*) are of this type. So are questions that ask for specific information (names, numbers). Closed questions often begin with such words as *do you/did you, when, who, how many.*

Examples of Closed Questions

Do invoices go directly from you [the accounts payable clerk] to the treasurer's office for payment?

When did you install your new customer billing software program?

How many data entry personnel did your sales department lose last year?

Did you make any contributions to charity last year? Do you have receipts for them?

Who is responsible for making product quality decisions in this area?

Closed questions are useful for keeping an interview on target and for confirming information because they limit the interviewee's answers to the specific question posed. Relying on them too heavily, however, can prevent your obtaining a view of the big picture.

A thorough list of open and closed questions should prepare you for an initial interview. If you are conducting a follow-up interview, however, you may want to obtain fuller answers to material previously provided. In that case, you should prepare probing questions as well.

Probing questions help interviewers dig beneath the surface of respondents' answers to uncover the underlying story. Interviewers use probing questions when a respondent's answer seems vague or evasive. In many cases, all that obscures the underlying story is an incomplete or overly general answer.

Examples of Probing Questions

Auditor: Why did your company change over to an ERP system?

Controller: Well, many of our competitors have gone over to it, and it has features that our old system didn't provide.

Auditor [probing]: What are some of these features? Why are they important?

In other cases, however, the respondent may be deliberately avoiding the question, perhaps fearing to go too deeply into confidential or potentially damaging information:

Cost Accountant: Can you tell me why this new product is using a higher amount of direct labor time than the engineers expected?

Production Supervisor: Um, well, we've had a bit of a problem with turnover of personnel in that shop area.

Cost Accountant [probing]: Oh, I see. Yes, turnover can be tough. There's all that training time you have to invest to bring new people up to speed. What do you think is causing this turnover?

Production Supervisor: Well, it's hard to say. Lots of reasons, I guess.

Cost Accountant [probing]: I understand. It's usually hard to pinpoint a single source for problems on the job. But what do you think are some of the *main* problems?

Production Supervisor [Looking away]: Oh, well . . . Some of the guys who left had a lot of gripes about the shop foreman.

Cost Accountant [restating and probing]: So you're saying that some of the people who left had complaints? Can you be more specific or give me some examples?

To get complete information in a case like this one, where the interviewer suspects a particular individual might be at fault, there is a temptation to lead the interviewee with loaded questions. Resist it! Loaded questions are those that embed the expected answer: "Oh, so the people left because of the shop foreman's policies, right?" People tend to respond unconsciously to the embedded cues in such questions, which have a built-in bias; because of this bias, the answers they elicit should not be considered valid.[12] Instead of asking biased questions, try restating the interviewee's answer; doing so may lead the interviewee to elaborate and give you the information you need. If restatement does not work, keep probing gently. Remember to pace your probing questions judiciously: Too many at once may seem like a cross-examination.

In practice, probing questions frequently come to the interviewer's mind during the course of the interview as the interviewee responds to questions. Often, the interviewer does not plan probing questions in advance because that would require the interviewer to anticipate the interviewee's answers. We consider some further examples next.

In this example of a list of questions for an initial interview, the interviewer, Ted Graham, is an internal auditor at a finance company where a network-based computer system for securitizing receivables has been recently put in place. (*Securitization* is the process of converting receivables and other assets into securities that can be traded in capital markets.) Ted is questioning the person in charge of securitizing accounts receivable in an effort to understand the system's internal controls. Notice how the list combines open and closed questions to elicit a detailed overview of the system:

Initial-Interview Questions

1. What are the criteria for deciding to securitize a receivable?
2. What percentage of receivables do we try to keep on a regular basis?
3. What are the steps involved in securitizing the receivables? How are the accounts selected?
4. Who determines the time, interest rate, and other criteria for securitizing the receivables?
5. Who determines whether an account gets charged off? Who approves the charge-offs?
6. What types of reports are done after the securitization takes place?
7. How are accounts rolled on and off securitization?
8. When we receive payments from the securitized receivables, are they applied specifically? Are they prorated on the number of securitizations we have?
9. What is our overall return on securitizing the receivables versus waiting for the receivables to be paid by the consumer?

10. When an account is set up in securitization and the company continues to purchase on the account, are the additional purchases considered our receivables?

Of the questions in this example, four are open (1, 3, 6, and 7). Unless the interviewee's answers are unusually thorough, each of these four could easily lead to probing questions, which the interviewer would devise on the spot.

Internal Auditor: Who determines whether an account gets charged off?

Securitization Manager: That would be Samantha Ellerby.

Internal Auditor: Who approves the charge-offs?

Securitization Manager: She basically approves them herself.

Internal Auditor [probing]: What do you mean "approves them herself"?

Securitization Manager: She can enter the charge-off into the system and doesn't need any other person's OK to make the entry go through.

Internal Auditor [probing]: Oh, that's interesting. Has it always been that way?

Securitization Manager: Yes. That's the way the system has always been. Back in the old days, we didn't have many personnel to do all of this, and so I guess it was just easier to have one person take care of it.

Internal Auditor [probing]: I see. Could you tell me more about the duties that Samantha has in this area?

The other six questions in the auditor's list (2, 4, 5, 8, 9, and 10) are closed and will most likely lead to specific, short answers. Although these questions could also lead the interviewer to probe for further information, they are less likely to do so than the open four.

Conducting the Interview

Because businesspeople are busy, it is important to begin your interview on time, to state the purpose of the interview to the interviewee, and to indicate how much of the interviewee's time you plan to need. Interviews make some people nervous, so be sure to break the ice before you begin and establish rapport with the interviewee from the start.

Breaking the Ice and Establishing Rapport   Depending on the purpose, content, and parties to the interview, putting an interviewee at ease may take as little as a friendly handshake or as much as a carefully orchestrated conversation. Whatever the circumstances, remember that the most important factor in launching the interview is to create rapport between yourself and your interviewee. Though friendly comments about common topics help to break the ice, genuine rapport is less a matter of social interests than it is of trust. Your goal at the beginning of any interview, therefore, should be to make your interviewee trust you as a competent, fair, and dependable person.

Many factors contribute to the level of trust you inspire in others; your credentials and your reputation play a large role. The way you present yourself—how prepared you are, how prompt you are, how professional you seem—is similarly important. Less obvious factors are also significant, however. One of these factors is nonverbal communication.

According to experts, people feel rapport with those whose nonverbal communication is in sync with their own. Communicators who trust one another tend to mirror each other's body language and vocal intonations; those whose nonverbal signals clash tend to lack rapport.[13] One of the ways to build rapport, then, is to observe the kinesic, proxemic, and vocalic signals your interviewees send and to mirror subtly these behaviors as much as possible. If your interviewee leans forward as she is speaking, for example, wait 20 to 30 seconds and then lean slightly forward yourself. If she smiles, smile back. If she crosses her legs or folds her arms, follow by doing the same. Mirror the pitch and rhythm of her speech. Once you have synchronized your body language with that of your interviewee, test the level of rapport by changing your posture or slowing down your questions. Your interviewee should soon respond by mirroring your cues.[14] If this response does not occur, you need to work further on establishing rapport.

Asking Your Questions   When you feel assured that your interviewee is at ease, get down to business. Explain the purpose of the interview (to gather information for an audit; to get information to help the client/interviewee make retirement plans; to discover the accounting information system needs of the accounts receivable department; to learn about the financial demands of faculty staffing plans for a new major at a university). Explain how this interview fits into the larger context of interviews you are conducting at the company or interviews you will conduct with the client.

Use your prepared questions to guide the interview, but be ready to revise your questions and to improvise as you go along. Use active listening techniques to understand what the interviewee is telling you, both explicitly, in terms of facts and opinions, and implicitly, in terms of the feelings underneath. By listening carefully to both levels of response, you will be able to determine when you need to change directions or to probe for further detail. As we noted earlier, an interviewer's probing questions most often result from actively listening to the respondent's answers. Indeed, the active listening techniques of *restatement* and *reframing* create probing questions, illustrated in the following interview where an auditor is asking the client's cashier about her duties:

Auditor: I understand that you've been working for the company for quite some time now.

Cashier: Yes, that's right. Ten years in June.

Auditor: Could you describe for me your cash-handling duties?

Cashier: Sure. Well, when the customers' money comes in from the showroom or in the mail, it comes straight to me. I enter everything into the CRL [cash remittance list] screen, and transmit copies of it to Peggy [the cash manager], Al in Accounts Receivable, and Jane in General Ledger. Then I prepare the deposit slip.

Auditor [noticing from the company's procedures manual that another individual is supposed to prepare the deposit slips]: I see. So you are responsible for writing up the deposit slip each day?

Cashier: Yes, that's right. I didn't used to do it, but two years ago when Peggy went on maternity leave, I started doing it. When she came back, she was so busy that it just sort of got left to me. You know, to save her the trouble.

Auditor: So you and Peggy agreed between yourselves that you would take over writing up the deposit slips?

Cashier: Yes. We didn't think it was a big deal. I mean, her desk is right across the room from mine and it seemed silly to have her go through the hassle every day when I had the time to do it. It's been no problem so far.

Auditor: Yes, I see. So no one has had a problem with the arrangement?

Cashier: Oh, I don't think that anyone else knows about it. It's no big deal, so we didn't announce it or anything.

Auditor: Is the treasurer aware of it?

Cashier: No, probably not. Unless Peggy told him. You'll have to ask her about that.

Auditor: OK, thanks. Now, let's continue with your description of your other duties . . .

Notice that the auditor gently reframes the cashier's statements into probing questions in an effort to coax the truth from the cashier. If instead he were to directly accuse her of having bent the rules, she no doubt would have become defensive and might not have told the auditor everything she knew.

Taking Notes   Unless you are blessed with a perfectly photographic memory, you will need to take complete and accurate notes during the interview. Note taking presents certain problems, however.

- Note taking makes many people uncomfortable. Watching someone write down their words may make interviewees self-conscious and hesitant to speak.
- Slow or clumsy note taking can slow the pace of the interview.
- Conspicuous note taking can diminish the relaxed conversational atmosphere essential to successful interviews.

For these reasons, it is a good idea to handle note taking as unobtrusively as possible. Explain to your interviewee at the start that you want to take notes to help you remember the interview accurately. Use a small writing pad or inconspicuous electronic notebook and assume a relaxed posture while recording information. Some interviewers use laptop computers for note taking, but the machines themselves and the keyboard sounds can be quite distracting.

Try to preserve the conversational atmosphere while you are writing. If you must ask the interviewee to pause or slow down, simply do so politely. Do not try to write down every word; instead, use whatever shorthand you have developed for recording college lectures.

Here are some other techniques for taking good notes[15]:

1. *Use the Cornell split-page format.* On each page of your notes, draw a vertical line, top to bottom, 1.5 inches from the left edge of the paper. Write your notes to the right of the line. For longer answers, take notes on additional pages and use numbers to key your notes to the questions on the master sheet. Reserve the area to the left of the line for key word clues and sample questions. Fill in the left-hand column when you review your notes.

2. *Write notes in outline form.* Or use a rough outline to organize information. Do not worry about making your outline a formal one; simply try to group information in categories as your interviewer speaks. After the interview, go back to your notes and assign priorities to the information by numbering segments. Outlines are particularly useful for open questions because they help organize information that may be presented in a disorganized way.

3. *Write notes in paragraphs.* When it is difficult to follow the organization of interviewees' responses, take notes in informal paragraphs. Do not try to write complete sentences. Simply jot down phrases.

4. *Use key words.* Key words (or phrases) are those words that contain the essence of the information. They include technical terms, names, numbers, and the like. Key words call forth images of other words; one key word can trigger the recall of a whole cluster of ideas. A few key words can form a chain from which you can reconstruct an entire interview.

5. *Use a "lost" signal.* Invent a signal—such as "X" or a question mark—that you can write in your notes to indicate that you are confused or dissatisfied with part of an answer. When an interviewee's answers are incomplete or confusing and you feel it is inappropriate to stop, record your "lost" signal in your notes. Later, when you can return to that point, probe or ask for clarification.

6. *Label and date all notes.* Always record the date, time, and location of the interview, the names of the person or persons interviewed, and the name of the engagement or project. Be sure to record the phone number and e-mail address of the person you are interviewing. You may need to check back later to confirm content.

Concluding the Interview   Before ending the interview, go back over any points you still have questions about, and make sure direct quotes are worded properly. You may want to summarize the main points covered and ask whether the interviewee wants to add anything. Then close the interview with an expression of thanks.

Documenting the Interview   Write up your notes as soon as possible, before you begin to forget details. Convert your notes from shorthand to complete sentences and record them in a permanent computer file. The table below offers a model for this step. The notes are from the same internal auditor we encountered earlier, Ted Graham. Here, the auditor is questioning Rob Barnes, the representative from Johnson & London, LLP, the international public accounting firm that designed the company's accounting information system, about the follow-up and monitoring services that Johnson & London will be providing.

Interview with Rob Barnes 7/10/00

Questions	*Responses*
Will J&L perform upgrades? What is the nature of your contract to service our system if there is a problem? What is your response time? How will any fixes or upgrades be tested in the system?	J&L may perform upgrades. They are under contract for the system and for the first 180 days must service it for free. The guaranteed response time is 7 days. Rob Barnes dials into the J&L system and allows the consultants to enter changes/correct the error. The change goes into a test directory, and after it is thoroughly tested is moved into production by Rob or one of his staff.
Is there a setting that forces a user to change a password? Are there reports that can be used to monitor the application?	There is no setting that can force a user to change a password. There are audit reports that can be created showing the user who was responsible for modifying the data.
Is there a limit to the number of users we are allowed to have on the system? Is there any type of stipulation in the contract?	No. The contract states that there is *not* a stipulated number of licenses to which the company is restricted.
Are failed network log-ins monitored?	They are not being reviewed in any way. Corporate technology is not using any tool to determine failed log-ins.
Are there any tables currently being used that need to be changed periodically (e.g., rate tables, transaction tables, other)?	There are tables that need to be changed on a periodic basis.
What reports are you looking at daily? Weekly? Monthly?	Rob is looking at the wire transfer and the supporting activity report on a daily basis. Monthly, he is looking at the reports that go to the public and at all supporting reports associated with them.

The type of documentation in the table would be adequate as support for a meeting in which the accountant would summarize the interview orally, perhaps to his or her supervisor or to other auditors on the team. Afterward,

| Figure 6.1 |

File Memo Documenting Interview

MEMO

TO: File
FROM: Ted Graham
DATE: July 12, 2000
RE: **Securitization Application System Audit**

As part of the audit of the J&L securitization and reporting system, I interviewed Rob Barnes to determine whether adequate controls exist for introducing and maintaining program changes in the *Account Master* system. The interview took place at his office on July 10, 2000. Rob's responses, summarized below, suggest the system does not yet provide sufficient controls to prevent or detect unauthorized program changes.

J&L is responsible under the contract to perform upgrades, corrections, and changes to the system. Rob dials in and J&L's consultants enter the change he requests. The change goes into a test directory where it is thoroughly tested. Rob reviews the daily wire transfer and supporting activity report every day. He looks monthly at the reports that go to the public. Based on Rob's knowledge of the system and regular reviews, he has identified a number of areas in which additional controls are needed:

1. Though the system can create audit reports showing who was responsible for a change, it cannot at present force a user to change a password. To tighten security, the system needs a feature for locking out certain passwords and forcing changes.
2. The contract contains no restriction on the number of possible users.
3. At present, everyone in IT is expected to make periodic changes to tables and has the access to be able to do so. To put restrictions in place, the department will have to change job responsibilities.
4. IT is not monitoring failed log-ins in any way.
5. To put the proper controls in place, J&L will need to create an interface between the network ID and the J&L user ID.

however, the accountant should create more formal documentation of the interview in the form of a memo to the file or a narrative that serves as part of a report. Figure 6.1 illustrates the file memo that documents Ted's interview with Rob Barnes. To draft such documents, use the principles described in Chapters 2, 3, and 4. Chapters 10, 11, and 12 provide further examples of interviews and interview documentation in managerial accounting, auditing, and tax work.

SPEAKING AND LISTENING IN MEETINGS

In addition to interviews with clients and co-workers, accountants spend considerable time in other meetings of many kinds. Although you will attend, and possibly even lead, meetings during your first years in the workplace, the time you spend in such meetings will increase as you rise in your career. By the time you reach the level of senior manager or partner, you may spend over 50% of your workday in meetings.[16]

Because so much business planning, problem solving, and information transfer occurs in meetings, they represent perhaps the most important site of oral communications in the professional workplace. They are also one of the most expensive. A recent study estimated that meetings can cost an organization as much as $300 to $700 per hour;[17] another study estimated that over 30% of the time spent in meetings is unproductive, wasting $37 billion per year.[18] Considering the enormous cost that meetings represent to companies, it is easy to understand why developing effective meeting skills is important to your career.

There is another, more immediate reason why you should work to develop effective meeting skills: Meetings often draw together individuals from different levels of the organization. Entry-level accountants attend and participate in meetings, but higher level people commonly lead those meetings. Thus, meetings are an important forum in which entry-level people can demonstrate their credibility, competence, and skill to those who will be making decisions about their career advancement. By offering relevant information and well-thought-out suggestions, by asking and answering questions in an informed, intelligent manner, and by actively listening to your peers and superiors, you demonstrate your professionalism and promotion-worthiness to all who are at the meeting. Even if you are not leading the meeting, take the time to prepare well for it so you can participate effectively.

Types of Meetings

Most of the meetings accountants attend can be classified into one of four types:

1. Update meetings and briefings
2. Problem-solving meetings
3. Planning meetings
4. Business development meetings.

Update Meetings and Briefings   In update meetings, accountants relay factual information to their clients and co-workers. For example, members of an audit team might meet with their audit supervisor each week to update her—and each other—on what they accomplished and discovered while auditing during the week; or a corporate financial analyst might update his CFO each month with a description of how that month's sales measured up to the company's forecast.

Update meetings may be relatively informal, especially when they occur one on one between people who work closely together and are on friendly, casual terms. One-on-one meetings can sometimes be quite formal, however, when hierarchical differences exist between the participants. Group update meetings tend to be somewhat more formal than one-on-one meetings, simply because more people attend.

Because the purpose of update meetings is to relay information, an e-mail message or memo can often do the job just as well. Deciding whether to hold an update meeting or simply to send a memo should always depend on the people involved and on how important the information is.

Whereas update meetings usually occur between people who are familiar with the context of the communication, briefings involve providing instructions or detailed explanations to those who know less about the topic than you do. Accountants often find themselves in situations where they need, for example, to explain the results of their work to clients who are not well versed in accounting techniques. A CPA might have to explain to a small business owner the significance of certain items on the financial statements. A cost accountant for a large fast-food restaurant chain might have to explain to a product development trainee how to determine how much a new food product will cost to make.

If you are to brief another individual about accounting matters, you must truly understand the subject matter because you will, in fact, be teaching that person about your work. Being certain of the material you are trying to communicate will give you the confidence you need to be an effective teacher. As with update meetings, briefings that are long and/or complex may call for visual support. The instructions in Chapter 7 on preparing oral presentations will give you the guidelines you need.

Problem-Solving Meetings   The goal of a problem-solving meeting is to have the participants come up with ideas with which to solve their company's, firm's, or client's problem(s). For example, a meeting might be held by a software implementation team to discuss problems that have arisen during roll out of the new system; or a meeting might be held by a business owner and the company's controller, sales manager, and production manager to come up with ways to reverse recent declines in the company's sales and profits.

The leader's role in a problem-solving meeting is to stimulate discussion among all the participants, to help them generate ideas for solving the problem(s) at hand, and to lead them toward solutions. Organizations use numerous techniques to achieve these ends, including brainstorming sessions, visualization strategies, round-robin discussions, and various systems for prioritizing ideas and voting on solutions. In Chapter 8 we describe several of these techniques and show how groups use them to carry out collaborative communication projects.

Planning Meetings   Accountants participate in planning meetings to organize and prepare for upcoming projects or engagements. Auditors normally begin engagements with planning meetings, and accountants in the private sector work with management in planning meetings of various kinds. Some planning meetings are loosely structured: The participants give and gather information, generate ideas, and attempt to foresee problems that might arise on a project or engagement. Other planning meetings are highly structured with agendas that dictate the ordering of discussion of timetables, scheduling, and deadlines for the upcoming project or engagement.

Chapter 10 describes a planning meeting involving a corporate project team. Chapter 11 provides an example of an audit planning meeting.

Business Development Meetings   As the practice of public accounting becomes more diverse and increasingly competitive, firms are exploring ways in which to market their services to both new and existing clients. Even many local accounting firms now employ marketing specialists to help them develop their client base and to train their accountants to effectively promote the services that the firm offers. One of the major roles of the accounting firm partner has always been that of salesperson, but today, all of a firm's professionals, even staff accountants, are expected to enhance the firm's public image and to develop new business where possible.

A public accounting firm might hold a business development meeting to assess an existing client's needs and to explore ways to offer additional services; or, after an engagement proposal is written, senior members of a firm might meet with a potential client's management to develop business through a formal proposal presentation.

In your first years as an accounting professional, you undoubtedly will attend and participate in many meetings. Use this experience to cultivate your meeting communication skills because you will eventually be asked to lead meetings.

Preparing to Participate in Meetings

To prepare for meetings that you will *not* be leading, follow these steps:

1. Find out who will attend the meeting.
2. Review the agenda and make sure you understand the purpose of the meeting.
3. Study all materials relevant to the agenda topics.
4. Jot down a list of questions to ask during the meeting.

Finding out in advance who will be attending the meeting—both peers and superiors—allows you to think about how to build your workplace rapport with those people. Reviewing the agenda and relevant documents prepares you to answer questions intelligently in case any are put to you. Preparing meaningful questions of your own not only helps clarify material for yourself; it also gives you the opportunity to speak at the meeting. Try to contribute in a useful way to every group meeting that you attend.

Preparing to Present Information in Meetings

If you are asked to present information at a group meeting, follow these steps:

1. Prepare for the meeting by summarizing the information in a way that listeners can easily grasp. For informal meetings, write a summary on a single sheet of paper. At the top, note the topic of the meeting and the date. Group together the points you want to make into clear categories, much as you would group questions for an interview. Format the summary with bullets and write in clear, simple language. Print copies of the summary and distribute them to your listeners; retain one copy to speak from for yourself. For more formal meetings, you may want to prepare more extensive handouts or computer presentations. See Chapter 7 for instructions on preparing formal oral presentations and computer-supported visual aids.
2. Begin your presentation by explaining your purpose clearly (to report on progress on the installation of a new accounting software system; to convey information gathered on a new client prospect).
3. Move through your material point by point, using a pleasant yet professional tone.
4. Use active listening to ensure that you understand your listener's comments and questions.

Preparing to Lead a Meeting

If you will be leading a meeting, it is your responsibility to use participants' time constructively. Business meetings can be great time wasters (and therefore money wasters) if they are not carefully planned. Leaders of effective meetings prepare detailed agendas that structure time and activities, inform participants beforehand of goals and expected outcomes, and keep the meeting focused on results.[19]

Begin to prepare to lead your meeting by making sure you understand the issues at hand:

1. Research background information thoroughly.
2. Collect up-to-date facts, numbers, and so forth.
3. Schedule your meeting in an appropriate location—one that has adequate space for comfortable seating as well as the hardware needed for the presentations that will be given.
4. Order refreshments (if any).
5. Check with participants and schedule the meeting for the most convenient time for all concerned.
6. Once the subject, place, date, and time of your meeting have been set, send a notice inviting the participants to attend.

Informing Your Participants   Announce the meeting well in advance. Whether you notify the participants by voice mail, e-mail, or in person, be sure to also send written (paper) notification that includes the time, location, and purpose of the meeting. In that notification, clearly state the purpose of the meeting, as the notice in Figure 6.2 does. Send your meeting participants any materials they should review before attending the meeting. Ask them to do so and to bring the materials with them to the meeting. If any participants are expected to present information or deliver reports, give them as much advance notice as possible and explain specifically what you want them to do.

Writing Your Agenda   Agendas are essential for effective meetings. A properly crafted agenda structures a meeting by specifying the topics to be covered, the people responsible for covering those topics, and the time allocated to each activity.

The agenda is the leader's most important tool for keeping a meeting on track. If someone wanders off the topic, you can use the agenda to pull the discussion back where it belongs. You can say to the person who is digressing, "That's a good point, although it's not on our agenda for today. I'll make a note of it, and we can consider it at next week's meeting." In this manner, you are not criticizing the person; you are using the agenda to keep the process properly structured. Similarly, the agenda can help you take control of a meeting in which someone is dominating the discussion. You can say, "That's interesting—can we relate that back to our agenda?" Or you can say, "That's interesting, but let's hear from other people on the topic too."[20]

Figure 6.2

Memo to Announce a Meeting

> ## MEMO
>
> **TO:**   John Cassidy, Elaine Pettis, Max Alonzo, and Gregg Chan, Production Supervisors; Carl Hindman, Assistant Controller, James Callahan and Mary Alexyev, Cost Accountants
> **FROM:**   Jean Trumble, Controller
> **SUBJECT:**   Cost Accounting Quarterly Update Meeting
> **DATE:**   June 28, 2000
>
> Our regular update meeting is scheduled for Thursday, July 5, at 3 P.M. in the executive conference room. At the meeting, John, Elaine, Max, and Gregg will give us their quarterly production report summaries, and Carl will demonstrate the new data-entry procedures for raw material usage.
>
> I look forward to seeing all of you next week.

Agendas, of course, can vary in style and length, but they should all contain the following elements:

1. Purpose, date, and time of the meeting
2. Opening remarks
3. Reminders of previous meetings; committee and/or background reports
4. Items of business, including who is responsible for covering each item and how much time is allocated to discussion
5. Concluding comments.

The content of the "Items of Business" section of your agenda will vary depending on the type and purpose of meeting you are planning. In the boxes that follow are some suggestions appropriate for the agendas of update meetings and briefings, planning meetings, problem-solving meetings, and business development meetings.

Items of Business: Update Meeting or Briefing Agenda

1. list of the items to be introduced, or
2. list of the items to be described, or
3. list of the items to be demonstrated
4. topics on which the participants will speak
5. designated discussion period.

Items of Business: Problem-Solving Meeting Agenda

1. description of the problem to be resolved
2. discussion of issues involved
3. discussion of ideas for solving problem
4. vote or agreement on decisions/solutions
5. summary of results/solutions.

Items of Business: Planning Meeting Agenda

1. description of plan to be created or agreed upon
2. individual planning issues to be discussed (organized from most to least important or grouped by the person responsible for that segment of the plan)
3. designated discussion period.

Business Development Meeting Agenda

1. introduction of the meeting participants
2. statement of the meeting's purpose
3. introduction to the firm or company
4. description of client benefits
5. designated question and answer period.

Figure 6.3 shows an agenda for a group problem-solving meeting. In the agenda, the controller for a local cable television company outlines the course of a meeting to be held among the accounting, sales, and operations managers to discuss ways the company could increase revenues and cut costs. The controller has been asked to lead the meeting by the CEO, who will not be present so as to foster a more relaxed environment for the meeting participants. The controller must run a meeting where all participants will feel free to speak openly and to offer ideas and solutions to problems. She constructs her agenda to provide structure to the meeting but to allow for flexibility of discussion.

In the agenda illustrated, the meeting leader initially provides some structure by reading a message from the CEO (providing direction to the group), by reviewing the background of the company's problems, and by having her assistant go over the financial information, which is distributed to the participants a few days before the meeting. The next part of the agenda creates a framework for the group to generate ideas about possible solutions and to discuss their relative merits. Finally, the agenda keeps the group focused on getting results by building in segments for prioritizing and voting on solutions. This type of agenda helps participants achieve outcomes during the time they spend together.

Preparing Your Notes   Although the agenda provides an outline and a structure, you should prepare notes for leading a meeting. If the subject matter is relatively simple, a few brief notes in the margins of your agenda will suffice. If you are giving detailed information, however, such as how to use a new data-entry system, you will need to have notes detailed enough to supply you with facts and reminders about what you intend to say. If you are leading a planning or problem-solving meeting, jot down questions to stimulate ideas in case the discussion begins to wind down.

Leading the Meeting   Arrive early to check the meeting room, to arrange your materials (agenda, notes, visual aids, if any), and to test the audiovisual equipment. As the participants arrive, greet them in a friendly way and chat with them casually. At the appointed time, however, get down to business. Begin the meeting whether everyone is present or not. Nothing annoys busy people more than to have to wait for meetings to begin, and waiting for latecomers penalizes those who are punctual. Open with your welcoming remarks and introduce any participants who do not know each other. Then begin to follow your agenda.

Figure 6.3

Agenda—Problem-Solving Meeting

AGENDA

Rocky Mountain Cable Company
Profit Enhancement Session
February 15, 2001

1. Opening remarks—Alexis Waterson, Controller
   Reading of memo from the CEO
   (5 minutes)
2. Backgrounds on problems and financial summary—Alexis
   Waterson
   (10 minutes)
3. Discussion of ways to increase sales—Ann Damien, Jonathan
   Hacker, and Buddy Wilson
   - customer base
   - product diversification
   - advertising and promotion
   - quality of product/service
   - other
   - (20 minutes)
4. Discussion of ways in which to decrease operating costs—Otis
   Campbell, Edgar Lewis, Sue Byrne, Jaime Norris
   - line servicing costs
   - efficiency improvement
   - service call costs
   - office/administrative costs
   - other
   - (20 minutes)
5. Priority ranking of solutions—All
   (30 minutes)
6. Vote on top five solutions—All
   (10 minutes)
7. Summary and Closing—Alexis Waterson
   (5 minutes)

If you are leading a briefing or an update meeting where you are providing information, introduce each of your agenda items, provide supporting information, and ask participants to hold questions until the end so the meeting does not become a question and answer session. If you are leading a planning meeting or an update meeting where you are seeking to obtain information, introduce each topic and solicit information from the participants using mostly open questions; probe for information, if necessary, by using the techniques you learned earlier in the chapter in the section on interviewing.

If you are leading a formal business development meeting such as a proposal presentation, introduce the members of the firm present to the prospective client; then deliver your oral presentation (see Chapter 7 for guidelines). In less formal meetings of this type, simply begin with friendly conversation to break the ice; then describe the services you can offer the client based on your understanding of that client's needs.

If you are leading a problem-solving meeting, remind the group of what problem(s) must be addressed. Use your agenda to bring up issues the participants are familiar with, and, if necessary, call on people to get the conversation rolling. To lead effectively, avoid seeming judgmental or critical of the participants' ideas or comments. If the discussion gets off track, politely guide it back to the agenda. If you create a comfortable meeting environment, your participants will probably feel more inclined to speak their minds.

Sample Meeting: Rocky Mountain Cable Company

Let's listen in on the meeting being led by Alexis Waterson, the controller of Rocky Mountain Cable Company.

Preparation   To ensure the best use of time at the meeting, Alexis has used proven techniques for problem solving to help participants begin generating ideas in advance of the meeting. A week before the meeting, she distributed to each participant a questionnaire about ways to increase sales and cut costs. When each participant had submitted his or her written responses to the questionnaire, Alexis summarized the responses, distributed the summary to everyone, and asked participants to bring the written summary to the meeting. In doing so, Alexis prepared the participants to contribute to the discussion by stimulating their ideas on the topics beforehand and by giving them time to think about the topics on their own.[21]

Discussion   At the problem-solving session, it is Alexis's job to facilitate free discussion but to keep the session on track. As a result of her thorough preparation, the participants have a number of good ideas for increasing profitability. At one point, however, the conversation flows so freely that the meeting begins to get off the track. Otis Campbell, an operations manager, makes a comment that diverts the focus:

Ann (sales manager): Why don't we try offering, for a limited time period, some of those new movie channels? We've had several calls from current customers asking for them, and if we did it, we would be offering more movie channels than the competition.

Otis (operations manager): Yeah, have you seen the promotional spots for that new channel that's all westerns? They were running a John Wayne marathon last month, and this month I think it's Clint Eastwood. You know, I think the spaghetti western is an unappreciated art form . . .

Alexis must bring the discussion back into focus, but she must be careful not to offend Otis because he and other participants may then feel inhibited about contributing. She handles the situation diplomatically.

> *Alexis [bringing the discussion back on track]:* You know, that does sound like an attractive idea for bringing in some new customers, although we'll have to look at the costs involved. Let's add it to the list. Any other ideas for bringing in new sales revenue?

By turning her attention away from Otis and toward the other members of the group, Alexis encourages discussion from all participants and without allowing any one individual to dominate the session.

Prioritizing Ideas Throughout the discussion, Alexis has recorded the ideas for increasing sales and decreasing costs on flip chart paper, which she has posted around the room. At the end of the time allocated for discussion, Alexis helps the group prioritize their ideas. She distributes 3 × 5 cards to the participants and asks each person to rank the ideas generated by the group. Working independently, participants write a single idea on each card and arrange the cards in a stack, from the most effective idea to least effective. Then Alexis asks the members to read aloud the idea on the top card in their stacks. She records these as "Round 1: Top Priority Solutions" on her flip chart, posts the paper on the wall, and repeats the process, round by round, until all the ideas have been recorded.

At this point, the group studies the priority rankings to see how close they are to consensus. After discussion, they narrow the list to the following ten ideas:

1. Specifically assign sales reps to personally cover the territories and to build rapport with customers.
2. Decrease advertising in those areas where we have little/no competition (Salida, Pueblo, Cañon City) and use the advertising dollars to regain ground in the Colorado Springs area.
3. Add new, exciting channels to basic service in the Colorado Springs area. Offer those channels at an extra charge in our stronger areas.
4. Look into feasibility of providing telephone and Internet services as a bundled package with cable.
5. Run all shopping, sports, and news channels 24 hours per day.
6. Offer more promotional "try-it" offers with premium channels.
7. Conduct/outsource an efficiency study of our line servicing operations.
8. Adopt an activity-based tracking system for service calls.
9. Look into feasibility of hiring more part-time line persons and telephone service reps.
10. Consider streamlining administrative functions/positions.

Voting on Solutions To arrive at solutions that can be implemented, Alexis asks the group to vote for the top five priorities. (Because this meeting is small and informal, the group decides by voice vote. In larger or more formal problem-solving meetings, decisions might be made through a series of secret votes.)[22]

These are just a few of the techniques that you might use in workplace meetings. For a fuller discussion of group dynamics, team decision making, and collaborative communications, see Chapter 8.

Closing and Following Up Your Group Meeting

Let the group know when the meeting time is almost at an end. Briefly go over the highlights of what was discussed, and, if relevant, give instructions for what to do next. Always thank your participants for their time.

Soon after the meeting has concluded, the leader (or secretary) of the meeting should briefly summarize in writing any decisions made, ideas generated, and/or problems solved. At the conclusion of Rocky Mountain Cable Company's meeting, Alexis writes the memo in Figure 6.4, which she e-mails to all the meeting participants.

The guidelines in this chapter will help prepare you for the interviews and meetings you will participate in on the job. For the many occasions when

---

Figure 6.4

Follow-Up Memo to a Group Problem-Solving Meeting

MEMO

TO: Ann Damien, Jonathan Hacker, and Buddy Wilson, sales managers; Otis Campbell, Edgar Lewis, Sue Byrne, operations managers; Jaime Norris, accounting manager

FROM: Alexis Waterson, controller

SUBJECT: Follow-up to meeting

DATE: February 16, 2001

Thanks to all for a great problem-solving session yesterday. We came up with some terrific ideas, and I will be passing them along to Stan [the CEO] when I meet with him on Friday.

Here is a summary of the ideas we came up with, in priority order:

Ways to Improve Sales:

1. Decrease advertising in those areas where we have little/no competition (Salida, Pueblo, Cañon City) and use the advertising dollars to regain ground in the Colorado Springs area.
2. Add new, exciting channels to basic service in the Colorado Springs area. Offer those channels at an extra charge in our stronger areas.
3. Look into feasibility of providing telephone and Internet services as a bundled package with cable.
4. Conduct/outsource an efficiency study of our line servicing operations.
5. Adopt an activity-based tracking system for service calls.

participating in meetings means presenting information formally, use the information in Chapter 7.

NOTES

[1] M. Knapp, *Essentials of Nonverbal Communication* (New York: Holt, Rinehart and Winston, 1980).

[2] The literature on nonverbal communication is abundant. In addition to Knapp, useful general sources include J. K. Burgoon, D. B. Buller, and W. G. Woodall, *Nonverbal Communication: The Unspoken Dialogue* (New York: Harper & Row, 1989), and Dale G. Leathers, *Successful Nonverbal Communication: Principles and Applications* (New York: Macmillan, 1986).

[3] John L. Waltman and Steven P. Golen, "Detecting Deception During Audit Interviews," *The Internal Auditor,* vol. 50, no. 4 (August 1993): 61–63. The authors maintain that hand-to-face movements often suggest deception. In addition to covering the mouth with the fingers, these gestures include placing a single finger to the mouth, scratching the nose with the index finger, and (in men) stroking the mustache.

[4] Burgoon et al., *Nonverbal Communication,* p. 324.

[5] William E. Nolen, "Reading People," *The Internal Auditor,* vol. 52, no. 2 (April 1995): 50.

[6] Waltman and Golen, "Detecting Deception."

[7] Ibid.

[8] Ernest Stech and Sharon A. Ratliffe, *Working in Groups: A Communication Manual for Leaders and Participants in Task-Oriented Groups* (Skokie, IL: National Textbook Company, 1982), pp. 25–27.

[9] Waltman and Golen, "Detecting Deception."

[10] Mary Munter, "Cross-Cultural Communication for Managers," *Business Horizons* 36 (May-June 1993): 69–79.

[11] Ibid.

[12] Thomas R. Craig, "Effective Interviewing Skills for Auditors," *Journal of Accountancy,* vol. 172, no. 1 (July 1991): 121–126.

[13] Kerry L. Johnson, "How to Gain Your Client's Trust—Fast," *The CPA Journal,* vol. 63, no. 9 (September 1993): 40–42.

[14] Ibid.

[15] David B. Ellis, *Becoming a Master Student* (College Survival, Inc., 1985), pp. 122–123.

[16] Lillian H. Chaney and Julie A. Lyden, "Managing Meetings to Manage Your Time," *Supervision* 59 (May 1998): 13.

[17] This calculation assumes a meeting attended by eight managers. Ibid.

[18] Survey of a thousand business leaders conducted by Hofstra University and Harrison Consulting Services. Ibid.

[19] Steve Kaye, "Turn Meetings into Results," *Industrial Management,* vol. 40, no.5 (September-October 1998): 10–11.

[20] Michael Finley, "Subduing the Loudmouth: How to Keep Dominating People from Dominating Meetings," *Manage,* vol. 44, no. 3 (January 1993): 7–10.

[21] The method Alexis used combines the Delphi technique, described in Chapter 8, with a form of nominal group technique for problem solving. Philip L. Roth, Lydia L. F. Schleifer, and Fred S. Switzer, "Nominal Group Technique: An Aid to Implementing TQM," *The CPA Journal,* vol. 65, no. 5 (May 1995): 68–69.

[22] Ibid.

EXERCISES

1. **Communication task:** Using a tape recorder to record your communication, explain one of the accounting concepts listed here to a friend who has no knowledge of accounting. During your explanation, ask for feedback to make sure your listener understands you, and pay attention to the nonverbal cues your listener sends to indicate understanding and receptivity to your message. After you have finished, play back the tape and evaluate how clearly you explained the concepts and how well you attended to your listener's verbal and nonverbal feedback. In addition, ask your listener how effectively you communicated. Then write a critique of your communication, incorporating your own insights and your listener's suggestions. What suggestions can you make for improving your communication skills based on this exercise?

   Topics for Explanation:

   - Cash versus accrual accounting
   - Relevance versus reliability
   - Financial accounting versus managerial accounting
   - The purposes of an audit report
   - Information presented on a balance sheet

2. **Communication task:** Choose at least two different communication settings and formally observe the nonverbal feedback of *others* around you. You may observe the nonverbal feedback of two people holding a conversation in a social setting; of students and the instructor in a class you attend, preferably a small one; of members and leaders at a club, student council, fraternity or sorority meeting; or of employees at an office where you work. Observe at least two different communication settings and pay special attention to the kinds of messages nonverbal behaviors send (comprehension/confusion, receptivity/withdrawal, friendliness and trust/suspicion and skepticism, and so forth). Take notes on your observations and your interpretations of them. Be sure to consider kinesics, proxemics, and vocalics, as described in the chapter.

   Write a two-page report documenting the date, time, place, participants, and nature of the communication, your observations and interpretations of nonverbal feedback that occurred, and any conclusions you may have reached from your observations.

3. **Communication task:** While working for an international public accounting firm, you have been told that several CPAs from your firm will soon be going on a one-year international assignment to three different developing areas: (1) China, (2) Latin America, and (3) the Middle East. Your manager has asked you to choose any one of these three areas and to research cultural differences, customs, and communication and business practices that could have an impact on the success or failure

of your firm's business there. Prepare a two- to three-page report, which will be distributed to the staff going abroad, highlighting information gathered in your research.

4. **Scenario:** You are an internal auditor for a large corporation. Your job frequently requires you to interview other employees to understand and document the company's systems and to investigate unusual items or unexplained differences in account balances. Knowing when to use restatement to clarify the information being given to you is important when preparing accurate workpapers and reports; knowing when to use reframing to show sensitivity to a speaker's feelings is important when developing a rapport and obtaining all the information you need.

   Communication task: For each of the following interview situations, determine whether a restatement or a reframing would be more appropriate, and briefly explain why. Also, develop an appropriate interviewer response for each.

   a. You are investigating a large difference between the physical count and perpetual inventory records of one of your firm's manufacturing plants. The plant controller says, "We're asked to take a physical inventory so often, it would be no wonder if our counts are off. You have no idea what a hassle it is to take inventory as often as you folks ask us to."

   b. You are documenting the procedures used to operate a petty cash fund at a branch office. The secretary who handles petty cash says, "When someone comes to me and asks to be reimbursed out of our petty cash fund, I ask them to fill out a petty cash voucher and staple their receipt to it. My boss approves the voucher, and I make the payment from the fund."

   c. You are investigating a possible abuse of the expense account system for company salespeople. While you are talking with the accounts payable supervisor she says, "When each expense report is submitted, we follow company procedures by checking its clerical accuracy and verifying that receipts are attached, when they are required."

   d. You are evaluating whether the firm's Allowance for Doubtful Accounts is adequate, considering the large number of past due accounts and a recent downturn in the economy. The accounts receivable manager states, "Our accounts receivable clerks have done everything possible to collect past due amounts, but we are very shorthanded and don't have time to make as many phone calls to the overdue accounts as we should. I don't know what more we can do."

   e. You are trying to document why one of the company's divisions was over budget on several expenditures last month. While explaining the variance, the division controller says, "I'll tell you why we are over budget on repair and maintenance expense this month. It's because top management cuts my budget by 15%, then says I shouldn't spend more money. When a machine breaks, I have to have it fixed, or operations are going to stop totally."

f. You are analyzing the impact of a possible change in depreciation methods on the company's income statement. The fixed asset accounting supervisor says, "Manufacturing machinery is depreciated using the straight-line method over a ten-year life, but vehicles are depreciated using the units-of-activity method over an estimated 100,000-mile useful life."

5. Communication task: Contact one of the people listed and arrange an interview about the subject indicated:
   a. A graduate of your school who is working as an accountant (interview about his or her career).
   b. An officer of a student accounting association (about the benefits of membership and methods of joining).
   c. An officer of the local CPA association (about the benefits of membership for students and practicing accountants).
   d. A fellow student who is working as an accounting intern (about the work he or she does for the firm or company and opportunities for internships).
   e. A fellow student who has held a part-time or summer job in an accounting firm (about the work he or she does for the firm or company and opportunities for jobs).
   f. A professor who works as a practicing accountant (about the ways his or her practice enhances teaching).
   g. A member of the accounting staff at your university (about his or her career).
   h. A recruiter for a CPA firm or corporation (about the qualifications the organization seeks in new accounting hires).

Before the interview, do the following:

Review relevant documents—learn more about the firm, company, or association by researching it on the Internet or, if it is a publicly held company, through the SEC EDGAR (Electronic Data Gathering, Analysis, and Retrieval) database. If you are researching a small firm or a student association, ask your contact how you can get background information about the company.

Familiarize yourself with the names of key people—if possible, learn the names of your contact's secretary, assistant, supervisor, or fellow officers. Try to find out the name of the organization's president, treasurer, or controller.

Gather information about the person you will be interviewing—ask your contact for a copy of his or her résumé, if one is available. If your contact is a fellow student or a graduate of your school, look in yearbooks or other college records for information about his or her majors, clubs, activities, and leadership activities.

Decide on goals for the interview—what do you want to know? Are you interested in specific information about the position your contact holds, general information about the organization, potential job opportunities in accounting, differences between public and corporate accounting? Write down your goals in complete sentences to guide you during your interview. **Prepare a detailed set of questions**—include some open questions and some closed questions.

6. **Communication task:** Conduct the interview you planned in exercise 5. Be sure to present yourself promptly and professionally. During the initial minutes of the interview, break the ice and establish rapport. Observe the kinesic, proxemic, and vocalic signals your interviewee sends and mirror these behaviors as much as possible, to establish rapport. Following the many interviewing techniques and guidelines in the text, conduct your interview. Keep in mind that probing questions are generally not planned in advance but are asked in response to the interviewee's answers to get more complete details about a particular topic. Take notes during your interview, using the methods explained in the chapter. Close the interview by clarifying any points and thanking the interviewee.

   Write up your interview notes as soon as possible, using the file memo format shown in the text.

7. **Scenario:** You are a CPA who provides personal financial planning services. One of your clients, Eva Edwards, has recently inherited $100,000 and would like to invest it. She has asked you for guidance about the types of investments she should consider.

   Communication task: Prepare a list of questions for an initial interview with Eva. Include both open and closed questions to obtain a detailed understanding of her investment goals and susceptibility to risk.

8. **Scenario:** During the past few months, it has become clear to several people in your department that outdated technology is contributing to a number of inefficiencies. Your supervisor has recognized your knowledge and expertise with computers and has asked you to lead a department meeting to determine what technology might be acquired during the next 12 months to solve the department's problem. The information you gather will be used to develop a budget proposal for new equipment and software.

   Communication task: Prepare a set of notes describing the specific steps and actions that you need to take before the meeting to accomplish your goal and be an effective leader.

9. **Communication task:**
   a. Prepare a brief memo announcing the meeting described in exercise 8. Using your notes, assign tasks to participants (make up names) and specify what materials you would like each participant to bring to the meeting. Make up other details you believe are necessary.
   b. Prepare an agenda for the meeting. Assume your department manager, Jacob Green, will be present to give the opening remarks, and the director of information and technology, Harriet Smith, will be

present to provide guidance about the feasibility of suggestions made by the department.

10. **Scenario:** You served as secretary at a recent problem-solving meeting to generate ideas for reducing the use of printers throughout your company. The notes you took are given below.
    Communication task: Write a follow-up memo to the meeting participants.

Arkanes, Inc.
Printer Use Meeting
1/25/00—3 P.M.—Conference Room

Present: Sally Heist, Kevin White, Jill Able, Mark Peterson, Mike Barnes, me

Problem: Rising cost of paper and toner cartridges; need to reduce printing volume

Background: Company printing costs—$240,000/year; increasing at avg. of 20%/yr. over past 3 years

Ideas:
6 Don't print e-mails.
3 Proofread on computer, not printouts.
2 Send memos as attachments to e-mail.
1 Educate employees about problem (committee of Sally, Jill, and Mark to do this).

7 Charge departments for actual costs or cost/page.
4 No personal use of printers (Internet printouts, etc.).
8 Have fewer printers—less convenient to print.
5 Send large jobs to print shop on disk (lower cost/page).

Priorities: See numbers.

CHAPTER 7

Oral Communications: Presentations and Visual Support

Although the communication involved in leading meetings and participating in discussions is largely informal, accountants must still prepare for those activities. Even when following an agenda very closely, participants in a discussion communicate informally, speaking off the cuff, questioning and answering one another, listening and responding to one another. But accountants often need to present information formally as well. A formal oral presentation is frequently the best way to communicate information that requires extended explanation and/or justification because a presentation combines the power of the spoken word with the structure of the written text. A well-prepared oral presentation can convey a message more effectively than a written document or extemporaneous speech because it balances well-organized verbal content and oral delivery with appealing and memorable visual support.

Like their other oral communications, the presentations accountants make most often take place in meetings. For example, a corporate financial analyst might make a presentation to colleagues about conducting specialized information searches on the World Wide Web; a tax manager with a public accounting firm might give a prospective client a PowerPoint presentation proposing services that the firm offers; a team of cost accountants might present its report on the operational efficiency of certain production divisions to a high-level management group; a business advisory consultant, speaking at a professional accounting conference, might deliver an hour-long presentation on how to develop a business advisory practice; or a senior auditor might do a presentation to a group of auditor trainees about the SEC and auditing publicly traded companies. This chapter offers general guidelines for preparing for oral presentations, for creating appropriate visual support, and for delivering presentations effectively. In the chapters that follow, you will find examples of oral presentations based on real-world communications in private and public accounting.

ORAL PRESENTATIONS IN MEETINGS

Presentations in small meetings are usually more informal than those accountants deliver at large meetings and conferences. In a small, informal meeting, the speaker may stand (or even sit) at a conference table, close to her listeners, and address them in a conversational style. She may illustrate her points with printed handouts; she may write key words on a white board while she speaks; she may project transparencies onto a screen or run through a slide show on a large computer monitor to keep her audience focused on her main ideas. Listeners may raise questions or make comments during the presentation, requiring the speaker to supply impromptu answers. Sometimes, these questions and comments lead to a discussion that interrupts the presentation for a period of time; sometimes the interruptions are brief.

In some small meetings, however, and in most large ones, the speaker may stand at some distance from the audience, perhaps behind a podium equipped with a microphone, and address the audience using a formal speaking style. The audience will probably withhold questions and comments until the presenter has finished speaking. In these more formal presentations, the speaker will probably use a computer-generated slide show for visual support. The slide show itself might include an array of multimedia effects, such as audio, video, animation, and links to the World Wide Web.

Sometimes presentations are supported by more elaborate technologies than even the most complicated computer slide shows. Indeed, technological advances in recent years have been revolutionizing the way oral presentations are made. Since the mid-1990s, many corporations and firms have supplemented face-to-face meetings with computer-mediated communications that lessen the expense and inconvenience of bringing people together in one place. The technology used to create computer-mediated meetings is quite diverse, running the gamut from e-mail systems with video windows for oral interchanges to videoconferencing technology that broadcasts presentations via satellite to locations all over the globe.[1]

Some companies, for example, are using technology to conduct annual shareholder meetings. Since 1996, when the SEC approved the use of the World Wide Web for shareholder transactions, companies such as Hewlett-Packard and Bell & Howell have used the Internet to "meet" with shareholders and present information. Hewlett-Packard posts audio clips from the annual meeting to its company Web site. Bell & Howell goes further, conducting "virtual" shareholder meetings through the Web; participants send queries over the Internet, and the queries are read aloud and answered by the company president.[2]

Videoconferencing is also increasingly popular in firms and companies as a way to present information to large groups, especially in organizations with well-developed intranet capabilities. Ernst and Young, for example, delivers many of its training programs as videoconferences using its extensive intranet. Presentations for these videoconferences are carefully orchestrated and often make use of highly sophisticated audio and video technologies as well as elaborate visual support.[3]

These technologies will become more commonplace in the near future, and you may be involved in various forms of electronic presentation as your career develops. The presentations you will make early in your career, however, will most likely be fairly traditional ones, delivered to small groups and supported by simple visual aids. By learning the basics of traditional presentations, you will master skills that you can transfer to other presentation formats.

A Word About Stage Fright

If the idea of speaking to a group of clients or colleagues intimidates you, you are not alone. Many seasoned speakers and performers admit to stage fright even after many years' experience. And small groups can be just as intimidating to a potential speaker as large groups, especially if the boss is present! Thorough preparation can help reduce your anxiety, however. By organizing your ideas and drafting carefully, preparing appropriate visual aids, and practicing your delivery, you can gain the confidence you need to make your presentations a success.

PLANNING YOUR PRESENTATION

Analyzing Your Audience and Purpose

As we have emphasized throughout this text, the audience you are addressing should play a major role in structuring your communications, as should the purpose you want to achieve. In the case of oral presentations, an understanding of your audience and purpose is especially important. Unlike readers of a written communication, who can simply toss a document aside if it does not engage their interest, the audience of a presentation is a captive one. Common courtesy dictates that listeners sit through your presentation unless pressing concerns force their departure, and, of course, the smaller the meeting, the more difficult it is for a listener to leave while you are talking. For these reasons, it is important to get as much information about your audience as you can so you can plan your presentation to meet their needs.

Fortunately, most presenters can collect a good deal of information about the audience in advance. A cost accountant working with the company's production supervisors would understand that the production team's performance is judged, in part, by how well it manages its product costs. The production supervisors need to understand how their product costs are accounted for so they can know how to improve their operating practices. Because the accountant and the supervisors work at the same company, the accountant knows what information he can assume the supervisors have and what specialized terms and concepts he needs to explain.

An investment research analyst working with a group of her firm's investment brokers would understand that the brokers need information to help them understand the securities they sell to their clients. The research analyst could assume a certain level of knowledge from the brokers and could use the specialized terminology that is common in her industry.

A public accountant presenting a proposal to a client will have researched that client's company, financial history, future plans, and key staff. He will try to determine what motivates the client and which of the services he can offer will be most useful to the client. A CFO reporting to stockholders will know that her audience is primarily interested in factors affecting the company's financial performance—present and future. She knows, for example, that her audience wants information about plant expansion initiatives, plans for major borrowing or stock issuance, and inventory-level projections, which will help them predict the company's financial growth.

Much as writers use their audience analysis to keep their documents reader-based, speakers use prior knowledge about the audience to keep the presentation listener-based.

Organizing Your Information

The principles you learned in Chapters 2 and 4 apply to organizing oral presentations as well as to drafting written documents.

Informative Presentations: Most-to-Least-Important Structure If the purpose of your presentation is to inform, organize your information from most to least important by clearly identifying your main point and following up with details. For example, a tax accountant would adopt this structure to inform his clients about opportunities for tax savings in the next tax year. The accountant would begin his presentation by describing the provisions in the tax law that permit deductions for, say, a home office and would compare projected taxes without these deductions to those with the deductions taken. The accountant would then describe other potential savings, such as those from enrolling in the client's employer's flexible spending plan and those from deducting actual automobile expenses rather than using the mileage allowance, in descending order of amounts to be saved.

Persuasive Presentations: Problem/Solution Structure If your purpose is to persuade, however, begin by convincing your listeners that they have a problem to be solved or a need to be filled. Unless you convince your listeners that a problem exists, they will not care about the solution you are proposing. For example, if you are a senior cost accountant for a manufacturing company and are presenting a capital expenditure request for an expensive piece of machinery on behalf of one of the production divisions to the company's CFO and controller, begin by describing the equipment currently used for manufacturing; what its problems are; how much time/money/person power it wastes; what the new machinery can do; how it can cut production costs and streamline operations; which competitors, if any, are already using it and the results they are obtaining. Only then, after you have created a vivid picture of the problem in your listeners' minds, should you state your proposal.

DRAFTING YOUR PRESENTATION

Introduction

Your introduction should achieve four objectives: It should catch your listeners' attention, establish your credibility as a speaker, establish the context and purpose of your remarks, and forecast the structure of the presentation. Throughout your talk, use rhetorical techniques, such as repeating key words and using examples, to keep your listeners on track.

Catch Your Listeners' Attention   Whether you are presenting results of your financial analysis to your company's CFO, proposing an engagement to prospective clients, or addressing an auditorium full of colleagues at a professional meeting, you must make your listeners want to listen to you. In some informal settings, opening with humor is an effective way to do so.

> **Example:** An information systems manager, at a briefing for AIS staff about an upcoming electronic commerce audit, opens with a slide containing a few Internet jokes: "You know you're addicted to the Internet when . . . you spend half of the plane trip with your laptop on your lap and your child in the overhead bin. . . . you check your e-mail. It says "no new messages"—so you check it again . . ."

Only use humor, however, when you are certain it will be well received: when the environment is casual and relaxed, when you are acquainted with your listeners, when you are speaking to a group at your own level in the organization. When the setting is more formal—an address to supervisors, partners, or company executives, a meeting with new or potential clients—open instead with information that rivets their attention.

> **Example:** The CFO, at the year-end meeting of a manufacturing company's top executives, opens his presentation by saying, "The numbers are in, and the news is good: This year, Alpha Robotics topped $14 million in sales on projections of $8.3 million. Better yet, our gross profit is up by $1.7 million. We're doing something right!"

> **Example:** A business advisory consultant with a public accounting firm is presenting a report on systems improvement to convince her client, a midsized manufacturing company, of the need to purchase and implement an Enterprise Resource Planning (ERP) software system. "Industry analysts predict that by 2002, 87% of Fortune 1000 companies will be using Enterprise Resource Planning software to run all of their business applications. And because of the growing demand for ERP programs from middle-sized companies, such as yours, who cannot afford the typical two-year implementation time, vendors such as SAP and J.D. Edwards have developed strategies for rapid implementation, which in many cases will now require as little as nine months!"

Establish Your Credibility as a Speaker   Whatever the context, you must also make your listeners believe in you: in your authority to speak on the subject, in your reliability as a presenter of information. The most important contributors to your credibility are these:

- your educational background (bachelor's, master's, or PhD degree from a college or university)
- your professional credentials and licensure (CPA, CMA, CIA, etc.)
- your position in the firm or company that you represent (senior, manager, or partner in a public accounting firm; accountant, controller, financial analyst, manager, CFO of a private company; research analyst or broker for an investment firm, etc.)
- your demeanor (calm, self-assured)

- your appearance (well groomed, appropriately dressed)
- the quality of your content.

In small, informal meetings, your listeners will probably be familiar with your education, your credentials, and your position. After all, most of the presentations you will make early in your career will be to co-workers and clients who know you or at least know the organization you represent. In large-group presentations, speakers are usually introduced by members of the association, company, or board hosting the meeting. To help the person introducing you to establish your credibility, write a one- or two-paragraph biographical sketch highlighting your educational background, your credentials, your current position, your experience, and any special achievements you have attained (see Figure 7.1). Give this sketch to the person introducing you before the meeting begins.

Establish the Context and Purpose of Your Remarks   When you are presenting to a group, you must give enough background to orient that person who is least familiar with the subject to your material and your purpose.

Example: As the business advisory consultant (see preceding example) continues in her presentation to her client, she provides background on the ERP

Figure 7.1

Presenter's Biographical Sketch

Michael J. Taylor, MBA, CPA

Michael Taylor is a senior business consultant for the public accounting firm, Adams, Beeler, and Cunningham, PC, in Seattle, Washington. He has built the firm's relatively new business consulting practice to include such clients as the Seattle school district, Northwest Bank Corporation, and Laney Pharmaceuticals. Before joining A,B,&C in 1998, Michael was for three years operations finance manager at Evenstem, Inc., a pharmaceutical division of Biohealth, Inc., where he managed new product projects across a variety of functional areas. Michael began his accounting career at the international public accounting firm, Johnson & London, LLP, in 1993 as a staff, and then senior, auditor, specializing in audits of accounting information systems. He also has had experience as a marketing representative for a Fortune 500 computer and telecommunications equipment provider.

Michael received a BS in accounting from Washington State University in 1993 and an MBA from the University of Seattle in 1999.

system software package that she has selected for her client: "Our research shows that SAP's R-3 system performs best in allowing its users (in your case, primarily your accounting team and operations managers) to gather and synthesize data about activities taking place in the organization. Because people all across the company will be entering data as activities take place, and because R-3 gathers and sorts that data quickly, accurately, and comprehensively, your users will get detailed, up-to-the-minute information about, for example, sales, production planning, materials management, internal and external accounting, cash management, and product data management. You'll be able to support your cross-functional project planning efforts with better data and highly sophisticated forecasting. The package will help you speed up and make more efficient the processing of your customer orders, and it can even produce customized reports that compare actual results to planned results on a real-time basis."

Forecast the Structure of the Presentation   You have heard the advice before: Tell them what you're going to tell them; tell them; then tell them what you told them. By explaining your presentation's structure in advance, you give listeners a scaffolding on which to hang the content of your remarks. This scaffolding helps listeners follow your remarks because it allows them to anticipate what is coming and to categorize information as you present it.

> **Example:** "I'm going to talk with you today about SAP's R-3 system and how it would suit your company's needs. First, I'll explain how the program works; then I'll give you a brief demonstration, using actual data from various functional areas across your company. Finally, I'll show you how you can put R-3 into place for a minimum of cost and trouble."

Use Rhetorical Techniques That Keep the Listeners on Track
Like the writer who must lead his reader through his document, the presenter must find ways to keep his listeners on track during his oral presentation. Here are some techniques.

Limit Your Points   Listeners can process only so much information at once. The most effective presentations are those that cover a single topic (or at most two or three).

> **Example:** In a monthly update meeting, a corporate financial analyst presents to his company's executive committee (the CEO, CFO, COO, and other upper-level executives) the key financial ratios for the month. Although the analyst has calculated an entire battery of financial indicators, including a variety of liquidity, turnover, leverage, and profitability ratios, he chooses to present only those ratios that allow the executives to evaluate certain aspects of the company's monthly operations. For the regular quarterly meeting, the analyst expands his presentation to include turnover ratios (for inventory, accounts receivable, and total assets) and profitability ratios (return on total assets, return on stockholders' equity, and earnings per share) because those ratios help answer the questions on which that meeting focuses—respectively, how effectively the company is using its assets and how successful management has been in generating returns to shareholders. If management has questions about other financial information, the analyst can convey the answers later in writing or in another presentation.

Repeat Key Words and Phrases As we saw in Chapter 2, repetition is an effective tool for anchoring information in memory. By repeating key words and phrases in similar positions in a paragraph, writers keep readers focused on the topic at hand. Such repetition is even more important in oral communications because the audience (usually) does not have the benefit of a written text to which they can refer for clarification if they become confused. Effective speakers repeat key words throughout their presentations to help keep listeners focused on their main idea.

> **Example:** In a presentation by a public accountant to a client who is considering having his company's Web site certified by the CPA WebTrust,[4] the accountant uses key words that remind the client of why he wants the service: "A lack of ***security*** is the number-one reason given by nonbuyers for not purchasing products online." "Having credible assurance about the ***security*** of online transactions would greatly increase online purchasing of products and services." "Nearly half of online shoppers say the CPA WebTrust seal would make them more likely to purchase products and services online because CPA endorsement renders a company's Web site more ***secure.***"

Use Concrete Examples to Illustrate Your Points Abstract theories and complicated explanations put listeners to sleep. To keep your listeners' attention, support any general statements you make with examples that the listeners can easily visualize.

> **Example:** A consultant from a large public accounting firm is making a presentation to one of its clients, Golden Opportunity, Inc., a for-profit corporation that owns and operates several junior colleges in the Midwest. He is explaining why colleges and universities should use activity-based costing. After describing the costing system in a general, theoretical way, the consultant gives his audience a concrete example of how the system affects its users:
>
> *Presenter:* Let's look at the case of Alexander Junior College, a small private institution in Nebraska that implemented an activity-based costing system last year. The system has already helped administrators make more accurate budget projections because they can now *specifically* identify and measure costs associated with various services.
>
> Here's why: The system makes use of an on-screen computer form that personnel fill out every time they provide a particular service. By filling in the appropriate boxes on the screen, the person specifies what activity took place, what personnel were involved, what resources were used, and how much time was spent. Let's say Suzy Student comes to the career center to meet with Cathy Counselor about getting a job. They spend 45 minutes researching the job market on the Internet and another hour working on Suzy's résumé. At the end of the session, Cathy records the time she spent with Suzy and the services she performed by using code numbers that correspond to various types of services typically delivered by the career center. This information goes into the system, which calculates the direct costs of Cathy's time and associated indirect costs.
>
> With everyone on campus keeping these records, Alexander's administration gets a highly targeted cost statement every month, one that allows them to see exactly where their service efforts, as well as dollars, are being spent.

Reinforce Your Message with Appropriate Visual Aids   Experts maintain that visual aids determine, to a great extent, how much of a presentation the audience will retain after the presenter has finished speaking. One study estimates that after three days, listeners retain 65% of a message presented with visual aids and only 10% of a message presented without them.[5] Because visual aids play such an important role in audience retention, presenters should use them to reinforce their main points (those they want the audience to take away from the presentation).

Preparing Visual Aids and Presentation Graphics

Computer-based slide shows are the most common type of visual support for oral presentations. Using software such as Microsoft PowerPoint, Corel Presentations, and Harvard Graphics, it is easy for anyone to generate visually appealing slide shows that can be projected directly from a computer or converted into transparencies for lower-tech overhead projection. Because this software is almost universally available, audiences have come to expect computer-generated slides or overhead transparencies in almost all business presentations.

Creating Visual Aids to Highlight Information   In addition to using the techniques just described, therefore, the speakers in our examples would support their verbal content with visual aids to keep their listeners focused on their main ideas. The accountant proposing CPA WebTrust to her client would no doubt reinforce her main point—the security WebTrust provides—by highlighting this key word on an overhead or slide (see Figure 7.2).

Providing assurance about a Web site's security is what marketing specialists call the "unique selling proposition" (USP) of CPA WebTrust; in a proposal, the speaker should emphasize the USP in as many ways as possible. By displaying her slide as she talks about the advantages of CPA WebTrust, the accountant reinforces the product's USP. The bulleted list on her slide provides a *visual anchor* for the idea she is communicating in words. A visual anchor helps the audience retain the message because it remains in place in the visual field, whereas the speaker's words disappear in the flow of speech.

In addition to reinforcing key points, visual aids help listeners understand complex ideas. Without visual aids, the consultant describing activity-based costing at Alexander Junior College might leave his listeners with only a vague idea of the process involved. As he speaks about the on-screen form, the activities, the personnel involved, and so forth, the audience is confronted with a number of variables that are difficult to visualize. By reproducing the computer form on a slide, however, the presenter can easily show his audience exactly how the college calculates the costs of employees' time (see Figure 7.3). Using an electronic pointer, the presenter can indicate as he speaks where each item is recorded and how the totals are derived. This step-by-step illustration helps the audience to understand the process.

Figure 7.2

PowerPoint Slide Highlighting Key Words

Feel Secure . . . with CPA WebTrust

- Security = Customers' Top Concern

- More Security = More Customers

- Security Assurance = More $$$

Figure 7.3

PowerPoint Slide Reproducing On-Screen Form

Alexander Junior College

	Career Development Department				
	Cathy Counselor				
	December 19xx				
Account Title:	Account #:	Day:	Hours:	Student:	Resources:
Résumé Services	1000-0001	15	1	Suzy Student	
Mock Interviewing	1000-0002				
Counseling/Advice	1000-0003				
Job Market Research	1000-0004	15	0.45	Suzy Student	Internet
Internship Services	1000-0005				
Networking Services	1000-0006				
Database Maintenance	1000-0007				
Alumni Services	1000-0008				
Other	1000-0009				

Creating Visual Aids to Communicate About Numbers: Tables, Charts, and Graphs By far the most important visual aids for accountants, however, are those which present numerical relationships in ways that are easy to grasp. Although accountants must know how to support their presentations with the general visual aids that all business presenters use—bulleted lists of key points, illustrations, flowcharts, and the like—they must also develop special skill with visual aids that display numbers effectively and translate numbers into images. We noted in Chapter 4 that tables, charts, and graphs help readers understand quantitative relationships because they render numerical relationships in spatial terms, and in doing so, allow readers to process those relationships as concrete visual images rather than as abstractions. Tables, charts, and graphs are helpful in reports and workpapers, but they are even more important in oral presentations, where listeners have a limited time in which to process information.

Remember: Most people do not communicate as easily with numbers as accountants do. In fact, for nonaccountants, numerical data sets can be intimidating, and many experienced nonfinancial businesspeople cannot easily draw conclusions from complex numerical information. For these reasons, converting numerical data into graphics is essential for presentations to nonaccounting audiences. Moreover, because graphic displays are easier for everyone to process than verbal discussions of numbers, use them wherever possible in presenting to other accountants as well.

Guidelines for Graphics Effective graphics present information clearly and persuasively. Effective graphics encourage efficient decision making because they allow listeners to get the point more quickly than verbal content alone can do. Although computer software makes it possible for anyone to create elaborate graphics, strive for simplicity in graphic presentation rather than for fancy effects. To create graphics that do the job, follow these guidelines from Edward R. Tufte's well-known source, *The Visual Display of Quantitative Information.*[6] Your graphics should:

- Show the data clearly.
- Induce the viewer to think about the substance rather than about the design.
- Avoid distorting what the data sets say.
- Present many numbers in a small space.
- Make large data sets coherent.
- Encourage the eye to compare different pieces of data.
- Reveal the data at several levels of detail, from a broad overview to the fine structure.
- Serve a reasonably clear purpose: description, exploration, tabulation, and so on.
- Be closely integrated with the statistical and verbal descriptions of the data set.

Tables Tables are the best way to display large amounts of data in a compact format. Tables have less visual appeal than other graphics, but they make

Figure 7.4

Sample Tables

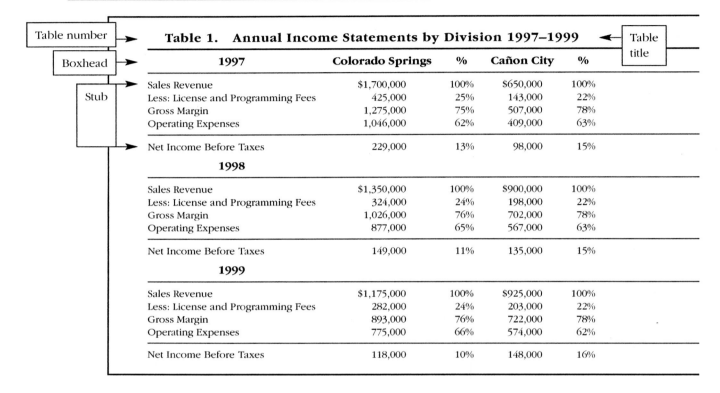

Table number → **Table 1. Annual Income Statements by Division 1997–1999** ← Table title

Boxhead →

Stub →

1997	Colorado Springs	%	Cañon City	%
Sales Revenue	$1,700,000	100%	$650,000	100%
Less: License and Programming Fees	425,000	25%	143,000	22%
Gross Margin	1,275,000	75%	507,000	78%
Operating Expenses	1,046,000	62%	409,000	63%
Net Income Before Taxes	229,000	13%	98,000	15%
1998				
Sales Revenue	$1,350,000	100%	$900,000	100%
Less: License and Programming Fees	324,000	24%	198,000	22%
Gross Margin	1,026,000	76%	702,000	78%
Operating Expenses	877,000	65%	567,000	63%
Net Income Before Taxes	149,000	11%	135,000	15%
1999				
Sales Revenue	$1,175,000	100%	$925,000	100%
Less: License and Programming Fees	282,000	24%	203,000	22%
Gross Margin	893,000	76%	722,000	78%
Operating Expenses	775,000	66%	574,000	62%
Net Income Before Taxes	118,000	10%	148,000	16%

comparisons easy by presenting information in columns and rows. In accounting presentations, tables are particularly useful for laying out the data set on which the discussion or analysis is based. Because they are often quite detailed, tables are best presented to audiences on paper as handouts, although some presenters display simple tables on slides and transparencies as well.

Tables include the following elements:

Table title: The title describes the content and what it illustrates.

Table number: Tables are numbered separately from figures in written documents, and table numbers should appear on any tables presented on handouts or slides.

Table headings: This section includes descriptive column headings and specifies the units of measurement (dollars, millions, etc.).

Stub: The stub (the far left column of the table) lists the items being compared (assets, liabilities, equity; geographical factors; chronological factors, and so forth).

Body: This section presents the information in columns. If a numerical value is zero, place a zero. If you do not have information for an item, indicate that fact with an ellipsis (three spaced dots/. . .). If you are presenting

Pueblo	%	Salida	%	Total	%	Column headings
$1,200,000	100%	$590,000	100%	4,140,000	100%	Body
288,000	24%	118,000	20%	974,000	24%	
912,000	76%	472,000	80%	3,166,000	76%	
756,000	63%	377,000	64%	2,588,000	63%	
156,000	13%	95,000	16%	578,000	14%	
$1,400,000	100%	$600,000	100%	4,250,000	100%	
336,000	24%	120,000	20%	978,000	23%	
1,064,000	76%	480,000	80%	3,272,000	77%	
882,000	63%	378,000	63%	2,704,000	64%	
182,000	13%	102,000	17%	568,000	13%	
$1,480,000	100%	$760,000	100%	4,340,000	100%	
370,000	25%	160,000	21%	1,015,000	23%	
1,110,000	75%	600,000	79%	3,325,000	77%	
917,000	62%	471,000	62%	2,737,000	63%	
193,000	13%	129,000	17%	588,000	14%	

information leading to total amounts, perform the calculations and provide the totals.

Rules: Rules are the lines that separate elements in the table. The sections of the table are separated by horizontal rules (a rule separates the title from the heading section and encloses the table at the bottom). Columns may be set off by vertical rules if doing so improves clarity.

Source line: If you or your organization did not generate the data, indicate its source: "Source: U.S. Bureau of Labor Statistics, 1998."

Footnotes: Items needing explanation are marked with symbols (*) or, more often, superscript numbers. Footnotes appear below the source line.

Because so many of accountants' communications originate in spreadsheets and financial statements, which are always presented in tabular form, tables are one of the most common visual aids in accountants' presentations.

In Figure 7.4, which concerns the Rocky Mountain Cable Company, the fictitious company to which you were introduced at the end of Chapter 6, Alexis, the company's controller, has created several tables of data that illustrate the company's financial situation. She distributed the tables to the meeting participants a few days before the meeting so they could familiarize themselves with the information.

Figure 7.4

Sample Tables—*continued*

Table 2. Quarterly Income Statements by Division 1997–1999

Sales Division	Q197	Q297	Q397	Q497	Q198	Q298
Colorado Springs						
Sales Revenue	600000	400000	325000	375000	425000	325000
Less: License						
and Programming Fees	150000	125000	90000	60000	100000	80000
Gross Margin	450000	275000	235000	315000	325000	245000
Operating Expenses	325000	250000	260000	211000	250000	200000
Net Income Before Taxes	125000	25000	−25000	104000	75000	45000
Cañon City						
Sales Revenue	150000	165000	200000	135000	150000	250000
Less: License						
and Programming Fees	25000	29000	41000	48000	45000	45000
Gross Margin	125000	136000	159000	87000	105000	205000
Operating Expenses	85000	95000	110000	119000	140000	130000
Net Income Before Taxes	40000	41000	49000	−32000	−35000	75000
Pueblo						
Sales Revenue	240000	260000	340000	360000	350000	300000
Less: License						
and Programming Fees	60000	70000	75000	83000	85000	70000
Gross Margin	180000	190000	265000	277000	265000	230000
Operating Expenses	160000	170000	205000	221000	220000	195000
Net Income Before Taxes	20000	20000	60000	56000	45000	35000
Salida						
Sales Revenue	145000	150000	140000	155000	155000	135000
Less: License						
and Programming Fees	25000	26000	30000	37000	35000	30000
Gross Margin	120000	124000	110000	118000	120000	105000
Operating Expenses	88000	95000	95000	99000	95000	89000
Net Income Before Taxes	32000	29000	15000	19000	25000	16000

	Q398	Q498	Q199	Q299	Q399	Q499
	325000	275000	325000	275000	300000	275000
	90000	54000	90000	75000	65000	52000
	235000	221000	235000	200000	235000	223000
	215000	212000	225000	190000	215000	145000
	20000	9000	10000	10000	20000	78000
	240000	260000	280000	200000	240000	205000
	50000	58000	49000	52000	50000	52000
	190000	202000	231000	148000	190000	153000
	145000	152000	150000	140000	142000	142000
	45000	50000	81000	8000	48000	11000
	375000	375000	370000	385000	360000	365000
	90000	91000	85000	98000	92000	95000
	285000	284000	285000	287000	268000	270000
	250000	217000	230000	240000	200000	247000
	35000	67000	55000	47000	68000	23000
	160000	150000	175000	185000	190000	210000
	27000	28000	30000	37000	42000	51000
	133000	122000	145000	148000	148000	159000
	99000	95000	100000	125000	126000	120000
	34000	27000	45000	23000	22000	39000

Figure 7.4

Sample Tables—*continued*

Table 3. Operating Expenses by Quarter 1997–1999

1997	Colorado Springs
Labor: Line Maintenance and Technicians	422400
Materials and Supplies	53000
Depreciation Expense: Cable, Equipment, Plant	75000
Sales Commissions and Sales Rep Salaries	263000
Advertising and Promotion	104600
Administrative Salaries	70000
Rent, Utilities, Miscellaneous Overhead	58000
Total Operating Expenses	1,046,000
1998	
Labor: Line Maintenance and Technicians	306,000
Materials and Supplies	37000
Depreciation Expense: Cable, Equipment, Plant	75000
Sales Commissions and Sales Rep Salaries	195000
Advertising and Promotion	175400
Administrative Salaries	46000
Rent, Utilities, Miscellaneous	42600
Total Operating Expenses	877,000
1999	
Labor: Line Maintenance and Technicians	249250
Materials and Supplies	15,625
Depreciation Expense: Cable, Equipment, Plant	75000
Sales Commissions and Sales Rep Salaries	140000
Advertising and Promotion	232500
Administrative Salaries	41000
Rent, Utilities, Miscellaneous	21625
Total Operating Expenses	775,000

Graphs and Charts Graphs and charts (the terms are often used interchangeably) are better than tables for presenting interpretations of data. Although effective tables can lay out large amounts of data clearly and accurately, they do not highlight information very well. With graphs it is easy to make the relationships among data instantly apparent. The disadvantage of graphs, however, is that they are less accurate than tables. For this reason, careful communicators often present a data set in tabular form and then graph parts of that data to highlight the implications of those parts.

In her oral presentation to the meeting, Alexis translates the tabular information for her audience, which is composed of sales managers, operations

Cañon City	Pueblo	Salida	Total
135,000	297000	127000	981400
22100	36200	22150	133450
35000	50000	27000	187000
124000	200000	102000	689000
40900	75600	37700	258800
35000	55000	40000	200000
17000	42200	21150	138350
409,000	756,000	377,000	2588000
195,000	345,400	128000	974400
29000	44000	19600	129600
35000	50000	27000	187000
170000	250000	105000	720000
85050	88200	37800	386450
35000	55000	40000	176000
17950	49400	20600	130550
567,000	882,000	378,000	2,704,000
178600	368000	165000	960850
27,000	45,000	26,000	113625
35000	50000	27000	187000
168600	254000	140000	702600
114800	91700	47100	486100
35000	60000	40000	176000
15000	48300	25900	110825
574,000	917,000	471,000	2,737,000

managers, and accounting managers. Her translations consist of several graphs and charts that help her make certain points about the company's finances. For example, she uses bar graphs to compare sales growth and decline among the company's four sales divisions over the past three years and to illustrate how expenditures for advertising and promotion in those divisions have related to sales revenues generated. She uses a single-line graph to illustrate the trend in the company's overall sales performance over the past three years, a double-line graph to illustrate the shrinking profit margins of a problematic sales division, and a multiline graph to compare the trends in the sales performance of the company's four sales divisions over the past three years. She

Figure 7.5

Vertical Bar Graph

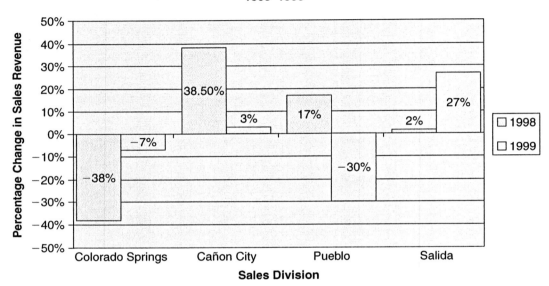

Rocky Mountain Cable Company
Year-to-Year Change in Sales Revenue
1998–1999

uses pie charts to illustrate the proportion of individual operating expenses to the company's total. She constructs a flowchart to depict the steps company personnel take to respond to customer service and repair requests.

In the following sections, we introduce you to these types of graphs and charts, explain the circumstances under which they should be used, and provide examples of bar graphs, line graphs, pie charts, and flowcharts.

Bar Graphs Bar graphs are particularly useful for drawing comparisons between items (like sales revenues and their related profits). They are also useful for showing how values for an item change over time (like quarterly production costs). In bar graphs, each bar represents a value for a particular item of interest. When the bars appear together on a graph with axes providing numerical values, dollar amounts, periods of time, and so on, the observer can judge how well or how poorly the company performed relative to other items of interest or to other points in time.

Although both horizontal and vertical bar graphs are common in professional communications, vertical bar graphs are better than horizontal ones for depicting amounts; therefore vertical bars are usually the most appropriate for accountants' communications. The vertical bar graph in Figure 7.5 illustrates the year-to-year percentage change in sales revenues for each of Rocky Mountain's four sales divisions. It makes obvious the problems the Colorado

Figure 7.6

Grouped Vertical Bar Graph

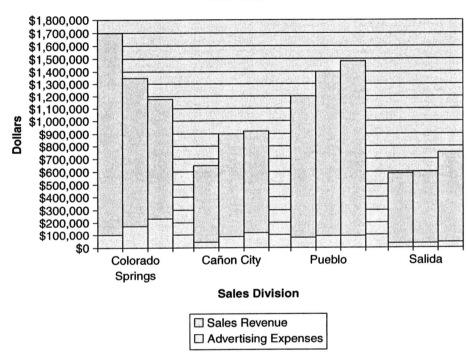

Rocky Mountain Cable Company
Advertising Expenses as a Proportion of Total Sales
1997–1999

☐ Sales Revenue
☐ Advertising Expenses

Springs and Pueblo sales divisions have experienced in terms of their sales revenues. (Each division, especially Colorado Springs, has lost considerable market share because new upstart cable companies have recently moved into the areas.)

To highlight more than one value for each item you are representing, use a *grouped bar graph*. The example in Figure 7.6 highlights the unusually inverse relationship between the advertising expenditures made by the Colorado Springs sales division and its resultant sales revenues each year, an indication that the division is spending proportionately more each year for advertising that is resulting in less sales revenue.

A few principles apply to the construction of any sort of graph:

1. Always label your *zero point,* and begin your graph at zero wherever possible. A graph that begins at zero usually represents its quantities more accurately than one that begins with other values. Graph (a) in Figure 7.7 has been given a zero point and presents its data

Figure 7.7

(a) Bar Graph with Zero Point; (b) Improved Bar Graph with Break Point

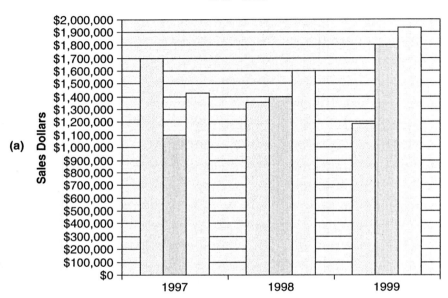

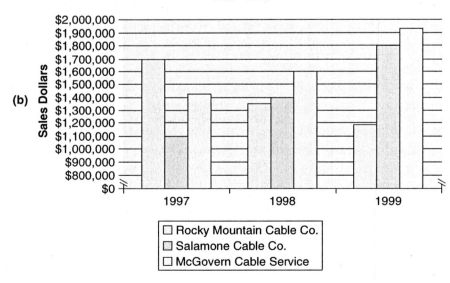

Figure 7.8

(a) Distorted 3-D Graph; (b) Accurate 2-D Graph

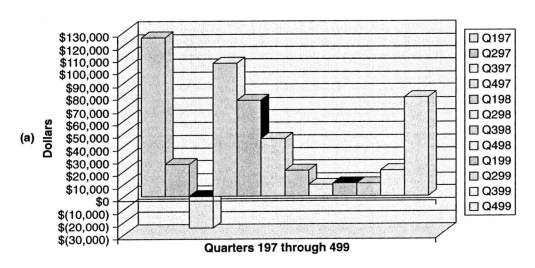

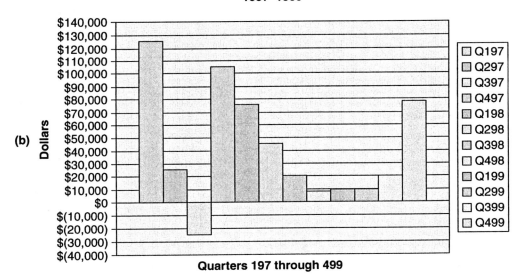

accurately. However, in this particular graph, the data points begin much later than zero, and as a result, much of the graph is wasted ink, comparing nothing in the lower one-third portion. To make the proportions look more normal and to save space, in the second graph (b), we have put a break in the scale, being careful to mark it clearly.

2. Divide both axes into equal units, beginning at the zero point or at your break point. Number the vertical axis from bottom to top, the horizontal axis from left to right. Label the units clearly. Place the caption for the vertical axis either at the upper left or vertically, along the axis. Place the caption for the horizontal axis below it.

3. Avoid 3-D effects. Although computer software can generate graphs with impressive-looking three-dimensional bars, these effects usually obscure rather than clarify the data. For example, it is not clear in Figure 7.8(a) whether the front or the back of each three-dimensional bar represents the quantity. The two-dimensional graph in Figure 7.8(b) makes the numbers clearer.

4. Use colors, shading, or simple fill effects (patterns available in your software) to distinguish the bars in your graph from one another, but be careful: Fancy fill effects are hard on the eyes. In fact, a leading expert on visual communication calls fancy patterns "chartjunk"[7] because they clutter charts and graphs, making them harder, rather than easier, to read. The dizzying effects in Figure 7.9(a) are examples of chartjunk. As you can see, the graph in Figure 7.9(b) is much cleaner and clearer.

Line Graphs Line graphs, like bar graphs, illustrate comparisons of numerical data, but what line graphs do best is to illustrate the *trends* that occur in the numbers over even intervals of time. As shown in Figures 7.10, 7.11, and 7.12, line graphs depict relationships among numbers as a series of points plotted along the intersections of two axes. The first example (Figure 7.10) is a simple single-line graph, which shows the trend, or pattern, of Rocky Mountain Cable Company's sales revenues, plotted by quarter, over the past three years.

Because several sets of numbers can be plotted on a line graph, line graphs allow for richer data representation than bar graphs do. Double-line graphs, which represent two data sets, often employ shading to emphasize the difference between the two lines, as in Figure 7.11, which illustrates the profit performance of the Colorado Springs sales division by shading the area found between the "sales revenue" line and the "total expenses" line.

Line graphs also are used frequently to compare multiple sets of data, such as data from several operation divisions of a company or from several competitors and the company. When constructing a multiple-line graph, use colors or symbols with clearly labeled captions to distinguish the items being compared. Figure 7.12 shows a multiple-line graph comparing the trends in sales performance for each of Rocky Mountain's four sales divisions.

Figure 7.9

(a) Bar Graph with Chartjunk; (b) Improved Bar Graph

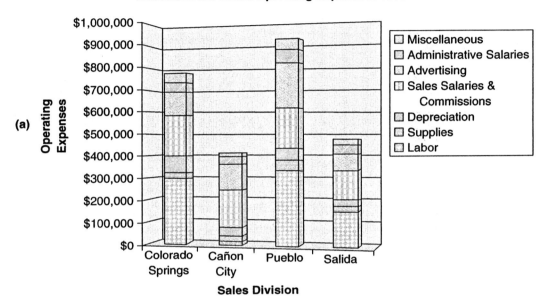

(a)

Rocky Mountain Cable Company
Allocation of Annual Operating Expenses: 1999

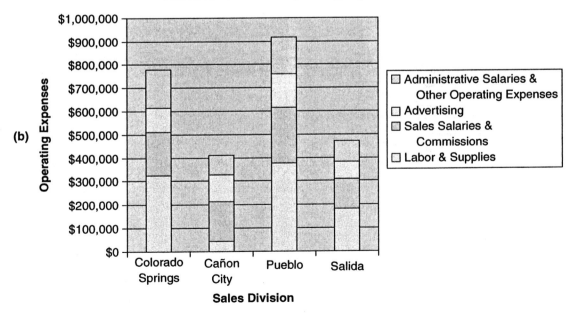

(b)

Rocky Mountain Cable Company
Allocation of Annual Operating Expenses: 1999

Figure 7.10

Single-Line Graph

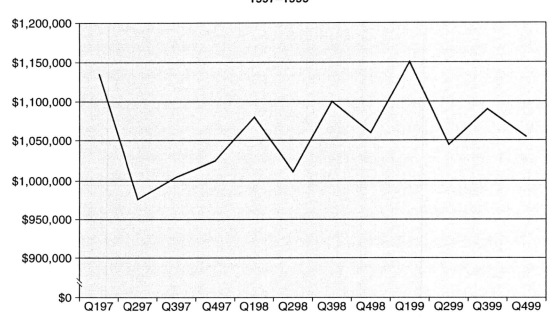

Rocky Mountain Cable Company
Total Sales Revenue
1997–1999

Many of the same principles apply to constructing line graphs as to bar graphs: Begin the axes at zero, wherever possible; clearly label all units and values; and avoid 3-D effects and chartjunk. Also realize that the angles in a line graph are determined by the number of points plotted. The line graph in Figure 7.13 shows Rocky Mountain Cable Company's net income before taxes, plotted by year for three years, and the graph in Figure 7.14 shows the company's net income plotted by quarter for three years. Notice that each of the lines in the first graph is composed of too few (only three) data points, and that the graph visually distorts the profit performance trends of the four sales divisions (the graph gives the impression that the patterns of Cañon City's, Pueblo's, and Salida's profit performances were virtually identical). Each line in the second graph is composed of 12 data points, and the graph more accurately represents the divisions' profit patterns: It shows the drastic fluctuations

Figure 7.11

Double-Line Graph

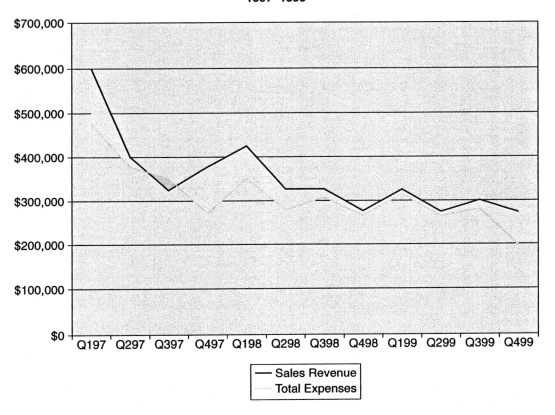

Rocky Mountain Cable Company
Colorado Springs Sales Division
Profit Performance
1997–1999

in Cañon City's performance over the course of the three years and the comparatively smooth trend in that of Pueblo and Salida. Figure 7.14 also gives a more detailed picture of the problems that have been experienced by the Colorado Springs division.

Set up your axes so your graph is wider than it is tall. Because we are accustomed to noticing deviations from the horizon, horizontally positioned graphs are more accessible to the eye than vertical ones.[8] Also, overly long vertical axes create graphic distortion because they make the differences

| Figure 7.12 |

Multiple-Line Graph

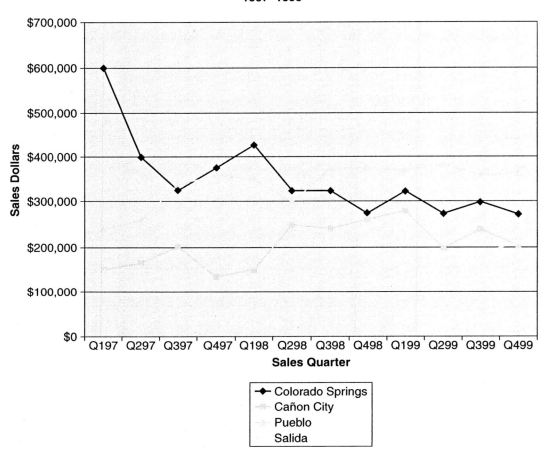

Rocky Mountain Cable Company
Trends in Sales Volume by Division
1997–1999

among values appear to be greater than they are. Horizontal axes that are too long distort relationships in the opposite direction, minimizing the differences among the values. Notice in Figure 7.15 how the visually accurate line graph shown in Figure 7.14 becomes distorted when either the vertical or horizontal axis is too long or too short.

Figure 7.15(a) makes the sales divisions' profit performances seem even more erratic than they actually are (the lines veer up and down in an exaggerated manner), and Figure 7.15(b), although still exhibiting erratic data patterns, tones down the impact of the problematic information.

Figure 7.13

Distorted Line Graph: Too Few Data Points

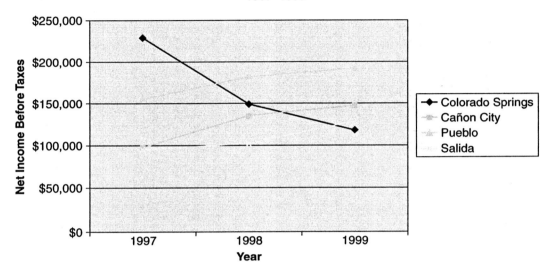

**Rocky Mountain Cable Company
Profit Performance by Division
1997–1999**

Figure 7.14

Effective Line Graph: Multiple Data Points

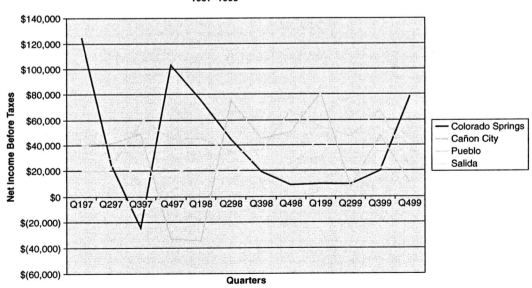

**Rocky Mountain Cable Company
Profit Performance by Division
1997–1999**

Figure 7.15

(a) Vertically Distorted Line Graph

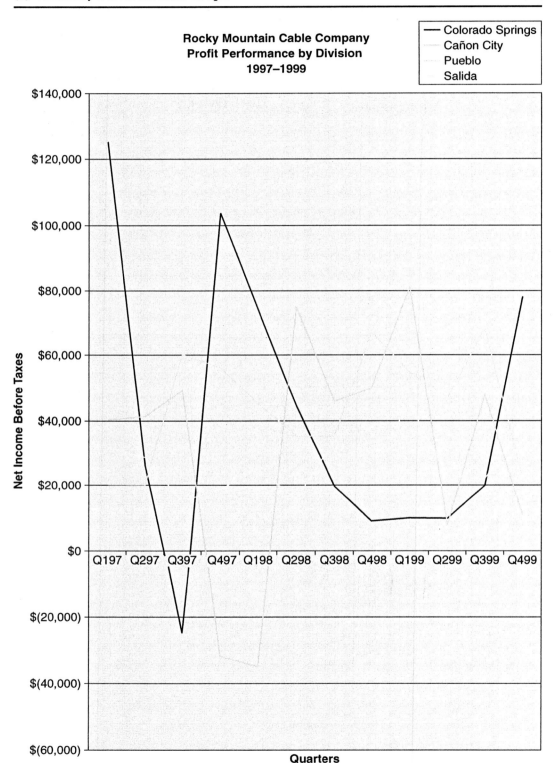

**Rocky Mountain Cable Company
Profit Performance by Division
1997–1999**

Legend:
— Colorado Springs
Cañon City
Pueblo
Salida

Y-axis: **Net Income Before Taxes**
$140,000
$120,000
$100,000
$80,000
$60,000
$40,000
$20,000
$0
$(20,000)
$(40,000)
$(60,000)

X-axis: **Quarters**
Q197 Q297 Q397 Q497 Q198 Q298 Q398 Q498 Q199 Q299 Q399 Q499

Figure 7.15

(b) Horizontally Distorted Line Graph

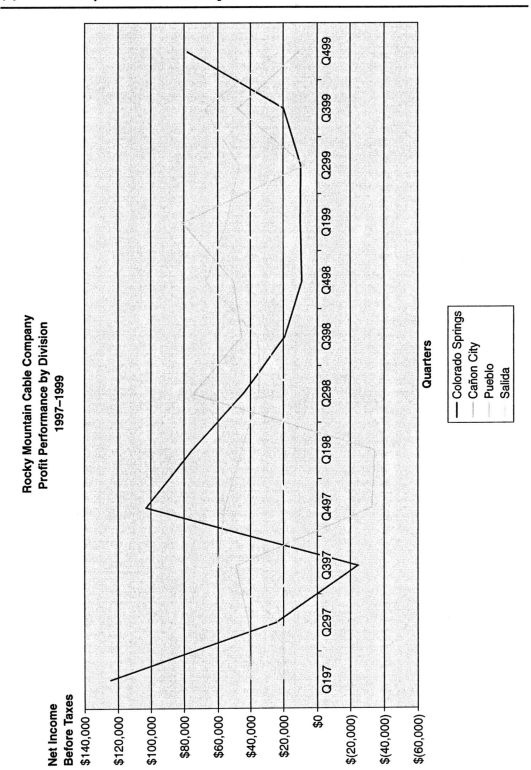

Rocky Mountain Cable Company
Profit Performance by Division
1997–1999

Pie Charts Pie charts present the relationship of parts to each other and to the whole. The advantage of pie charts is that they are very simple; they present data in a way in which the least number-savvy observer can easily understand. Pie charts are good for illustrating, for example, what proportion of an office supply budget is spent on which types of items or what proportion of a multinational company's total production output is generated by each of its plants around the world. A disadvantage of pie charts is that they present information in a relatively superficial way. They are best used to supplement more accurate and detailed depictions of data, such as tables.

To create pie charts, follow these guidelines:

1. Begin the slices of the pie at 12 o'clock and divide the pie working clockwise (unless your software moves counterclockwise, as some programs do).
2. Make the first slice your largest value and move in descending order around the pie.
3. Display no more than five or six numbers/slices. A lot of information is difficult to represent, and as the slices become smaller, relative differences are harder to perceive.
4. Label the slices horizontally, inside each slice if possible, and give the percentage value of each slice.
5. Keep your pie charts two dimensional; three-dimensional charts distort the relative values of the slices.
6. As with bar graphs, use colors or simple patterns to distinguish the slices from one another.
7. To highlight one section of the pie, pull out ("explode") that slice from the whole. (Most computer programs can separate slices for you.)
8. Make sure your percentages add up to 100%.

The chart in Figure 7.16 shows what problems arise if these principles are violated. The chart, prepared by Alexis's well-meaning student intern, attempts to illustrate the proportion of individual operating expenses to the total. But it contains too many data items, or slices, places data labels confusingly outside of the wedges, and uses chartjunk. Instead of serving its intended purpose—to stimulate discussion about ways to curb expenses—this chart is more likely to confuse the people at the meeting.

After consulting with Alexis, the intern corrects the pie chart, following good charting principles. The improved graph (Figure 7.17) explodes only one slice to highlight the largest expense, avoids fancy fill patterns and 3-D effects, and combines some of the smaller expense categories so there are fewer slices. The result is a pie chart that will help the group focus on those expense areas that are of relative financial consequence.

Flowcharts A flowchart is a diagram of the sequence of steps in a process or system. Flowcharts use symbols to depict the procedures, documents, and files that are involved in the process or system, with connective lines showing the direction or flow of information. A good flowchart helps its user understand the

Figure 7.16

Problematic Pie Chart

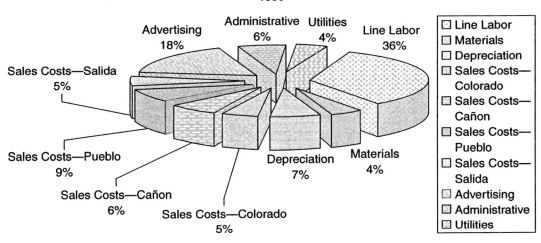

Rocky Mountain Cable Company
Total Operating Expenses
1999

Figure 7.17

Improved Pie Chart

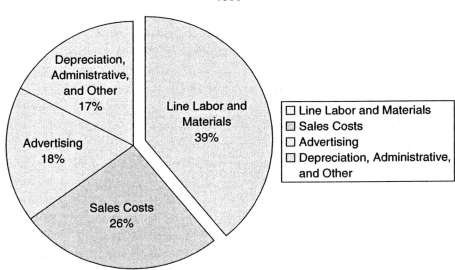

Rocky Mountain Cable Company
Total Operating Expenses
1999

Figure 7.18

Flowchart

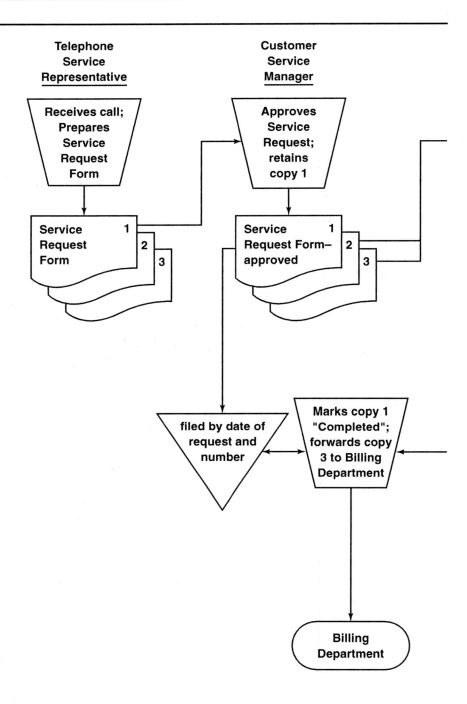

Figure 7.18

Flowchart—*continued*

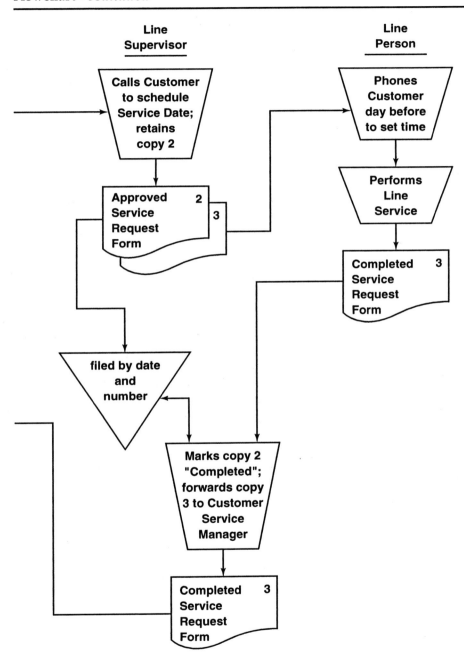

nature of the process or system being described, the duties of the people involved, and the physical flow of information being processed.

Flowcharts are widely used in audit practice to help auditors understand their clients' systems of internal control. By drawing a picture of the activities that take place in an area of the client's transaction cycle, an experienced auditor can identify at a glance where problem, or weak control, areas exist. Flowcharts are also used by accountants in private companies to describe operational procedures and information system flows to help personnel understand how to carry out their duties or to establish accepted procedures for document flow and record keeping.

Flowcharting software can help you create professional quality flowcharts, but you can also produce legible, logical flowcharts by neatly drawing them using a flowchart symbol template, which can be purchased inexpensively in many college bookstores or office supply stores. Flowcharts usually begin at the upper left-hand corner of a page and flow from top to bottom and from left to right. Vertical columns contain symbols that depict procedures and documents that are handled by individual employees or departments. Lines and arrows indicate the direction of information and document flow. (Consult an auditing or accounting information systems textbook for symbol definitions.)

In Figure 7.18, Alexis's flowchart depicts the sequence of steps taken by Rocky Mountain personnel who handle customer service complaints. Notice that the typical vertical columns and top-to-bottom and left-to-right flow have been used.

More Tips on Graphics Whichever graphic devices you choose to reinforce your points, remember a few key principles:

- *Keep your terms consistent.* As we noted earlier, you will frequently create tables, graphs, and charts to clarify the numbers in a particular data set. Be sure to depict these numbers in the same terms: If your table represents numbers in thousands, for example, your charts and graphs should do so as well.
- *Introduce and explain all graphics in your presentation or your text.* Many communicators make the mistake of assuming that the graphics speak for themselves. These communicators simply confront the audience with a table, chart, or graph and expect the audience to draw the proper conclusions. Graphics are *support* materials, however, and they need to be introduced and explained. Never show a graphic before you have set up the context for it and explained its significance. In written communications and on handouts, always explain the graphic first and then place it immediately after the section of text it illustrates.

CREATING YOUR SLIDE SHOW

When you have finished drafting your presentation and creating your tables, charts, and graphs, you are ready to prepare your slide show. Figure 7.19 pre-

PowerPoint Slides—Guidelines for Creating Effective Presentation Support

Creating Presentation Support

1. Outline Your Presentation

2. Choose a "Look"

3. Insert Visuals

4. Produce Handouts

Outline Your Presentation

■ Outline View

■ Enter Text

   – Key Words Only

   – 3 or 4 Lines Per Slide

Figure 7.19

PowerPoint Slides—Guidelines for Creating Effective Presentation Support—
continued

Choose a "Look"

- Simple Fonts

- Large Type: 36/44 pt.

- Create Background

- Apply Design

Insert Visuals

- Clip Art

  - Picture Gallery

  - CD-ROM

  - World Wide Web

PowerPoint Slides—Guidelines for Creating Effective Presentation Support— *continued*

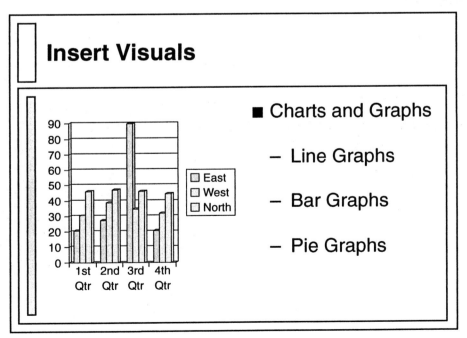

Figure 7.19
_____

PowerPoint Slides—Guidelines for Creating Effective Presentation Support—
continued
_____

Prepare Handouts

**Reasons why companies
adopt new software:**

■ Frequent downtime

■ Changes in reporting
   requirements

■ Current customized
   packages are hard to
   maintain

---

sents some slides with guidelines for creating effective presentation support using Microsoft PowerPoint, currently one of the most popular presentation software packages.

1. *Outline your presentation.* Working from your draft, use the software's outline feature to organize the points you want to make in each section of your presentation. PowerPoint will automatically convert your outline to a slide show, which, if properly designed, will create a visual road map for your listeners to follow as you speak. To create a clear road map, the slides should be uncluttered and easy to read. Do not list complete information about every point in your outline; instead, use key words, as the slides in Figure 7.19 do. Limit each section of your outline to three or four points only.

2. *Choose a look.* Decide which basic design you want to use: which background colors and accents, which kind of transition from slide to slide, and so forth. Although PowerPoint and other presentation software offer a wealth of backgrounds, design options, and transition effects, resist the urge to get fancy. A professional presentation should be understated and businesslike.

Also, be consistent in your design and in your slide-to-slide transition effects. Here are a few design tips:

- Stay with simple fonts such as Geneva, Chicago, New York, and Times.
- Use 44-point type for headers; 36-point type for body text.
- Choose a dark background and light text for slide shows.
- Choose a light background and dark text for overheads.
- Use photos and clip art selectively and sparingly.

3. *Insert graphics.* If you are using Excel, import your tables, graphs, and charts into your PowerPoint presentation slides. You may also want to make use of clip art, photographs, or illustrations to underscore the theme of your remarks or to add visual interest. Used judiciously, these elements can add a lot to your presentation. Your presentation software program should be equipped with a clip art gallery from which you may select standard images. Specialized images of all kinds are available on CDs as well as on the World Wide Web.

At the same time, however, remember that visual aids are *presentation support materials*. They should not be used merely for aesthetic reasons but always to enhance your message. The design elements you use in your support materials should reinforce the image you are trying to project and reflect your content appropriately. If you are discussing multinational initiatives in a client company, for example, you might include a graphic of a globe in the background of your slide. If you are presenting a progress report on objectives achieved, you might place a bright check-mark symbol next to each completed item.

4. *Produce handouts.* Although printed handouts are useful for presenting complex or detailed data, such as tables, they can distract your listeners from your presentation by inviting them to read what is in their hands. Therefore, try to keep your handouts as simple as possible. One way to provide handouts that are not too distracting is to print copies of your slides with accompanying "notes" spaces next to each slide. As the sample in Figure 7.20 shows, your listeners can use these handouts to reinforce the key points you make in your presentation by filling in notes as they go along. You can supplement these handouts with printed tables and other written text as necessary.

Remember: Always print a hard copy of your slide show. Computer equipment can be unreliable. If your equipment fails at a crucial moment, and you have a hard copy, you can quickly generate a set of handouts to distribute to your listeners.

Rehearsing Your Presentation

After you have drafted your presentation and prepared your visual aids, rehearse your presentation to check timing and to practice your delivery. If you are a highly experienced public speaker, you may simply want to run through the presentation once or twice, coordinating your slides with your oral delivery.

Figure 7.20

Handout to Accompany an Oral Presentation

CPA WebTrust—General FAQs

- What is Electronic Commerce?
- What is CPA WebTrust?
- Why is CPA WebTrust needed?
- Why are CPA's offering CPA WebTrust?

CPA WebTrust—General FAQs

- How do I know that a Web site has received the CPA WebTrust service?
- What does the CPA WebTrust Seal mean?
- Who issues the WebTrust Seal?
- Where can I obtain copies of the WebTrust Standards?

Background

- Joint AICPA/CICA Team Effort
- Dual Focus
    - Build the practice for the profession
    - Promulgate user-oriented measurement criteria
- Timing
    - Announced Sept. 16, 1997

Most people, however, benefit from more extensive rehearsal. Try practicing your presentation in front of a mirror. As you speak, watch for the following behaviors:

1. *Facial expression.* Does the look on your face show that you're frightened? Do you look frozen and tense? Relax your facial expression and smile at your audience. If you are afraid of speaking in front of a group, practice smiling at yourself while you are talking. It will help you relax.

2. *Eye contact.* Are you looking into the mirror or down at your notes? Looking listeners in the eye helps keep their attention and inspires confidence in you as a speaker. Do not "read" your notes; do not "talk to" the slide you are discussing. Look into the mirror as if your reflection were a member of your audience and talk to that reflection.

3. *Hand movements.* Do your hands get in the way of your message? Avoid hand gestures that will distract your audience. If you are planning to sit during your presentation, find a comfortable position for your hands (crossed palm-to-elbow on the table or folded in your lap, for example) and keep them in that position except when switching slides or pointing to highlight information. If you are planning to stand, practice speaking with your hands at your sides. If that feels unnatural, try holding an electronic pointer or a few pages of notes to give your hands something to do. Or you may want to rest one hand lightly on the podium while you speak.

4. *Speed of delivery.* Many people speak in a rush when they are nervous, which makes it difficult for listeners to follow their presentations. Force yourself to speak slowly, to articulate clearly, and to pause after important points. If you are worried about your speed, use a tape recorder and play your presentation back until you are satisfied with the pace of your speech.

Delivering Your Presentation

Before the meeting at which you will make your presentation, check out the room to ensure that you have adequate space for your laptop, if you are using one, for your handouts, and for any other materials you plan to bring. If you plan to connect your laptop to a monitor and/or a projector, do a trial run with the equipment. Make sure the connections work properly, audio and video channels are functioning (if required), and the resolution is sharp enough on the screen. If you are presenting your slides as transparencies on an overhead projector, make sure the projector is positioned so it will not obstruct participants' view of you or of the screen. Also check to see that the projector's relationship to the screen allows for proper focus and image size. Test the light bulb on the projector and find out where spare bulbs are kept.

If you are not sure that water will be available, bring a small bottle of your own and a cup. Many people experience "dry mouth" when speaking in public (even to small groups). A sip of water from time to time will alleviate this problem.

To begin your presentation, smile at your listeners and summarize for them what your presentation will cover. If you are standing, position your feet comfortably and stand still. Find a friendly pair of eyes and focus your initial remarks toward that person. As you loosen up, move your eyes from person to person. Do not let your eyes dart about, however; instead, establish eye contact with a person and hold that contact until you have articulated an entire thought. Then, move your eyes on to another person.

Face your listeners, not the screen or computer monitor. If you must turn to your visual aids, turn, point or gesture in the appropriate direction, and speak. Then turn around and face your audience again.

To conclude your presentation, thank your audience, and ask if anyone has questions. Answer any questions as fully as possible. If you do not know the answer, simply say, "I don't know" or "I haven't studied that part of the problem yet" and offer to find the answer later. After the question and answer period is over, thank the audience again, gather your materials quickly, and be seated.

CONCLUSION

In the professional workplace, you will find that your opportunities to present information to others will vary greatly. They may range from casual and simple to elaborate and highly structured. As you gain experience, your presentation skills will become more polished, and speaking in front of others will become second nature. You will learn your own favorite strategies for overcoming public speaking anxiety, for orchestrating oral presentations, and for displaying data through graphics. This chapter will help you begin to master the basics for presenting information to groups large and small.

NOTES

[1] LaTresa Pearson, "Get Connected with Cutting-Edge Presentation Tools," *Training* 33 (September 1996): 10; Lynda Bell Sereno, "Meetings Get an Electronic Boost," *The Business Journal* 13 (January 22, 1996): 23.

[2] Joseph McCafferty, "The Virtual Shareholder," *CFO: The Magazine for Senior Financial Executives* 14 (August 1998): 15.

[3] Pearson, p. 10.

[4] The CPA WebTrust, which is based on principles and criteria developed by the AICPA, is an assurance service that focuses on business-to-consumer electronic commerce. A WebTrust-certified CPA completes an examination based on measurable criteria of the applicant company and issues a report attesting to the company's business practice disclosures, transaction integrity controls, and information protection controls.

[5] T. C. Smith, *Making Successful Presentations: A Self-Teaching Guide* (New York: Wiley, 1991), p. 58.

[6]Edward R. Tufte's *The Visual Display of Quantitative Information* (Cheshire, CT: Graphics Press, 1983) is the best general source on graphics. The SEC follows Tufte in the section on graphics in its *Plain English Handbook (http://www.sec.gov/news/handbook.htm)*. Other useful sources include J. V. White, *Using Charts and Graphs: 1000 Ideas for Visual Persuasion* (New York: R.R. Bowker, 1984), and Walter E. Oliu, Charles T. Brusaw, and Gerald J. Alred, "Designing and Using Visual Aids," in *Writing That Works: How to Write Effectively on the Job* (6th ed.) (New York: St. Martin's Press, 1998), pp. 339–374.

[7]Ibid.

[8]Tufte, *The Visual Display of Quantitative Information.*

EXERCISES

1. **Scenario:** You are a CPA and CFE (Certified Fraud Examiner) and have been asked to make a presentation on the general topic of fraud in the business world today, with no further specific information given. Before preparing your presentation, you need to consider the purpose of your presentation and understand the audience to whom you will be speaking.

   Communication task: For each of the following groups, explain what purpose you want to achieve and how an understanding of your audience will affect the aspects of fraud you address and the degree of technical information you present.

   a. A group of students at a university accounting society meeting.

   b. A group of auditors attending a Continuing Professional Education course.

   c. A group of small business owners.

2. **Scenario:** You work for ACE Systems, a software development company specializing in accounting information systems. You have contacted a prospective client, Ambler Services, whose director of information systems had browsed your Web site and decided that he would like to receive additional information about your software. You have analyzed Ambler's current accounting information system and realize it is very outdated and lacks many of the time-saving features found in ACE software. In addition, Ambler's current software cannot be expanded as the company grows. Your prospective client has agreed to listen to a presentation about ACE accounting system software. An accounting intern working for your firm has prepared the following outline for the presentation that you plan to make to Ambler Services.

   Communication task: After considering the purpose of your presentation, revise the outline to accomplish your goals more effectively. Eliminate any information that you believe is not relevant to the goals of this presentation and add any information you believe is necessary.

ACE Systems
Accounting Information Systems Software
Client Presentation for Ambler Services
May 10, 2000

I. Introduction
  A. History of ACE Systems
  B. Types of software available from ACE
  C. Company expertise with accounting information systems (AIS)
  D. Satisfied clients
II. Personal background
  A. Education and professional credentials
  B. Position in the firm
  C. Personal experience with AIS
III. Overview of ACE accounting systems
  A. Strengths—what makes it better than the competition
  B. Weaknesses—things currently in development
IV. Demonstrate how ACE software works
V. How ACE software would benefit Ambler Services
VI. Conclusion

---

3. **Communication task:** Create an outline for a presentation about the structure and operation of the FASB (Financial Accounting Standards Board), as if you were preparing it for a group of first-year accounting students. Consider the purpose of your presentation: Is it an informative presentation or a persuasive presentation? Consider the audience and keep your content listener-based.

4. **Communication task:** Using your computer's software, create a title page slide and one or two introductory information slides for the beginning of presentations on *two* of the following topics. Do not spend a lot of time researching your topics—the objective of this exercise is to *evaluate the design* of your slides, not to gather information about the subject.
  a. Structure of the U.S. federal income tax.
  b. The SEC (Securities and Exchange Commission).
  c. International accounting standards.
  d. Health care fraud.
  e. Accounting practices in the entertainment industry.
  f. Environmental accounting issues.
  Choose at least three different, but relevant, design options for each presentation. Evaluate the pros and cons of each in both slide show mode and as printouts. Does the design complement and enhance

your presentation? Does it reflect your content? Does it reinforce the image you are trying to project? Is the text clearly visible? Are the fonts easy to read? Add transition effects from slide to slide. Is the transition from slide to slide smooth and not too distracting? Consider getting the opinions of several other people. Prepare a written report, analyzing the options you considered, including printouts of each, and including a conclusion about your best option for each presentation.

5. **Communication task:** For each of the situations given here, determine if the data would be best presented as a table, a pie chart, a line graph, a bar graph, or a flowchart. For each situation, also explain briefly why you chose the method of presentation you did.
   a. Comparing sales for each of the four industry segments in your business.
   b. Showing the proportion of net income derived from each industry segment.
   c. Showing growth in net income for the past five years.
   d. Showing the documents and procedures for handling petty cash.
   e. Illustrating the components of revenue.
   f. Showing ten different ratio calculations for a company this year and last year, along with industry averages.
   g. Providing a trend analysis of gross profit for the past five years.
   h. Contrasting net income by international region.
   i. Comparing Big Five CPA firms with respect to total revenues, total employees, and percentage of annual revenues for accounting and auditing services, tax services, and consulting work.
   j. Illustrating the method used to process false invoices by a criminal who defrauded a company.

6. **Communication task:** For each situation and set of data provided, create either a pie chart, a line graph, or a bar graph, including appropriate titles, data labels, legends, and/or gridlines to make your chart understandable. Keep in mind that your chart should not be too cluttered and should clearly illustrate the point you are trying to make.
   a. Comparison of Median Losses of Different Types of Check Tampering Schemes*

Type of Scheme	Median Losses
Altered Payee	$82,500.00
Authorized Maker	136,000.00
Concealed Check	62,000.00
Forged Endorsement	25,000.00
Forged Maker	90,129.00

*Data from *Occupational Fraud and Abuse* by Joseph T. Wells, Obsidian Publishing Company, Inc. © 1997.

b. Comparison of The Walt Disney Company sources of revenues in 1998 and 1997.**

Revenues (in millions)	1998	1997
Creative Content	$10,302	$10,937
Broadcasting	7,142	6,522
Theme Parks and Resorts	5,532	5,014
Total	$22,976	$22,473

c. Trend analysis of revenues and net income for The Walt Disney Company.

(in millions)	1998	1997	1996	1995	1994
Revenues	$22,976	$22,473	$18,739	$12,151	$10,090
Net Income	1,850	1,966	1,214	1,380	1,110

7. **Communication task:** Assume you will be giving a 10- to 15-minute presentation to your class. After discussing possible options with your instructor, choose a topic relevant to the content of your course and appropriate for a relatively short presentation. (a) Prepare a brief written analysis of your audience and purpose and develop an outline of the information you plan to present. (b) Draft your presentation, using the guidelines given in the text.

8. **Communication task:** Create presentation slides to accompany your presentation. Use templates and design elements appropriate for your topic that support and enhance your presentation. Add graphics such as clip art, photographs, illustrations, graphs, and charts to anchor ideas in the listeners' minds and to reinforce your verbal message. Print a copy of your presentation and have your instructor or classmates critique your presentation.

9. **Communication task:** After you have drafted your presentation and prepared your visual aids, rehearse your presentation to check timing and to practice your delivery. Use the suggestions in the text to improve your oral delivery. After you have practiced several times, ask a friend to listen to your presentation and to critique you on the following points:

- Is your facial expression relaxed?
- Are you smiling at the audience?
- Are you looking at the audience?
- Are you talking to the audience (as opposed to reading your notes or talking to the slides)?
- Are your hands fairly still and not distracting?

**Data for (2) and (3) from The Walt Disney Company 1998 Annual Report.

- Are you speaking slowly enough?
- Are you speaking clearly and distinctly?
- Do you pause after important points?

10. **Communication task:** As arranged by your instructor, deliver your presentation to your class, another group of students, or a group of faculty. Before the presentation, check the room and equipment to make sure everything is working properly. Look at your presentation slides from the view of the audience to be sure they are clearly visible. Prepare handouts for your audience and organize any other materials you plan to use. At the designated time, deliver your presentation using the advice given in the chapter.

CHAPTER 8

Collaborative Communication

Thus far, we have focused primarily on the skills you need to communicate *as an individual*. It is equally important, however, that you know how to write and develop presentations *as a member of a group*. No matter where you work—in a small business, a bank, a major corporation, or a public accounting firm—you will find that communicating on the job frequently involves collaborating with others. As we noted in Chapter 6, a large percentage of accountants' oral communications occur in meetings where several people work together to solve problems, plan projects, develop business, and advise clients. Moreover, research shows that professional writing in all sectors of the workplace is, to some extent, collaborative writing.[1] One study of 200 college-educated businesspeople, for example, found that 74% wrote collaboratively at least some of the time. Another study reported that nine out of ten professionals surveyed wrote as members of a group on the job.[2]

What is true of the workplace in general is especially true for the accounting profession. Because accounting provides the foundation for business planning, control, and reporting, accountants often find themselves at the center of the collaborations that drive business. Experienced accountants regularly lead audit planning meetings, spearhead proposal writing teams, and offer consultation to business planning groups. Entry-level accountants frequently work as members of such teams and contribute to projects anchored by others.

TECHNOLOGIES OF GROUP COMMUNICATION

The global economy of the twenty-first century increasingly involves collaboration on complex tasks, bringing people from various specialties and geographic locations together via group communication technologies. To foster communications among geographically disparate workers, multinational firms and corporations are relying more and more on groupware—that is, on technologies that permit teleconferencing, computer conferencing, document conferencing, group decision support systems (GDSS), and the like.[3] Groupware participants communicate through telephones, through computer screens, and sometimes through a combination of both.

Although the more sophisticated of these options may not be available to students, many of them are routinely used in the workplace, and it is likely you will use some of them on the job. Whether you are sitting around a table with a few other people or participating in an international video conference, your contribution will be strengthened by a knowledge of group communication principles.

Here are two examples of collaborative communication involving accountants. Although the first is a traditional face-to-face situation and the second is a hi-tech interaction, they are both anchored in similar communication techniques.

Example: A project development company in the southeastern United States is planning to build a multimillion-dollar plant to manufacture chemical fertilizer. The project developers must win the approval of the state legislature on the one hand and must sell their project to investors on the other.

To develop the necessary proposals, the project director works with the engineering firm her company has selected for the job. Although she consults frequently with the firm's engineers about technology options, it is not the engineers who are her major collaborators on the proposals. It is the company's in-house accountants. At every step of the proposal process, the project director confers with the accountants on information vital to the business plan—ways to predict profitability ratios for the technology options; ways to take advantage of federal, state, and local tax incentives; ways to work with banks on debt structuring and capital investment strategies. The accountants not only generate numbers for her; they also help her interpret numbers and evaluate financial alternatives.

Throughout the planning process, the accountants record their information in cash flow analyses, financial summaries, profitability projections, and other documents. These numerical data are supported by the project director's write-ups of notes she has taken during her frequent consultations with the accountants on the implications of these data. At the end of the process, the project director synthesizes in a project proposal the numerical data and the interpretations provided by the accountants with information from the engineers and others who will be involved in the project. Although the project director is the primary author of the final product, the backbone of the proposal will be information drafted by accountants.

Example: The audit client of a large international accounting firm has recently expanded its manufacturing and marketing interests to Europe, specifically to France, Germany, and Great Britain. After being engaged by the client to expand the audit scope to include the new European divisions, the responsible partner at the firm sets up an electronic meeting among the New York office's audit team (the partner himself, the engagement manager, and senior), and the assigned accounting firm associates in the Paris, Frankfurt, and London offices. One purpose of the online multinational meeting is to enable everyone involved in the expanded audit to learn about the client's new European business operations, legal and tax concerns, and financial performance. Another purpose of the meeting is to allow the group to discuss audit approach strategies and to coordinate specific audit tasks.

The partner in New York initiates the meeting using software that allows multiple users to log on simultaneously from different locations. Using their individual keyboards and screens, the audit team discusses audit matters in real time by typing questions and comments. As the participants type, their information instantly appears on all participants' screens so that an ongoing electronic discussion occurs. At the end of the meeting, the New York partner saves the discussion's text as a computer file. Later, he summarizes the discussion in a memo to the group. He retains one copy in the electronic engagement file and transmits copies via e-mail to all team members. Then, using the information in the file, he creates a computer software slide show highlighting the team's strategies and time lines for the upcoming multinational audit. He uses the slide show to support the oral presentation he delivers the following week to the client's upper-level financial and accounting officials (the vice president for finance, the chief financial officer, the controller, etc.) to update them on the audit plan and to co-ordinate time lines for cooperative work between the accounting firm and the client's accounting staff.

These scenarios represent just two examples of the numerous ways accountants collaborate on communication tasks. Here are some other ways you can expect to work collaboratively as a professional accountant:

You may

- work on a team that employs oral and written communications to solve problems
- submit/transmit drafts to a supervisor, who provides written feedback for your revision
- incorporate written information from experts into a document of your own
- blend your own writing with company boilerplate authored by others
- participate with others in electronic brainstorming sessions
- provide technical information orally or in writing to a team leader, producing a multisource presentation
- plan, draft, and revise a document or oral presentation with others
- coordinate, edit, and format the writing of several other people into a single document
- write up and present the results of an extended team problem-solving or analytical project

In each of these cases your contribution will intermingle with that of others; the authorship of the document, presentation, or project—and the responsibility for it—will be shared to some degree. The sharing involved in such projects requires more than strong writing skills. Anyone working with others toward a common goal must possess skills in interpersonal communication, conflict management, delegation, planning, and negotiation. This chapter offers guidelines for developing these important skills.

ADVANTAGES OF COLLABORATIVE COMMUNICATION

Although collaborating usually takes more time than working alone, it has several important advantages:[4]

Collaboration enlarges the knowledge base. Collaborative projects often involve cross-functional teams. By pooling expertise, collaborators can generate a document that none of them could have produced alone.

Collaboration promotes "reader-based" writing. Because collaborators share their drafts with others in the group, they serve as readers for one another. The process of reading and commenting on others' writing helps refine the sense of audience for all those working on the project.

Collaboration creates shared "ownership" of projects. Having a stake in the outcome of a collaborative task pulls people together, enhances communication, and promotes sharing of expertise, all of which boost productivity.

Collaboration helps acculturate new employees to the organization's procedures and values. Working with more experienced members of the organization helps new employees learn the ropes and recognize the values that drive the corporate culture. Because collaboration often brings together people from different areas and levels of the organization, it helps new employees to see how their individual efforts contribute to the big picture.

TYPES OF COLLABORATIVE COMMUNICATION AT WORK

Collaborative communication in the workplace ranges from the simple sharing of ideas to formally scheduled multiauthor projects. Although distinctions among the types of collaboration are, in actual practice, blurry, we can distinguish between two general types:

Primary-author collaboration, in which a single individual controls the collaboration, using information and feedback from others; and

Multiauthor collaboration, in which several people share authority and decision-making responsibility for the final document, presentation, or plan.

Primary-Author Collaboration

The collaborations described earlier exemplified this type of group communication, in which a single person anchors, controls, and coordinates the writing process while working with a number of collaborators, contributors, and readers (see Figure 8.1). The primary author in such a collaboration is usually designated in advance and assigned responsibility for the project by someone else.

The primary author

- plans the collaboration, sets the schedule, and divides the tasks
- interviews or confers with contributors to the project
- solicits written material, graphics, and numerical data
- leads group meetings
- compiles the drafts submitted by collaborators
- circulates a master draft for readers' comments
- solicits revisions from collaborators
- drafts the final manuscript and/or visual support materials
- edits the final manuscript and/or visual support materials
- has the document and/or visual support materials produced

Figure 8.1

Primary-Author Collaboration—Accounting Firm Engagement Proposal

At Big Five firms, engagement proposals are usually products of primary-author collaboration. The firm's marketing director is generally appointed primary author, and accountants from staff to partner level contribute to the writing process. The marketing director might begin the process by calling a meeting including staff accountants, seniors, managers, and partners of all divisions involved. After explaining the opportunity for the engagement, the marketing director solicits information on possible approaches to the client and ways of adding value to basic services. She specifies what information she needs from each collaborator; at that point, each contributor either writes up the information or schedules an appointment with the project leader to convey the information orally. After making their contributions, the group might meet again as a whole, or individuals might work one on one with the marketing director to revise their sections. The marketing director is responsible for pulling the contributions together and creating the proposal.

In collaborations such as this one, each contributor works with the primary author to help produce a collectively created document. But the individuals do not work with one another, and control of the final product rests with one person, the project team leader.

Multiauthor Collaboration

The second type of collaboration involves a far more complex process, one in which collective decision making replaces centralized authority. In multiauthor collaboration, each member of the project team shares in planning the group's goals, working methods, leadership, deadlines, quality criteria, and so forth. Such collaborations usually occur on projects where consensus is important, that is, in situations where people with diverse expertise and divergent points of view must reach mutually acceptable conclusions that can be expressed in mutually acceptable language.

This form of collaboration is especially common in the professional workplace,[5] where highly educated people perform specialized job functions. It is more challenging than primary-author collaboration because it involves *sustained interaction* and *negotiation of consensus* among team members at every stage of the process. But these very challenges make multiauthor collaboration the preferred method for projects demanding high levels of accountability and expertise.

Even the simplest forms of multiauthor collaboration can involve negotiation and sharing authority.

> **Example:** Imagine for a moment that you are an accountant at a large corporation. You and your supervisor are drafting a report explaining why your cost projections for a new manufacturing process, which has been in place for six months, were drastically understated. If time permits, you and your supervisor might work on the cost analyses together, discussing reasons for the mistaken projections and reaching agreement about how to organize the document, how to present the figures, and how to present recommendations for accounting for the cost discrepancies incurred and for restating the projections for the remainder of the year. This process would ensure maximum input from you both, but it would be time consuming.
>
> Given the time pressures of the workplace, it is more likely that you would perform the analyses by yourself, write a draft, and turn it over to your supervisor for review. Your supervisor might respond by writing his or her own draft or by asking you to restructure, refocus, and clarify what you have written. In either case, a cycle of rewrites would ensue until you arrived at a draft that satisfied you both.
>
> At each step of this cycle, both writers would consider options, rewrite material, and offer alternatives in response to one another. The final document would be enriched by the differing frames of reference and expertise that you and your supervisor have both brought to bear on the writing task. Although the two of you may not have agreed on every point, the finished product is acceptable to both of you. It represents a *negotiated consensus* of your original material and your supervisor's input.

When multiauthor collaboration occurs between two people or in a small, familiar group, achieving consensus can be a relatively simple matter. But when collaborating on the job means working with large teams of people with differing knowledge and expertise, consensus becomes harder to reach. In complex multiauthor collaborations, negotiating consensus can require weeks or months of work in a series of formally scheduled meetings. Such is the case in the following example and in its diagram in Figure 8.2.

> **Example:** Accountants, lawyers, and others at a large public utility work together each year to prepare the company's 10-K report to the Securities and Exchange Commission (SEC). The process is initiated each fall by the staff in

Figure 8.2

Sample Multiauthor Collaboration—Preparation of a 10-K Report

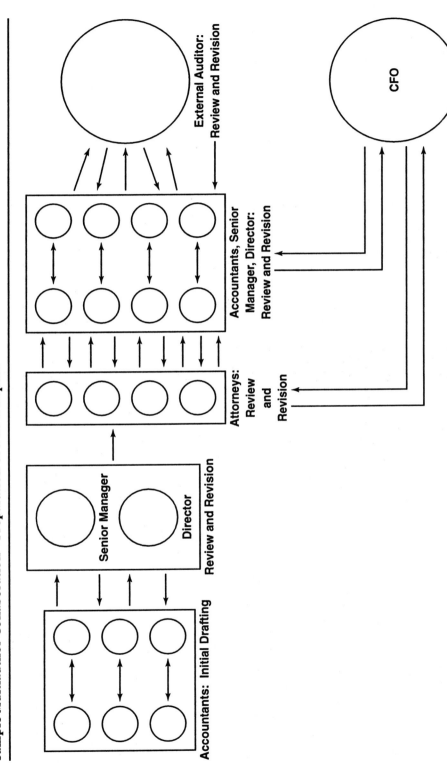

External Auditor: Review and Revision

CFO

Review and Revision

Accountants, Senior Manager, Director: Review and Revision

Attorneys: Review and Revision

Senior Manager

Director

Review and Revision

Accountants: Initial Drafting

regulatory accounting, the department responsible for external reporting. The dozen people in this department range from junior-level staff accountants to managers with years of experience in SEC reporting and public utility accounting. The production of the 10-K report involves a complex collaboration among the accountants in the regulatory department, the corporate attorneys, and the external auditors, all of whom must reach consensus on the content and the language of the report.

To begin the process, the accountants work in teams of two, dividing the reporting tasks among themselves. One member of each team prepares the numbers and written analyses while the other member reviews the work. The documents are then forwarded to the senior manager, who reviews them for accuracy and completeness, and to the director, who focuses on high-risk issues and narrative consistency. Documents may cycle back for revision once or several times during this initial stage.

When the accountants are satisfied with their report, it is passed on to the company's attorneys, who review the entire document for conformity with SEC regulations. The attorneys meet with the accountants and discuss the text line by line, questioning language, adding qualifications, tightening explanations. During meetings that may last for days, the two groups engage in lengthy negotiations until they craft language that will satisfy external regulations as well as create a readable report. Each revision is made by consensus of everyone present.

Next, the entire report is reviewed by an external auditor. If the auditor has problems with any part of the report, it is sent back to the regulatory accounting department for revision, after which it is once again discussed with the attorneys. The final step is review by the chief financial officer, who may make additions or send the report back through the cycle for further revision. The process is not complete until all parties to the project—accountants, attorneys, external auditors, and corporate executives—are satisfied with the document.

EFFECTIVE COLLABORATION: PUTTING IT INTO PRACTICE

Whether you contribute to a project anchored by someone else, engage in a document cycle with one other person, or participate in an elaborate, extended project involving many people and numerous meetings, you will at some point collaborate on the job. The remainder of this chapter offers practical guidelines to prepare you to do so.

The Structure of Groups

Group work in business settings is conducted in various ways, and different tasks call for different group structures. The interactive group—in which team members gather together, face-to-face, in the same room—is the structure most people associate with group work. With interactive groups, members have the advantage of mutual stimulation because team members can build on one another's ideas, process the nonverbal, as well as the verbal, messages of others, and respond simultaneously to ideas. When group tasks involve helping one another, bringing some members "up to speed" on concepts or procedures, or arriving at consensus, the interactive format is often the best choice.[6]

The interactive format is not the most productive one for other collaborative tasks, however. When the goal is to generate ideas—as in many types of planning and problem-solving projects—studies have repeatedly shown "nominal" groups to be more effective than interactive ones.[7] In nominal groups, the individual members work separately on a problem or task. The members feed their work to a group leader who summarizes the responses or compiles them in a master list. Some nominal groups meet face-to-face for later stages of group work; some never meet interactively at all. Computer-mediated communication has made it easier for organizations to use the nominal group structure. Because so much collaborative work begins with a process of idea generation, nominal groups are quite common, at least in early phases of a collaboration.

Generating Ideas

Brainstorming is the technique most groups use to get ideas flowing. In an oral brainstorming session, group members come together and take turns contributing ideas orally while the group leader writes the contributions down on a flipchart, whiteboard, or blackboard. Although the rules for brainstorming can vary, they usually require that members volunteer ideas without censoring them, withhold comment or criticism on the ideas others contribute, and let one person speak at a time.[8] In some small groups (six or fewer), this oral process can be quite effective. In larger groups, however, the need to take turns can slow down individual creativity because team members must wait so long to build on others' comments or volunteer new ideas of their own; and in groups where certain members dominate, the oral format can inhibit the contributions of other members. In many organizations, therefore, brainstorming is conducted electronically.

Electronic brainstorming is a form of computer-mediated communication that can involve geographically separated groups as well as those in the same location. Electronic brainstorming is usually conducted via specially designed software that allows each group member to view other members' contributions and build on others' ideas. For geographically disparate groups, electronic brainstorming usually takes place over intranets. Group members type their ideas into a computer that has a second "window" showing the ideas generated by others who are simultaneously brainstorming the problem.[9] For electronic brainstorming groups at the same location, many organizations have constructed specially-designed computer facilities with networked workstations.[10] As members enter their ideas into the computers, each person's contribution appears on a large screen that is visible to all.[11] A group leader helps keep the brainstorm on track by synthesizing responses and steering members to respond to new questions on the topic. For people who are naturally shy, for those on teams with their bosses, or for groups that would otherwise be dominated by certain members, anonymity can be a catalyst for the flow of ideas.

The Value of Conflict

Any group seeking an outcome that all members can accept inevitably experiences conflict. Indeed, conflict is the engine of the group process, providing the energy that drives creative thinking and problem solving. Thus collaborators should not avoid conflict but rather learn how to value and utilize their differences. Remember that the purpose of collaboration is to draw on differing perspectives and areas of expertise; collaborators must not rush to consensus before airing their differences. In other words, they must learn to differentiate their positions before integrating them.

By clarifying how they differ, group members have the chance to consider the broadest possible range of options. Groups that try to minimize conflict and stifle difference cheat themselves by agreeing prematurely on important decisions or by allowing certain members to dominate. Successful groups generate a wealth of ideas and tolerate the disagreements over ideas, information, conclusions, and opinions that arise from their differing perspectives. Such disagreement is a necessary step to reaching a common position on the final product and a prerequisite for high-quality group work.

Managing Conflict Constructively   To use conflict to your advantage in collaborative work, you must learn to encourage and manage conflict at each stage of the writing process: as you plan the project, brainstorm, and prewrite, consider initial drafts of your document or presentation, compare revisions, compile visual support, edit, and prepare the document for production. Here are some guidelines for constructive conflict management:

Emphasize cooperation, not competition. In your discussions, do not try to establish who is right and who is wrong, whose contribution is better, whose is worse. Instead, focus on exploring different perspectives to achieve the best possible outcome for the group.

Involve each member in group discussions. At the beginning of the process, establish a structure that includes all participants in every discussion. Ask each member to state his or her position clearly to get comments and reactions from other members. Treat each member's contribution with respect.

Highlight contrasting viewpoints. Encourage each member to analyze data, drafts, and approaches to the writing task and share those analyses with the group. This process will help you uncover weaknesses in your information, inadequacies in reasoning, failures to focus on the audience, failures to write for your reader, and areas where more research is needed.

Use good speaking and listening skills. Phrase your messages clearly, ask for feedback on messages sent, and ensure that your nonverbal signals are congruent with your verbal communications. In responding to others, restate and reframe the ideas they have conveyed and try to view their messages from their perspectives.

Be critical of ideas, not persons. A critical stance toward ideas, information, drafts, and revisions is essential in group work, but be sure to deliver your criticism in a context of appreciation for others' competence. Try to convey, "I disagree with your current position," not "That's a stupid idea."[12]

Ways to Prevent Groupthink   "Groupthink" is a theory of how group dynamics can create pressures to conform and thus get in the way of effective decision-making.[13] Groups that avoid conflict, downplay individual doubts, and assume consensus that is not there are guilty of groupthink. The strategies described in the previous section help groups tolerate conflict long enough to avoid groupthink and make decisions that represent the group's best effort.

As we noted in Chapter 6, numerous other techniques are used to help groups achieve true consensus and avoid groupthink. The Delphi technique, which is used in nominal groups to generate ideas and to support decision-making, involves several rounds of written questions and responses with each round summarized by the group leader.[14] Groups also use various voting systems to prioritize ideas and arrive at good decisions. Among these systems the most common are referendum voting (simple yes/no/abstain votes), multiple choice voting (given a set of several options, select a certain number), and preference ranking (rank the order of preference for a set of options).[15] Moreover, as we noted earlier, computer-based Group Decision-Support Systems (GDSS) help groups structure the process of their work from conception to final decision. GDSS leads group members through idea generation, discussion, prioritizing, voting, and consensus and does so in ways that help the group resist premature closure.[16] Because many universities now have intranets and sophisticated computer classrooms, you may have the chance to participate in computer-mediated group work before you enter the job market. Here are a few techniques you can use to avoid groupthink in student group work whether you are using electronic communications or not:

Critical evaluator. At each phase of the process, assign a member the role of critical evaluator. This person should make objections and air doubts about the discussions and decisions to help keep others from minimizing their disagreements.

Devil's advocate. Assign one or more group members the duty of challenging those who support the majority opinion about the document. Ask these devil's advocates to represent unpopular positions in the group to ensure that a range of opinions is represented.

Second-chance meeting. When you have reached a preliminary consensus on any part of the document or project, postpone the decision until you have held a second-chance meeting in which each member can express any doubts before reaching closure.[17]

Planning the Project

Bringing any collaborative communication task to a successful conclusion requires careful planning and time management as well as an understanding of group dynamics and process writing skills. Follow the seven steps listed next to lay the groundwork for a successful collaborative document or presentation.

1. *Appoint a group leader.* If your project involves primary-author collaboration, the group leader may have been previously assigned. In most Big Five engagement proposals, as we have seen, the firm's marketing director serves as group leader for the production of the document. He or she solicits information from different divisions, meets with each contributor, leads group meetings to discuss drafts and clarify objectives, and drafts the final document.

In a multiauthor collaboration, the group usually needs to select its own leader. Because group members share responsibility for the final product, the leader is primarily a project manager who keeps the collaboration on track, coordinates members' work and communications, and serves as liaison with management. Ideally, a group leader for this kind of collaboration should possess strong organizational, management, and listening skills, a diplomatic communication style, and an ability to bring projects in on deadline.

The group should assess each member as impartially as possible to determine who will perform these duties most effectively.

2. *Define the task/problem.* On the job, your task may be clearly defined for you. At other times, you will have to formulate a problem and define how your group will solve it. In class, your instructor may assign a multiauthor project involving the subject matter you have been studying and define the problem for you. On the other hand, you may have to analyze a case to formulate the problem for yourselves.

Whatever the source of the project, begin by making sure each group member understands the task. People bring different assumptions and conceptual frameworks to any task, and these differences can result in serious problems if not handled from the beginning. Together, you should specify in writing what you are trying to achieve. Use the worksheet provided in Figure 8.3. Each group member should receive a copy of the task statement and use it as a guide throughout the project.

Figure 8.3

Sample Task Statement Worksheet

WORKSHEET

Group Members:

Group Leader:

Project Title:

Audience(s):

Purpose/Desired Outcome:

Data Needed:

Special Factors (federal or state regulations; client history; etc.):

Definitions of Technical or Unfamiliar Terms:

Projected Completion Date:

3. *Analyze individual strengths.* When you work by yourself on writing projects, you probably work in certain habitual ways. You may always begin by making a list of the information you need, collecting that information, and creating an outline of your document. You may develop a sense of the whole document in your mind—complete with chains of argument, examples, and details—before you sit down at your computer. You may move quickly to completion, with plenty of time to revise before the deadline.

In writing collaboratively, however, you will find that others may not compose as you do. You may find yourself working with someone who procrastinates about getting started. This person may keep researching and mulling over the writing task until the deadline is practically at hand. Only then will he begin to write, and he will revise along the way, trying out one idea and then another, restructuring, rethinking, and arriving at a conclusion through the process of writing itself.

This person's method of writing is not necessarily inferior to yours. It is merely different. In fact, your colleague's tendency to leave conclusions open ended may be a valuable resource that helps the group explore all sides of important issues. Although differences in approach to the composing process, task orientation, and time management can be frustrating, an awareness of differences is important to group productivity. Such awareness can help groups make good decisions about how to divide a project into tasks and delegate those tasks appropriately.

Research has shown that different types of personalities display predictably different approaches to the writing process.[18] Some people, for example, approach a writing task by talking to others about it. These people tend to generate ideas easily by talking and discover their direction as they go along. Others prefer to plan alone, conceptualizing the whole document before beginning to write. Whereas writing is a process of discovery for the former, it is for the latter a matter of transcribing an already complete "internal document."

Some people begin composing by collecting data and organizing these data in a sequential step-by-step fashion. They work best with explicit instructions and clearly defined tasks; they want guidelines for preparing the document and want to follow them. Others begin with a general sense of patterns among data; they are less interested in explicit instructions, preferring to develop their own approaches to the task.

Some write by categorizing information into rational structures and filling in those structures with detail. Others write by envisioning the reader and accommodating that reader's needs and interests. Some move quickly into a composing task; others resist narrowing a task, preferring to consider possibilities and gather information until the last minute.[19]

With so many different approaches to the writing process, each member of a collaborative team needs to become aware of his or her writing process so potential problems can be identified and anticipated.

The worksheet in Figure 8.4 can help you begin to identify your habits, strengths, and weaknesses as a writer. Each group member should complete the worksheet and then meet with other members to discuss the responses.

Figure 8.4

Sample Self-Analysis Worksheet

WORKSHEET

Circle one choice from each pair. If both choices appeal to you, circle the one that describes your most common behavior. When you have completed the worksheet, write a paragraph or two describing your usual approach, from prewriting through editing.

To get started, I like to: a) Talk with others to get ideas flowing. b) Concentrate on the assignment by myself.

a) Figure out my thesis while I'm writing. b) Get a mental picture of the whole before I start.

a) Collect lots of facts. b) Develop my approach before researching.

a) Outline my ideas and data. b) Let structure emerge as I write.

a) Think about my main points. b) Think about my reader's needs.

a) Research quickly; begin writing early. b) Keep researching; consider different approaches.

To compose, I like to: a) Write freely until I catch my focus. b) Transcribe what's in my head.

a) Write about the data I've gathered. b) Write about my ideas.

a) Work from my outline. b) Watch my structure develop.

a) Focus on my information. b) Focus on my reader.

To revise, I like to: a) Do it as I go along. b) Write a full draft first and then rewrite.

a) Talk with others about my draft. b) Work from written feedback.

To edit, I am good at: a) Catching typos. b) Eliminating wordiness.

a) Getting the mechanics right. b) Tightening sentences.

My greatest strength as a writer is ————————————————

My greatest weakness as a writer is ———————————————

What most often causes writer's block for me is ———————————

My ideal collaborator would be someone who ————————————

When you have thoroughly investigated your different strengths and weaknesses, you are ready to assign tasks.

4. *Divide and delegate tasks.* Sometimes the project itself suggests an appropriate division of labor based on areas of expertise. For example, a manufacturing enterprise, having won a bid to manufacture products for a large international customer, prepares a capital expenditure authorization, a formal written document that provides elaborate details about how the product will be made and at what cost. The senior financial analyst might divide responsibilities for writing sections of the authorization document according to the functional areas in which each project team member works. Individuals from the cost accounting group, the financial analysis group, the product engineering group, and the marketing group might each contribute text to the document, which would be drafted to provide upper-level management with a complete overview of the operational and financial aspects of the new manufacturing contract.

On the other hand, you might divide tasks based on parts of the writing process. In class, for example, you may plan the project with the other students in your group while assigning research to one or two people (prewriting). You may agree to divide the drafting equally among yourselves by assigning one person to go over the drafts to unify voice and style (revising), another to the editing of the final manuscript, and another to creating graphics and presentation support.

5. *Establish procedures.* As we have seen, the dynamics of group work can be problematic. Everyone is busy, and many collaborative projects require work beyond regular job responsibilities or class meeting times. Co-workers from the same office often find scheduling meetings difficult; co-workers from different locations—and students with differing schedules—almost always have trouble meeting with one another. To minimize the potential for serious difficulties, anticipate problems from the beginning and clarify not only *what* will be done but *how* it will be done.

Will geography and schedules permit group members to get together regularly? If not, consider conducting meetings via conference call or computer conference.

Phone conferences. If group members can all be available at the same time, conference calls are a convenient alternative to face-to-face meetings. Most business telephone systems permit calls among multiple users, and many personal systems do as well. Using the conference call function, the group leader may call each member, one after the other, at an appointed time, adding him or her to the conference call. Phone conferences are ideal for groups whose members work in different buildings and for those whose members are separated geographically.

Computer conferences. As we noted earlier in the chapter, computer conferences are becoming more and more common in the business world. Groups whose members are physically distant but can agree on meeting times may choose to meet via synchronous computer conferences, as our global audit team did. In such conferences, each member is online at the same time, logged on from an individual workstation. Participants in synchronous conferences can communicate in writing, or they can use voice and even video channels to conduct meetings.

When schedule conflicts and physical distance make it difficult to meet, groups can communicate in asynchronous conferences. By sending e-mail to a central location, posting comments to a computer bulletin board, or using any of a number of group authoring software products, group members can communicate in writing by leaving messages in a location accessible to the entire group. Each member can retrieve and respond to messages as his or her own schedule permits.

Be sure to discuss the possibilities of phone and computer conferencing at this stage of your project. Write down phone numbers, e-mail addresses, and hours available for meetings. Discuss whether group members have access to special communication technologies that would facilitate conferencing.

Next, consider how the group leader will announce meetings. In person? By phone? Via e-mail? How will records of meetings be kept and distributed? Is accuracy important enough to merit a tape recorder?

Finally, discuss the methods the group will use to manage conflict and to avoid groupthink while fostering consensus. Ask yourselves how your group will assess progress and evaluate outcomes.

Use the worksheet in Figure 8.5 to clarify procedures. Circulate copies to all members of your group.

6. *Create a schedule.* Setting up and monitoring deadlines is one of the most important aspects of collaborative work. In addition to a completion date for each phase of the project, the schedule should include checkpoints for each task, dates and times of all meetings, and specifications of the person responsible for each step. Create your schedule by working backward from the final deadline. Use the time line worksheet in Figure 8.6 to help you.

Notice that this sample time line leaves enough time between checkpoints for flexibility. The group begins planning almost three months before the deadline and allows a full month between the planning meeting and the first draft due date. In addition, the group builds in time for two revisions: the first one performed by each member on his or her own draft, and the second, performed by a member selected for personal skill in revision and editing. The columns headed *status* and *further action required* provide a place for the group to check its progress, reassign deadlines in case a member is running late, and assign additional work if necessary. (Although it is very important that all group members meet the deadlines agreed on, the schedule must not be so tight that the project is jeopardized should a member fail to do so.)

7. *Draft individually; revise as a group.* Ideally, each group member should produce a draft of each part of the project, and the group should use meetings to discuss the drafts, cull the best elements of each one, and produce a composite draft. This procedure ensures that the final product represents each contributor's best efforts. When the composite draft is complete, one person should revise it further to create a consistent voice.

The remainder of this chapter illustrates how a student team in an undergraduate tax course used the guidelines in this chapter to complete a multiauthor, multidocument writing project.

Figure 8.5

Sample Group Procedures Worksheet

WORKSHEET

Name of Project:
Group Members:
Group Leader:
Procedures

Conducting Meetings
    Face to face/when/where
    Conference calls/when/how
    Computer conferences/when/how
    Combination (explain)

Scheduling Meetings
    Who will call meetings?
    How often?

Recording Meetings
    Who will keep records?
    How (tape recorder, notes)?
    How will records be distributed?

Communicating Between Meetings
    Phone? List members' numbers:
    E-mail? List members' addresses:

Managing Conflict
    How will group involve each member?
    How will group highlight contrasting viewpoints?
    Who will be critical evaluator/when?
    Who will be devil's advocate/when?

Assessing Progress
    What are we trying to evaluate?
    How? (Attach evaluation instrument)

Figure 8.6

Sample Time Line Worksheet

WORKSHEET

Name of Project:
Group Members:
Group Leader:

Task	Member Responsible	Status	Date	Further Action Required
Oral Presentation	Terry		4/22	
Slide Show Production	Kate		4/15–4/20	
Report Production	Chris		4/15–4/20	
Final Corrections	Jim		4/13	
Meeting 5: Final Proofing	All		4/11	
Final Ms. Production	Chris		4/5–4/10	
Final Edit	Jim		3/28–4/2	
Meeting 4: Assemble Illustrations	Chris/Kate		3/25	
Approve Draft	All			
Revision 2	Kate		3/12–3/24	
Meeting 3: Group Review	All		3/11	
Revision 1	All		3/5–3/10	
Meeting 2: Assemble Draft and Preliminary Illustrations	All		3/4	
Individual Drafting	All		2/15–3/3	
Research Complete	Terry/Jim		2/15	
Meeting 1: Plan Project	All		1/28	

Meeting Times	Recorder	Date
Meeting 5 8–10 a.m.	Terry	(4/11)
Meeting 4 1–3 p.m.	Kate	(3/25)
Meeting 3 1–3 p.m.	Jim	(3/11)
Meeting 2 8–10 a.m.	Chris	(3/4)
Meeting 1 1–3 p.m.	Terry	(1/28)

The team was charged with preparing for a new tax client an individual federal income tax return and a letter to the client explaining the return and providing instructions for filing.[20]

After an initial meeting in which they selected a leader, the group defined its task, using a task statement worksheet (Figure 8.7). Next, they agreed on procedures for group interaction (Figure 8.8) and created a time line of tasks (Figure 8.9). At this point, each member completed the Writing Process Self-Analysis Worksheet (see Figure 8.4) and produced a written summary of it to share with the group (Figures 8.10a, b, and c). Notice that one group member mentions needing to talk with others early in the process to generate ideas and opinions; another describes having difficulty getting started. Initial meetings to discuss the scope and direction of the project are very important for writers such as these. Although each member reports working from an outline, two of the three say that they continue researching after the outline is completed and the drafting begun. In contrast, the third describes gathering data, outlining, and "transcribing" his thoughts from the outline. In groups such as this one, it is

---

Figure 8.7

Completed Task Statement Worksheet

WORKSHEET

Group Members: Kerri Jones, Dennis Davis, Joe Smith
Group Leader: Dennis Davis
Project Title: Tax Engagement Project
Audience(s): Charles and Joanne Martin
Managing Partner, Ms. Ross
IRS

Purpose/Desired Outcome: To present an accurate representation of Charles and Joanne Martin's tax liability, to maximize deductions for the Martins, and to achieve all possible tax savings.

Data Needed: Charles Martin's W-2 for 1996
Social Security numbers: Charles, Joanne, and children
Filing status: Married filing jointly or separately
Dependency status of their children

Special Factors: Details on Martins' change of residence
Details on Charles Martin's business expenses

Definitions of Technical or Unfamiliar Terms: N/A

Projected Completion Date: April 15, 1997

Figure 8.8

Completed Group Procedures Worksheet

WORKSHEET

Name of Project: *tax engagement project*

Group Members: *Dennis Davis, Kerri Jones, Joe Smith*

Procedures

Group Leader: *Dennis Davis*

Conducting Meetings
Face to face/when/where *3-4 times weekly*
Campus library (evening)
Cabor Hall Rm 1 (T, Th 12:30-1:30)
Conference calls/when/how
Computer conferences/when/how
Combination (explain)

Scheduling Meetings
Who will call meetings? *Dennis*
How often? *approximately 3-4 times a week, including class meetings.*

Recording Meetings
Who will keep records? *Kerri*
How (tape recorder, notes)? *notes*
How will records be distributed? *in the form of minutes distributed the day after the meeting.*

Communicating Between Meetings
Phone? List members' numbers: *Kerri → 555-1234*
Dennis → 555-3456
Joe → 555-6789
E-mail? List members' addresses: *Kerri → Kaj@email.tu.edu*
Dennis → ddd@email.tu.edu
Joe → jas@email.tu.edu

Managing Conflict
How will group involve each member? *by collaborating individual efforts to achieve a balanced joint agreement.*
How will group highlight contrasting viewpoints? *by analyzing the pros and cons of each individual effort to develop an overriding consensus.*
Who will be critical evaluator/When? } *through each phase of the project,*
Who will be devil's advocate/When? } *the team will alternate roles as both critical evaluator and devil's advocate.*

Assessing Progress
What are we trying to evaluate? *the tax liability of Charles and Joanne Martin.*
How? (Attach evaluation instrument) *see attachments. Additional forms may be added once all information is received.*

Figure 8.9

Completed Group Time Line

Time Line

Name of Project: Tax Engagement Project
Group Members: Dennis Davis, Kerri Jones & Joe Smith
Group Leader: Dennis Davis

Task	Member Responsible	Status	Date	Further Action Required
Meeting 6: **Prepare for Client Meeting**	All		4/7	
Prepare Agenda	Kerri		4/6	
Deliver Documents	Dennis		4/3	
Produce Minutes	Kerri		4/2	
Meeting 5: **Final Proofing**	All		4/2	
Prepare Agenda	Kerri		4/1	
Produce 1996 1040	Dennis		4/1	
Produce Transmittal Letter	Joe		4/1	
Produce Short Report	Joe		4/1	
Final Edit	Kerri		3/31	
Produce Minutes	Kerri		3/31	
Meeting 4: **Assemble Illustrations Revise Drafts**	All		3/31	
Prepare Agenda	Kerri		3/30	
Draft Individual Transmittal Letters and Short Reports	All		3/29	
Research Memos	Joe		3/29	
Make Individual Information Inquiries	All		3/28	
E-Mail Transmission of Individual Work Assignments Memo	Joe		3/28	
Produce Minutes	Kerri		3/28	
Meeting 3: **Assemble Illustrations Revise Drafts**	All		3/28	
Produce Time Line	Dennis		3/28	
Make General Information Inquiry	Dennis		3/28	
Prepare Agenda	Kerri		3/27	
Draft Individual Work Assignments Memo	All		3/27	

Figure 8.10 a and b

Writing Self-Assessment Statement

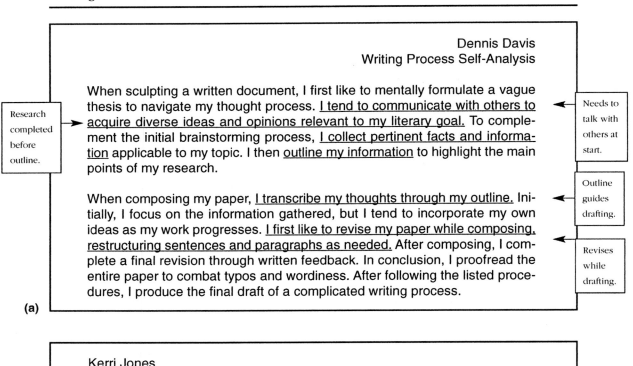

Dennis Davis
Writing Process Self-Analysis

When sculpting a written document, I first like to mentally formulate a vague thesis to navigate my thought process. I tend to communicate with others to acquire diverse ideas and opinions relevant to my literary goal. To complement the initial brainstorming process, I collect pertinent facts and information applicable to my topic. I then outline my information to highlight the main points of my research.

When composing my paper, I transcribe my thoughts through my outline. Initially, I focus on the information gathered, but I tend to incorporate my own ideas as my work progresses. I first like to revise my paper while composing, restructuring sentences and paragraphs as needed. After composing, I complete a final revision through written feedback. In conclusion, I proofread the entire paper to combat typos and wordiness. After following the listed procedures, I produce the final draft of a complicated writing process.

Research completed before outline.

Needs to talk with others at start.

Outline guides drafting.

Revises while drafting.

(a)

Kerri Jones
Writing Process Self-Analysis

When I begin to work on a paper or project, I have the most trouble pinpointing a specific topic. Once I finally decide on a topic, however, I move forward nicely. The first thing I do after I decide on my topic is to begin researching the topic. I usually spend a few hours doing this in the beginning. I develop my thesis from this research. This thesis allows me to outline the course my paper or project will be taking. The outline provides me with a guide to follow; however, it does not limit me to a certain course. As I begin writing, I continue to research. This research aids in answering questions I may develop throughout the paper. I write a full draft of my paper this way.

Once I have a completed rough draft, I read it over and make corrections accordingly. I also print a copy out and give it to either a friend or a teacher to proofread. I take any suggestions I receive and adjust my work as I feel it should be. I then type up a new draft and proofread it. Usually this draft is my final draft.

Needs to brainstorm with others at start.

Outline precedes completion of research.

Revises using input from others after drafting.

(b)

Figure 8.10 c

Writing Self-Assessment Statement

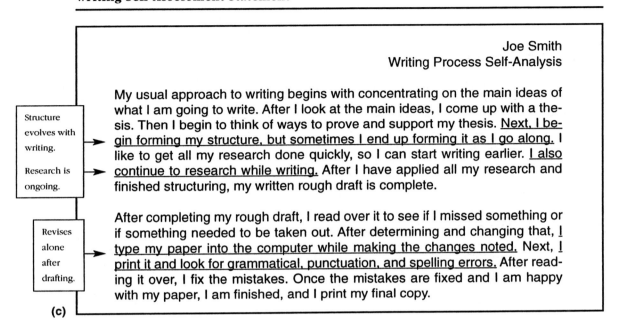

Joe Smith
Writing Process Self-Analysis

Structure evolves with writing.

Research is ongoing.

My usual approach to writing begins with concentrating on the main ideas of what I am going to write. After I look at the main ideas, I come up with a thesis. Then I begin to think of ways to prove and support my thesis. <u>Next, I begin forming my structure, but sometimes I end up forming it as I go along.</u> I like to get all my research done quickly, so I can start writing earlier. <u>I also continue to research while writing.</u> After I have applied all my research and finished structuring, my written rough draft is complete.

Revises alone after drafting.

After completing my rough draft, I read over it to see if I missed something or if something needed to be taken out. After determining and changing that, <u>I type my paper into the computer while making the changes noted.</u> Next, <u>I print it and look for grammatical, punctuation, and spelling errors.</u> After reading it over, I fix the mistakes. Once the mistakes are fixed and I am happy with my paper, I am finished, and I print my final copy.

(c)

important for all members to understand their differing writing processes before the writing begins. With an understanding of these differences, members can use the group process techniques described in this chapter to plan how they will make effective use of their differences. Otherwise, the people who like to keep researching and incorporating new material throughout the entire drafting phase will annoy the person who researches, outlines, and drafts in sequential order.

As the team's time line in Figure 8.9 indicates, the students met frequently to review progress and to synthesize drafts. The minutes illustrated in Figure 8.11 show their record keeping. Note that the minutes begin by indicating who was present and at what time the meeting began, summarize in list format actions taken, and close by indicating what time the meeting ended. The minutes also show how the group combined individual drafts of the transmittal letter to produce a collaboratively written document.

To produce the multiauthor transmittal letter, the students were asked to write individual drafts and instructed to meet, critique each draft, and compile the best elements of each draft into a single collaboratively written document. Figures 8.12a, b, and c show the individual drafts the students produced.

As they compared their drafts, the group members noticed some common weaknesses:

■ Each of the drafts offers more information than the clients need. It is not necessary, for example, to explain how taxable income was calculated

Figure 8.11

Minutes from Group Meeting

MINUTES

Tax Engagement Project—Group #4 (Davis, Jones, Smith)
April 5, 1997

1. Called meeting to order at 12:30 p.m. in Room 108 of Cabor Hall, 1st Floor.

2. Joe printed out all tax forms and schedules we need to complete the final 1040 for our client.

3. Reviewed each member's transmittal letter. Pieced parts from the different letters together to form a final transmittal letter. Typed up the final letter. Added a signature request and the date by when it needed to be filed. Printed out final letter request.

4. Kerri reminded all the members of the group to initial each memo they write.

5. Dennis began copying information from the rough draft of the 1040 onto the final copy of the 1040.

6. Scheduled next meeting for Saturday, April 7, 1997 at 1:00 p.m. in Campus Library, 1st Floor.

7. Meeting adjourned at 1:49 p.m.

(draft 1); nor is it necessary to break down the amounts saved in each deduction (draft 2). And information on future tax savings (draft 3) more appropriately belongs in the tax planning report (to be included in the client's packet) than in the transmittal letter. For the final document, the group decided to eliminate all of this information.

■ Each of the drafts uses language that is inappropriate for nonexpert readers (we took out all of your *deductions for AGI,* we were able to deduct $6,500 of employee business expenses, *net of reimbursements,* from taxable income, . . . the $4,400 reimbursement Mr. Martin received under *an accountable plan*). This language was changed for the final draft as well.

Working together, the group crafted a final document that drew on the best elements of each draft, condensed explanations, recast technical language, and assumed an appropriate rhetorical stance to the reader. They used the

Figure 8.12a

Client Letter Draft No. 1

LETTER

Dennis Davis

Dear Mr. and Mrs. Martin:

After looking at all the information provided, we have finished your form 1040 and arrived at your tax refund. As you requested, we marked no $$ for the presidential election campaign. We concluded that the wisest way for you to file is married filing jointly. You have five exemption deductions that you were able to claim in 1996: one each for you and your spouse, and three for your children. The total of your wages, salaries, and tips was $40,345.

To arrive at total income, we had to include your interest and dividend income of $284 and $170, which comes to $40,799 for total income. To arrive at AGI, we took out all of your deductions for AGI. The only deduction for AGI that we could deduct was your moving expenses. Not all your moving expenses were deductible. The only two amounts that were deductible were .10 a mile for transportation and $800 for the moving company. After taking out these amounts we arrived at an AGI of $39,900. Next, to arrive at taxable income we had to take out the larger of your itemized or standard deductions. Your itemized deductions were far more than your standard deductions. Your itemized deductions were far more than your standard deductions for the year. Your itemized deductions were comprised of:

(Take from form 1040)

We are happy to inform you that your refund will be $1,500. Please sign your tax forms and mail them to the IRS in the enclosed envelopes by April 15, 1997.

Sincerely,

Annotations:

Paragraph jumps from point to point.

Overkill: Reader does not need this information.

Jargon

Good, clear "action in closing."

Figure 8.12b

Client Letter Draft No. 2

LETTER

Kerri Jones

Dear Charles and Joanne,

We would like to inform you that we have successfully completed your 1996 income tax return. We are delighted to announce that you will be receiving a $1,500 tax refund from the federal government. In 1996 your income totaled $40,799. As a result of the information you provided us, we were able to reduce your taxable income to maximize your refund.

> Omit or move.

Because you moved over 50 miles from your previous residence, we were able to reduce your taxable income by $809: $800 for the moving van expenses and $9 for car mileage at 10 cents per mile. However, the meal expenses incurred during travel and the security deposit placed on a new apartment are nondeductible personal expenses.

> Needs clarification.

> Does reader need/want this much detail?

As a result of the taxes and interest paid, we were able to further reduce taxable income by $13,259. Under the law, we were then entitled to reduce your taxable income by $2,550 per family member.

Additionally, we were able to deduct $6,500 of employee business expenses, <u>net of reimbursements</u> from taxable income. However, the meal and lodging expenses not related to overnight business travel are nondeductible. Nonetheless, those related to overnight business travel, and all business-related entertainment, are only 50 percent deductible.

> Jargon

Finally, we diminished the tax due by the qualifying amount of child-care expenses, or $960. These procedures summarize the contributing factors that led to the maximization of your refund. Please file your tax forms in the enclosed envelope. Without any complications, your refund will be issued in 40 days.

> Does reader need to know this point?

We hope you are pleased with the results of our analysis. We thank you for your business and wish you a safe and healthy year.

> Date needed.

Sincerely,

> Good closing.

Figure 8.12c

Client Letter Draft No. 3

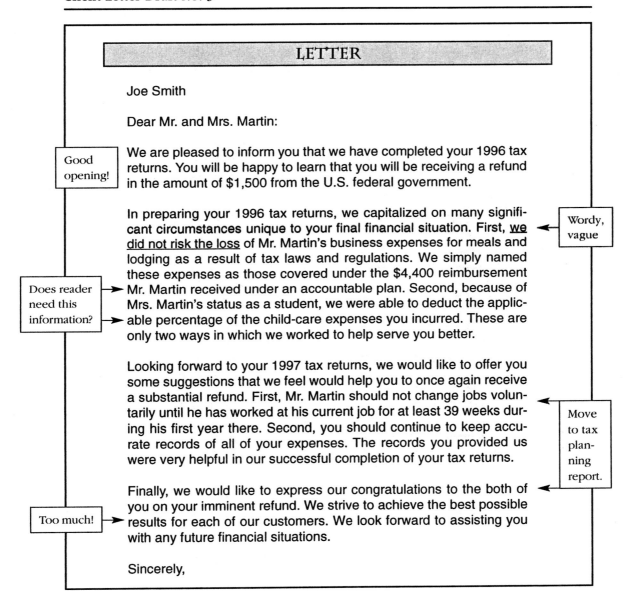

LETTER

Joe Smith

Dear Mr. and Mrs. Martin:

Good opening!

We are pleased to inform you that we have completed your 1996 tax returns. You will be happy to learn that you will be receiving a refund in the amount of $1,500 from the U.S. federal government.

In preparing your 1996 tax returns, we capitalized on many significant circumstances unique to your final financial situation. First, <u>we did not risk the loss</u> of Mr. Martin's business expenses for meals and lodging as a result of tax laws and regulations. We simply named these expenses as those covered under the $4,400 reimbursement Mr. Martin received under an accountable plan. Second, because of Mrs. Martin's status as a student, we were able to deduct the applicable percentage of the child-care expenses you incurred. These are only two ways in which we worked to help serve you better.

Wordy, vague

Does reader need this information?

Looking forward to your 1997 tax returns, we would like to offer you some suggestions that we feel would help you to once again receive a substantial refund. First, Mr. Martin should not change jobs voluntarily until he has worked at his current job for at least 39 weeks during his first year there. Second, you should continue to keep accurate records of all of your expenses. The records you provided us were very helpful in our successful completion of your tax returns.

Move to tax planning report.

Finally, we would like to express our congratulations to the both of you on your imminent refund. We strive to achieve the best possible results for each of our customers. We look forward to assisting you with any future financial situations.

Too much!

Sincerely,

Figure 8.13

Client Letter, Written Collaboratively

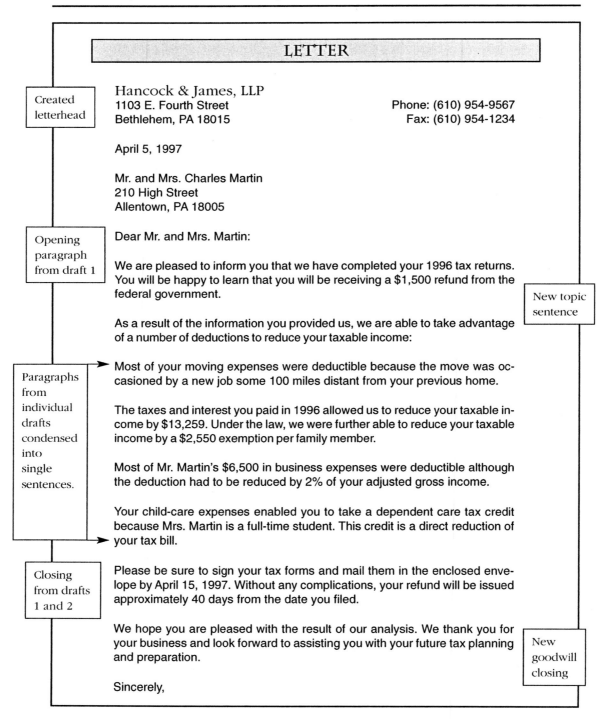

Created letterhead

Hancock & James, LLP
1103 E. Fourth Street
Bethlehem, PA 18015

Phone: (610) 954-9567
Fax: (610) 954-1234

April 5, 1997

Mr. and Mrs. Charles Martin
210 High Street
Allentown, PA 18005

Opening paragraph from draft 1

Dear Mr. and Mrs. Martin:

We are pleased to inform you that we have completed your 1996 tax returns. You will be happy to learn that you will be receiving a $1,500 refund from the federal government.

New topic sentence

As a result of the information you provided us, we are able to take advantage of a number of deductions to reduce your taxable income:

Paragraphs from individual drafts condensed into single sentences.

Most of your moving expenses were deductible because the move was occasioned by a new job some 100 miles distant from your previous home.

The taxes and interest you paid in 1996 allowed us to reduce your taxable income by $13,259. Under the law, we were further able to reduce your taxable income by a $2,550 exemption per family member.

Most of Mr. Martin's $6,500 in business expenses were deductible although the deduction had to be reduced by 2% of your adjusted gross income.

Your child-care expenses enabled you to take a dependent care tax credit because Mrs. Martin is a full-time student. This credit is a direct reduction of your tax bill.

Closing from drafts 1 and 2

Please be sure to sign your tax forms and mail them in the enclosed envelope by April 15, 1997. Without any complications, your refund will be issued approximately 40 days from the date you filed.

We hope you are pleased with the result of our analysis. We thank you for your business and look forward to assisting you with your future tax planning and preparation.

New goodwill closing

Sincerely,

opening paragraph from draft 3. They combined statements from drafts 1 and 2 for the closing and together added a final goodwill statement requesting future business. For the body of the letter, they summarized the key paragraphs of each letter in a sentence or two, introduced them with a topic sentence, and formatted them in a bulleted list. Look at their revision in Figure 8.13.

CONCLUSION

The techniques and worksheets provided in this chapter will help you bring any collaborative project to a successful conclusion. Remember these points:

- Manage conflict constructively
- Choose your group leader carefully
- Define your task clearly; put it in writing
- Assess and discuss the strengths of each individual in the group
- Establish procedures for group interaction; put them in writing
- Create a schedule with reasonable deadlines and stick to it
- Draft individually; revise as a group

Whether you are anchoring a primary-author collaboration, contributing to a collaborative project directed by someone else, or working as one of several individuals on a multiauthor project, these guidelines will help you do effective group work.

NOTES

[1]James Paradis, David Dobrin, and Richard Miller, "Writing at Exxon ITD: Notes on the Writing Environment of an R & D Organization," in *Writing in Nonacademic Settings,* eds. Lee Odell and Dixie Goswami (New York: Guilford Press, 1985): 281–308; Evelyn Jaffe Schreiber, "From Academic Writing to Job-Related Writing," *IEEE Transactions on Professional Communication* 36, no. 4 (December 1993): 178–184; and Craig Hansen, "Writing the Project Team: Authority and Intertextuality in a Corporate Setting," *Journal of Business Communications* 32, no. 2 (April 1995): 103–122.

[2]Lisa Ede and Andrea Lunsford, *Singular Texts/Plural Authors/ Perspectives on Collaborative Writing* (Carbondale: Southern Illinois University Press, 1990).

[3]Mary Munter, "Meeting Technology: From Low-Tech to High-Tech," *Business Communications Quarterly* 61, no. 2 (June 1998): 80–87.

[4]The advantages listed here are adapted from Mike Markel in *Technical Communication: Situations and Strategies,* 4th ed. (New York: St. Martin's Press, 1996): 48–49.

[5]Lester Faigley and Thomas P. Miller, "What We Learn from Writing on the Job," *College English* 44, no. 6 (October 1982): 557–569.

[6]Robert I. Sutton and Andrew Hargadon, "Brainstorming Groups in Context: Effectiveness in a Product Design Firm," *Administrative Science Quarterly,* vol. 41, no. 4, December 1996: 685–718.

[7]More than 80 studies have found nominal groups more effective in generating unique, high-quality ideas than interactive groups. See Alan R. Dennis and Joseph S. Valacich, "Group, Sub-Group, and Nominal Group Idea Generation: New Rules for a New Media?" *Journal of Management,* vol. 20, no. 4, Winter 1994: 723–737; Philip L. Roth, Lydia L.F. Schleifer, and Fred S. Switzer, "Nominal Group Technique: An Aid in Implementing TQM," *The CPA Journal,* vol. 65, no. 5, May 1995: 68–69; Michael Diehl and Wolfgang Stroebe, "Productivity Loss in Idea Generating Groups: Toward a Solution of the Riddle," *Journal of Personality and Social Psychology,* vol. 53, 1987: 497–509.

[8]Alex F. Osborn, *Applied Imagination: Principles and Procedures for Creative Problem-Solving* (New York: Scribner's, 1957).

[9] Brent R. Gallupe, Lana M. Bastianutti, and William H. Cooper, "Unblocking Brainstorms," *Journal of Applied Psychology,* vol. 76, no. 1, 1991: 137–143; Joseph S. Valacich, Alan R. Dennis, and Terry Connolly, "Idea Generation in Computerbased Groups: A New Ending to an Old Story," *Organizational Behavior and Human Decision Processes,* vol. 57, 1994: 444–467.

[10]Dennis and Valacich, 1994.

[11]Lynne M. Scalia and Benjamin Sackmary, "Groupware and Computer-Supported Collaborative Work in the College Classroom," *Business Communications Quarterly,* vol. 59, no. 4, December 1996: 98–111.

[12]Adapted from David W. Johnson and Frank P. Johnson, *Joining Together: Group Theory and Group Skills* (Englewood Cliffs, NJ: Prentice Hall, 1987): 245–246.

[13]Clark McCauley, "Group Dynamics in Janis's Theory of Groupthink: Backward and Forward," *Organizational Behavior and Human Decision Processes,* vol. 73, nos. 2/3, February/March 1998: 142–162; Irving L. Janis, *Victims of Groupthink* (Boston: Houghton Mifflin, 1972).

[14]Philip L. Roth, Lydia L.F. Schleifer, and Fred S. Switzer, "Nominal Group Technique: An Aid in Implementing TQM," *The CPA Journal,* vol. 65, no. 5, May 1995: 68–69.

[15]B. Gavish, J. Gerdes Jr., and S. Sridhar, "CM3: A Distributed Group Decision Support System (Computer-Mediated Meeting Management)," *IIE Transactions,* vol. 27, no. 6, December 1995: 722–734.

[16]Lynne M. Scalia and Benjamin Sackmary, "Groupware and Computer-Supported Collaborative Work in the College Classroom," *Business Communications Quarterly,* vol. 59, no. 4, December 1996: 98–111.

[17]Johnson and Johnson, p. 122.

[18]George H. Jensen and John K. DiTiberio, "Personality and Individual Writing Processes," *College Composition and Communication* 35, no. 3 (October 1984): 285–300.

[19]Adapted from Jensen and DiTiberio.

[20]This assignment was based on the federal tax laws and forms in effect for the tax year 1996.

EXERCISES

You will play the role of accountants who work for a regional accounting firm in its Advisory Services Division. Teams of three or four students will evaluate the business possibilities of these clients, each of whom is considering starting up a new business.

Client Profiles

- **John Reilly** is a recent retiree from a large financial house in an East Coast city with a population of approximately 400,000. The downtown area has a thriving financial district, and most people live on the outskirts, where there are two large malls (one of either side of town).

John plans to use part of his nest egg to live his dream—to run his own pub! He has asked your advice about whether he should rent or buy a building and whether he should open his pub in center city or on the outskirts near one of the malls. He is prepared to part with $50,000 of his nest egg to use for a down payment (if he buys), equipment, supplies, redecorating, inventory of food and drink, and marketing.

John is married to Alma, who is also retired, and they would like to maintain a lifestyle similar to their current one by clearing $80,000 per year before taxes.

- **Katie Wilson** is a recent graduate of the Fashion Institute, and her parents have given her a graduation gift of $50,000 with which to start her own boutique. She wants to locate her business near a major midwestern city, ideally in a suburban area where many malls, both upscale and budget, are located.

  Katie needs help deciding what kind of market (and clothing) she wants to target, and she will require $40,000 per year in profits before taxes to support herself. Her $50,000 graduation cash is available for leasing space in a mall, for decorating, and for purchasing a start-up inventory of clothing.

- **Jessica Smith and Joanne Larsen** are recent Beauty Academy graduates and have decided to form a partnership to open and operate a hair salon. They plan to open their salon in a West Coast university town, where the population diminishes by approximately 80% of the student body during the summer months. Jessica and Joanne need business start-up advice as well as advice on how to manage the seasonal nature of their future clientele.

  Jessica and Joanne each has $2,500 to contribute toward the business, which will require equipment, furniture, supplies, inventory of products to sell, and redecoration of the facilities, which will be rented. They each require $20,000 per year before taxes for living expenses.

The Engagement

The engagement requires creating a business plan consisting of three sections:

The marketing plan: A description of your product or service and of possible marketing strategies. Consider the trends and outlook for the industry, your client's service and how to differentiate it, traits and demographics of potential customers, and the nature of any competition.

The operating plan: A description of strategies for operating the business, such as facilities, number of employees, equipment needs, and organizational structure. The plan should also include a cost-benefit analysis for alternative locations, prices, and volumes.

The financial plan: Five-year projected income statements, balance sheets and statements of cash flows, with any notes and disclosures; a description of funds that will be needed and the team's recommendation for obtaining those funds.

Your research should include both print and electronic sources.

Collaborative Writing Tasks

1. As a group, develop a plan for managing the engagement. Then write a memo to the firm's partner-in-charge, Michael McKeever, in which the team summarizes its plan for managing the engagement.

   a. Appoint a group leader and define the team's task by completing a Task Statement Worksheet (Figure 8.3). Analyze the strengths of team members by individually completing the Writing Process Self-Analysis Worksheet (Figure 8.4) and then meeting to discuss the responses.

   b. Divide and delegate tasks and establish procedures for completing the project. Complete a Group Procedures Worksheet (Figure 8.5).

   c. Create a schedule by completing a Time Line Worksheet (Figure 8.6).

   d. Using the multiauthor approach discussed in this chapter (individual drafting, group revising), write the memo summarizing your plan.

   e. Attach all worksheets and drafts for Mr. McKeever's review.

2. As a group, produce the appropriate written documentation for a meeting in which you will discuss the team's plan for managing the engagement with the firm's partner-in-charge, Mr. McKeever.

   a. Complete all worksheets (see number 1).

   b. Prepare a written agenda for the meeting.

   c. Using the multiauthor approach discussed in this chapter (individual drafting, group revising), write a memo inviting Mr. McKeever to the meeting.

   d. Attach all worksheets and drafts for Mr. McKeever's review.

   e. Conduct the meeting (with your instructor or a class member assuming the role of McKeever).

   f. Prepare minutes of the meeting for submission to Mr. McKeever.

3. Use the multiauthor approach to write the marketing plan for your client's prospective business. The plan should be in the form of a short report (see Chapter 5).

   a. Complete all worksheets (as listed earlier).

   b. Individually: Conduct research and write a memo to the client file describing the results of research you have performed. Correctly record Web site addresses, references to articles or other publications, names of individuals interviewed, and so on.

   c. As a group: Summarize these memos to create an initial draft of the plan.

   d. Conduct a meeting to review the draft. Appoint one group member to maintain minutes of team meetings. Minutes should provide information on who was present at the meeting, what was discussed, who contributed particular ideas and efforts toward the project, and important conclusions that were drawn.

   e. Conduct an interim meeting with the client (your instructor or a designated class member) during which the team discusses its preliminary findings and the proposed marketing plan. Ask the client for ideas and suggestions, and be willing to consider incorporating them into the plan.

f. Working together, revise the marketing plan to incorporate the client's ideas and submit to the client in the form of a report.

g. Attach all worksheets and drafts.

4. Produce a transmittal letter to the client summarizing the report.
   a. Individually: Draft a transmittal letter.
   b. As a group: Create a single multiauthor letter that draws on each individual's draft.
   c. Attach all worksheets and drafts.

5. Follow the guidelines in tasks 3 and 4 to produce a report and transmittal letter describing the operating plan. Attach all worksheets and drafts.

6. Follow the guidelines in tasks 3 and 4 to produce a report and transmittal letter describing the financial plan. Attach all worksheets and drafts.

7. Use the multiauthor approach to combine the marketing, operating, and financial plans in a substantial report to the client that provides details and explanations of findings, ideas, and recommendations. The report should be accompanied by a transmittal letter. Attach all worksheets and drafts.

CHAPTER 9

Communicating Financial Information: Annual Reports and 10-Ks

To communicate about their financial performance, companies use the language of accounting. All businesspeople need to understand this language because it is the standard means of communicating about numbers in the business world. In most business environments, accountants are responsible for monitoring business transactions, translating them into accounting language, and recording them in the accounting records. When accountants compile the accumulated records in a standardized, logical fashion, these records become the client's or company's financial statements. These statements provide the basis for all of the company's significant external communications about its operations and performance.

For publicly traded companies, these external communications frequently involve disclosures mandated by the Securities and Exchange Commission (SEC). Established in the wake of the 1929 stock market crash to enhance the integrity of U.S. financial markets, the SEC requires all publicly traded companies to make periodic public disclosures about their financial performance. Among the most important of these disclosures are annual reports—the Form 10-K Annual Report (10-K Report) and the Annual Report to Shareholders (Annual Report)—that companies must issue after the close of each fiscal year. In these reports, companies provide timely and accurate information on their past year's financial performance, including details on their operations, holdings, assets, income, the price of their stock, and other matters relevant to their financial health.

Many interested parties, including private investors, investment analysts, stockbrokers, credit and bond rating analysts, and others, consult annual reports for information about a company and the quality of its financial performance. Some of these people, in turn, use their analyses and interpretations to communicate to other interested parties who are making strategic business decisions about, for example, investing in the company's stock or lending the company money.

As an accounting student, you will most likely study annual reports in your financial accounting course while you are beginning to master the terms and concepts of financial accounting and learning to analyze financial statements. Although you may never be called on to write sections of an annual report, you will spend much of your career communicating about financial information. The principles that shape annual report writing—and that allow companies to communicate financial data to various audiences, including nonfinancial readers—will be useful to you in many contexts, from corporate accounting to tax and audit practice.

In this chapter, we introduce you to annual reports as communication tools for corporations. We focus on the analyses involved in these communications as well as the rhetorical principles that shape them. Then we examine the ways that members of the investment community use annual reports.

COMMUNICATING FINANCIAL INFORMATION THROUGH THE 10-K REPORT

The purpose of the 10-K Report is to furnish the government, and thereby the general public, with complete information about companies in which the public invests its money. The 10-K Report contains the full audited financial statements for the year as well as other financial information specified by the SEC. The 10-K Report is due 90 days after the company's fiscal year-end or by March 31 of each year, and it must be filed electronically, under the commission's Electronic Data Gathering, Analysis, and Retrieval system (EDGAR).[1, 2]

After the 10-K Reports are filed, SEC members review them to see that they are complete, that they comply with standards of financial reporting such as GAAP and FASB rules, and that they are comparable in quality to reports filed in prior years and to those filed by other companies in similar industries.

Contents of the 10-K Report

The 10-K Report normally includes the following:[3]

1. Identification information about the company such as address, employer ID number, and so forth
2. Description of the properties owned by the company
3. Description of any legal proceedings and possible litigation losses
4. Detailed financial information, including
   - a multiyear summary of key financial information
   - the financial statements: the statement of earnings, the balance sheets, the statement of cash flows, and the statement of shareholders' equity
   - notes to the financial statements, which amplify or explain items in the financial statements themselves
   - the independent auditors' report
   - recent stock price information
   - quarterly summaries of unaudited financial data
5. A "Management's Discussion and Analysis," which discusses trends, events, or other uncertainties that are likely to have effects on the company's future operations or financial affairs[4]
6. Names and addresses of directors and officers of the company

7. Information about directors, executive officers, and executive compensation
8. Signatures of responsible individuals.

Because 10-K Reports are essentially compliance documents—prepared to demonstrate that the company is operating properly according to governmental regulations—they are almost always written collaboratively by staff from a company's legal department as well as by its accountants, managers, and executives. The job of attorneys on the drafting team is to ensure that the language of the report is sufficiently inclusive on the one hand and sufficiently precise on the other to protect the company from charges of misrepresentation. Because the authors must consider potential liability issues, 10-K Reports are usually full of legal and technical language, elaborate definitions and disclaimers, and high levels of detail. The sample in Figure 9.1 from the 1997 10-K Report of Guess?, Inc., illustrates the formal style as well as the rhetorical situation typical of 10-K Reports.

From the first page, you can see that the report is set up to provide required data; the only information on the page is that requested by the SEC, and it is requested in a series of closed questions ("Exact name of registrant as specified in its charter, IRS Employer Identification No.," and so forth). This initial form structures information as a summary but permits only certain pieces of information to appear. The rigid structuring ensures that the data the company communicates to its publics through the SEC is standardized and therefore easily comparable to that of other companies.

Disclaimer About "Forward-Looking Statements"

Figure 9.2, an excerpt from Part I of Guess?, Inc.'s 10-K Report, begins with a legal disclaimer about "forward-looking statements." This disclaimer is necessary to protect the company from litigation should the projections in its statements prove to be incorrect. Under the Private Securities Litigation Reform Act of 1995, companies are encouraged to make statements projecting future earnings, plans, and performance because such information can be helpful to investors. Indeed, companies are given "safe harbor" from liability in making such statements as long as the statements are clearly labeled "forward-looking" and accompanied by language cautioning that actual results could differ from the projections stated.[5]

Notice that the authors of the Guess?, Inc. report have been careful to explain that its projections are not factual ("Readers are cautioned not to place undue reliance on these forward-looking statements . . .") and to note that they appear in the 10-K Report, in other documents, and possibly in oral comments from management. To distinguish further these statements from facts about past and present performance, the authors identify words typically used in these statements: *believe, expect, anticipate, optimistic, intend, aim, will.* The additional information, to which the reader is referred in the last line of that section ("refer to Item 7 . . ."), goes into much greater detail on the subject, as Figure 9.3, p. 284, illustrates.

Figure 9.1

Sample Excerpt from 10-K Report

SECURITIES AND EXCHANGE COMMISSION
Washington, D.C. 20549

FORM 10-K

☒ ANNUAL REPORT PURSUANT TO SECTION 13 OR 15(d) OF THE SECURITIES EXCHANGE ACT OF 1934, for the Fiscal Year Ended December 31, 1997

Commission File Number 1-11893

GUESS ?, INC.
(Exact name of registrant as specified in its charter)

Delaware	**95-3679695**
(State or other jurisdiction of incorporation or organization)	(I.R.S. Employer Identification No.)

1444 South Alameda Street
Los Angeles, California 90021
(213) 765-3100
(Address, including zip code, and telephone number, including area code)

Securities registered pursuant to Section 12(b) of the Act:

Title of Each Class	**Name of Each Exchange on Which Registered**
Common Stock, par value $0.01 per share	New York Stock Exchange

Securities registered pursuant to Section 12(g) of the Act:
None

Indicate by check mark whether the registrant (1) has filed all reports required to be filed by Section 13 or 15(d) of the Securities Exchange Act of 1934 during the preceding 12 months (or for such shorter period that the registrant was required to file such reports) and (2) has been subject to such filing requirements for the past 90 days.

☒ Yes   ☐ No

Indicate by check mark if disclosure of delinquent filers pursuant to item 405 of Regulation S-K is not contained herein, and will not be contained, to the best of registrant's knowledge, in definitive proxy or information statements incorporated by reference in Part III of this Form 10-K or any amendment to this Form 10-K. ☒

As of March 6, 1998, the aggregate market value of the voting and non-voting common equity stock held by non-affiliates of the registrant was $42,095,644.

As of March 6, 1998, the registrant had 42,902,035 shares of Common Stock outstanding.

Figure 9.2

Disclaimer for "Forward-Looking Statements," Guess?, Inc. 1997 10-K Report

PART I

ITEM 1. Business

Important Factors Regarding Forward-Looking Statements

Various forward-looking statements have been made in this Form 10-K. Forward-looking statements may also be in the registrant's other reports filed under the Securities Exchange Act of 1934, in its press releases and in other documents. In addition, from time to time, the registrant through its management may make oral forward-looking statements.

Forward-looking statements generally refer to future plans and performance, and are identified by the words "believe," "expect," "anticipate," "optimistic," "intend," "aim," "will" or similar expressions. Readers are cautioned not to place undue reliance on these forward-looking statements, which speak only as of the date of which they are made. The registrant undertakes no obligation to update publicly or revise any forward-looking statements.

For additional information regarding forward-looking statements, refer to Item 7, "Management's Discussion and Analysis of Financial Condition and Results of Operations."

General

Guess ?, Inc. ("the Company" or "Guess"), founded in 1981 by the Marciano brothers, designs, markets, distributes and licenses one of the world's leading lifestyle collections of casual apparel, accessories and related consumer products. The Company's apparel for men and women is marketed under numerous trademarks including Guess, Guess ?, Guess U.S.A., Guess Collection and Guess ? and Triangle Design. The lines include full collections of denim and cotton clothing, including jeans, pants, overalls, skirts, dresses, shorts, blouses, shirts, jackets and knitwear. In addition, the Company has granted licenses to manufacture and distribute a broad range of products that complement the Company's apparel lines, including clothing for infants and children, activewear, footwear, eyewear, watches, home products and other fashion accessories. Revenue generated from wholesale and retail operations and from licensing activities, were 48.5%, 41.9% and 9.6%, respectively, of net revenue in 1997. The Company's total net revenue in 1997 was $515.4 million and net earnings (including the favorable effect of a $4.0 million change in accounting) were $37.5 million.

Company Products. The Company derives its net revenue from the sale of Guess men's and women's apparel worldwide to wholesale customers and distributors, from the sale of Guess men's and women's apparel and its licensees' products through the Company's network of retail and factory outlet stores primarily in the United States and net royalties from worldwide licensing activities. The following table sets forth the net revenue of the Company through its channels of distribution.

	Year Ended December 31,					
	1997		1996		1995	
	(in thousands)					
Net Revenue:						
Wholesale operations	$250,040	48.5%	$288,046	52.2%	$270,931	55.7%
Retail operations	215,873	41.9	209,828	38.1	169,428	34.8
Net revenue from product sales	465,913	90.4	497,874	90.3	440,359	90.5
Net royalties	49,459	9.6	53,288	9.7	46,374	9.5
Total net revenue	$515,372	100.0%	$551,162	100.0%	$486,733	100.0%

Figure 9.3

Cautionary Language About Forward-Looking Statements, Guess?, Inc. 1997 10-K Report

Important factors that could cause actual results to differ materially from the registrant's forward-looking statements, as well as affect the registrant's ability to achieve its financial and other goals, include, but are not limited to, the following:

The Company's inability to identify and respond appropriately to changing consumer demands and fashion trends could adversely affect consumer acceptance of Guess products.

A decision by the controlling owner of a group of department stores or any other significant customer to decrease the amount purchased from the Company or to cease carrying Guess products could have a material adverse effect on the Company's financial condition and results of operations.

The inability of the Company to control the quality, focus, image or distribution of its licensed products could impact consumer receptivity to the Company's products generally and, therefore, adversely affect the Company's financial condition and results of operations.

The failure of the Company to continue to enhance operating control systems could adversely affect the Company's financial condition and results of operations.

Factors beyond the Company's control may affect the Company's ability to expand its network of retail stores, including general economic and business conditions affecting consumer spending.

A general failure by the Company to maintain and control its existing distribution and licensing arrangements or to procure additional distribution and licensing relationships could adversely affect the Company's growth strategy, which could adversely affect the Company's financial condition and results of operations.

The extended loss of the services of one or more of the Principal Executive Officers could have a material adverse effect on the Company's operations.

The Company's operations may be affected adversely by political instability resulting in the disruption of trade with the countries in which the Company's contractors, suppliers or customers are located, the imposition of additional regulations relating to imports, the imposition of additional duties, taxes and other charges on imports, significant fluctuations in the value of the dollar against foreign currencies or restrictions on the transfer of funds. Also, a substantial increase in customs duties could have an adverse effect on the Company's financial condition or results of operations.

The inability of a manufacturer to ship the Company's products in a timely manner or to meet the Company's quality standards could adversely affect the Company's ability to deliver products to its customers in a timely manner.

No assurance can be given that others will not assert rights in, or ownership of, trademarks and other proprietary rights of Guess. In addition, the laws of certain foreign countries do not protect proprietary rights to the same extent as do the laws of the United States.

Although such explanations may seem elaborate, they are common in documents such as disclosure reports that could be subject to legal dispute. The language of the remainder of Part I is similarly legalistic, characterized by specifically enumerated items and precise figures: "The lines include full collections of denim and cotton clothing, including jeans, pants, overalls, skirts, dresses, shorts, blouses, shirts, jackets and knitwear . . . . Total net revenue (in thousands) $515,372 (1997), $551,162 (1996), $486,733 (1995)." These enumerations represent an effort on the part of the drafting team to be specific on the one hand and comprehensive on the other, that is, to be both legally adequate and technically accurate.

Plain English Guidelines

As you observed in Chapter 3, legal and technical language can make documents hard to read, and, as in the case of the Guess?, Inc. sample, 10-K Reports are often quite difficult for their intended audience (the general public) to comprehend. To help 10-K Reports achieve their purpose—disclosing essential information about a company's finances and operations—the SEC has issued guidelines for simplifying their language. These guidelines are compiled in the SEC's *Plain English Handbook,* available since 1998 in hard copy or on the Web (http://www.sec.gov/news/handbook.htm). The handbook, which contains excellent advice on clear communication in Annual Reports, 10-K Reports, and other disclosure documents, stresses the importance of audience awareness, reader-based organization, and clean, concise style. It also offers practical suggestions for graphing numerical data and for designing documents for easy readability.

THE RELATIONSHIP BETWEEN THE 10-K REPORT AND THE ANNUAL REPORT TO SHAREHOLDERS

Much of the information in the 10-K Report must be included in the Annual Report to Shareholders (commonly known as the Annual Report), which is sent to shareholders with or before the solicitation of proxies for the annual election of directors. Because these reports overlap to a great extent, and because they are usually prepared at the same time, companies are not required to repeat in the 10-K Report information they are disclosing in the Annual Report.[6] They can instead incorporate financial information by reference from the Annual Report into the 10-K.[7] If a company chooses this option, its Annual Report must comply with the reporting requirements specified for the 10-K Report; the required information must be incorporated via electronic exhibits in the EDGAR filing. If a company does not choose this option, it has considerable latitude in preparing the Annual Report: It may satisfy reporting requirements by filing a complete 10-K and simply appending a summary of financial information—including the audited financial statements and management's discussion and analysis—to the proxy statement it sends to shareholders.[8] Most companies prepare fairly elaborate Annual Reports, however, and use them as key public relations documents. In fact, a typical Annual Report is a glossy, full-color document, copiously illustrated and expensively printed on high-quality paper, a visual representation of the company's image and financial success.

Contents of the Annual Report to Shareholders

Although Annual Reports vary in size, content, and style, they are usually divided into two sections: an introduction and a financial section. The introduction, which focuses on public relations, typically contains (1) a letter to shareholders from the CEO and chairman of the board, and (2) an overview of the company's philosophy, products, current position, and plans for the future.

The first section is usually printed on high-quality, glossy paper and may include color photographs, maps depicting the company's operational locations, and other attractive visuals. The financial section typically contains the information found in the 10-K Report:

- a multiyear summary of key financial information
- management's discussion and analysis
- the financial statements and notes
- the independent auditors' report
- other information from the 10-K.

The financial section is often printed on a different paper stock from the first section to make it easy for readers to distinguish between them.

SAMPLE ANNUAL REPORT TO SHAREHOLDERS: GAP INC., 1997

To illustrate how companies communicate through their Annual Reports, we focus in this chapter on the 1997 Annual Report of Gap Inc., the global clothing retailer. We examine how principles of verbal and visual communication are used to promote the company to the public and to represent financial data.

Introductory Overview

The first section of the Gap Inc. report—like the opening of most Annual Reports—is written to foster positive public relations and to present the company in the best possible light to shareholders and potential investors. This introductory section is written for a wide audience, one that includes nonfinancial readers as well as readers with high levels of expertise in business and finance. The purpose of this section is to encourage investment in the company by impressing readers with good news about the company's annual performance and projecting an optimistic view of the future. In many cases, the company's communication specialists or marketing personnel write this opening section, using nontechnical language and a variety of visual effects to make the text as broadly accessible as possible.

Gap Inc.'s introductory overview begins with a two-page spread, shown in Figure 9.4, that sets the tone and theme of the report.

Notice that these two pages communicate similar information and reinforce each other: They distill from the financial statements the information most likely to appeal to a wide audience—sales, earnings, and stock value—and present it in three ways: as numbers in a table, as values on a bar graph, and as a segment of narrative prose. Although this threefold presentation makes use of nonverbal elements (tabular numbers, graphs), it is structured according to the principles of effective writing you learned in Chapter 2: from most important to least important, from general summary to specific details. Unlike a written document, which follows a linear organization, however, this two-page presentation is arranged in a *spatial* pattern. The elements that compose it—the table, the graphs, the prose—are laid out as separate blocks that draw the eye back and forth.

Let's look at how this layout leads readers first to the main message ("We're Growing!") and then guides them to more detailed, supporting information. Imagine that these two pages are divided into quadrants, as depicted in Figure 9.5, p. 290.

Lower Left: Bar Graphs   The bar graphs in the lower left quadrant, (a), are the first element to draw the reader's attention because the bars are the largest and darkest images on either page. These graphs, which depict a healthy rise in net sales, net earnings, and earnings per share over a five-year period, convey the basic general message of growth. Although they represent rough figures only, these graphs provide an upbeat introduction to the rest of the report. Their configuration—rising from the lower left corner of the page toward the upper right quadrant—draws the eye to the second element, the opening paragraph of prose.

Upper Right: Text Block   The text in section (b), which introduces the letter to shareholders from the CEO and chairman of the board, reiterates the good news presented in the bar graphs: "Gap Inc. is growing like never before." The size of the type in this paragraph is at least twice as large as that of any other text in the spread, and the main message is printed in boldface. These typographic features mirror the appearance of the bar graphs, which are also printed light to dark. Together, the elements in these two quadrants set the theme for the report, much as a summary statement does in a purely verbal text.

Upper Left: Table   The next sentence in the shareholder letter invites the reader to look back at the financial highlights in the upper left quadrant, (c)—"One look at the financial statistics in this report should be evidence enough"—and begins to introduce supporting detail for the main theme. The table, which presents more precise numbers and more categories of data than the graphs do, communicates the company's profitability and financial position to readers with enough business knowledge to understand the difference between, say, basic net earnings per share and diluted net earnings per share.

It is the numbers in the upper left quadrant that explain the information introduced in the bar graphs and alluded to in the opening of the shareholders' letter: net sales, net earnings, and so forth. Let's look for a moment at the relationship among these textual elements. The bar graph of net earnings in the lower left quadrant shows a steady growth in earnings from 1993 through 1997, with the exception of flat growth between 1994 and 1995. What is not clear from the graph, however, is the rate at which that growth took place. The percentage change in earnings from year to year, which can be discovered only in the table, has declined significantly from 1996 to 1997

Figure 9.4

Introductory Overview, Gap Inc. 1997 Annual Report

Financial Highlights

	Fifty-two Weeks Ended January 31, 1998	Fifty-two Weeks Ended February 1, 1997	Fifty-three Weeks Ended February 3, 1996
OPERATING RESULTS ($000)			
Net sales	$6,507,825	$5,284,381	$4,395,253
Percentage change year-to-year	23%	20%	18%
Earnings before income taxes	$ 854,242	$ 748,527	$ 585,199
Percentage change year-to-year	14%	28%	11%
Net earnings	$ 533,901	$ 452,859	$ 354,039
Percentage change year-to-year	18%	28%	11%
PER SHARE DATA			
Net earnings–basic	$1.35	$1.09	$.85
Net earnings–diluted	1.30	1.06	.83
Cash dividends	.20	.20	.16
STATISTICS			
Net earnings as a percentage of net sales	8.2%	8.6%	8.1%
Return on average assets	17.9%	18.2%	16.3%
Return on average shareholders' equity	33.0%	27.5%	23.5%
Current ratio	1.85:1	1.72:1	2.32:1
Number of stores open at year-end	2,130	1,854	1,680
Comparable store sales growth (52-week basis)	6%	5%	0%

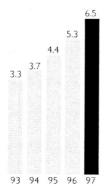

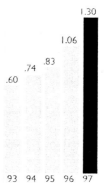

Net Sales
(in billions of dollars)

Net Earnings
(in millions of dollars)

Earnings Per Share–Diluted
(in dollars)

Dear Shareholders: This year, our message to you is simple: Gap Inc. is growing like never before. One look at the financial statistics in this report should be evidence enough. In every key category—net sales, net earnings, return on equity, earnings per share—we achieved significant increases in 1997. And we're quite proud of that.

But we're even more excited about our growth beyond the numbers. Building on the momentum we created in 1996—when we repositioned ourselves not as a retailer, but as a portfolio of global brands—we set new standards in nearly every facet of our operations. From the subtle but critical adjustments we made in our behind-the-scenes business processes to the bold approach we took to marketing our brands and broadening our customer base, we demonstrated that this Company has just begun to tap its potential for growth.

With this in mind, we embarked on an aggressive initiative to win more market share—increasing our percentage of the U.S. apparel market and landing *Advertising Age's* Marketer of the Year honors along the way. And indeed, the Gap, Banana Republic and Old Navy brands seemed to be everywhere in 1997. Recognizing that maturity doesn't necessarily preclude growth, we acquired more square footage of new real estate than in any year prior, adding 21 percent to Gap Inc.'s retail footprint around the world. We opened 298 stores—many of them in markets once considered unpromising—breaking the 2,000-store mark on our way to a year-end total of 2,130. To fuel that growth, we hired and trained an unprecedented number of employees, watching as the

Gap Inc. team swelled to more than 100,000 people worldwide during the Holiday peak season. Meanwhile, we expanded our corporate facilities in San Francisco and New York, broke ground for our fifth U.S. distribution center and expanded the reach of our global sourcing network by establishing offices in several new markets.

We also increased our marketing expenditures, making sure we stayed connected with consumers through high-profile multimedia advertising, unique brand promotions and strategic exposure in the media. We established an exciting commercial presence on the Internet, enhancing our Web site with an innovative online store that enables customers to purchase Gap merchandise from nearly anywhere in the United States using a computer. And we set the stage for our return to the mail order business, developing the infrastructure for Banana Republic's soon-to-debut catalog operation.

Driven by a passion for innovation and a focus on quality, we grew stronger and more confident through every quarter of 1997. Now, looking toward the challenges of the 21st century, we believe we are better positioned than ever before to build, enhance and protect the value of the Gap Inc. brands.

Figure 9.5

Two-Page Spread, General-to-Specific Organization

Financial Highlights

Dear (...)

Gap Inc. is growing like never before. One loo... (...) financial statistics in this report should be evidence (...) igh. In every key category—net sales, net earnings, return o(...)uity, earnings per share—we achieved significa(...) creases in 1997. And we're quite proud of that.

(b)

But we're even more excited about our growth beyond the numbers. Building on the momentum we created in 1996—when we repositioned ourselves not as a retailer, but as a portfolio of global brands—we set new standards in nearly every facet of our operations. From (...) subtle but critical adjustments we made in our b(...) the-scenes business processes to the bold (...) ch we took to marketing our brands and b(...) ng our customer base, we demonstrated th(...) mpany has just begun to tap its potential (...) n.

With this in mind, we (...) on an aggressive initiative to win more (...) re—increasing our percentage of (...) rel market and landing Advertis(...) r of the Year honors along the way. Ann(...)

(...) Recognizing th(...) aturity

to be th(...)

doesn't necessarily pre(...)

square footage of new real estate than in prior, adding 21 percent to Gap Inc.'s retail footprint around the world. We opened 298 stores—many of them in markets once considered unpromising—break- ing the 2,000-store mark on our way to a year-end total of 2,130. To fuel that growth, we hired and trained an unprecedented number of employees, watching as the

Ga(...) team swelled to more than 100,000 people wide during the Holiday peak season. Meanwhile, (...) expanded our corporate facilities in San Francisco (...) d New York, broke ground for our fifth U.S. distribution center and expanded the reach of our global sourcing network by establishing offices in several new markets

We also increased our marketing expenditures, making sure we stayed connected with consumers through high- profile multimedia advertising, unique brand promotions and strategic exposure in the media. We established an exciting commercial presence on the Internet, enhancing our Web site with an innovative online store that enables customers to purchase Gap merchandise from nearly anywhere in the United States using a computer. And we set the stage for our return to the mail order business, developing the infrastructure for Banana Republic's soon-to-debut catalog operation.

(d)

(...) Banana Republic and Old Navy brands we(...)

Driven by a passion for innovation and a focus on quality, we grew stronger and more confident through every quarter of 1997. Now, looking toward the challenges of the 21st century, we believe we are better positioned than ever before to build, enhance and protect the value of the Gap Inc. brands.

	Fifty-two Weeks Ended January 31, 1998	Fifty-two Weeks Ended February 1, 1997	(...) Ended (...)uary 3, 1996
OPERATING RESULTS ($000)			
Net sales	$6,507,825	(...),381	$4,395,253
Percentage change year-to-year	23%	(...)0%	18%
Earnings before income taxes	$ 854,242	748,527	$ 585,199
Percentage change year-to-year	14%	28%	11%
Net earnings	$ 533,901	$ 452,859	$ 354,039
Percentage change year-to-year	18%	(...)%	11%
PER SHARE DATA			
Net earnings—basic	$1.35	$1.09	$.85
Net earnings—diluted	(...)	1.06	.83
Cash dividends	.2(...)	.20	.16
STATISTICS			
Net earnings as a percentage of net sales	8.2%	8.6%	8.1%
Return on average assets	17.9%	?.2%	16.3%
Return on average shareholders' equity	33.0%	?(...)%	23.5%
Current ratio	1.85:1	1.(...)	2.32:1
Number of stores open at year-end	2,130	1,85(...)	1,680
Comparable store sales growth (52-week basis)	6%	5%	0%

(c)

(a)

Net Sales
(in billions of dollars)

6.5
5.3
4.4
3.7
3.3

93 94 95 96 97

Net Earnings
(in millions of dollars)

534
453
354
320
258

93 94 95 96 97

Earnings Per Share–Diluted
(in dollars)

.83
.(...)4
.60

93 94 95 96 97

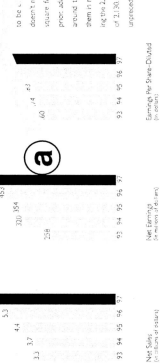

(from 28% to 14%). These figures tell the reader that although Gap Inc.'s earnings have been rising each year, its 1997 earnings rose at a slower rate (by approximately half) than did its earnings of the year before. This example illustrates that many of the important financial facts about a company are clear only in those sections of the Annual Report which present the numbers in their primary state, that is, in tables of raw numbers and in the financial statements themselves. The graphical, or secondary, representations of data can give the reader only a superficial understanding of the company's financial position and profitability.

Lower Right: Text Block   The prose in the remaining quadrant, (d), elaborates on the tabular data for those readers who want more narrative detail or for those who are uncomfortable with numbers. Throughout this portion of the letter, the CEO and chairman of the board summarize the reasons for the year's economic growth depicted in the table:

> [W]e embarked on an aggressive initiative to win more market share . . .
> [W]e acquired more square footage of real estate than in any year prior, adding 21 percent to Gap Inc.'s retail footprint around the world. We opened 298 stores . . . breaking the 2,000-store mark on our way to a year-end total of 2,130. To fuel that growth, we hired and trained an unprecedented number of employees, watching as the Gap Inc. team swelled to more than 100,000 people worldwide during the Holiday peak season.

By combining various techniques of visual and verbal communication, the authors of this report have maximized the impact of the important opening section. By choosing a spatial organization, they have been able to condense a great deal of information into a concise, readable format, one designed to keep readers' attention and thus increase the chances that the rhetorical purpose—to encourage investment in the company—will be achieved. (When you have to present technical information persuasively to nonfinancial audiences, remember that techniques such as these can help make your points easy to grasp.)

Financial Review Section

As important as the introductory section is for fostering positive public relations, the heart of the Annual Report is the financial section. The financial section has the same rhetorical purpose as the 10-K: to fulfill as accurately and succinctly as possible the SEC's disclosure requirements and to convey detailed financial data to shareholders and potential investors. The Annual Report is more likely than the 10-K to be read by a broad audience including nonfinancial readers, however. For this reason, companies often use a variety of techniques to make the financial data accessible to such an audience. In addition to using tables, in which financial statements are always presented and which sophisticated readers can easily understand, the authors of many Annual Reports present numerical information with charts, graphs, and other visuals that help the average reader understand the implications of the data. Moreover, because the overall purpose of the Annual Report is to encourage investment in the company, preparers of Annual Reports often organize the information in the financial section so as to represent the company in the best possible light (without, of course, misrepresenting its performance).

Financial Summary   A close look at the Gap Inc. 1997 report reveals how rhetorical techniques such as organization and visual support can achieve these goals. The financial section opens with a graphical summary of "key financial statistics" (Figure 9.6) followed by a ten-year summary of selected financial data (Figure 9.7, pp. 296–297). The financial data presented—ten years of statistics on operating results, stock values, and retail sites—is one of the items required for the 10-K/Annual Report,[9] but SEC disclosure rules do not specify where the summary must be placed. By placing the ten-year summary at the beginning of the financial section, the authors of the Gap Inc. report affirm the company's favorable financial position and continuing growth.

Bar Graphs   The bar graphs in Figure 9.6 reinforce the report's main theme ("We're Growing!"), although they do not convey this message quite as strongly as the visual summary in Figure 9.4. The earlier illustration depicts the statistics more selectively, showing those that enjoyed the most dramatic incline. Moreover, the smaller data set in Figure 9.4 (five years instead of ten) makes the vertical rises of the graphs seem more extreme. In Figure 9.6, the ten-year graphs show a less dramatic, yet still positive, growth trend, with steady growth represented in four of the six graphs. Because the financial section of an Annual Report presents more detailed performance figures than the introductory section does, more categories are included in the graphed summary so that the company's performance is presented more broadly.

In two of the graphed categories, however (Return on Average Shareholders' Equity and Sales Per Average Gross Square Foot), the 1997 numbers are down from high points in 1991 and 1992, respectively. Return on Average Shareholders' Equity is one of the many measurements of companies' financial performance that the investing community considers when determining the value of shares of stock. Despite some downturn in the category during the period from 1992 to 1995, the graph in Figure 9.6 shows that Gap Inc. has rebounded in the past two years; therefore the graph conveys a positive message to investors and potential investors. Sales Per Average Gross Square Foot is a common performance measurement among companies that sell merchandise in stores. This measurement is often included in the Annual Reports of such companies. The graph of Gap Inc.'s Sales Per Average Gross Square Foot shows that the company's 1992–1995 sales were increasing at a rate that was slower than the rate of increase in store floor space. The dip in the graph indicates that the company's significantly expanded floor space was not generating a proportionately expanded amount of sales revenue. Perhaps this phenomenon could be explained by Gap Inc.'s in-store marketing technique of creating an open, roomy atmosphere in which to shop, and by the stores' making a point of not displaying as much inventory per square foot as they once did. Or perhaps the company opened new stores in less desirable locations because the best locations were already taken, causing the company's stores, on average, to decline in productivity. But regardless of the reason for the decline, the

Figure 9.6

Graphical Ten-Year Summary of Selected Financial Data

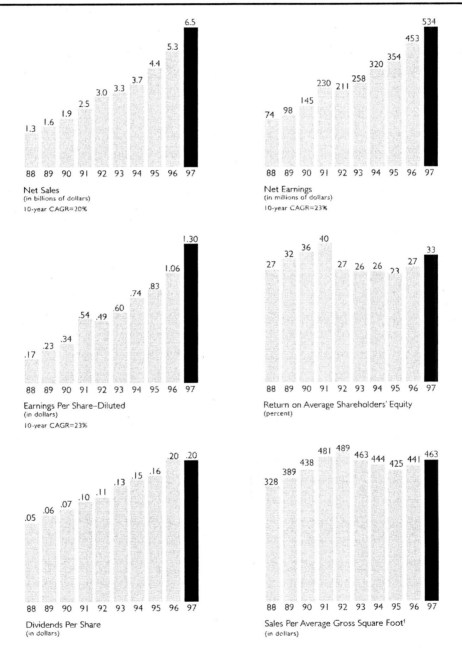

Net Sales
(in billions of dollars)
10-year CAGR=20%

Net Earnings
(in millions of dollars)
10-year CAGR=23%

Earnings Per Share–Diluted
(in dollars)
10-year CAGR=23%

Return on Average Shareholders' Equity
(percent)

Dividends Per Share
(in dollars)

Sales Per Average Gross Square Foot[1]
(in dollars)

1 52-week basis.

graph in Figure 9.6 still manages to convey a positive message: Gap Inc. is regaining ground in terms of the productivity of its sales floor space.

Tables   The tabular summary shown in Figure 9.7, which immediately follows the bar graphs, is the first element of the report scrutinized by sophisticated investors and financial professionals. Because these expert readers know exactly what information they are looking for, they may not even look at the introductory section of the report (with its simplified and marketing-oriented language), going instead directly to the numbers in the financial section. For this reason, anything essential conveyed in the introduction needs to be repeated in some form here. Accordingly, the authors of the Gap Inc. report have reiterated the introduction's message of growth by beginning the financial section with the ten-year financial summary and by making its highlights visually concrete through the graphical support of a table.

The table of ten-year data contains information that allows readers to assess Gap Inc.'s liquidity (current ratio), profitability (earnings per share), and solvency and equity positions (debt-to-equity ratio). In fact, the table is a product of financial analysis performed by the company for the benefit of the Annual Report readers. Because investors and potential investors are typically interested in a company's plans and capacity for growth, many items in this table describe the company's growth history and/or expectations for future growth: Property and equipment and merchandise inventory—assets a merchandiser needs to be able to generate sales—all increased substantially in 1997; long-term debt (a common indicator of a company's intention to expand) rose from zero to almost $500 million; and the number of stores opened (298) and square footage of store space (15.3 million) each increased significantly from the prior year.

These summary elements not only launch the financial section with a strongly positive message, but they also tend to offset the relatively negative language of the legal disclaimer about forward-looking statements that begins the management discussion (see Figure 9.8, p. 298). The disclaimer, which protects the company from liability should management's projections not be realized, is printed in smaller type than the rest of the discussion (the proverbial *fine print*); the type is readable, but small enough to subordinate the text of the disclaimer to the more important text that follows—the body of the management's discussion and analysis (MD&A).

Management's Discussion and Analysis   The MD&A, which explains the financial statements, is one of the most important parts of the Annual Report (and the 10-K). The section is a required disclosure item, one the SEC scrutinizes very carefully. The discussion gives management's analysis of the four basic financial statements: the statement of earnings, the balance sheets, the statement of cash flows, and the statement of shareholders' equity. Its purpose is to help investors understand the company's financial affairs from management's point of view. In the MD&A, management must provide information about liquidity, capital resources, and results of operations. The MD&A must also disclose any currently known trends, events, or uncertainties that may have material results on the company's operations or future finances.[10] At most companies, the MD&A is carefully reviewed by the accountants and at-torneys as well as by management because it is one of the elements of the Annual Report that can expose the company to serious liability.[11]

As the opening of the Gap Inc. MD&A illustrates (Figure 9.8), the MD&A also provides reasons for increases or decreases in sales, expenses, and income. Be-ginning with a table of net sales figures for the last three years, the text then gives reasons for the growth from one year to the next. The SEC's instructions for preparing the MD&A require such explanations; when the financial statements reveal material changes from year to year, management must describe the causes for these changes in the context of the company's business as a whole.[12] In Gap Inc.'s MD&A, these explanations are written in simple, straightforward language: "The total net sales growth for all years presented was attributable primarily to the increase in retail selling space. . . . The increase in net sales per average square foot in 1997 and 1996 was primarily attributable to increases in compara-ble store sales" (meaning that the increase in net sales came from both old and new stores, not just from a bulge of initially large sales from brand-new stores).

Another crucial function of the MD&A is the explanation of any facts that could have potentially adverse effects on the company's operations. Indeed, these types of disclosures have become increasingly important in recent years. In 1989 the SEC issued detailed instructions for explaining such conditions and uncertainties,[13] and since then has brought numerous enforcement proceed-ings against companies on the basis of inadequate MD&As.[14] Figure 9.9, p. 299, illustrates the sorts of facts that must be disclosed.

The first paragraph of this section addresses risks to Gap Inc. shareholders as a result of a share repurchase program and of its foreign operations; the second, possible financial threats from political instability and currency fluctu-ations in the 40 countries where the company does business; the third, poten-tial losses associated with year 2000 computer-system issues. In each para-graph, management explains what steps have been taken to avoid or offset these adverse effects ("The Company entered into various put options con-tracts [and] . . . foreign exchange contracts to reduce exposure to foreign cur-rency exchange risks"; "[T]o date the instability in Asia has not had a material adverse effect on the Company's ability to import apparel"; "The costs associ-ated with [the Y2K] effort are expected to be incurred through 1999 and are not expected to have a material impact on the results of operations, cash flows, or financial condition. . . ."). At the same time, however, the discus-sion makes the risks clear ("[N]o assurances can be given that [the instability in Asia] will not have such an effect in the future"; "[N]o assurances can be given that the company will be able to completely identify or address all the year 2000 compliance issues. . . ."). Although these risks are presented in a bal-anced way, they are clearly identified as potential areas of uncertainty, as re-quired by the rules of disclosure.

The management discussion and analysis in the Gap Inc. report is presented, for the most part, in prose with little visual support aside from simple tables. This simplicity reflects the minimalist image conveyed throughout the report (as well as in Gap Inc.'s stores and advertisements). In the financial sections of many An-nual Reports, you will find verbal and visual communications combined in more elaborate ways to direct readers' attention to information that management

Figure 9.7

Tabular Ten-Year Summary of Selected Financial Data

Ten-Year Selected Financial Data

	Compound Annual Growth Rate			1997 52 weeks	1996 52 weeks
	3-year	5-year	10-year		
OPERATING RESULTS ($000)					
Net sales	21%	17%	20%	$6,507,825	$5,284,381
Cost of goods sold and occupancy expenses, excluding depreciation and amortization	....	....	....	3,775,957	3,093,709
Percentage of net sales	....	....	....	58.0%	58.5%
Depreciation and amortization[a]	—	—	—	$ 245,584	$ 191,457
Operating expenses	....	....	....	1,635,017	1,270,138
Net interest (income) expense	....	....	....	(2,975)	(19,450)
Earnings before income taxes	17	20	21	854,242	748,527
Percentage of net sales	....	....	....	13.1%	14.2%
Income taxes	—	—	—	$ 320,341	$ 295,668
Net earnings	19	20	23	533,901	452,859
Percentage of net sales	....	....	....	8.2%	8.6%
Cash dividends	—	—	—	$ 79,503	$ 83,854
Capital expenditures	....	....	....	483,114	375,838
PER SHARE DATA					
Net earnings–basic[b]	21%	21%	23%	$1.35	$1.09
Net earnings–diluted[c]	21	22	23	1.30	1.06
Cash dividends	....	....	....	.20	.20
Shareholders' equity (book value)[d]	....	....	....	4.03	4.02
FINANCIAL POSITION ($000)					
Property and equipment, net	18%	16%	24%	$1,365,246	$1,135,720
Merchandise inventory	26	15	14	733,174	578,765
Total assets	19	19	23	3,337,502	2,626,927
Working capital	15	19	21	839,399	554,359
Current ratio	....	....	....	1.85:1	1.72:1
Total long-term debt, less current installments	....	....	....	$ 496,044	....
Ratio of long-term debt to shareholders' equity	....	....	....	.31:1	N/A
Shareholders' equity	5	12	19	$1,583,986	$1,654,470
Return on average assets	—	—	—	17.9%	18.2%
Return on average shareholders' equity	....	....	....	33.0%	27.5%
STATISTICS					
Number of stores opened	20%	21%	10%	298	203
Number of stores expanded	....	....	....	98	42
Number of stores closed	....	....	....	22	30
Number of stores open at year-end[e]	12	10	10	2,130	1,854
Net increase in number of stores	....	....	....	15%	10%
Comparable store sales growth (52-week basis)	....	....	....	6%	5%
Sales per square foot (52-week basis)[f]	....	....	....	$463	$441
Square footage of gross store space at year-end	19	19	15	15,312,700	12,645,000
Percentage increase in square feet	—	—	—	21%	14%
Number of employees at year-end	14	16	18	81,000	66,000
Weighted-average number of shares–basic[b]	....	....	....	396,179,975	417,146,631
Weighted-average number of shares–diluted[c]	....	....	....	410,200,758	427,267,220
Number of shares outstanding at year-end, net of treasury stock	—	—	—	393,133,028	411,775,997

[a] Excludes amortization of restricted stock, discounted stock options and discount on long-term debt.
[b] Based on weighted-average number of shares excluding restricted stock.
[c] Based on weighted-average number of shares adjusted for dilutive effect of stock options and restricted stock.
[d] Based on actual number of shares outstanding at year-end.
[e] Includes the conversion of GapKids departments to their own separate stores. Converted stores are not classified as new stores.
[f] Based on weighted-average gross square footage.

	Fiscal Year							
1995 53 weeks	1994 52 weeks	1993 52 weeks	1992 52 weeks	1991 52 weeks	1990 52 weeks	1989 53 weeks	1988 52 weeks
$4,395,253	$3,722,940	$3,295,679	$2,960,409	$2,518,893	$1,933,780	$1,586,596	$1,252,097
2,645,736	2,202,133	1,996,929	1,856,102	1,496,156	1,187,644	1,006,647	814,028
60.2%	59.2%	60.6%	62.7%	59.4%	61.4%	63.4%	65.0%
$ 175,719	$ 148,863	$ 124,860	$ 99,451	$ 72,765	$ 53,599	$ 39,589	$ 31,408
1,004,396	853,524	748,193	661,252	575,686	454,180	364,101	277,429
(15,797)	(10,902)	809	3,763	3,523	1,435	2,760	3,416
585,199	529,322	424,888	339,841	370,763	236,922	162,714	125,816
13.3%	14.2%	12.9%	11.5%	14.7%	12.3%	10.3%	10.0%
$ 231,160	$ 209,082	$ 166,464	$ 129,140	$ 140,890	$ 92,400	$ 65,086	$ 51,585
354,039	320,240	258,424	210,701	229,873	144,522	97,628	74,231
8.1%	8.6%	7.8%	7.1%	9.1%	7.5%	6.2%	5.9%
$ 66,993	$ 64,775	$ 53,041	$ 44,106	$ 41,126	$ 29,625	$ 22,857	$ 18,244
309,599	236,616	215,856	213,659	244,323	199,617	94,266	68,153
$ .85	$ .76	$ .62	$ .51	$ .56	$ .36	$.24	$.18
.83	.74	.60	.49	.54	.34	.23	.17
.16	.15	.13	.11	.10	.07	.06	.05
3.80	3.17	2.59	2.05	1.59	1.10	.80	.65
$ 957,752	$ 828,777	$ 740,422	$ 650,368	$ 547,740	$ 383,548	$ 238,103	$ 191,257
482,575	370,638	331,155	365,692	313,899	247,462	243,482	193,268
2,343,068	2,004,244	1,763,117	1,379,248	1,147,414	776,900	579,483	481,148
728,301	555,827	494,194	355,649	235,537	101,518	129,139	106,210
2.32:1	2.11:1	2.07:1	2.06:1	1.71:1	1.39:1	1.69:1	1.70:1
----	----	$ 75,000	$ 75,000	$ 80,000	$ 17,500	$ 20,000	$ 22,000
N/A	N/A	.07:1	.08:1	.12:1	.04:1	.06:1	.08:1
$1,640,473	$1,375,232	$1,126,475	$ 887,839	$ 677,788	$ 465,733	$ 337,972	$ 276,399
16.3%	17.0%	16.4%	16.7%	23.9%	21.3%	18.4%	16.2%
23.5%	25.6%	25.7%	26.9%	40.2%	36.0%	31.8%	27.0%
225	172	108	117	139	152	98	106
55	82	130	94	79	56	7	N/A
53	34	45	26	15	20	38	21
1,680	1,508	1,370	1,307	1,216	1,092	960	900
11%	10%	5%	7%	11%	14%	7%	10%
0%	1%	1%	5%	13%	14%	15%	8%
$425	$444	$463	$489	$481	$438	$389	$328
11,100,200	9,165,900	7,546,300	6,509,200	5,638,400	4,762,300	4,056,600	3,879,300
21%	21%	16%	15%	18%	17%	5%	6%
60,000	55,000	44,000	39,000	32,000	26,000	23,000	20,000
417,718,397	421,644,426	417,905,336	412,629,996	407,007,521	401,965,082	399,847,754	410,942,274
427,752,515	431,619,827	428,937,902	427,068,347	423,687,625	419,978,006	420,619,541	434,112,567
431,621,976	434,294,247	435,746,184	432,555,714	427,570,002	423,792,090	421,654,212	421,576,368

Figure 9.8

Excerpts, Management's Discussion and Analysis, Gap Inc. 1997 Annual Report: Legal Disclaimer and Interpretation of Financial Statements

Management's Discussion and Analysis of Results of Operations and Financial Condition

The information below and elsewhere in this Annual Report contains certain forward-looking statements which reflect the current view of Gap Inc. (the "Company") with respect to future events and financial performance. Wherever used, the words "expect," "plan," "anticipate," "believe" and similar expressions identify forward-looking statements.

Any such forward-looking statements are subject to risks and uncertainties that could cause the Company's actual results of operations to differ materially from historical results or current expectations. Some of these risks include, without limitation, ongoing competitive pressures in the apparel industry, risks associated with challenging international retail environments, changes in the level of consumer spending or preferences in apparel, and/or trade restrictions and political or financial instability in countries where the Company's goods are manufactured and other factors that may be described in the Company's filings with the Securities and Exchange Commission. Future economic and industry trends that could potentially impact revenues and profitability remain difficult to predict.

The Company does not undertake to publicly update or revise its forward-looking statements even if experience or future changes make it clear that any projected results expressed or implied therein will not be realized.

Results of Operations

NET SALES

	Fifty-two Weeks Ended Jan. 31, 1998	Fifty-two Weeks Ended Feb. 1, 1997	Fifty-three Weeks Ended Feb. 3, 1996
Net sales ($000)	$6,507,825	$5,284,381	$4,395,253
Total net sales growth percentage	23	20	18
Comparable store sales growth percentage (52-week basis)	6	5	0
Net sales per average gross square foot (52-week basis)	$463	$441	$425
Square footage of gross store space at year-end (000)	15,313	12,645	11,100
Number of:			
New stores	298	203	225
Expanded stores	98	42	55
Closed stores	22	30	53

The total net sales growth for all years presented was attributable primarily to the increase in retail selling space, both through the opening of new stores (net of stores closed) and the expansion of existing stores. An increase in comparable store sales also contributed to net sales growth in 1997 and 1996.

The increase in net sales per average square foot in 1997 and 1996 was primarily attributable to increases in comparable store sales.

COST OF GOODS SOLD
AND OCCUPANCY EXPENSES

Cost of goods sold and occupancy expenses as a percentage of net sales were 61.8 percent in 1997, 62.2 percent in 1996 and 64.2 percent in 1995.

The .4 percentage point decrease in 1997 from 1996 was primarily attributable to a .6 percentage point decrease in occupancy expenses, partially offset by a decrease in merchandise margin. The decrease in occupancy expenses as a percentage of net sales was primarily attributable to leverage achieved through comparable store sales growth.

The 2.0 percentage point decrease in 1996 from 1995 was due to a 1.2 percentage point increase in merchandise margin combined with an .8 percentage point decrease in occupancy expenses as a percentage of net sales. The increase in merchandise margin was driven by increases in initial merchandise markup and in the percentage of merchandise sold at regular price. The decrease in occupancy expenses was primarily attributable to the effect of the growth of the Old Navy division, which carries lower occupancy expenses as a percentage of net sales when compared to other divisions, and leverage achieved through comparable store sales growth.

Figure 9.9

Excerpt, Management's Discussion and Analysis, Gap Inc. 1997 Annual Report: Potential Risks to Future Operations

During fiscal 1997, the Company entered into various put option contracts in connection with the share repurchase program to hedge against stock price fluctuations. The Company also continued to enter into foreign exchange forward contracts to reduce exposure to foreign currency exchange risk involved in its commitments to purchase merchandise for foreign operations. Additional information on these contracts and agreements is presented in the Notes to Consolidated Financial Statements (Note E). Quantitative and qualitative disclosures about market risk for financial instruments are presented on page 38.

The Company pursues a diversified global import operations strategy which includes relationships with vendors in over 40 countries. These sourcing operations may be adversely affected by political instability resulting in the disruption of trade from exporting countries, significant fluctuation in the value of the U.S. dollar against foreign currencies, restrictions on the transfer of funds and/or other trade disruptions. The current financial instability in Asia is an example of this instability, which could affect some suppliers adversely. Although to date the instability in Asia has not had a material adverse effect on the Company's ability to import apparel, and therefore on the Company's results of operations and financial condition, no assurances can be given that it will not have such an effect in the future.

The Company is addressing the need to ensure that its operations will not be adversely impacted by software or other system failures related to year 2000. A program office was established in 1997 to coordinate the identification, evaluation and implementation of any necessary changes to computer systems, applications and business processes. The costs associated with this effort are expected to be incurred through 1999 and are not expected to have a material impact on the results of operations, cash flows or financial condition in any given year. However, no assurances can be given that the Company will be able to completely identify or address all year 2000 compliance issues, or that third parties with whom the Company does business will not experience system failures as a result of the year 2000 issues, nor can the Company fully predict the consequences of noncompliance.

wants to emphasize. Indeed, the SEC's instructions for reporting to shareholders encourage companies to "utilize tables, schedules, charts, and graphic illustrations to present financial information in an understandable manner."[15]

Financial Statements and Notes

Readers considering investing in a company or lending a company money can glean important information about that company's liquidity, profitability, solvency, and future prospects from the Ten-Year Summary of Financial Highlights and the MD&A. They should view this information with some skepticism, however, because it has not been audited by independent auditors. Although presumably truthful (because the SEC *does* investigate complaints about misleading language in Annual Reports), the information in these sections may be presented with some degree of management "spin" that makes the company look good.

The most objective financial information in the Annual Report is the audited financial statements. Through an audited balance sheet, income statement, and statement of cash flows, a company communicates its financial position and operating results in its least digested form and with an independent auditor's opinion on the reliability of the information. Therefore, the reader may place greater reliance on the information in the audited financial statements than on anything else in the Annual Report (see later section on auditors' reports).

Although financial statements are composed of raw financial data, their structure and content are nevertheless shaped by concerns with audience and purpose. In fact, the format, content, and organization of financial statements have evolved over the last century to serve the basic objectives of financial reporting articulated by the FASB in SFAS No. 1: to provide information that is "useful," "comprehensible," and "helpful" to current and potential investors and creditors in making investment and credit decisions.[16] In other words, the financial statements are intended to communicate financial information in an effective manner that suits the intended audience—a concept we have been stressing throughout this textbook. Let us look at how the content of the financial statements is organized to achieve that goal.

Structure and Content of the Financial Statements Companies maintain complex accounting records, collecting data in hundreds or even thousands of individual accounts. To communicate efficiently the results of operations, companies summarize the individual accounts by grouping them according to their function or purpose. For example, a company may have several different bank accounts, and each bank account may have its own account number within the chart of accounts. When it is time to prepare financial statements, those accounts are summarized (combined) and classified as *cash* on the balance sheet because readers may be interested in how much cash the company has on hand but probably do not need to know the individual balances being kept in various banks.

This classification process, when applied to all of a company's accounts, produces the line items we are accustomed to seeing on financial statements, such as *cash, inventory, accounts payable, retained earnings, sales, wages expense,* and so on. These items are further summarized into broader classifications, or categories, and are called the *elements* of the financial statements. FASB requires accounting information to be categorized by these elements, which consist of *assets, liabilities, equity, contributed capital, distributions, revenues, expenses, gains, losses,* or *net income* or *loss,*[17] so that users of the financial statements will be able readily to locate information about a company's economic resources, its creditors' and owners' claims to those resources, and the changes that have occurred during the year to those resources and claims.[18]

To make the financial statements even more user friendly, preparers classify the asset and liability elements by liquidity: current and noncurrent assets, and current and long-term liabilities. These classifications help financial statement users to perform analyses. For example, a supplier who is considering selling merchandise on account to Gap Inc. will be interested in the company's liquidity (its ability to pay its short-term liabilities) and, therefore, in its current assets and current liabilities. However, the lenders who recently extended Gap Inc. its ten-year notes would have been concerned with the company's solvency (its ability to pay its long-term liabilities) and, therefore, with its long-term assets and liabilities (among other things). In either case, the interested parties are able to find the precise information they need quickly and easily because of the statements' efficient organization.

Thus, by summarizing and classifying account balances, by reporting the summarized accounting information using a set of standardized financial statement elements, and by classifying short- and long-term assets and liabilities on the balance sheet, businesses communicate to the public their financial position and operating results in a manner that is recognizable, understandable, and highly usable to the business and investing community. (To review Gap Inc.'s 1997 classified balance sheet, consult the company's Web site at www.gap.com/onlinestore/gap/company/fin.annual.97.)

Users of Annual Reports   Companies' financial statements are based on historical accounting information; that is, they contain information about what has already taken place. But investors and other users of the statements are usually interested in how the company is going to perform in the future. These users study Annual Reports to compare a company's historical data over time as an aid to predicting its potential future performance. Although an individual line item on an income statement or balance sheet does not tell a reader much about the future, an analysis of how that item has changed over time can suggest where the company is going.

Financial professionals, such as investment firm research analysts and brokers, corporate financial analysts, and credit rating and bond rating research analysts, spend their careers analyzing companies' financial information in their efforts to predict how the value of companies' stocks and bonds may rise and fall. Although a complete discussion of financial analysis is beyond the scope of this textbook, we present here a simple illustration of how an investor might use the financial information in the 1997 Gap Inc. Annual Report to assess the company's plans for future growth. (To see how Gap Inc. fulfilled its 1997 Annual Report's predictions for financial growth, review the company's 1998 Annual Report at www.gap.com/onlinestore/gap/company/fin.annual.98.)

Using the Gap Inc. Annual Report   Here is an excerpt from the asset section of Gap Inc.'s 1997 balance sheet. We have selected three of the company's balance sheet items that could indicate an increased capacity for growth:

(in $000s) **Assets**	**1/31/98**	**1/31/97**
Property and Equipment (long-term assets)		
Furniture and equipment	$1,236,450	$960,516
Land and buildings	154,136	99,969

Liabilities and Shareholders' Equity		
Long-Term Liabilities		
Long-term debt	$496,044	$ -0-

Because a company uses its assets to generate income and to acquire more assets with which to generate even more income, changes in a company's assets can help describe its ability to grow. By adding furniture and equipment (which increased by 29%) and acquiring more real estate (which increased by 54%), Gap Inc. evidently has invested in "room to grow." But we cannot be sure just from reading the balance sheet that these increases indicate plans for future store and facilities expansion. We must return to the MD&A for management's explanation of the reasons for the increases in property and equipment:

> The increase in capital expenditures [i.e., the additions to property and equipment] in 1997 from 1996 was primarily attributable to the number of stores opened, expanded and remodeled, as well as the expansion of headquarters facilities. . . . In 1997, the Company completed construction of a headquarters facility in San Bruno, California for approximately $60 million. . . . .To further support its growth, the Company continues to explore alternatives for additional headquarters facilities in San Francisco and San Bruno, California. The Company acquired land in 1997 in San Francisco and in the fourth quarter entered into a purchase contract to acquire additional land in San Bruno. Also during 1997, the Company commenced construction on a distribution center in Fresno, California for an estimated cost at completion of $60 million.

Here, management provides details about its increase in property and equipment during the year, and some of those details do point to future growth: Constructing a new headquarters facility and beginning construction of a distribution center indicate that Gap Inc. expects to need more space in which to conduct the administration and distribution activities of the company. In addition, the company acquired more land during the year for future building projects. Although the MD&A goes on to project the number of new stores and store expansions it will undertake in the next year, it is by no means certain that those numbers will be fully realized.

The balance sheet excerpt also shows that the company issued approximately $500 million in new long-term debt (that line item rose from $0 to $496,044,000). This large amount of new debt may be intended for funding expansion, but we cannot tell from the balance sheet alone why the debt was issued. We can refer to the notes to the financial statements to discover the terms and conditions of the debt issue (see next section), but for an explanation of the intended uses of the borrowed funds, we should turn again to the MD&A:

> To provide financial flexibility, the Company issued $500 million of 6.9 percent, 10-year debt securities in fiscal 1997. The proceeds from this issuance are intended to be used for general corporate purposes, including store expansion, brand investment, development of additional distribution channels and repurchases of the Company's common stock pursuant to its ongoing repurchase program.

Although, according to the MD&A, some of the $500 million will be used for expansion in terms of the number of stores and the extent of distribution channels, management also reveals that the company plans to use at least some of the borrowed funds to buy treasury stock. Notice that it is not made clear how much of the new debt will go toward funding operational expansion. Although readers have learned much about Gap Inc.'s new debt issue, they may still be left wondering whether it arose from a commitment to operational expansions or to boosting stock prices by buying treasury stock. Nevertheless, this example illustrates how the financial statements work hand in hand with management's discussion and analysis to give Annual Report readers as comprehensive a picture of the company as possible.

Notes to the Financial Statements   Interested parties may obtain additional information about a company's financial condition by reading the notes to its financial statements. In fact, the notes give supplemental information that is often critical to having a complete picture of the company's situation. Notes to the financial statements, in general, serve three primary functions: (1) they provide descriptions of the accounting rules and methods that the company has used to develop its accounting information, such as depreciation and inventory methods; (2) they provide supporting detail about specific line items in the financial statements, such as descriptions of bond covenants and detailed property and equipment schedules; and (3) they provide information about items that are not listed on the financial statements but warrant disclosure, such as pending lawsuits or stock option plans.

Here is an excerpt of the note that describes the terms and conditions of Gap Inc.'s new long-term debt issuance:

> During fiscal 1997, the Company issued long-term debt which consists of $500 million of 6.9 percent unsecured notes, due September 15, 2007. Interest on the notes is payable semi-annually. The fair value at January 31, 1998 of the notes was approximately $526 million, based on the current rates at which the Company could borrow funds with similar terms and remaining maturities.

By making dates more specific than the explanation in the MD&A does, this note provides the sort of supporting detail mentioned earlier.

The Auditors' Report

The auditors' report indicates whether the company's financial statements present fairly the company's financial position in accordance with generally accepted accounting principles. If the auditors have rendered an unqualified, or so-called clean opinion, then the reader of the financial statements may have confidence in the statements. If the financial statements have received a modified opinion in the auditors' report, that report must specifically describe the nature of the items in the statements which were of concern or needed explanation. Gap Inc. received an unqualified opinion in its 1997 auditors' report; therefore, the reader may rely on the financial statements because the auditors assert that, in their opinion,

> [S]uch consolidated financial statements present fairly, in all material respects, the financial position of the Company and its subsidiaries as of January 31, 1998 and February 1, 1997, and the results of their operations and their cash flows for each of the three fiscal years in the period ended January 31, 1998 in conformity with generally accepted accounting principles.

PREPARATION OF THE 10-K AND THE ANNUAL REPORT

The production of both the 10-K Report and the Annual Report is a complex communication process involving multiple contributors, various categories of information, and, often, cycles of drafting, revising, and editing over the company's fiscal year. It is a process that draws input from many functional areas, most importantly, from the accounting department, the legal department, and management. As we noted earlier, the Annual Report overlaps significantly with the 10-K Report, although the filing deadline for the former is determined by the date of the annual meeting and the mailing of proxy materials to shareholders, and the filing deadline of the latter is set by the SEC (March 31 or 90 days after the close of the fiscal year). In many companies, the preparation of these reports involves a number of interrelated processes that recur on an annual cycle.[19]

The following timetable shows a typical production cycle for a company's Annual Report to Shareholders and 10-K Report. The timetable assumes a December 31 fiscal year-end and an April 30 annual meeting date.[20]

Date	Action
January 10 (110 days before annual meeting)	Accountants, attorneys, and management agree on timetable and allocate responsibility for collecting information and preparing drafts of the Annual Report and the 10-K Report.
January 20 (70 days before 10-K filing date)	Accountants begin preparing financial tables and statements for 10-K and Annual Report. Management begins drafting MD&A, letter to shareholders, and other text for Annual Report.
January or February	The board of directors meets to authorize time and place of annual meeting and set a record date for notice and voting.
February 6 (54 days before 10-K filing date)	Management circulates first draft of MD&A and text of annual report to attorneys, accountants, and other officers of the company.
February 15 (44 days before 10-K filing date)	Accountants circulate draft of financial statements to management. Management completes second draft of MD&A and other text for Annual Report.
March 9 (22 days before 10-K filing date)	Full draft of Annual Report circulated, in substantially final form, among attorneys, accountants, and officers for final review and approval.
March 19 (12 days before 10-K filing date)	Form 10-K circulated, in substantially final form, among attorneys, accountants, directors, and officers for comment. Signature pages delivered (with request for quick return).
March 28	Form 10-K must be filed with SEC within three days.

Date	Action
March 31 (March 30 in leap years)	Last day to file Form 10-K with SEC and exchanges or Nasdaq. Any portions of the Annual Report, such as the MD&A, incorporated by reference in the Form 10-K, are required to be filed as 10-K exhibits.
April 1 (March 31 in leap years)	Last day to request a 15-day extension for filing the Form 10-K.
April 1 (30 days before annual meeting)	Annual report and proxy material mailed to shareholders and stock exchanges or Nasdaq. Annual report mailed to SEC for filing; proxy materials filed with SEC.

CONCLUSION

Until the computer revolutionized information storage and transmission, 10-K and Annual Reports existed in hard-copy form only. Potential investors and others interested in the performance of a company could obtain copies of these reports by mail upon request. Although the reports were available to anyone under this system, their actual circulation was limited to shareholders and to others who bothered to request them by phoning or writing the company or the SEC. With the advent of computerized databases in the 1980s, however, commercial services began storing Annual Reports—minus their sometimes elaborate graphics—as electronic files. Electronic storage made Annual Reports easily accessible to industry users, to university communities, whose libraries often subscribed to the services, and to other subscribers.

Since the advent of the World Wide Web in the mid-1990s, Annual Reports (and 10-Ks, filed electronically through EDGAR) have become much more widely available to a broad range of readers. Companies eager to reach potential investors have begun posting their Annual Reports on Web sites, and these documents are now available at the click of a mouse to anyone with Internet access. In the last five years, the Web has become a key source of financial information for many in the investment industry as well as for private investors seeking to learn about companies' financial performance.

Until very recently, most companies have simply posted their Annual Reports to their Web sites without taking full advantage of Web technology to lead readers through information. Because the Web's integrative potential can make financial research easy for investors, however, the AICPA has taken steps to encourage the adaptation of Annual Reports to hypertext formats. Through its FASB Web site (www.fasb.org), the AICPA has posted a hypertext version of an Annual Report for a fictitious company, FauxCom,[21] to illustrate how the Web can enhance financial reporting to the public. Those seeking information on the company can navigate the report through the hyperlinks that connect related items of data. For readers seeking specific information, such navigation vastly simplifies the research process.

Helping investors gather information efficiently from Annual Reports serves the best interests of companies because Annual and 10-K Reports are the foundation documents on which the investment community relies for research, analysis, and decision making. Tools that make annual reports accessible to readers— whether they be the *Plain English Guidelines,* electronic filing systems, company Web pages, or hypertext models such as that offered by FauxCom—help companies achieve the basic objectives of financial reporting and help both individuals and professionals make well-informed investment decisions.

NOTES

[1]Carl W. Schneider, Jason M. Shargel, and Richard A Silfen, *Now That You Are Publicly Owned* (New York: Bowne), p. 3. Available upon request from the United States Securities and Exchange Commission.

[2]Since May 6, 1996, all public domestic companies have been required to file their 10-K Reports on EDGAR. With the exception of investment firms, companies are not required, however, to submit their Annual Report to Shareholders on EDGAR. "Important Information About EDGAR," http://www.sec.gov/edaux/wedgar.htm. December 19, 1998.

[3]For complete information on requirements for the 10-K Report and the Annual Report, see the following SEC publications (available upon request): *The Form 10-K Report, Regulation SK, Regulation SX,* and *Proxy Rules, Regulation 14D.*

[4]Schneider, Shargel, and Silfen, p. 3.

[5]Carl W. Schneider and Jay A. Dubow, "Forward-Looking Information: Navigating the Safe Harbor," *The Business Lawyer* 51 (August 1996): 1071–1100. As a result of the 1995 Reform Act, the following definitions of forward-looking statements were added as section 27A of the Securities Act of 1933 and section 21E of the Securities Exchange Act of 1934:

1. a statement containing a projection of revenues, income (including income loss), earnings (including earnings loss) per share, capital expenditures, dividends, capital structure, or other financial items;
2. a statement of the plans and objectives of management for future operations, including plans or objectives relating to the products or services of the issuer;
3. a statement of future economic performance, including any such statement contained in a discussion and analysis of financial condition by the management or in the results of operations included pursuant to the rules and regulations of the [Securities and Exchange] Commission;
4. any statement of the assumptions underlying or relating to any statement described in subparagraph (a), (b), or (c),
5. any report issued by an outside reviewer retained by an issuer, to the extent that the report assesses a forward-looking statement made by the issuer; or
6. a statement containing a projection or estimate of such other items as may be specified by rule or regulation of the Commission.

[6]Schneider, Shargel, and Silfen, p. 4.

[7]General Instruction G to Form 10-K, United States Securities and Exchange Commission.

[8]Schneider, Shargel, and Silfen, p. 4. The information that must be sent to shareholders is specified in the SEC *Proxy Rules,* section 14a-3.

[9]Item 301 of *Regulation S-K* (s229.301a) requires companies to file selected financial data for each of the last five fiscal years and (229.301b) any additional fiscal years necessary to keep the information from being misleading.

[10]Schneider, Shargel, and Silfen, p. 3.

[11]Klaus Eppler, "Preparing the Management's Discussion and Analysis," *Preparation of Annual Disclosure Documents, 1997,* vol. 2 (Practicing Law Institute), pp. 91–200.

[12]Eppler, pp. 100–101.

[13]United States Securities and Exchange Commission, Release Nos. 33-6835 and 34-26831.

[14]Eppler, p. 93.

[15]SEC *Proxy Rules,* section 14a-3(b) (11).

[16]Financial Accounting Standards Board, "Objectives of Financial Reporting by Business Enterprises," *Statement of Financial Accounting Concepts No. 1* (Stamford, CT: FASB, 1978).

[17]Financial Accounting Standards Board, "Elements of Financial Statements," *Statement of Financial Accounting Concepts No. 6* (Stamford, CT: FASB, 1985).

[18]Financial Accounting Standards Board, "Objectives of Financial Reporting by Business Enterprises," ibid.

[19]Schneider, Shargel, and Silfen, p. 25.

[20]Timetable adapted from Schneider, Shargel, and Silfen, Appendix D-1-6.

[21]"Model Company Goes Online," *Journal of Accountancy* 185, no. 6 (June 1998): 17.

EXERCISES

1. **Scenario:** As a potential investor, you are researching information on the fast-food industry. The first company you have decided to investigate is McDonald's. Using the SEC's EDGAR database (www.edgar-online.com), find McDonald's 1998 10-K Report.

   Writing task: As you read McDonald's 1998 10-K, identify the major sections of the report and write a brief overview of each part. Then write a summary of the most important information you found in the 10-K.

2. **Scenario:** To research McDonald's further, you have decided you want to read its Annual Report. Using the McDonald's Web site (www.mcdonalds.com), locate the company's most recent Annual Report. As an alternative, you may contact the McDonald's Investor Relations Department by e-mail, telephone, or letter to request a hard copy of the Annual Report.

   Writing task: As you read McDonald's Annual Report, identify its major sections and write a brief summary of each section. Then select a paragraph from the section headed "What's Been Happenin'" and a paragraph from the section headed "Year in Review." Write a memo to your instructor explaining how the differences in content, vocabulary, and tone in these two passages reveal differences in their audience and purpose.

3. **Writing task:** Compare and contrast the contents of the McDonald's Annual Report with the contents of its 10-K Report. Make notes of your observations. Write a memo to your instructor discussing the

differences between the 10-K and the Annual Report in the light of their differing purposes. (If you did not complete Exercise 1, you will need to obtain a copy of McDonald's 10-K through the SEC's EDGAR database—see Exercise 1 for the Web address.)

4. **Scenario:** To supplement your research on McDonald's, you have decided that you need to know whether any changes have occurred that may affect the company's operations and financial situation since the Annual Report was issued. Using the World Wide Web, obtain two recent press releases related to McDonald's or to other companies in the fast-food industry whose performance might affect McDonald's.
   Writing task: Write a one-page report describing how the information you obtained may affect the market price of McDonald's stock and explain why you believe that will occur. Be prepared to share in class the information you obtained.

5. **Scenario:** To obtain a broader perspective on the company than its own press releases provide, you have decided to consult several business publications for articles on McDonald's and its position in the fast-food industry. Locate two such articles from the *Wall Street Journal, Barron's, Business Week,* or other business publications.
   Writing task: In a brief report, summarize each of the articles and analyze how the information they contain is similar to or different from the information you obtained from the Annual Report and 10-K. Explain how analyzing the viewpoints of others helps you better understand a company.

6. **Scenario:** You are an accountant working in the financial accounting department of a major corporation. Jamie Anderson, vice president of finance, who oversees your firm's financial reporting process, has asked you to review the SEC's *Plain English Handbook.* She would like you to prepare a report summarizing the *Plain English* guidelines and identifying the basic elements of plain English according to the SEC.
   Writing task: After researching the SEC's *Plain English* guidelines, prepare the report for the vice president of finance. (Review Chapter 5 for information on report writing.)

7. **Scenario:** The vice president liked your report and decided that the company should implement the *Plain English* guidelines in its 10-K and Annual Report for the upcoming fiscal year. She has asked you to help train the other accountants in your department to make the transition from their present writing practices to those recommended by the SEC. She has given you the following excerpts of Notes to the Consolidated Financial Statements from the 1996 and 1997 Annual Reports of Baltimore Gas and Electric Company (BGE), one of the first companies in the United States to adopt the *Plain English* guidelines for its external reporting. She wants you to ana-

lyze these "before" and "after" excerpts and to explain exactly how the *Plain English* guidelines made the "after" samples clearer.

a. **(Before) Impairment of Long-Lived Assets** Long-lived assets subject to the requirements of Statement of Financial Accounting Standards No. 121, *Accounting for the Impairment of Long-Lived Assets and for Long-Lived Assets to Be Disposed Of,* are evaluated for impairment through a review of undiscounted expected future cash flows. If the sum of the undiscounted expected future cash flows is less than the carrying amount of the asset, an impairment loss is recognized.

(After) Evaluation of Assets for Impairment Statement of Financial Accounting Standards No. 121, *Accounting for the Impairment of Long-Lived Assets and for Long-Lived Assets to Be Disposed Of,* applies particular requirements to some of our assets that have long lives (some examples are utility property and equipment, and real estate). We determine if those assets are impaired by comparing their undiscounted expected future cash flows to their carrying amount in our accounting records. We recognize an impairment loss if the undiscounted expected future cash flows are less than the carrying amount of the asset.

b. **(Before) Amortization** Nuclear fuel expenditures are amortized as a component of actual fuel costs based on the energy produced over the life of the fuel.

(After) Amortization Expense Amortization is an accounting process of reducing an amount in our Consolidated Balance Sheets evenly over a period of time. When we reduce amounts in our Consolidated Balance Sheets we increase amortization expense in our Consolidated Statements of Income. An amount is considered fully amortized when it has been reduced to zero.

c. **(Before) Long-Term Debt** The discount or premium and expense of issuance associated with long-term debt are deferred and amortized over the original lives of the respective debt issues. Gains and losses on the reacquisition of debt are amortized over the remaining original lives of the issuances.

(After) Long-Term Debt We defer (include as an asset or liability in our Consolidated Balance Sheets and exclude from our Consolidated Statements of Income) all costs related to the issuance of long-term debt. These costs include underwriters' commissions, discounts or premium, and other costs such as legal, accounting and regulatory fees, and printing costs. We amortize these costs over the life of the debt. When we incur gains or losses on debt that we retire prior to maturity, we amortize those gains or losses over the remaining original life of the debt.

d. **(Before) Subsidiary Information** Diversified businesses consist of the operations of the Constellation Companies, HP&S, EP&S, and Constellation Energy Source, Inc. (formerly named BNG, Inc.).

(After) Information About Our Subsidiaries Our diversified business subsidiaries are organized in three groups: (1) Our power generation, financial investments, and real estate businesses, (2)

Our energy marketing businesses, and (3) Our home products and commercial building systems businesses.

Writing task: Write a memo to the vice president analyzing the samples and explaining the changes that improved them (you may want to consult Chapter 3 as well). Consider the following questions as you study the samples: How do the "after" versions indicate a greater awareness of the reader than the "before" versions do? What specific techniques have been used to simplify language and clarify content?

8. **Scenario:** You work in the financial accounting department of a publicly held corporation, and you have been asked to adapt several financial statement notes to comply with the *Plain English* guidelines.

   Writing task: Revise each of the following traditional notes to make them clearer and easier to read.

   a. **Property and Equipment** Property and equipment are stated at cost, with depreciation provided using the straight-line method. Estimated useful lives of assets are as follows: buildings—up to 40 years; leasehold improvements—lesser of useful lives or lease terms; equipment—3 to 15 years.

   b. **Stock Split** In May 2000, the company effected a two-for-one split of the company's common stock, by means of a special stock dividend. Stockholders' equity has been restated to give retroactive recognition to the stock split in prior periods by reclassifying from retained earnings to common stock the par value of additional shares issued pursuant to the split. In connection with the common stock split, the company amended its corporate charter to increase the company's authorized common stock from 2.0 billion shares to 4.0 billion shares. All share and per share data included herein have been restated to reflect the split.

9. **Communication task:** Obtain a copy of McDonald's most recent Annual Report and turn to the Report of Independent Auditors.

   a. In one or two paragraphs, summarize the content of the report.

   b. Discuss in class the significance of the auditors' report to the Annual Report to Shareholders.

10. **Scenario:** You are a consultant, hired to analyze and make suggestions for future changes to the graphic displays (tables, charts, graphs) of various companies' Annual Reports.

   Communication task: Obtain copies of several companies' Annual Reports, including The Walt Disney Company 1998 Annual Report. Look at the graphic displays included in the reports. Read the written descriptions that accompany the graphics.

   a. Write a one- or two-paragraph description of how The Walt Disney Company communicates its financial information in graphic form. What types of graphs and charts are used? What information is displayed graphically? Why do you think this information was chosen rather than other data? What information would a company generally not display in graphic form?

b. Discuss in class: What changes to the graphic display would you suggest for this Annual Report? What information might be important to shareholders and creditors that was not presented in graphic form? What other approaches to presenting graphic information could the company have used?

CHAPTER 10

Communication and Managerial Accounting

Accountants working in private industry at the beginning of the twenty-first century face communication challenges hardly imaginable a few decades ago. Changes in the corporate workplace, brought on by restructuring, globalization, and fast-developing information technology, have redefined the role of management accountants in key business processes. As the transactional dimension of accounting has become automated, the traditional responsibilities of the management accountant—to gather and record information, to prepare financial statements, to monitor the financial results of operations—have expanded; in today's corporate environment accountants are often involved in strategic planning and decision support, performance measurement, process re-engineering and design, and other activities demanding excellent communication and interpersonal skills.[1] One study describes the transition this way: "It was symbolic of the narrow role of corporate accountants in the past that they were viewed as naysayers, or 'corporate cops'. . . . Now, in many leading-edge companies, accountants are sought out as facilitators in decision making. Their input is prized for a breadth of perspective that is based on a broad, comprehensive understanding of business."[2]

Management accountants' input is valuable because they are uniquely positioned not only to understand all phases of an organization's business but also to appreciate the ways in which the financial function intersects with marketing, information systems, engineering, production, and other functional areas. For this reason, management accountants are often integral members of cross-functional teams engaged in planning, product and project development, re-engineering, and other strategic activities. On such teams, the accountants are expected to do more than simply circulate a spreadsheet or "provide the financial perspective": They are expected to help the team understand the implications of financial alternatives, to work through problems and find solutions, to communicate the value of their work to corporate management, and to obtain the resources needed to achieve their goals.[3]

To fulfill these responsibilities, management accountants need highly developed communication skills. Because they routinely work with nonfinancial managers and staff, management accountants must be skilled at digesting numerical information into structures that these audiences can understand. They must be able to judge which forms of representation—raw numbers, narrative prose, tables, charts, and/or graphs—will be most effective with a given audience. They must know how to place details into context so their listeners can grasp the significance of financial facts to the big picture and do so quickly and efficiently. Because the work of planning, decision making, and business development often occurs in meetings, management accountants must be skillful oral communicators, who know how to interact productively with others and to make effective presentations.

In this chapter, we study the communications of a management accountant as he participates in the planning process for a capital expenditure decision at a manufacturing company. We examine the ways accountants present information to a mixed audience of nonfinancial managers and technical experts, the rhetorical choices they make to represent financial information to those audiences, the roles they play in problem solving and collaboration, and the written documentation they produce.

In management accounting, and specifically in management reporting, there must be a balance between substance and form. The style, method, and means of communication are critical to the success of management reporting. Information is of little value unless it can be exchanged and communicated. . . . As management accountants we need to avoid real and imagined dullness and accept that substance without form is of little value.

Source: Peter Murray, "Mastering Management Reporting," *Australian Accountant,* October 1994

THE ACCOUNTANT'S ROLE IN CORPORATE PLANNING AND CONTROL

Planning is an ongoing activity in any company, and it derives from the information that accountants gather, maintain, and communicate. From the business plan that launches a company, through the strategic plan that sets its goals, to the budget plan that drives its daily activities, the company's accountants serve as an indispensable support team to management, providing financial information essential to the planning process. Controlling the expenses associated with those plans is an ongoing activity as well, one that requires constant financial comparisons between projected and actual revenues and costs. To support the planning and control functions, companies employ a variety of accounting, finance, and other professionals. Many young accountants enter the profession as corporate financial accountants, cost accountants, or financial and/or economic analysts. These jobs are not only entries into rewarding careers in corporate administration and management; they are also excellent proving grounds for young professionals eager to learn how companies operate and to gain experience that will lead them upward on their career ladders.

Financial accountants provide the foundation for the company's planning because they are the backbone of its financial record-keeping and reporting systems. Under the direction of the company's controller, they maintain the financial records, tie balances together by looking for discrepancies, ensure compliance with accounting and reporting rules, prepare financial statements, and often assist with the preparation of the company's 10-K Report to the SEC and the Annual Report to Shareholders. (See Chapter 9 for a discussion of those reports.)

Cost accountants, also supervised by the controller, anchor the company's control systems by monitoring costs of production in manufacturing enterprises, producing specialized cost reports, assisting in the preparation of budgets, and performing tasks such as variance analysis and capital expenditure postaudits, which allow management to see how well the company has performed compared to expectations.

Financial analysts support both planning and control by synthesizing the information generated by their companies' financial and cost accountants and conducting ratio analysis, identifying trends, and forecasting what might take place in the future. Their work puts financial information in context, helps management see its implications, and guides management's decisions about present control issues and future plans.

Strategic Planning

The strategic plan describes a company's long-term goals and the objectives by which it will achieve them. Although most companies try to involve everyone in the planning process, they usually designate a strategic planning team from among top management to spearhead and carry out that process. The planning team studies the company's current situation in terms of its financial health, labor force, production capacity, product positioning, and strength among its competitors. The company's financial accountants, cost accountants, and financial analysts support the strategic planning team by researching the subject, gathering and analyzing the data, and creating the forecasts needed to perform the self-study on which the planning process rests.

Capital Expenditure Planning

As part of its strategic planning, a company may consider initiating various capital projects, such as adding new product lines, building new facilities, acquiring new equipment, and so forth. To develop the plan for the project, management normally creates a cross-functional team that may include members from production, sales, engineering, research and development, human resources, and accounting. The role of management accountants on such teams is to help other members understand, at each step of the process, the financial impact of the alternatives being considered. The communications involved in this work are the subject of this chapter and are discussed in detail later.

Budgeting

A company's budget quantifies the objectives of its strategic plan in terms of dollars. The budget also plays an important communication role within the organization, reminding managers of the resources they have available to them and of their commitment to the strategic plan that was agreed upon.

Under the supervision of the controller, management accountants gather information from all functional areas of the company to prepare the budget. The accountants meet with budgeters to clarify requests, explain the nature of dollar constraints, and give reasons for denial of budget requests (if necessary). The accountants then compile the budget and run the proposed cost and revenue projections through the budget accounting system, developing a budget, which is, in fact, a set of forecasted cost reports and financial statements. With these spreadsheets, the accountants may continue to meet with budgeters to discuss ways to achieve objectives at a lower cost and to ensure that the budget anticipates an acceptable level of performance. In these instances, production personnel, who may have to defend their budget requests, need to understand the accountant, and the accountant needs to understand how production operates to earn credibility as a champion for the budget.

Controlling: Variance Analysis

The control function involves keeping actual financial results in line with those planned. Accountants let managers know how well operations are progressing by preparing performance reports that show the difference, or variance, between actual results and planned results in the company's revenues, costs, and profits. Accountants' variance analyses allow management to take appropriate action to correct the problem (enhance sales, boost production, increase advertising, and so forth).

Controlling: Capital Expenditure Postaudits

Just as companies monitor actual results against projected results throughout the fiscal year, they also monitor the outcomes of capital expenditure projects. The procedure by which they do so is called a *postaudit*. In a postaudit, the accountants compare the actual results for the project—in terms of costs, revenues, and return on investment—with the projections on which the project was based. Postaudits, along with variance analyses that are performed as the project materializes, allow management to determine whether the project has met expectations and to take corrective action if it has fallen short in some way.

MANAGEMENT ACCOUNTANTS AND CAPITAL EXPENDITURE PLANNING

The role of accountants on project development teams is a crucial one, and accountants are particularly important team members when product development is the goal. Experts estimate that between 75% and 90% of a product's costs are already determined at the end of the product's design;[4] therefore, a team needs accountants' input in every phase of product design to manage costs effectively. As the experts on cost data and finance, the accountants help the team assess the financial feasibility of the product and project cost estimates that they will need to win decision makers' approvals along the way. In addition, it is often the management accountant on the team who develops the financial section of the capital expenditure proposal if a new plant facility or new equipment is needed to manufacture the product.[5]

The skills needed for effective work on project development teams include flexibility, imagination, and an ability to communicate with others on their own terms. The accountant has to know how to handle resistance and conflict, how to help the team anticipate costs without making members feel that cost issues are dictating the design. According to one management accountant, "To do this job well, you have to be a person who likes to work with people."[6]

Accountants also need to remember that nonfinancial people usually find raw financial data to be, in the words of one expert, "intrinsically unattractive and generally unstimulating."[7] Accountants must realize that their function is to bridge the gap between that information and those who need to use it by presenting it in a logical and appealing way.

The management accountant must become an integral part of the . . . creative effort . . . evolving from a financial perspective to a team perspective. . . . According to a management accountant, "At first, I dealt mainly with financial people. I was not a core team member. I was brought in on an as-needed basis at the beginning for target cost issues and at the end of the process as they were going to ask for funding. Now, I deal with development engineers, CAD, and marketing. I am a core team member involved in all major decision points. I help the team think of costs as an important issue; for example, if the designers add or delete parts, I help them think about the cost implications and tradeoffs."

Source: Julie H. Hertenstein and Marjorie B. Platt, "Why Product Development Teams Need Management Accountants," *Management Accounting (USA)*, April 1998

The next section shows you how one company's management accountants carried out these responsibilities on a cross-functional capital expenditure project planning team.

NEW PRODUCT DEVELOPMENT AT MILLENIUM NUTRITIONAL SUPPLEMENTS, INC.

Millenium Nutritional Supplements, Inc., is an international, publicly traded company that manufactures and sells vitamins and mineral and herb supplements to large discount department chains, drugstores, and health and nutrition chain stores around the world. The company prides itself on being on the cutting edge of nutritional advances, and it has recently acquired the rights to market a unique form of the popular natural food supplement chlorella, which is manufactured in France using a patented process. The current manufacturer has agreed to supply the product, trade named Beta-rella, to Millenium for the next two years, but beginning June 1, 2002, Millenium will have to manufacture the supplement itself.

The Cross-Functional Project Team

The upper management of Millenium has designated a cross-functional team of company professionals to evaluate the two manufacturing options available: (1) to redesign and remodel an existing factory in Minneapolis, Minnesota, or (2) to use empty space in a new facility that currently manufactures a similar product in Málaga, Spain (near where the primary ingredient, an alga, is harvested from the Mediterranean Sea). The team is composed of colleagues from product engineering, plant engineering, production, distribution, marketing, sales, and accounting. The team accountant is Joe Markley, a corporate accountant with three years of product and facility accounting experience. Joe worked last year as assistant to a senior corporate accountant on another new product team, and so he has some experience working as a member of a cross-functional team.

The team's assignment is to assess the desirability of the two manufacturing options. Joe Markley's role is to determine the financial desirability of each option, to communicate that information to the team, and to participate in making a recommendation to upper management. Joe will also need to acquire and develop the data necessary to prepare the financial information for presentation at the formal recommendation meeting with upper management as well as to write the financial section of the capital expenditure proposal.

The Initial Project Team Meeting

The project manager, Dave Dwyer, coordinates all of the team's activities, provides overview and assistance to team members both individually and in groups, and makes sure that team members are keeping to the project timetable. Dave calls an initial meeting of the project team by sending an e-mail message to each team member, along with the agenda for the meeting (see Figure 10.1).

Notice that the agenda is organized appropriately for an informative, or update, meeting: from most to least important. (For more information on designing meeting agendas, refer to Chapter 6.) Because the meeting's purpose is to bring the team together and to inform members about the project and their assignments, the meeting begins with an introduction of the team members. Next, the project manager and plant engineers describe, respectively, the background of the project and each of the plant facilities under consideration. And finally, after a brief discussion of responsibilities and timetables, time is allotted for the team members to ask questions. Dave Dwyer knows it is also important to allow time during the meeting for the team members to discuss schedules and to coordinate how they will transfer information during the project.

Figure 10.1

First Project Team Meeting Agenda

AGENDA

Millenium Nutritional Supplements, Inc.
Beta-rella Manufacturing Facility Project
Agenda
Initial Team Meeting
March 12, 2000 10 A.M.

1. Opening remarks—Dave Dwyer, project manager
2. Introduction of team members—Dave Dwyer
   - Elaine Wycoff and Tom Lukins, plant engineers
   - Chip Allwell, product engineer/Beta-rella specialist
   - Jane Parker, marketing (North America)
   - Joe Markley, accounting
   - Jean-Pierre Pau, distribution manager
   - Sophie Laval, quality assurance
   - Enrico Cadiz, Spain liaison
3. Project background—Dave Dwyer
4. Overview of existing Minnesota facility—Elaine Wycoff, plant engineer
5. Overview of Spain location—Tom Lukins, plant engineer
6. Team member responsibilities and timetable—Dave Dwyer
7. Discussion
8. Adjournment

The Managerial Accountant's Role on the Team

Collecting the Data   The role of project accountant Joe Markley at this meeting is to learn as much as he can about the two plant facilities and to arrange for his fellow team members to send him the cost data he will need to perform his financial analysis of each option. Joe's work assignment involves gathering data for each of the two site options about the following:

- costs of plant remodeling (for the Minnesota site only)
- costs of equipment and its installation and employee retraining (from the plant engineers)
- costs to produce and package Beta-rella (from the product engineer and quality assurance expert)
- costs to ship and distribute Beta-rella (from the distribution manager)
- costs to market the product (from the marketing manager).

As Joe receives the data from the team members, most often in the form of an e-mailed message or small spreadsheet, he accumulates it in a spreadsheet file of his own. (See Figure 10.2, Accountant's Project Data File.) Joe will later compile the data into a more readily understandable format for presentation to the team.

In the course of collecting data, Joe receives an e-mail from the distribution manager, Jean-Pierre Pau, giving shipping cost figures that are surprising to Joe. Jean-Pierre writes that if Millenium were to produce Beta-rella in Spain, it would cost 2 cents per bottle to ship the finished product to the United States for sale; but if Beta-rella were manufactured in Minnesota, the cost of shipping the primary raw material, chlorella algae, to the United States would be 15 cents per bottle. Joe wonders about this large shipping cost discrepancy, and he requests a meeting with Jean-Pierre.

> *Joe:* Hi, J.P. Thanks for seeing me on such short notice. I'll just need a minute of your time.
>
> *Jean-Pierre:* No problem, Joe. What's up?
>
> *Joe:* Well, first let me thank you for getting your shipping cost information to me so quickly. But I did want to ask you about the large difference between the cost to ship the raw material from Spain to Minnesota versus the cost to ship the finished product. *[Joe approaches the subject with an "open" question, leaving Jean-Pierre to explain the matter, at least initially, in his own way.]*
>
> *Jean-Pierre:* Yes, there is a big difference between those shipping costs. But I was sure to calculate them meticulously.
>
> *Joe:* Oh, I have great confidence in your work, J.P. It's just that I am still learning about our international shipping procedures and about this new product, for that matter. Could you please explain to me how the shipping would work under either scenario? *[Noticing that Jean-Pierre seems a little defensive, Joe quickly reassures him by taking the blame himself for not understanding. He then continues to probe with another open question.]*
>
> *Jean-Pierre:* Sure, I'd be glad to. You see, our primary raw material, the chlorella alga that comes from the Mediterranean Sea, is very sensitive and loses much of its potency quickly if not kept under proper conditions. If we decide to manufacture in Minnesota, we will have to ship the unprocessed chlorella in special containers and in air-conditioned vessels.
>
> *Joe:* I see. That does sound expensive. So the shipping route would be the same, but we would have to invest in containers and request air-conditioned cargo bays in the ships? *[As Joe gets closer to his answer, he asks a "closed" question for specific details.]*
>
> *Jean-Pierre:* Oh, it's more than just that. This stuff has to be air freighted. Four to six weeks on a boat just won't work. The stuff would be useless by the time it got to Minnesota.

Joe: Now I'm starting to get the picture. And what about shipping the finished product? Could that be done by sea? *[Another closed question for specific information]*

Jean-Pierre: Absolutely. Once the chlorella has been processed and put into capsules, it can be sent by slow boat, as a finished product, to our U.S. distribution centers on the East and West Coasts. That saves us a lot on freight.

Joe: It sure does. Thanks for your explanation, J.P.

Jean-Pierre: You're welcome, Joe. See you at the meeting tomorrow.

Satisfied with the shipping cost information, Joe now has all of the raw data he needs from the team members. With it, he calculates two key figures that he will use in his financial comparison of the two site options: the initial capital expenditure required and the cost to manufacture each bottle of Beta-rella. Applying trend information he obtained, Joe also prepares sets of forecasted income statements for the first ten years of the project (Figure 10.2) and using these forecasts, he calculates the net present value for each site option.

Notice in Joe's data file that the Spain site is the lower cost location in terms of both initial capital expenditure required and manufacturing cost per unit. The net present values, which Joe has calculated, also support that determination. Now he must work with his information to make it clear and readily comprehensible for the team.

Summarizing and Organizing the Data for Presentation   As Joe prepares his data for the team's next meeting, he realizes that he cannot merely hand out copies of his data file. Even though the team members are experienced in working with numbers to a certain extent, wading through spreadsheets that contain a variety of data and trying to distill from them what is important would waste everyone's time. So Joe plans to *summarize* his data by including on his presentation slides only those facts and figures most relevant to the team's recommendation; he also plans to *organize* the data in order of most to least important.

Visual Display of Data: Pie Charts   Joe knows from experience that the financial side of the team's recommendation will be based primarily on a comparison of the amounts of initial capital expenditure required and on which location can manufacture the product at the lowest manufacturing cost per unit. As you can see in Figure 10.3, pp. 326–327, he summarizes the capital expenditure information for each site on his first slide (a) and summarizes the total cost per unit information for the sites on the second slide. On slides (b) and (c), Joe breaks down each per unit total manufacturing cost by its components (direct materials, direct labor, overhead, and shipping costs) so that team members can see and discuss specifically why the cost per bottle of Beta-rella is greater in Minnesota than it is in Spain. By using pie charts to illustrate the cost components, Joe not only communicates the dollar amounts of each component efficiently but also illustrates each component as a proportion of the total per unit cost.

Figure 10.2

Accountant's Project Data File

Spain facility

Source	Data Item	Amount
Lukins	Square footage	10,000
Lukins	Remodeling costs	none
Lukins/Laval	Packaging and processing equipment	$2,000,000
	Total initial capital outlay	**$2,000,000**
Lukins	Training costs	none
Allwell/Laval	Materials	$1.00
	Overhead	$0.40
Lukins	Labor	$0.25
Pau	Shipping cost	$0.02
	Total cost to manufacture	**$1.67/btl**

Minnesota facility

Source	Data Item	Amount
Wycoff	Square footage	10,000
Wycoff	Remodeling costs	$7,000,000
Wycoff/Laval	Packaging and processing equipment	$6,000,000
	Training costs (onetime cost to retrain existing employees)	$500,000
	Total initial capital outlay	**$13,500,000**
Wycoff		
Allwell/Laval	Raw materials	$1.15
	Plant overhead	$0.60
Wycoff	Direct labor	$0.22
	Total cost to manufacture	**$1.97/btl**

Visual Display of Data: Line Graph   Next, Joe plans to present forecasted income statement information to show the team the expected revenues, operating expenses, and profits of each site. Because presenting all 20 income statements would overload the team members with more details than they need, Joe creates a multiline graph for each site that illustrates how sales, marketing and sales costs, and net income are expected to pan out in the first ten years of Beta-rella production (slides [d] and [e]).

Joe then chooses to show just two income statements for each site, one for Year 1 and one for Year 5, on slides (f) and (g). Joe chooses to present Year 1 because he expects that team members will want to know the magnitude of the difference in profits between the two site options. Because sales vol-

Figure 10.2

Accountant's Project Data File—*continued*

Data for forecasted income statements

Source	Data Item	Amount
Parker	Sales volume—year 1	5,000,000 btls
Parker	Selling price	$14/btl
Parker	Anticipated sales trend	5% increase through year 5 no increase years 6–10
Lukins/Allwell	Anticipated manufacturing cost annual increase	5% increase through year 5 3% increase years 6–10
Parker	Marketing and sales costs—year 1	$40,000,000
Parker	Anticipated marketing and sales cost trends	steady through year 5 5% decrease years 6–10
Corporate	General and administrative costs—year 1	$12,000,000
Corporate	Anticipated general and administrative cost increase	5% per year
Corporate	Cost of capital	10%

ume and operating expenses are expected to increase at the same steady rate through Year 5, Joe decides it is unnecessary to present the income statements for those years. After Year 5, the company's marketing manager expects sales volume to level off (no longer increase) and marketing and sales costs to decline, and so that year warrants presentation in Joe's view because the product reaches maturity and profits no longer continue to rise at the same rate as in Years 1 through 5. Because Years 6 through 10 are expected to be similar to Year 5, Joe chooses not to present those income statements to the team.

On the last slide, (h), Joe provides the sites' net present value figures, which reinforce his first two slides by showing that the Spain site has the higher net present value.

Presenting the Information to the Team and Participating in Making the Decision   Joe presents his financial information to the team at its next regular meeting by showing his slides and describing his determinations verbally. During his presentation, Joe not only must communicate his prepared information effectively; he must also be prepared to answer questions that the team members might ask. He brings along a copy of his data file so he can refer to it if necessary. (See Chapter 7 for detailed advice on delivering oral presentations.)

During its deliberations, the team must evaluate more than the financial aspects of each site option; it must also consider any qualitative issues that could affect the success of either or both of the sites. As the Beta-rella team discusses the strengths and weaknesses of each site, they try to address any

Figure 10.2

Accountant's Project Data File—*continued*

			Forecasted Income	
	Year 1	Year 2	Year 3	Year 4
Sales	$70,000,000	$73,500,000	$77,175,000	$81,033,750
Cost of Goods Manufactured and Sold	$8,350,000	$8,767,500	$9,205,875	$9,666,169
Gross Profit	$61,650,000	$64,732,500	$67,969,125	$71,367,581
Operating Expenses				
Marketing/Sales Expense	$40,000,000	$40,000,000	$40,000,000	$40,000,000
General and Administrative	$12,000,000	$12,600,000	$13,230,000	$13,891,500
Total Operating Expenses	$52,000,000	$52,600,000	$53,230,000	$53,891,500
Net Income	$9,650,000	$12,132,500	$14,739,125	$17,476,081

Net Present Value: $104.5 million

			Forecasted Income	
	Year 1	Year 2	Year 3	Year 4
Sales	$70,000,000	$73,500,000	$77,175,000	$81,033,750
Cost of Goods Manufactured and Sold	$9,850,000	$10,342,500	$10,859,625	$11,402,606
Gross Profit	$60,150,000	$63,157,500	$66,315,375	$69,631,144
Operating Expenses				
Marketing/Sales Expense	$40,000,000	$40,000,000	$40,000,000	$40,000,000
General and Administrative	$12,000,000	$12,600,000	$13,230,000	$13,891,500
Total Operating Expenses	$52,000,000	$52,600,000	$53,230,000	$53,891,500
Net Income	$8,150,000	$10,557,500	$13,085,375	$15,739,644

Net Present Value: $83 million

possible problems that could arise: The distribution manager describes the problems that could be experienced by operating within a long international supply chain; the Spain liaison addresses possible complications due to differences in working culture, language, and computer systems; and Joe informs the group about the possible impact of doing business with the new Euro currency. Figure 10.4, p. 328, shows the slides Joe uses to summarize what he has learned.

After considering all aspects of the manufacturing sites in question, the Beta-rella team comes to an agreement that the Spain site should be recommended. It is now the job of the project manager, Dave Dwyer, to communicate the team's recommendation to upper management, who have the power to give the go-ahead to the project.

Presentation of the Team's Recommendation to Management

At their next regularly scheduled meeting, Dave Dwyer will make a formal presentation to Millenium's executive committee, which consists of the company president and vice presidents for marketing, sales, operations, finance, product development, and human resources. Dave writes a memo to request placement on the agenda and e-mails it to the company president's secretary (see Figure 10.5, p. 329). Dave uses proper memo-writing technique (see Chapter 4) for a simple, single-point message: His opening paragraph establishes context and purpose, his body paragraph begins with a topic sentence

Statements—Spain Site

Year 5	Year 6	Year 7	Year 8	Year 9	Year 10
$85,085,438	$85,085,438	$85,085,438	$85,085,438	$85,085,438	$85,085,438
$10,149,477	$10,453,962	$10,767,580	$11,090,608	$11,423,326	$11,766,026
$74,935,960	$74,631,476	$74,317,857	$73,994,830	$73,662,112	$73,319,412
$40,000,000	$38,000,000	$36,100,000	$34,295,000	$32,580,250	$30,951,238
$14,586,075	$15,315,379	$16,081,148	$16,885,205	$17,729,465	$18,615,939
$54,586,075	$53,315,379	$52,181,148	$51,180,205	$50,309,715	$49,567,176
$20,349,885	$21,316,097	$22,136,709	$22,814,625	$23,352,396	$23,752,236

Statements—Minnesota Site

Year 5	Year 6	Year 7	Year 8	Year 9	Year 10
$85,085,438	$85,085,438	$85,085,438	$85,085,438	$85,085,438	$85,085,438
$11,972,737	$12,331,919	$12,701,876	$13,082,933	$13,475,420	$13,879,683
$73,112,701	$72,753,519	$72,383,561	$72,002,505	$71,610,017	$71,205,754
$40,000,000	$38,000,000	$36,100,000	$34,295,000	$32,580,250	$30,951,238
$14,586,075	$15,315,379	$16,081,148	$16,885,205	$17,729,465	$18,615,939
$54,586,075	$53,315,379	$52,181,148	$51,180,205	$50,309,715	$49,567,176
$18,526,626	$19,438,140	$20,202,414	$20,822,300	$21,300,302	$21,638,578

and then develops his point with details, and his closing paragraph requests action.

Although he will present the results of the team's study orally rather than in writing, the project manager will, in fact, deliver a *recommendation report* to the executive committee at the June 10 meeting. The report, presented via key words on PowerPoint slides, is constructed according to the principles of sound report writing (see Chapter 5). Dave begins with a summary of the team's work and its recommendation, followed by sections explaining the background of the project, comparative data used and the rationale for the recommendation, and, finally, a conclusion. Figure 10.6, pp. 330–332, shows the PowerPoint presentation that Dave creates for the Executive Committee meeting. Note that Dave has included Joe Markley's slides (presented earlier at the team meeting) in his presentation.

Although the project manager delivers the presentation to the Executive Committee, the team accountant attends the meeting as well in case members of the Executive Committee want detailed answers about the financial assumptions the team used. Therefore, Joe Markley prepares for the meeting as if he were going to present the financial information himself. He thinks about possible questions the executives might ask and gets ready to answer questions about, for example, the projected costs to manufacture, the net present value assumptions, the sales growth rates, or the possible impact of the Euro economy in Spain. He brings with him his original data file so he can look up specific numbers if necessary. He knows that the meeting offers him a unique opportunity to make a good impression on influential people in the company.

Figure 10.3

Presentation Slides—Summarized Financial Data

a.
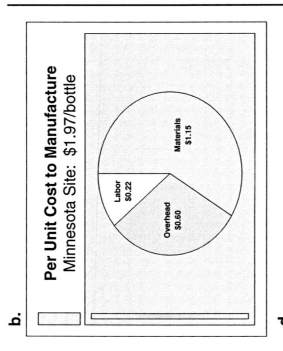

Initial Capital Expenditures

■ Minnesota Site   **■ Spain Site**

■ Minnesota Site		■ Spain Site	
▪ Remodeling costs	$7,000,000	▪ Packaging and processing equipment	$2,000,000
▪ Packaging and processing equipment	$6,000,000		
▪ Training costs (onetime cost to retrain existing employees)	$500,000		
▪ **Total initial capital outlay**	**$13,500,000**	▪ **Total initial capital outlay**	**$2,000,000**

b.
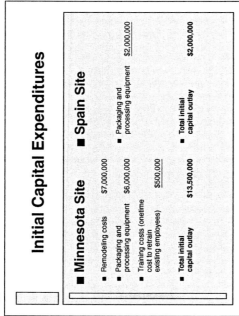

Per Unit Cost to Manufacture
Minnesota Site: $1.97/bottle

c.
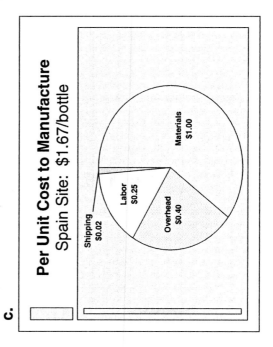

Per Unit Cost to Manufacture
Spain Site: $1.67/bottle

d.
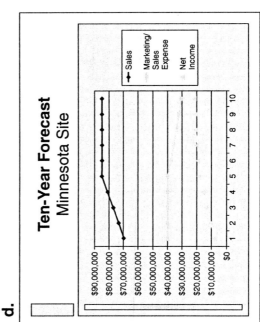

Ten-Year Forecast
Minnesota Site

Figure 10.3

Presentation Slides—Summarized Financial Data—*continued*

f. Forecasted Income Statements: Year 1

■ **Minnesota Site**

Sales	$70,000,000
Cost of Goods Manufactured and Sold	$9,850,000
Gross Profit	$60,150,000
Operating Expenses:	
Marketing and Sales	$40,000,000
General and Administrative	$12,000,000
Total Operating Expenses	$52,000,000
Net Income	**$8,150,000**

■ **Spain Site**

Sales	$70,000,000
Cost of Goods Manufactured and Sold	$8,350,000
Gross Profit	$61,650,000
Operating Expenses:	
Marketing and Sales	$40,000,000
General and Administrative	$12,000,000
Total Operating Expenses	$52,000,000
Net Income	**$9,650,000**

h. Net Present Value

■ **Minnesota Site**   *$83 million*

■ **Spain Site**   *$104.5 million*

e. Ten-Year Forecast
Spain Site

(chart with y-axis from $0 to $90,000,000, x-axis years 1–10; legend: Sales, Marketing/Sales Expense, Net Income)

g. Forecasted Income Statements: Year 5

■ **Minnesota Site**

Sales	$85,085,438
Cost of Goods Manufactured and Sold	$11,972,737
Gross Profit:	$73,112,701
Operating Expenses:	
Marketing and Sales	$40,000,000
General and Administrative	$14,586,075
Total Operating Expenses	$54,586,075
Net Income	**$18,526,626**

■ **Spain Site**

Sales	$85,085,438
Cost of Goods Manufactured and Sold	$10,149,477
Gross Profit:	$74,935,960
Operating Expenses:	
Marketing and Sales	$40,000,000
General and Administrative	$14,586,075
Total Operating Expenses	$54,586,075
Net Income	**$20,349,885**

Figure 10.4

Presentation Slides—Qualitative Information

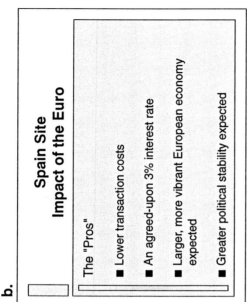

Figure 10.5

Memo Requesting Time on the Agenda

> ## MEMO
>
> **To:** Kathy Green, Executive Assistant to the President
> **From:** David Dwyer, Capital Project Manager
> **Subject:** Placement on Executive Committee Meeting Agenda
> **Date:** June 1, 2000
>
> Because the Beta-rella project team has concluded its study, I am writing to request placement on the agenda for the June 10, 2000, meeting of the Executive Committee.
>
> As project manager, I intend to present the team's recommendation for site selection to the Executive Committee. My presentation will take approximately ten minutes, and we should assume another ten minutes for a question and answer period. I will need access to the conference room's screen projection hardware for my PowerPoint presentation.
>
> Management is anxious to move on Beta-rella, and your help in getting the project on the agenda will allow us to do that. Thank you for your assistance, and if you have any questions, please e-mail me or call me at extension 8540.

The Capital Expenditure Proposal

We noted in Chapter 5 that reports often are written as the result of a proposal; as in this case, however, recommendation reports often lay the groundwork for proposals. Here, the capital expenditure proposal, or the formal request for funding, will be written after the Executive Committee has accepted the recommendation put forward in the report, and it will draw on much of the information presented there (see Figure 10.7, p. 333).

It is most often the job of the project manager to act as the primary author of a collaboratively written capital expenditure proposal for the project once the team's recommendation has been accepted by management. Because the capital expenditure proposal is such a large document and must contain so many details from a variety of specialized areas of the company, the project manager, in addition to drafting sections of the proposal himself, draws on material furnished to him by his team members. (Refer to Chapter 8 for a detailed discussion of collaborative writing.)

The first one or two pages of a capital expenditure proposal typically contain a summary of project engineering criteria and detailed financial information.

Figure 10.6

Presentation to Executive Committee—PowerPoint Slides

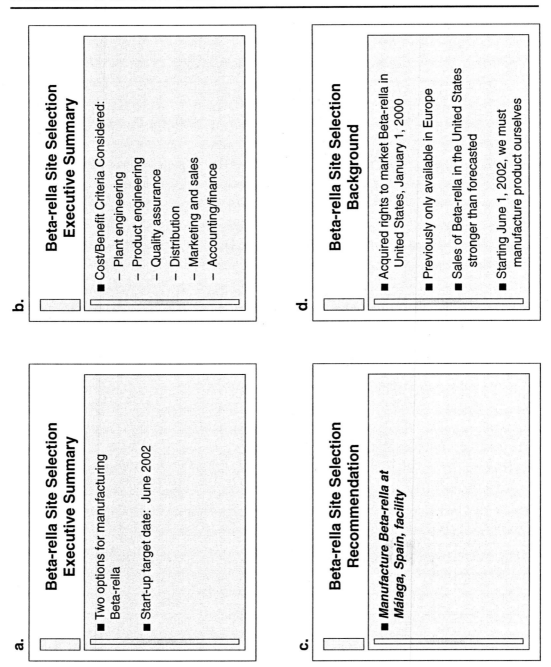

Figure 10.6

Presentation to Executive Committee—PowerPoint Slides—*continued*

e.

Beta-rella Site Selection Background

■ Option 1: Málaga, Spain
 – Factory space is available
 – Some new equipment required
 – Similar products already manufactured there
 – Skilled labor force in place
 – Raw material source close by

f.

Beta-rella Site Selection Background

■ Option 2: Minneapolis, Minnesota
 – Major plant remodeling needed
 – Much new equipment required
 – Labor force training required

g.

Initial Capital Expenditures

■ **Minnesota Site**   ■ **Spain Site**

■ Remodeling costs $7,000,000
■ Packaging and processing equipment $6,000,000
■ Training costs (onetime cost to retrain existing employees) $500,000

■ Total initial capital outlay $13,500,000

■ Packaging and processing equipment $2,000,000

■ Total initial capital outlay $2,000,000

h.

Per Unit Cost to Manufacture
Minnesota Site: $1.97/bottle

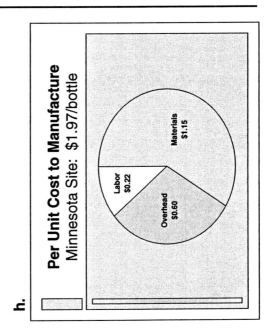

Labor
$0.22

Overhead
$0.60

Materials
$1.15

Figure 10.6

Presentation to Executive Committee—PowerPoint Slides—*continued*

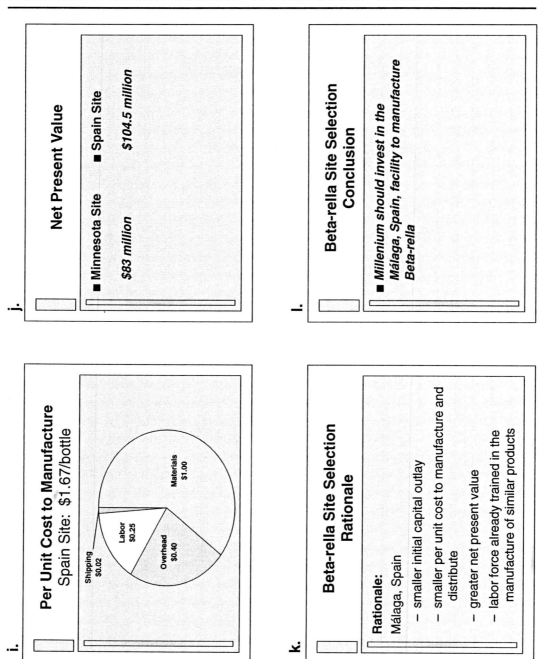

Figure 10.7

Capital Expenditure Proposal

> ## PROPOSAL
>
> ### Background
>
> On January 1, 2000, Millenium acquired the rights to market the nutritional supplement Beta-rella in the United States. Before that time, the supplement, which is produced in Agde, France, using a unique, patented manufacturing process, has only been available in Europe. Since launching the product on January 1, we have experienced stronger sales of Beta-rella in the United States than our forecasts predicted.
>
> Beta-rella's current manufacturer will supply us with the product until June 1, 2002, but beginning then, we will have to manufacture the product ourselves.
>
> Two manufacturing facility options are available to us:
> 1. to add the manufacture of Beta-rella to our new facility in Málaga, Spain, or
> 2. to redesign and rehab our existing Minneapolis factory.
>
> ### Proposal
>
> We propose that the company manufacture Beta-rella at its newly constructed facility in Málaga, Spain.
>
> ### Benefits
>
> The benefits of choosing to manufacture Beta-rella at our Málaga, Spain, facility are as follows:
>
> - The initial capital expenditure will be only $2 million, which will purchase the few pieces of processing and packaging equipment needed to produce Beta-rella in the unused factory space.
> - The per unit cost to manufacture will be minimized due to lower raw material costs and lower allocated overhead.
> - The investment's net present value will be maximized ($104.5 million).

Figure 10.7

Capital Expenditure Proposal—*continued*

■ The labor force is already trained in the manufacture of similar products.

Rationale and Comparative Costs

Our presumption of the benefits described above is based on the following financial and qualitative studies of the Málaga, Spain, site. The alternative site in Minneapolis, Minnesota, was also studied and found to be less desirable.

Initial Capital Outlay

	Spain Site	Minnesota Site
Packaging and processing equipment	$2,000,000	$6,000,000
Remodeling costs		$7,000,000
Training costs (onetime cost to retrain employees)		$ 500,000
Total initial capital outlay	**$2,000,000**	**$13,500,000**

By choosing to manufacture Beta-rella in Spain, Millenium will save approximately $11.5 million in initial capital expenditures.

Per Unit Cost to Manufacture

	Spain Site	Minnesota Site
Direct materials	$1.00	$1.15
Direct labor	.25	.22
Overhead	.40	.60
Cost to ship finished product to United States	.02	
Cost per bottle:	**$1.67**	**$1.97**

By choosing to manufacture Beta-rella in Spain, Millenium will save 30 cents per bottle in manufacturing costs. Assuming a first-year volume of 5 million bottles, Millenium will save $1.5 million, or approximately 18%, in manufacturing costs in the first year, and this percentage of savings is presumed to continue annually through Year 10 of the project. (See the appendix to this proposal, which contains the ten-year forecasted income statements for both sites.)

Figure 10.7

Capital Expenditure Proposal—*continued*

Net Present Value

Based on the ten-year forecasted income statements (see appendix to this proposal), and a cost of capital rate of 10%, the following net present values were calculated:

Spain Site	Minnesota Site
$104.5 million	$83 million

Although either site would be expected to render a positive net present value, that of the Spain site is higher by $21.5 million, indicating that it is the more desirable choice.

Qualitative Issues

- The products currently being manufactured in the Málaga, Spain, facility are similar in production process and packaging to Beta-rella. As a result, the labor force at that plant is already trained and ready to begin manufacturing Beta-rella immediately.
- The Málaga, Spain, facility is located near the Mediterranean Sea, where the primary ingredient of Beta-rella, the chlorella alga, is harvested. Chlorella is highly sensitive to environmental conditions, and, if we were to manufacture Beta-rella in Minnesota, it would likely be very costly and risky to ship in its raw state.
- Although the European economy is currently in a transitional and volatile state, the Euro situation is expected to stabilize in 2002, when the hard currency is introduced. The Euro is expected to create a larger, stronger economy and greater political stability in Europe, and we concur with many economists that now is an excellent time to invest in Europe.

Frequently, this information is presented in a columnar format with little or no prose accompanying it. The section provides a quick overview of the raw numbers and often follows corporate guidelines on a standardized form.

The second section of the proposal contains the project manager's written request for project funding. In many cases, the request follows the general guidelines for an internal proposal in that it attempts to persuade the audience by building an argument for the expenditure and using the following organization: background, the proposal, benefits, rationale and description of methods, and cost. (For more information on writing internal proposals, see Chapter 5.)

The project manager's report would typically conclude with a section titled "Implementation Plan," in which the manager would describe precise details about the timing of plant preparation and equipment purchases and about how and when the money will be spent.[8]

When the project manager finishes compiling the proposal, he transmits it to each team member, who reviews and approves it. The proposal is then sent to the first person or committee who must approve the capital expenditure. At some companies, the proposal may simply require the signature of the CFO or the company president; at other companies, the document may have to travel through a chain of individuals and/or committees who must all give their approval along the way. Upon final approval of the proposal, the capital expenditure may be made and the project gets underway.

CONCLUSION

Regardless of which of many roles the managerial accountant plays within his or her company, effective communication skills are required at every turn for the day's business to be carried out efficiently and productively and for the accountant to succeed in moving up the corporate ladder. In the next chapter, we look at how accountants who work as auditors with public accounting firms communicate effectively in their profession.

NOTES

[1]Gary Siegel and C. S. Kulesza, "From Statement-Preparer to Decision-Support Specialist: The Coming Changes in Management Accounting Education," *Management Accounting* (January 1996): 43–47. Sheryl Scobie, "The New Diversity of Financial Professionals," *CMA Magazine* (July-August 1998): 9–14.

[2]Siegel and Kulesza, p. 44.

[3]Julie H. Hertenstein and Marjorie B. Platt, "Why Product Development Teams Need Management Accountants," *Management Accounting* 79, no. 10 (April 1998): 50–56.

[4]Ibid., p. 50.

[5]Ibid., p. 53.

[6]Ibid.

[7]Peter Murray, "Mastering Management Reporting," *The Australian Accountant* (October 1994): 23.

[8]As we point out in Chapter 5, the elements of proposals can vary from one situation to the next. Some proposals include a "Benefits" section but no "Rationale"; in others, the section here entitled "Implementation Plan" is called "Description of Methods." Regardless of their differences, however, the common denominator of all proposals is the rhetorical purpose: to persuade.

EXERCISES

1. **Scenario:** You are working as an accountant for a publicly held corporation. From week to week you encounter a wide variety of situations that require your communication expertise.

   Writing task: For each of the following scenarios, analyze your audience and your message and determine which of the following means of communication you feel would be most effective: e-mail, one-on-one meeting, formal group meeting with agenda, informal meeting with several people, phone call, letter, memo, report, or presentation. In addition, for written communication and presentations, cite which forms of presentation you would include.

   a. You have been asked to provide a financial overview of the past fiscal year at a group meeting of your firm's sales force.

   b. The controller has requested that you research new accounting standards related to the company's investments and report back to her about changes that need to be implemented in the company's procedures.

   c. One of the student interns working under your supervision interpreted your firm's procedures incorrectly and you need to communicate the problem to him.

   d. The vice president of finance is preparing a proposal for financing to be presented to a group of banks. To obtain background information, he has asked you to summarize your firm's operations for the past five years.

   e. You have been asked to explain to a group of four or five auditors your firm's procedures for taking a physical inventory.

   f. The accounting society at your alma mater has asked you to represent managerial accounting on a panel discussion exploring careers in accounting.

2. **Scenario:** As a cost accountant for an international corporation you have been assigned to contact division managers throughout the world and request information about why significant expense items were over or under budget each month. Eventually you will use this information to prepare a variance report to management analyzing monthly budget to actual performance. You have drafted the following e-mail message as a template for managers to use whenever variances between actual and budgeted expenditures need to be explained.

   After you asked your supervisor what she thought of your message, she handed you a copy of this textbook, *The Accountant's Guide to Professional Communication: Writing and Speaking the Language of Business,* and suggested you read Chapters 3 and 4 and then revise your memo.

   Writing task: Reread Chapters 3 and 4 of this text, and then completely revise the memo here requesting the needed information from division managers. Be sure to use a professional communication style, a "you" attitude, a positive tone, and good overall organization.

MEMO

MEMORANDUM

To: {name}, Division Manager
From: Steven R. Luckenbill, Corporate Accountant
Date: {date}
Subject: Budget/Actual Expense Variances for {month} {year}

I am in receipt of your expense analysis report for {month} {year}. Pleased be advised that your expenditures in various categories, as specified below, deviate from the budget for this period by significant amounts. It is the responsibility of each division manager to explain certain variances to me so that I can report on them to corporate management and appropriate action can be taken by officers of the company, if they make a determination that it is necessary. Your financial performance this month is obviously not up to expectation and this can cause serious problems for the company as a whole, so it is important that we understand the problems so we can attempt to correct them. In order to accomplish my objectives and carry out my job responsibilities, you must respond with explanations for the attached budget variances. I expect you will be able to expedite this request due to its urgent nature.

{Listing of budget variances by account}

---

3. **Scenario:** You revised the e-mail message in Exercise 2 and have begun to use it to obtain information from division managers. When you called the northwestern U.S. division manager in Portland, Oregon, about his division's $250,000 overbudget expenditures for repair and maintenance expense he replied, "This expense variance problem is the same month after month! I don't know why they had to hire someone to harass us about it! Every year, we give you people at Corporate a realistic budget, and every year, you cut it, but you don't know the things that really need to be done. If you'd leave our budgets alone we wouldn't be over budget! I've been working for this company for 20 years and it's always the same—cut, cut, cut. That's why it looks like we spent too much this month! Equipment needs to be painted so it doesn't rust. If we don't paint it

we'll need to buy new equipment within a year or two. Engines and pumps have to be repaired when they stop running, or we don't earn the money this company needs to survive. There's nothing unusual about this month—we had *normal* expenditures for repairs and maintenance—I can't help if they look over budget to you people at Corporate."

Communication task:

a. Analyze the manager's response. Describe the tone of his reply. What might his tone indicate? Without actually writing a reply, describe the things you need to consider as you respond to him.

b. Assume you are unable to get any other specific information that would be useful in preparing your report. Write a paragraph, which will be included in the variance analysis report you prepare for management, explaining why the northwestern U.S. division was $250,000 over budget for repair and maintenance expense this month.

4. **Scenario:** As an accountant, you will regularly work as part of a team to accomplish certain tasks and objectives. Some of your team experiences will be positive and rewarding; others will be frustrating and disappointing. Analyzing the team encounters you have already experienced can help you understand what makes a team successful or unsuccessful, and thus help you encourage positive actions and avoid counterproductive actions when working in groups in the future.

Communication task:

a. Individually, analyze team experiences you have had during the past year or two. They could include team projects for classes you are taking, extracurricular activities in which you worked as part of a group, or teams that were part of your summer or part-time work or internship experiences. First, consider the most successful teams. List five or six reasons why you believe these teams were more successful than others. Next, consider the least successful teams. List five or six reasons why you believe these teams did not work well.

b. In groups of four to six students, compare and discuss the results of your analysis. Are there any factors common to your most successful teams? Are there any factors common to your least successful teams?

c. What did you learn from this exercise? How can you apply it to working in teams in the future?

5. Scenario: As a financial analyst for your company, you have compiled the following data related to your company's liquidity and certain industry averages.

Account	Balance at 12/31/00	Balance at 12/31/99
Cash	$15,000	$25,000
Current marketable securities	15,000	10,000
Accounts receivable (net)	45,000	55,000
Inventory	60,000	45,000
Fixed assets (net)	190,000	170,000
	$325,000	$305,000
Accounts payable	$50,000	$55,000
Long-term debt	100,000	110,000
Common stock	60,000	50,000
Additional paid-in capital	80,000	60,000
Retained earnings	35,000	30,000
	$325,000	$305,000

Account	Balance at 12/31/00	Balance at 12/31/99
Sales	$380,000	$350,000
Cost of goods sold	$265,000	$245,000
Net income	$15,000	$12,000
Ending accounts receivable (net) at 12/31/98		$50,000
Ending inventory at 12/31/98		$40,000
Industry averages:		
Current ratio		1.75
Acid-test ratio		1.20
Accounts receivable turnover		12.75
Inventory turnover		3.45

Writing task:

a. From the data given here, calculate ratios (to hundredths) and prepare a table summarizing the following measures of liquidity for both 1999 and 2000, as well as industry averages. Use the guidelines for preparing tables found in Chapter 7.

- the current (working capital) ratio
- the acid-test (quick) ratio
- the accounts receivable turnover
- the average collection period
- the inventory turnover
- the average days to sell the inventory

b. Prepare a short report in memo format to send to your company's CFO. Discuss the company's liquidity at December 31, 2000, commenting on trends as well as on your company's performance compared to industry averages. To the extent possible, forecast what might take place in the future based on what you know about the last two years.

6. **Scenario:** You have been asked to prepare an agenda for a meeting of cost accounting personnel in preparation for adopting a new activity-based costing system at your company. At the meeting, the vice president of finance will discuss the need for an improved costing system, which will permit better pricing decisions and more in-depth efficiency analyses. The controller will introduce the systems representative from FAST, Inc., who will be providing and installing the new ABC costing system software. The vice president of manufacturing will discuss the shortcomings of the current system.

   Writing task: Prepare an agenda for the meeting. Who would be best suited to making opening remarks at the meeting? Are there any other personnel you think should be invited or whose input would be helpful? Add any components that you feel the cost accountants will need to be fully informed and receptive to the system change. Be sure to allow time for a discussion and question and answer period.

7. **Scenario:** You are the accountant for a large law firm, Doran, Eisenberg, Miller and Norling. George Sands, president of Middleton Industries, a client of the firm, has contacted one of the firm's partners to complain about a recent invoice. The invoice was for $78,275 for the firm's successful defense of Middleton in a product liability suit. The firm bills clients on a hourly basis, plus expenses. The invoice included 145 hours of work at $150 per hour, 205 hours at $260 per hour, and expenses of $3,335 for travel and lodging related to the case. George Sands realizes it is standard practice for law firms to bill at an hourly rate, and he agrees that 350 hours was the approximate time spent on his case. However, he thinks all of the time should have been billed at the lower rate of $150 per hour, that $260 per hour is unreasonably high, and that this bill has resulted in a financial burden to his company and a very high profit for the law firm.

   Writing task: Using the professional writing guidelines in Chapters 3 and 4 of the text, write a letter to George Sands explaining and justifying the invoice. Include a brief explanation of the costs that are covered by your billing rate (associates are billed at $150, partners at $260), the different levels of experience that exist within a law firm, the benefits to Middleton Industries that resulted from the firm's work, and any other factors you believe would help him understand your fee while maintaining a good client relationship.

8. **Scenario:** You are a cost accountant working for Blue Jay Manufacturing, Inc. A new employee in the marketing department has asked you to explain a schedule of cost of goods manufactured to her because she is unfamiliar with this statement and does not understand how the company uses this information.

Writing task: Prepare a written explanation of the following Schedule of Cost of Goods Manufactured so that the new employee can understand it. Also, explain how the company might use this information.

Blue Jay Manufacturing, Inc.
Schedule of Cost of Goods Manufactured
For the month ended September 30, 2000

Work in process at September 1			$2,400
Manufacturing costs:			
Raw materials			
Beginning inventory of raw materials	2,500		
Purchases of materials	26,400		
Raw materials available for use	28,900		
Less: Ending inventory of raw materials	(4,100)		
Raw materials used		24,800	
Direct labor		15,000	
Variable overhead		4,500	
Fixed overhead		27,000	
Total manufacturing costs for the month			71,300
Total costs to account for			73,700
Less: Work in process at September 30			(5,200)
Cost of goods manufactured during September			$68,500

9. **Scenario:** As a corporate accountant, it important to you to obtain your Certified Management Accountant (CMA) certification and to remain active in professional organizations such as the Institute of Management Accountants and the Financial Executives Institute. As an active accounting professional, you are frequently asked to make presentations about management accounting at college career days or at accounting society meetings.

   Communication task: After reviewing Chapter 7 of this text, prepare a presentation about management accounting for an audience of college students. Use PowerPoint or other software to develop your presentation. You could include an overview of the CMA exam and other requirements to be a CMA, examples of the kinds of reports or analyses management accountants prepare, an explanation of the Standards of Ethical Conduct for Management Accountants, and/or other general information about management accounting as a career. Use visual representations of information whenever possible.

10. **Scenario:** You are an accountant in the office of the vice president of finance for New Designs, Inc. Top management recently met to discuss a proposal for major modifications to a local museum that had been developed by a team of New Designs' engineers. Although both the museum's board of trustees and the New Designs management team were very impressed with the proposal, they concluded that the costs for this project were too high, and either

the design must be modified to reduce costs or New Designs' proposal must be rejected.

Additional concerns involve timing: Because of the competitive nature of this project and the museum board's planning schedule, the revised proposal must be completed within the next two weeks. To revise the proposal within this time frame, the engineers, who have been working on this proposal for the past three months, will each need to work 80 to 100 hours per week until it is completed. If the proposal is rejected, New Designs stands to lose significant revenue in the next year and, as a result, could default on their loan payments.

Writing task: Because of your excellent communication skills, the vice president has asked you to draft a memo for his signature to the museum project engineering team informing them of this situation. Be sure to use a positive tone and follow the writing guidelines in Chapters 3 and 4. Make up any additional information you feel is necessary to draft the memo.

CHAPTER 11

Communication and Auditing

When an independent CPA firm undertakes an audit of a client company, it initiates one of the key communication processes in professional accounting: attesting to the quality of clients' financial information. Because a company might misrepresent its financial information—as a result of error, inadequate internal controls, or even deliberate manipulation of its records—users of that financial information need assurance from a disinterested and qualified monitor that the information accurately reflects the company's financial position. A report by an independent CPA firm provides such assurance. In issuing such a report, the CPA firm attests to the fact that the company's records can be relied on and that the company accounts for its business according to proper professional standards. Such communications place public accountants under a great responsibility because in making them, CPAs act as arbiters of financial reliability in the marketplace. The world of business depends on the assurance and attestation services that CPAs provide; every time they render opinions, CPAs put their professional reputations and that of their firms on the line.

One of the most common and important attestation services is the financial statement audit, the subject of this chapter. In a financial statement audit, accountants (typically members of a CPA firm) study a client company's balance sheet, income statement, and statement of cash flows to make a professional judgment about the reliability of these documents. As the result of performing a financial statement audit, the CPA firm offers assurances about these written records to the client company's audit committee, board of directors, shareholders and potential investors, government agencies (such as the SEC), creditors, and customers. Every time an accounting firm gives an unqualified or "clean" opinion on its client's financial statements, it is stating that the company's financial statements are free of material misstatement. It is also attesting to the fact that the company has presented its financial position, results of operations, and cash flows in conformity with generally accepted accounting principles (GAAP), and that the firm has gathered and evaluated evidence in accordance with generally accepted auditing standards (GAAS) in deriving its opinion.

Generally accepted auditing standards dictate that the accountant's audit work be adequately planned and supervised; that an understanding of internal control be obtained; and that the evidence obtained, auditing procedures applied, and testing performed provide sufficient competent information with which to form an opinion. To provide proof of having audited in accordance with these professional standards, auditors make elaborate written records of the audit procedures they perform to provide documentation and evidence of the tests and evaluations that were conducted. These written records, which include audit engagement letters, planning documentation, audit programs, and audit workpapers, do not merely convey a story of how the audit was conducted but sometimes also serve to protect the accounting firm in liability disputes. Should an accounting firm ever have to defend its audit opinion in a court of law, this documentation would serve as important proof of professional competence and of non-negligent conduct in performing the audit.

Auditing requires adherence to professional auditing standards, hard work, and a thorough understanding of the client's company. This understanding—essential to the audit process—depends on effective oral and written communications among the audit team, between the auditors and the client company, and between the auditors and the parties who will use the client's information. From the accounting firm's initial engagement proposal to its final auditor's report, a successful audit consists of gathering and evaluating evidence within an environment of honest and thorough communication.

COMMUNICATION EVENTS IN THE AUDIT ENGAGEMENT

In this chapter, we describe the communication events that typically take place during a financial statement audit. To give you an inside look at what it is like to perform an audit, we have modeled the audit we discuss on one actually performed by an independent CPA firm. By focusing on real-world examples of audit documents, particularly those generated by staff and senior accountants, we introduce you to the kinds of communication skills that are expected of new accountants in the audit field. The exercises at the end of the chapter give you the chance to practice and refine those skills.

Here is an overview of the communication events that *typically* occur before and during an audit engagement.

1. The accounting firm produces an **audit engagement proposal** for the potential client, describing the reasons why the client should choose to have the firm perform its financial statement audit. The proposal is almost always prepared by partners of the firm and/or by the firm's marketing department.
2. Once the accounting firm has won the client, a partner, often with assistance from the firm's legal department, prepares an engagement letter. The **engagement letter** is a contract stating the terms and conditions of the engagement, the services the auditor firm will perform, and the fees that will be charged.
3. After both parties have signed the engagement letter, an **audit planning meeting** takes place among the engagement partner, the engagement manager (a supervisory-level accountant responsible for managing several concurrent engagements), the audit senior, and the audit staff. At this meeting, the audit team discusses preliminary information gathered from the client and agrees on an audit plan and schedule.

4. Based on discussion at the audit planning meeting, the audit senior writes a **planning memo** for the engagement. This document formally summarizes planning activities for the engagement and helps members of the audit team to design the audit program.

5. The **audit program,** which lays out in detail the steps and procedures for the engagement, is either selected from a bank of prewritten programs and tailored to the individual client or is written from scratch to suit the special requirements of the audit about to be undertaken.

6. During all phases of the audit, **interviews with the client** take place, usually at the client's place of business. Staff and/or senior accountants interview client management and other key employees for information regarding various audit issues.

7. During the course of the audit, audit staff and seniors record the procedures they have performed, the evidence they have gathered, and the conclusions they have reached in the **audit workpapers.** Writing for the workpapers, the most common type of writing that new auditors do, includes **tickmark explanations, descriptive narratives, summaries,** and **analyses.**

8. As the audit draws to a close, the audit staff and senior typically write the **management comments,** which are descriptions of reportable conditions (significant deficiencies in the design or operation of internal control). After being reviewed by the client and, usually, by the audit manager and audit partner, the management comments are drafted into a formal **management comment letter.** This letter may also contain the auditor's recommendations for operational improvement.

9. At the end of the audit, the final **audit report** is compiled. The report usually consists of the **auditor's opinion letter,** the audited financial statements, and the notes to the financial statements.

As you can see, an audit consists of numerous oral and written communication events and many different types of documentation. There can be a variety of other kinds of communication unique to each audit, of course, and every accounting firm has its own preferred forms of written documentation. We focus in the next section, however, on the communication events you can expect to encounter in *any* audit (see Figure 11.1 on the following pages).

The sample documents and descriptions of meetings and interviews in this chapter have been derived from communications generated at a large public accounting firm during the audit of a manufacturing company. The audit senior, an accountant in his third year, was responsible for writing many of the original documents. (An audit senior typically performs more complex audit procedures than his staff does and is responsible for supervising the staff accountants assigned to the audit.) Although more senior members of the firm produced such documents as the proposal, the engagement letter, and the final audit report, staff accountants and seniors were responsible for the communications at the heart of the audit—the **agenda for the planning meeting,** the **planning meeting,** the audit **planning memo,** the **client interviews,** the **workpaper**

Figure 11.1
_____

Communication Events During a Typical Audit

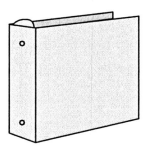

a. Engagement Proposal

Initiates the Audit Process

b. Engagement Letter

**Formalizes Contract Between Firm
and Client**

c. Audit Planning Meeting

Initiates Planning for the Audit

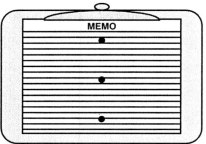

d. Audit Planning Memo

Summarizes Planning Meeting

e. Audit Program

Describes Audit Procedures

f. Interviews with Clients

**Solicit Facts and Data Needed for
Audit**

Figure 11.1

Communication Events During a Typical Audit—*continued*

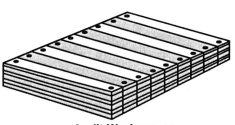

g. Audit Workpapers

Document Procedures Performed, Findings, and Conclusions

h. Management Comment Letter

Recommends Improvements to Client

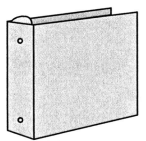

i. Audit Report/Opinion Letter

Concludes the Audit Process

From the time accountants begin writing working papers and having that work reviewed, the quality of their written work affects supervisors' assessments. At the senior level, for example, the accountant writes drafts of documents that the manager reviews. If an accountant's writing is weak, the manager must revise the work; over time, the manager may be less inclined to recommend the senior for other engagements. . . .

An accountant with excellent writing skills, by contrast, will be sought after by partners and managers alike. Possessing excellent writing skills is one sure-fire way to stand out.

Source: Gale Ruby Cohen
CA Magazine, March 1993

documentation, the **management comments,** and the **management comment letter.** Because these communications are among the most important that new accountants are involved in, and because new accountants are often judged by the quality of their communication skills, special care must be taken to ensure that these communication events are carried out in a polished and professional manner.

THE AUDIT ENGAGEMENT

The accounting firm's first formal communication with its prospective client is the proposal. The proposal outlines the services the accounting firm will provide, highlights special benefits the firm can offer the client, and estimates the fees for these services. A proposal is often brought to the client's place of business and delivered in an oral presentation. Customarily, proposals are prepared and presented by a partner, although senior-level auditors may contribute to the drafting and may accompany the partner to the presentation.

Because the audit services market has become more competitive in recent years, the quality of the proposal has become increasingly important for winning audit clients. Big Five and many large firms have their own marketing staff who assist the accountants in preparing attractive, convincing marketing pieces to help them win clients. Because potential clients can assume professional competence within CPA firms, firms use proposals to distinguish themselves from their competition by emphasizing special features such as personal, value-added service, unique industry knowledge and expertise, and money-saving ideas.

Chapter 5 provides information on writing proposals along with a sample engagement proposal. Chapter 7 offers tips and guidelines for making oral presentation of proposals.

THE AUDIT ENGAGEMENT LETTER

After the proposal has been accepted, the firm sends the client an engagement letter, spelling out what the firm will do and when, explaining the firm's responsibility for detecting errors and fraud, and confirming fees and billing arrangements. The engagement letter, in reality, is a contract between the accounting firm and the client, and it is always prepared and signed by someone in a position of considerable authority at the firm, usually a partner. Although you will probably not be called on to write an engagement letter during the early years of your career, Figure 11.2 provides an example of one for your information.

THE AUDIT PLANNING MEETING

Before the fieldwork begins on an audit engagement, the audit manager and audit partner decide on the overall strategy for the audit and convey these

Figure 11.2

Sample Engagement Letter

LETTER

Smith, Williamson, & Walker, LLP
85 Industrial Park Drive
Cincinnati, OH 45210
September 15, 1999

Mr. Chris E. Adams, Controller
Country Crafters, Inc.
636 Apple Street
Glenside, OH 45214

Dear Mr. Adams:

We are pleased to confirm our arrangements with you to audit the financial statements of Country Crafters, Inc., for the year 1999. Ms. Louise Jacobs, partner, will be responsible for the services that we perform for your company.

Our work will consist of an audit of the balance sheet at December 31, 1999, and the related statements of income, retained earnings, and cash flows. The financial statements are the responsibility of the company's management. Our responsibility is to express an opinion on the fairness of the presentation of those financial statements. Our audit will be conducted in accordance with generally accepted auditing standards. Those standards require that we plan and perform our audit to obtain reasonable assurance about whether the balance sheet is free of material misstatement, whether caused by error or fraud. However, because of the characteristics of fraud, particularly those involving concealment and falsified documentation (including forgery), a properly planned and performed audit may not detect a material misstatement. Therefore, an audit conducted in accordance with generally accepted auditing standards is designed to obtain reasonable, rather than absolute, assurance that the balance sheet is free of material misstatement.

An audit includes examining, on a test basis, evidence supporting the amounts and disclosures in the balance sheet. An audit also includes assessing the accounting principles used and significant estimates made by management, as well as evaluating the overall balance sheet presentation.

Figure 11.2
_____

Sample Engagement Letter—*continued*

We will report to the company matters coming to our attention during the course of our audit that we believe are reportable conditions. Reportable conditions are significant deficiencies in the design or operation of internal control that could adversely affect the company's ability to record, process, summarize, and report financial data consistent with the assertions of management in the balance sheet.

Our fee for audit services will be based on our regular per diem rates, plus travel and other out-of-pocket costs. Invoices will be rendered every two weeks and are payable upon presentation.

If you agree with the terms of our engagement described in this letter, please sign the enclosed copy and return it to us. We appreciate the opportunity to be of service to Country Crafters, Inc.

Sincerely,   Accepted by
Smith, Williamson, & Walker, LLP   Chris Adams [client]

---

plans to the audit senior. Then they meet with members of the audit team to discuss how the audit will be conducted and to agree on a plan for procedures and scheduling. The audit senior is frequently called on to prepare an agenda for the meeting and, in some cases, might even be responsible for leading the meeting.

Discussion at the planning meeting focuses on specific questions and details of implementation rather than on strategic issues, which have already been decided by senior members of the audit team. Nevertheless, the planning meeting offers staff and seniors a significant opportunity to demonstrate their communication skills and technical knowledge to those members of the firm who will be making crucial decisions about their career advancement. Staff accountants attending the meeting should thoroughly review in advance all preliminary documents, such as the previous years' workpapers, the client's Annual Reports and 10-Ks, accounting guides to the client's industry, FASB statements that might be unfamiliar to the group but relevant to the new client's industry, and so forth. The senior charged with preparing the agenda should think carefully about how the meeting can be most productively organized.

Figure 11.3 presents a sample agenda. Note how this agenda structures the time to be spent in the meeting. The audit senior, who is conducting the meeting, begins the meeting by presenting introductory topics himself. He has placed the audit manager's topics in the middle and has reserved the partner's

Figure 11.3

Sample Agenda for an Audit Planning Meeting

AGENDA

Audit Planning Meeting for Country Crafters, Inc.
October 10, 1999

I. Introduction to Country Crafters, Inc. (Ryan Worthington, audit senior)
   A. Client history
   B. Client's industry environment
   C. Key client management personnel

II. Time frame for the audit (Ryan)
   A. Timing of planning and preliminary fieldwork
   B. Timing of fieldwork and report preparation
   C. Budgeted billable hours for team members

III. Audit objectives and team expectations (Jerry Fields, audit manager)
   A. Audit objectives, materiality, and audit approach
   B. Roles of the audit staff members
   C. Role of the audit senior

IV. Firm's strategy and goals (Louise Jacobs, partner)
   A. Possible problem areas for new client audit
   B. Client's goals and expectations for future business growth
   C. Development of small business advisory services to the client.

---

discussion for last. This type of organization for a meeting leads the participants first through a sequence of interesting topics (details on the new client about whom the staff has probably been curious), devotes the middle to mundane but important considerations (scheduling and time constraints), and reserves the most interesting, even engaging topics for the end (discussion of possible problems and of ideas for expanding the firm's services to the client).

The agenda gets the meeting off to an energetic start, allows for some possible waning of interest, but then reenergizes the meeting toward the end. Other meeting strategies are possible, of course, but this strategy is generally reliable, especially for meetings of one hour or less. (See Chapter 6 for more advice on conducting meetings.)

THE AUDIT PLANNING MEMO

After the planning meeting takes place, staff or senior auditors may be called on to prepare a **planning memo** (see Figure 11.4), a formal written document that summarizes the plan for the audit and dictates to a large extent the content of the audit. To write the planning memo, the audit senior gathers

Figure 11.4

An Audit Planning Memo (excerpted)

MEMO

Country Crafters, Inc.
Audit Planning Memo
For Year Ended December 31, 1999

Client Background and Industry

Country Crafters, Inc., was founded in 1965 by Irene Havice and is a closely held corporation. Irene Havice owns approximately 55% of the company's stock; CEO Mary O'Reilly owns 30%; and Controller Chris Adams owns 1%. The company's other shareholders are various family members or independent small investors, none of whom individually own more than 2% of the company's stock.

As a result of aggressive acquisition of small, family-owned decorative country craft manufacturers, Country Crafters has grown rapidly in the last three years. The company has cornered a niche market in microwaveable pottery cookware and sells these items in national department stores as well as through many nationally distributed decorator housewares catalogs. Aside from the pottery line, which accounts for approximately 30% of the company's annual sales, Country Crafters also produces and sells dolls, toys, furniture, rugs, pillows and throws, jewelry, and clothing.

Audit Objectives

1. Issue the following reports upon completion of our audit:
   - Report on the financial statements
   - Management comment letter
2. Develop Ryan Worthington's skills as an audit senior and provide Kate Larsen and Claire Dufour (staff) with manufacturing audit experience.

Figure 11.4

An Audit Planning Memo (excerpted)—*continued*

> 3. Improve our firm's relationship with Irene Havice (majority owner) and Mary O'Reilly (CEO) in the interest of expanding our services into a business advisory engagement next year.

Engagement Timing and Staffing

Audit planning	October 15–31, 1999
Interim fieldwork	November 1–5, 1999
Final fieldwork and report preparation	January 15–February 25, 2000
Delivery of annual report and management comment letter	March 21, 2000

Staff		Budgeted Hours
Engagement Partner	Louise Jacobs	40
Engagement Manager	Jerry Fields	80
Engagement Senior	Ryan Worthington	300
Staff	Kate Larsen	200
Staff	Claire Dufour	200

Audit Strategy

To determine the audit strategy, S, W, & W first considered inherent risks to Country Crafters' continuing viability. We considered general economic conditions, relevant technological changes, competition from existing sources, and potential competition from new sources. We found significant risks from domestic competition and from growing markets in Mexico. Both the industry and Country Crafters are profitable, however, and are generating positive cash flows.

We also obtained and reviewed recent financial information for Country Crafters, including the prior years' workpapers (prepared by Henderson and Marks, CPAs). We conducted discussions with Country Crafters' management on matters of internal control.

Country Crafters' management has asked S, W, & W to help it assess the feasibility of opening its own line of retail stores in major shopping malls. During the course of the audit, team members should keep an eye open to any information that might be useful in a management advisory engagement subsequent to the audit.

Figure 11.4

An Audit Planning Memo (excerpted)—*continued*

Audit Program

A detailed audit program has been prepared and approved. The following is an overview of major accounts/audit areas.

<u>Cash</u>

Country Crafters maintains two bank accounts: a major operating account and a payroll account. Confirmations and requests for cut-off bank statements will be sent on both accounts. Returned confirmations will be reviewed against loan agreements, corporate minutes, etc.

We will trace and test prepared-by-client bank reconciliations and investigate interbank transfers.

<u>Inventory</u>

We will observe the client's taking of physical inventory (raw materials, work-in-process, and finished goods).

We will discuss with the client the company's inventory valuation procedures and pricing policies.

We will test the computational accuracy of the client's physical inventory sheets and will review those sheets for individually significant raw material, work-in-process, and finished good items.

---

preliminary information such as evaluations of the client's industry, business, and internal control system, results of analytical reviews performed, and assessments of various types of risks to the audit. He then organizes the information in a logical manner so he and his superiors can refer to it easily as they design the appropriate program for the audit.

Planning memos generally contain the following types of information:

- background on the client
- trends within the client's industry
- firm's objectives for the audit
- strategy for the audit
- schedule and timing plans
- synopsized audit program.

Figure 11.4 is an excerpt from a sample planning memo. Notice how the memo provides essential background information in summary form—that is, in a way that is concise and to the point—and outlines the audit schedule, staffing, and strategy with minimal detail. A more complete plan for the audit will be provided in the audit program.

THE AUDIT PROGRAM

Based on determinations made about the client through the planning process, the audit team supervisors (such as the partner, manager, and, perhaps, the senior) select and/or design an audit program appropriate for the client. The audit program is a detailed set of written instructions that describes the audit procedures and the sequence in which they will be performed. It is an important tool for controlling the progress and quality of the audit because it requires that the team specify the following in writing:

- the overall plan for the work
- details of required audit procedures, often in the form of instructions for staff accountants working on the audit
- a means of controlling the time spent on the audit
- evidence of the work performed on the audit.

Although staff auditors generally do not write these audit programs from scratch, they must be able to understand the technical language used. On occasion, they may be called on to make written modification(s) to existing audit programs. Audit seniors can be expected to write audit programs or parts of them, and these programs are usually evaluated by the audit manager and/or partner. Therefore, certainly audit seniors but even first-year accountants should be able to write clear and concise instructions.

Here are a few guidelines for writing instructions that others can follow easily:

1. *Use chronological order.* Properly written instructions create a step-by-step process for the reader.
2. *Number each step clearly.* Enumerating what to do first, second, third, and so forth, helps a reader stay on track.
3. *Treat closely related actions as a single step.*

Example: Determine which bank accounts need subsequent period cutoff statements and write a letter to the bank(s) requesting that these statements be mailed to our post office box.

Although this step describes two actions, the second is a direct follow-up to the first and therefore depends on it. Your instructions should clearly indicate this relationship.

4. *Use active voice and address the reader directly.* Writing directly to your reader makes it easy to keep your directions in the active voice (and therefore clear). Compare these two examples:

Example: The company's physical inventory should be observed via the firm's separate inventory observation program.

versus

Following the firm's separate inventory observation program, observe the company's taking of physical inventory.

The first sentence, which avoids addressing the reader directly, is impersonal and passive. The second sentence seems much more immediate: "Do this step next."

5. *Define any terms that may be unfamiliar to potential readers.* Compare these examples:

Example: Request, review, and summarize the client's IRMQ and compare results with prior years' file information.

versus

Request, review, and summarize the client's Insurance Risk Management Questionnaire (IRMQ) and compare results with prior years' file information.

6. *Test your instructions by following them yourself.* A trial run is the best way of checking your completeness and accuracy. A walk-through will show you immediately where you have left out important information, treated separate elements as single steps, or described procedures vaguely.

Figures 11.5 and 11.6 show excerpts from the audit program for Country Crafters. Notice how these instructions follow the guidelines outlined.

Audit programs are important to every phase of the audit because they contain the instructions that auditors need to complete the necessary audit procedures and because they document the auditors' compliance with firm and professional standards. As we noted earlier, much of the writing that staff auditors do is in fact to provide verification—in the workpapers—that the audit procedures in the program were performed and to note any reportable conditions (i.e., problems) that were detected.

INTERVIEWS WITH THE CLIENT

One of the auditor's main jobs is to gather thorough and accurate information about the client company's financial practices and systems of control. For this

Figure 11.5

An Excerpt from an Audit Program for Cash Audit Procedures

AUDIT PROGRAM

Audit Procedures

1. Send 12/31 confirmation requests for each bank account as well as for balances in savings institutions, certificates of deposit, and compensating balances. Use the standard confirmation forms to make these requests. Mail second requests if necessary.
2. Determine which bank accounts need subsequent-period cutoff statements and write a letter to the bank(s) requesting that these statements be mailed to our post office box.
3. Obtain prepared-by-client bank reconciliations and perform the following procedures:
   a. Trace the balance per bank on the reconciliation to the standard bank confirmation form received from the bank.
   b. Trace the balance per books to the general ledger, the trial balance, and the cash lead schedule.
   c. Review cash receipts and disbursements in each bank account for two months prior to and one month after 12/31 and perform other appropriate procedures to identify inter-bank transfer checks and deposits.

---

reason, fact-gathering interviews with employees of the client company represent a large part of any audit. Staff and senior accountants routinely conduct these interviews, which can include meetings with everyone from the company's account clerks to its chief financial officer.

The very nature of the audit process can make client interviewing a challenging communication task. It is the auditor's job, after all, to probe into the heart of the client's financial situation, to test systems and identify weaknesses, to review procedures and uncover discrepancies between policy and practice. The auditor must maintain an attitude of skepticism toward all information she receives, withholding judgment about the client's financial information until fieldwork has been completed. In the atmosphere of scrutiny and skepticism created by an audit, potential interviewees may feel defensive and even reluctant to cooperate with the audit team. This reluctance is especially likely among employees who feel uncertain about their job performance or have information they want to hide.

Interviews can be intimidating for auditors as well. The new auditor interviewing a chief financial officer, for example, could feel overpowered by the

Figure 11.6

An Excerpt from an Audit Program for Inventory

AUDIT PROGRAM

Audit Procedures

1. Use the firm's separate inventory observation program to review the company's taking of physical inventory.
2. Test the client's physical inventory sheets for computational accuracy:
   a. Trace counts taken during the physical inventory observation to the physical inventory sheets.
   b. On a test basis, compare tag numbers obtained during the physical inventory observation to those tag numbers noted on the inventory sheets. Investigate any irregular tag references.
   c. Reconcile the physical inventory sheets to the general ledger account balance. Investigate and explain any material discrepancies.
3. Determine the adequacy and appropriateness of allowances for scrap and obsolete inventory items, using the following procedures.

---

latter's relative maturity and business experience. If, in such a situation, the CFO seemed evasive, the auditor might find it hard to probe as deeply as necessary to uncover all the facts.

Because the relationship between auditor and client is a delicate one, auditors must approach client interviews with sensitivity and flexibility. By doing so, auditors can turn client interviews into an opportunity, not only to gather facts, but also to create a positive working relationship with the client. (For detailed information on interviewing, see Chapter 6.) The following checklist gives you a quick summary.

Tips for Successful Client Interviewing

1. Before meeting with the client, prepare by learning everything you reasonably can about the client's company, its organization, and problem areas.
2. Outline a plan for the interview, organize it by major subjects, and write down detailed questions that you intend to ask about each of those subjects. Use a mixture of open and closed questions to get the client talking but to keep him or her on track. *Remember:* Too many closed questions in a row make an interviewee feel interrogated!

3. Be punctual. Keeping people waiting is not only rude; it also makes them feel put down.
4. Begin the interview with a friendly smile and a firm handshake. Look the interviewee right in the eye. Smiles and straightforward eye contact put people at ease and create a positive first impression.
5. "Break the ice" with a comment on the weather, a sports triumph by the local team, a reference to an object on the interviewee's desk or wall.
6. Begin your interview with the simplest and least sensitive questions. Proceed to the more difficult questions only when your rapport with the client seems well established.
7. If the interviewee seems nervous or hostile, try adjusting the tempo of your speech, gestures, and even your breathing to those of your listener. Research shows that listeners feel most comfortable with speech rates that mirror their own.[1]
8. Take notes unobtrusively, and write up your notes as soon after the interview as you can.

During the Country Crafters audit, one of the staff auditors, Kate Larsen, became skeptical about the balance in the client's allowance for uncollectible accounts. She had noticed that the balance was distinctly lower than it had been in prior years while the amount of account sales for the year had grown. Her audit senior suggested that she make an appointment to discuss the matter with the company controller, Chris Adams. Because Kate was aware that the controller might feel defensive during an interview where he would be asked to justify the low balance in the allowance account, Kate planned to make an effort to break the ice before asking any probing questions. She jotted down a few notes with questions she wanted to ask the controller, and then went to his office punctually for the interview.

Kate: Good morning, Mr. Adams. Thank you very much for seeing me today on such short notice.

Chris: No problem, Kate, and please call me Chris. Would you like some coffee?

Kate: Thanks—that would be great. *[Chris pours the two cups of coffee.]* I must tell you that I'm very pleased to have been assigned to your company, Chris. Your company runs well and all your employees have been so helpful and friendly.
[Kate is breaking the ice by paying the company a compliment, and in so doing she indirectly pays Chris a compliment too.]

Chris: Yes, we've got a great team here in the accounting office. Mary (the CEO) and I try to maintain a family-like atmosphere here in administration, and it seems to be working very well.

Kate: [Taking her coffee] Thanks. *[They both sit down.]* Well, let me not take up too much of your valuable time this morning. I have just a few questions I'd like to ask you about the company's receivables.

[Kate shows respect for Chris and his busy schedule by promising to keep the meeting brief.]

Chris: Sure, go right ahead.

Kate: I've noticed that your sales in general have gone up this year— by the way, that's great!—and that your sales made on account have also gone up, which makes perfect sense. However, I also noticed that the allowance for uncollectibles has gone down as a percentage of year-end receivables. I was wondering about the reasons for this change in company estimates.

[Kate brings up the delicate issue—that the company is making a perhaps overly ambitious estimate of its uncollectible accounts—in a delicate manner. She simply states what she has seen in the accounting records without pointing a finger at the controller, even though he is the person who is probably responsible for making the decision to lower the estimate of uncollectible accounts. She poses the question as an open one, allowing Chris to respond in his own words.]

Chris: Well, you know, I am not the only one who decides on how to estimate the uncollectibles. The credit manager has a lot to do with it too.

[Chris evades Kate's question somewhat and even sounds a bit defensive.]

Kate: Yes, I see. It's perfectly logical that he would have a good idea of which customers were good risks and which were not, but I'm sure that you have your own insights into the situation. What is your understanding of the creditworthiness of your customers? *[Kate probes for Chris's explanation of the allowance.]*

Chris: Well, I do realize that other home decor manufacturers suffer more bad accounts than we do—I think the industry average is somewhere between 2% and 3% of credit sales—but we have very good customers. And some of them have somewhat unusual paying patterns. For example, Natural-Is-Nice, Sugarbox, Hall's, and Southern Style pay their invoices only once a year—in January when all their Christmas cash is rolling in.

Kate: Do you mean that even if they buy merchandise in March, it isn't paid for until the following January?

[Kate makes sure that she has understood his point by turning her question into a restatement of what Chris said. By asking him, in essence, to repeat what he was saying, she keeps him on the subject and gives him a little direction to keep talking about the subject of interest.]

Chris: That's right—and they always do pay. To my knowledge, none of our major customers are getting ready to go bankrupt and it sure would take a lot of the little guys defaulting to go beyond some $36,000 of allowance! In fact, for the last two years, we have written off less than 1% of our credit sales each year. I think that's pretty good.

Kate: Very impressive, considering what goes on industrywide. What do you think those other guys are doing wrong?

[Rather than asking Chris to defend his position, and perhaps risk making him defensive, Kate asks Chris for a critique of the company's competitors.]

Chris: I think many of them do business with little mom-and-pop gift and craft shops. You, know, shops whose owners go into it just for fun without doing their homework. Sometimes a little place like that can come and go in less than a year. We only sell to those places by insisting that they buy on credit cards, like Visa or MasterCard. We just don't take chances with small customers.

Kate: Very interesting. Well, thanks for giving me the scoop on this, Chris. I really appreciate your giving me some of your time.

Chris: Sure. Just let me know if you need anything else. I'll be here.

By relying on open questions in this preliminary interview, Kate has invited the interviewee to give his impressions of the situation in question. Open questions help build trust in audit interviews by encouraging interviewees to give their opinions and insights. Although Kate may still have some unanswered questions, she ends the interview when she is satisfied with the basic information obtained. Realizing that additional auditing work needs to be done to assess the allowance objectively, she politely closes the interview, leaving on good terms with the controller so that future interviews will be productive.

As soon as possible after meeting with the client, the auditor should assemble her notes and draft a memo summarizing the interview. Memos summarizing client interviews are addressed to the audit workpapers (treated in a later section of this chapter) and represent important documentation for the audit. Figure 11.7 illustrates how Kate might document her interview with the controller. In her memo, addressed to the file, Kate is not simply making notes for herself, but creating a record of part of the audit for multiple potential audiences:

1. her audit supervisor, who routinely reviews her work;
2. other members of the audit team, who may want to determine how this interview illuminates other aspects of the audit;
3. members of future audit teams, who may want to review the workpapers from this year's audit before beginning their own;
4. attorneys and/or court officials, should the audit later be subject to litigation by either party involved.

Kate writes up the interview in the form of a short report that summarizes the interview and defends a conclusion. As we pointed out in Chapter 5, many brief reports are presented in memo format, and much of the documentation created during the audit falls into this category. As you recall, reports should contain the following elements:

- An **introduction** summarizing the subject, purpose, and occasion of the report along with an explanation of how the report is organized.

Figure 11.7

Sample Memo Documenting Client Interview

MEMO

Date: December 17, 1999
To: 1999 Audit Workpapers/Country Crafters
From: Kate Larsen, staff auditor
Subject: Uncollectible Accounts Allowance Determination

On December 16, 1999, I held a discussion with Chris Adams, Country Crafters' controller, about the company's process for determining the Allowance for Uncollectible Accounts so that S, W, & W will be able to assess its adequacy.

The current allowance of approximately $36,000 represents 0.75% of the company's 12/31/99 accounts receivable. This amount is 1.25% lower than the 2% proportion that Country Crafters has historically maintained as its allowance. In addition, the controller has indicated that Country Crafters, for the past two years, has written off, on average, less than 1% of its credit sales. This percentage compares favorably to the norm in the home decor manufacturing industry, which, according to the controller, experiences bad debt write-offs of between 2% and 3% of credit sales nationally.

According to the controller, any customer having a balance in Accounts Receivable as of December 31 can be considered a reliable collection because customers' cash flows are in peak condition during and immediately after the Christmas shopping season, and most customers pay during this time.

The controller is confident that the current allowance of $35,692 is adequate to cover any potential losses. Here are the reasons he cites:

1. All of the major customers are paid up and none are in danger of declaring bankruptcy.
2. The number of small customers that could default would have to be very large to exceed the $36,000 allowance on the books.
3. The Over-90 Days balance appears high because several customers pay invoices only once a year. These customers (Natural-Is-Nice Company, Sugarbox Stores, Hall's Department Stores, and Southern Style Stores) pay their invoices in January regardless of their invoice dates or merchandise receipt dates.

Figure 11.7

Sample Memo Documenting Client Interview—*continued*

> In my opinion, S, W, & W will need to do further testing to assess the adequacy of the allowance for uncollectible accounts and to assess the validity of lowering the balance in the allowance to a smaller percentage of year-end receivables. See workpaper B-25 for further testing.

- A **background description** of the problem or situation that the accountant studied.
- An **explanation** of procedures performed to investigate the situation.
- A **conclusion** drawn from the application of principles and procedures to the problem or situation.

Let us look briefly at the ways Kate's memo conforms to these guidelines. It introduces the **context** and **purpose** of the memo in a one-sentence narration:

Example: *Context: [When]* On December 16, 1999, *[Who]* I held a discussion with Chris Adams, Country Crafters' controller, *[What]* about the company's process for determining the Allowance for Uncollectible Accounts . . .

Purpose: [Why] . . . so that S, W, & W will be able to assess its adequacy.

Any reader picking up the file will be immediately oriented to Kate's information.

The next two paragraphs summarize **the background** needed to support the conclusions the writer will draw at the end of the memo. Paragraph 2 identifies past and present allowances maintained by the company and compares these figures with the industry average:

Example: *[Present data]* The current allowance of approximately $36,000 represents .75% of the company's 12/31/99 accounts receivable.

[Past data] This amount is 1.25% lower than the 2% proportion that Country Crafters has historically maintained as its allowance. In addition, the controller has indicated that Country Crafters, for the past two years, has written off, on average, less than 1% of its credit sales.

[Comparative data] This percentage compares favorably to the norm in the home decor manufacturing industry, which, according to the controller, experiences bad debt write-offs of between 2% and 3% of credit sales nationally.

Other readers of the file need these comparative numbers to determine whether they can accept Kate's conclusions.

Paragraph 3 identifies **special circumstances in the case** that contribute to the company's confidence in the adequacy of its allowance:

> **Example:** *[Special circumstances]* . . . customers' cash flows are in peak condition during and immediately after the Christmas shopping season, and most customers pay during this time.

Paragraph 4 **presents the rationale** for that confidence by clearly and specifically itemizing the client's reasons for its confidence:

> **Example:** The controller is confident that the current allowance of $35,692 is adequate to cover any potential losses. Here are the reasons he cites:
> 1. All of the major customers are paid up and none are in danger of declaring bankruptcy.
> 2. The number of small customers that could default would have to be very large to exceed the $36,000 allowance on the books.
> 3. The Over-90 Days balance appears high because several customers pay invoices only once a year. These customers (Natural-Is-Nice Company, Sugarbox Stores, Hall's Department Stores, and Southern Style Stores) pay their invoices in January regardless of their invoice dates or merchandise receipt dates.

Notice that Kate takes care to attribute this rationale to *the company's controller*. At this point, she is not drawing a conclusion herself about the collectibility of these balances; rather she is documenting the client's position on the issue. A crucial difference exists between reporting the client's opinion on an issue and drawing a conclusion as a member of the audit team. Kate's memo makes that difference clear.

Paragraph 5 presents **the writer's judgment about the facts presented:**

> **Example:** *[Conclusion]* In my opinion, S, W, & W will need to do further testing to assess the adequacy of the allowance for uncollectible accounts and to assess the validity of lowering the balance in the allowance to a smaller percentage of year-end receivables. See workpaper B-25 for further testing.

Once again, Kate hedges her statement about the allowance with the phrase *In my opinion,* indicating that she is not stating a fact but making a judgment based on the facts she has at the time.

For more information on conducting and documenting client interviews, consult Chapter 6.

WRITING FOR THE AUDIT WORKPAPERS

Perhaps the most significant writing that staff accountants do involves writing for the workpapers.[2] Whether stored on paper or in electronic files, audit workpapers consist of records of evaluated numerical data and descriptions of procedures performed. Workpapers constitute the heart of the audit because they document the work performed. This documentation helps those who supervise and review the audit team and provides crucial support for the auditor's opinion.

According to Statement on Auditing Standards (SAS) No. 41, entitled "Working Papers,"

> working papers ordinarily should include documentation showing that
> a) The work has been adequately planned and supervised . . .
> b) A sufficient understanding of the internal control structure has been obtained to plan the audit . . .
> c) The audit evidence obtained, the auditing procedures applied, and the testing performed have provided sufficient competent evidential matter to afford a reasonable basis for an opinion . . .[3]

In order for workpapers to meet these authoritatively defined criteria, they must contain correct, complete information. They must make their often complicated content clear to any future auditor, providing adequate detail but without using vague or ambiguous language. Workpapers should also be succinct and concise so as not to waste the reader's time or lose the reader in unnecessary verbiage.

Here is an example of appropriate and inappropriate descriptions of findings resulting from the performance of an audit procedure for cash:

> **Example:** *Procedure:* Trace all outstanding checks appearing on a bank reconciliation as of a certain date to checks cleared in the bank statement of the subsequent month.
>
> *Inappropriate Description of Findings:* Nothing came to my attention as a result of applying the procedure.
>
> *Appropriate Description of Findings:* All outstanding checks appearing on the bank reconciliation were cleared in the subsequent month's bank statement.

The first description of findings is not a description at all; it is a conclusion drawn by the writer without supporting evidence. The phrases *Nothing came to my attention* and *applying the procedure* do not tell potential readers what steps the writer took to review the reconciliation. They simply ask the reader to take the writer's word for the findings. The second version appropriately describes how the writer reviewed the reconciliation against the later statement, thus providing proper documentation of audit procedures.

Types of Workpaper Writing

Writing for the workpapers takes several forms, the most common of which are **tickmark descriptions, narratives, summaries,** and **analyses of work performed.** Although auditors use these types of documentation in various sequences during the course of the audit, we have presented them here from the simplest type to the most complex.

Tickmark Descriptions of Procedures Performed The term *tickmarks* refers to annotations of the workpapers that auditors use to record their findings as they investigate the client's systems and review the supporting documents. The tickmarks themselves are usually symbols accompanied by brief notations. As they perform tests on their client's accounting data, auditors document, in detail, the procedures they followed by making notations on the various workpaper schedules. To keep these documents legible, the auditors place tickmarks—usually a number, letter, or symbol—next to the item investigated and keyed to a legend at the bottom of the document or on an attached page. The legend indicates what each tickmark means by providing a brief explanation of what the auditor investigated, what she found, and whether she was satisfied with the information. (Figures 11.8 and 11.9 illustrate, respectively, inappropriate and appropriate tickmark explanations and use letters of the alphabet as tickmarks keyed to explanations on a separate page.)

Tickmark explanations must be concise because the space available for them is often limited. They must be complete, however, and able to stand alone as substantive messages. Members of the audit team should not need to consult other documents or ask for clarification to understand the tickmark explanations on a workpaper.

In Figures 11.8 and 11.9, staff auditor Kate Larsen has performed substantive testing to determine whether the client's Allowance for Uncollectible Accounts is adequate. (See pp. 361–365 for a sample client interview and memo on the subject.) As the auditor investigated each past-due customer account, she made a tickmark next to each account.

In the first sample, Figure 11.8, Kate records the conclusions she reached without specifying what she found. Like the inappropriate description of findings on page 367, these "explanations" are not really explanations at all, but opinions about the collectibility of certain accounts that the auditor asks her readers to accept on faith. Readers of these documents will have to consult with the writer about details.

In Figure 11.9, however, the auditor explains in the tickmark legend exactly what she did and what she discovered as she reviewed each account. Tickmarks (a) through (d) describe the probable collectibility of specific accounts and the reasons for the auditor's assessments. Her explanations appropriately attribute evaluations of the customer to the client (B. Clayton). In tickmarks (e) and (f), the auditor describes details of the calculations she performed to come up with her own estimate of uncollectible accounts and explains why she thinks that the client's estimate is inadequate, considering current circumstances and trends.

Notice in (f) that the auditor has concluded that an item in the client's books (the Allowance for Uncollectible Accounts) may be in dispute and that the finding is carried forward to a more prominent summary worksheet. No doubt the audit senior and possibly even the manager and/or partner will review the summary worksheet; therefore, it is essential that the staff auditor make a clear and accurate record of what she has done and found.

Narrative Documentation of Operational Areas and Internal Control Testing

Narratives are descriptive accounts that document the auditor's investigation of the client's systems, how they are working, which key employees are performing which tasks, and how information is being processed. This documentation helps the auditor understand the functional areas he will be auditing and identify any areas of weak internal control that need consideration. As we noted in Chapter 3, narratives describe events in chronological order, explaining each step before moving on to the next. This

Figure 11.8

Workpaper Schedule with Inappropriate Tickmarks

WORKPAPER

COUNTRY CRAFTERS
WORKPAPER B-25
ALLOWANCE FOR UNCOLLECTIBLE ACCOUNTS

Procedures (from the audit program): S, W, & W will select for testing all customer accounts with balances over $5,000 in the Over-90-Days-Past-Due category to assess collectibility. To determine the adequacy of the client's Allowance for Uncollectible Accounts at December 31, 1999, S, W, & W will judge collectibility by considering discussions with the client, analyses of accounts receivable statistics, and historical trends.

Customer	Over-90 Balance
Natural-Is-Nice Company, Ltd.	16,825.27 (a)
Sugarbox Stores	13,749.76 (b)
Geddes-Markle Stores	23,337.08 (c)
TV Shopping Network	7,049.63 (b)
Hall's Department Stores	14,825.24 (b)
Country Catalogues, Inc.	21,787.22 (d)
Southern Style Stores	22,517.91 (b)
TOTAL	120,092.11

**S, W, & W Calculation of Uncollectible
Accounts Expected**

3% of Over-90 Balances	8,351.55 (e)
3% of 61–90 Balances	24,836.98 (e)
2% of 31–60 Balances	16,797.24 (e)
0.15% of 1–30 Balances	21,777.76 (e)
S, W, & W Expectation	71,763.53
Difference	(36,072.00) (f)
Recorded Balance per client's general ledger	35,691.53 G/L

Tickmark Legend

(a) Long-standing customer with good history. Account currently in dispute. Collection likely.

Figure 11.8

Workpaper Schedule with Inappropriate Tickmarks—*continued*

(b) Long-standing customer. Collection likely.

(c) Account was recently in dispute over customer's double dipping on its discount. Collection is likely.

(d) Account recently negotiated. Collection likely.

(e) 3% of the over-90-day and 61–90-day past-due accounts are thought to be uncollectible; less collectibility will be assumed for accounts that are less overdue, and 100% of current accounts will be presumed collectible.

(f) We feel the client's allowance is understated by about half. We will forward the matter to the Summary of Misstatements as a likely misstatement.

Figure 11.9

Workpaper Schedule with Appropriate Tickmarks

WORKPAPER

Tickmarks

(a) According to B. Clayton, Collections, this long-standing customer has a good payment history. This customer changed Accounts Payable managers this year and a dispute arose in which the customer insists that the amount over 90 was wired to Country Crafters; however, Country Crafters never received the money. The matter is being investigated and collectibility is assured due to the long-standing relationship with the customer.

(b) According to B. Clayton, Collections, this is a customer of long standing who has never defaulted on bills. As a result of the size and nature of the customer, this customer has the clout to fall delinquent occasionally in paying their bills. They always pay, however, and are expected to pay this over-90 balance as well.

Figure 11.9

Workpaper Schedule with Appropriate Tickmarks—*continued*

(c) According to B. Clayton, Collections, this matter was recently in dispute. Country Crafters believed that Geddes-Markle was "double dipping" on their discount. Geddes-Markle disagreed, and stopped paying bills while the question was in dispute, thus creating an overdue balance. Geddes-Markle has since admitted that it has been double dipping on its discounts, and payments have resumed with collectibility appearing apparent.

(d) According to B. Clayton, Collections, Country Crafters has had problems with this customer paying by the due date. It appears that terms have been worked out and repayment will occur. Clayton speaks with Country Catalogues on a daily basis and feels that collectibility is likely.

(e) Based on this analysis, 97% of over-90-days-past-due accounts are thought to be collectible. S, W, & W will estimate that the remaining 3% of the over-90-day balance is uncollectible. Additionally, we will assume that 3% of the 61–90-day balance is uncollectible, that 2% of the 31–60-day balance is uncollectible, that 0.15% of the 1–30-day balance is uncollectible, and that 100% of current accounts is assumed to be fully collectible. S, W, & W will use such percentages in developing our expectation of the Allowance for Uncollectible Accounts.

(f) The client's write-offs of uncollectible accounts, as well as its sales made on account, appear to have been decreasing in the past few years. For this reason, a decrease in the Allowance for Uncollectible Accounts appears to be warranted. However, the allowance as it currently stands in the client's books represents a disproportionately small percentage of the actual bad debt write-offs that occurred during 1999. We believe that our estimate, as calculated above, of approximately $72,000 would be a better reflection of potential future write-offs. Because the $36,072 difference between the client's estimate and that of S, W, & W is considered to be material, the matter will be forwarded to the Summary of Misstatements (Workpaper #I-5) as a "likely misstatement."

sequential order makes documentation easy to follow because it presents the tasks in the order in which they were performed. A well-written narrative is like a "flowchart in prose"—easy to follow, with each step clear.

The narrative in Figure 11.10 describes operational procedures within Country Crafters' purchasing and accounts payable departments. It is typical of

Figure 11.10

Sample Workpaper/Narrative

AUDIT PROGRAM

*COUNTRY CRAFTERS
SYSTEMS DOCUMENTATION OF
PURCHASING AND ACCOUNTS PAYABLE
1999 AUDIT ENGAGEMENT*

Any company employee may fill out a purchase requisition; however, all purchase requisitions must be approved by department supervisors. Once the requisition is approved, the white and pink copies are forwarded to the Purchasing Department and the yellow copy is maintained by the requisitioner.

The purchase requisition is filed in the Purchasing Department and entered by the purchasing clerk into the computerized accounting system, which creates a purchase order. The purchasing clerk prints out three hard copies of the purchase order: One copy is retained by Purchasing (in addition to the record that is maintained on the computer system), one copy is sent to the accounts payable clerk (pending receipt of goods), and one copy is sent to Receiving, a central facility where the majority of raw material shipments are delivered.

The receiving clerk compares quantities received to quantities ordered and notes any differences. Goods are forwarded with the annotated purchase order to the originator of the purchase requisition, who examines the goods and determines if they are acceptable. If no problems are noted, the originator of the purchase requisition signs the annotated purchase order and forwards it directly to Accounts Payable, with authorization to forward the invoice for payment. Simultaneously in Receiving, a receiving report is prepared and sent to the accounts payable clerk. The accounts payable clerk matches the invoice she received from the vendor to the original purchase order, the annotated purchase order, and the receiving report, and posts the transaction to the accounts payable ledger.

Any significant differences between purchase orders and invoices are brought to the attention of the purchasing clerk, who is responsible for investigating differences and coming to a reasonable compromise or solution with the vendor. If all supporting documentation has been collected and if there are no unresolved significant differences between the purchase order, annotated purchase order, receiving report, and invoice, the accounts payable clerk sends the invoice, with authorization for payment, as it becomes due to the Treasurer's Office for payment.

the documentation involved in the internal control portion of an audit. To begin a study of a client's internal control system, an auditor questions personnel, prepares internal control questionnaires to identify problem areas, and creates flowcharts depicting duties and functions of key personnel in various functional areas. When he has gathered his information, the auditor writes a narrative describing how the systems operate. Notice that the writer here has used chronological order to describe the purchasing and accounts payable systems and has presented his material using concrete detail. The flowchart in Figure 11.11 diagrams the steps described.

Summaries of Tests Performed   Once the auditor has fully understood and documented the operating procedures of the functional area under study, he begins performing tests of that area's internal controls to see if, in fact, the area is operating as it is supposed to. Of course, the auditor must document the testing he performs by describing what he did and any conclusions about the client's internal controls that he reached. The form of this internal control documentation can vary from firm to firm, but proper documentation always includes a description of the internal control in question and a summary of test(s) performed, along with the auditor's conclusion about the quality of that control.

The difference between summary documentation and narrative documentation rests primarily in the level of detail involved. Whereas narratives describe each step in a process, a series of procedures, or a chain of events, summaries highlight important information to give a general picture of events and actions. The summaries in the workpaper in Figure 11.12 (from the Country Crafters audit) illustrate the point. Rather than describing each test performed, the summaries explain in each case how the whole testing process was conducted. What emerges is not a set of discrete, specific descriptions, but a generalization about the effectiveness of the company's internal controls.

Analyses of Work Performed   After auditing each account, the auditor writes a memo to the file much like the one you saw in Figure 11.7 by Kate Larsen summarizing her client interview. The memos discussing account audits, however, focus on the quantitative data obtained, analyze any internal control issues raised from the audit, and offer the auditor's opinions on those issues. Although these memos often include sections of narration and summary, their function is specifically analytical; that is, they are written to discuss an issue raised by the facts of the audit in light of authoritative sources such as FASB Statements of Financial Accounting Standards (SFAS) and AICPA Statements of Position (SOP). It is important to note in these memos any problems encountered during the audit and to provide clear references to supporting documentation such as spreadsheets and references to relevant authority.

In Figure 11.13, the auditor analyzes whether Country Crafters has properly disclosed several *related-party transactions*. Statement on Auditing Standards No. 45[4] provides guidelines for identifying and disclosing transactions with entities defined as "related parties" under FASB SFAS No. 57[5]. These guidelines include requesting from client management the names of all related parties, interviewing management about transactions with these parties, reviewing the

Figure 11.11

Flowchart to Illustrate Narrative

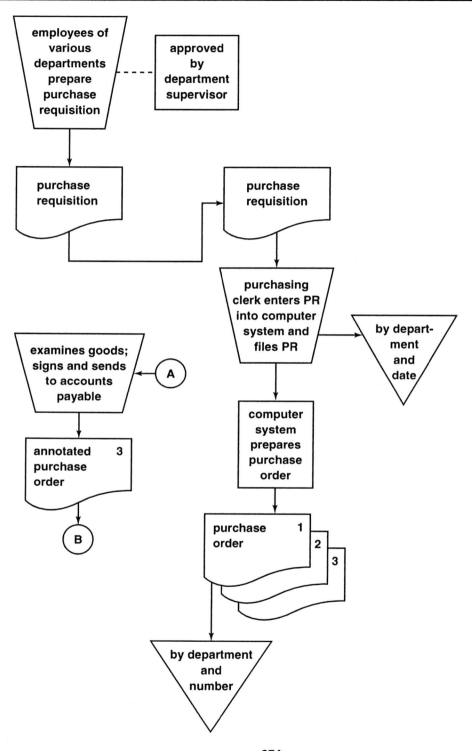

Figure 11.11

Flowchart to Illustrate Narrative—*continued*

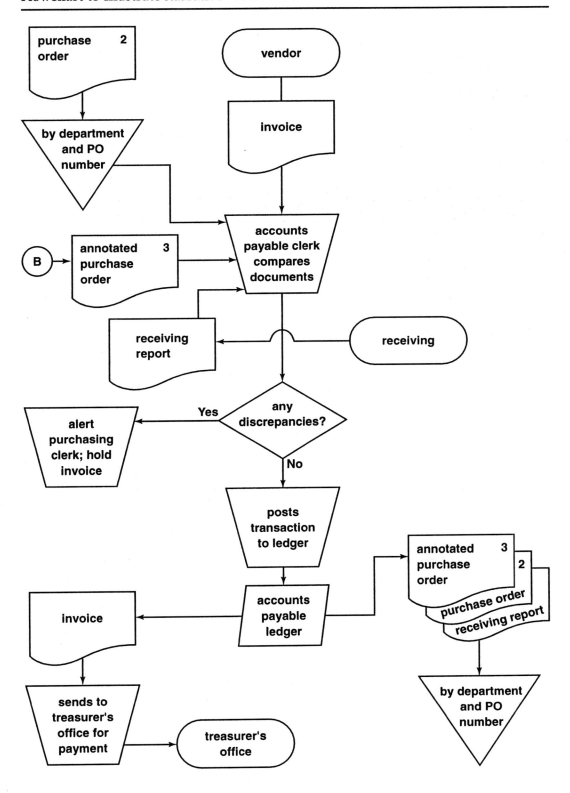

Figure 11.12

Sample Workpaper/Summary

WORKPAPER

COUNTRY CRAFTERS
TESTING OF INTERNAL CONTROL: PURCHASING
1999 AUDIT ENGAGEMENT

Desirable Control: Bank reconciliations are performed on a monthly basis.

Test of Control: S, W, & W tested this control by examining monthly reconciliations of the operating bank account. S, W, & W noted that each reconciliation was completed by the staff accountant on a timely basis. In addition, each reconciliation was reviewed and approved by the accounting manager on a timely basis. Based on a discussion with the accounting manager, S, W, & W noted that all monthly bank reconciliations are reviewed for accuracy, completeness, and timeliness.

Conclusion: Based on testing performed, this control appears to be functioning as intended and, therefore, contributes to the reliability of the purchasing, accounts payable, and cash disbursements systems.

Desirable Control: Periodic comparisons are made of actual expenses to budgeted expenses by the vice president of administration.

Test of Control: Based on an interview with the VP of administration and his staff, S, W, & W noted that comparisons of budgeted to actual expenses are performed periodically throughout the year. Accounts where actual expenses exceed budgeted amounts are investigated. In such instances, the VP of administration informs the appropriate department head of the situation and asks the department head for an explanation of the overage. In addition, the VP of administration reminds the department head that a budget transfer request should be prepared and submitted. Because of these periodic reviews and discussions with department heads, the VP of administration is able to identify problems that arise within departments purchasing raw materials as well as possible accounting errors/irregularities within the related purchasing accounts.

Conclusion: Based on testing above, it appears that this control is in effect and operating as intended.

Figure 11.12

Sample Workpaper/Summary—*continued*

Desirable Control: Purchase requisitions are approved by applicable department supervisor.

Test of Control: S, W, & W randomly selected 200 executed purchase requisitions from the file in the Purchasing Department and noted the applicable approval signature on each form. In a discussion with the purchasing manager (who supervises the purchasing clerk), it was noted that no purchase requisition is entered into the system as a purchase order without the appropriate approval signature.

Conclusion: Based on testing above, it appears that this control is in effect and operating as intended.

Figure 11.13

Sample Workpaper/Analytical Memo

MEMO

Date: January 31, 2000
To: 1999 Audit Workpapers
From: Claire Dufour
Subject: Identification of Related Parties

In accordance with SAS 45, S, W, & W has considered related-party transactions and relevant disclosures. To identify related parties and related-party transactions, as they are defined in SFAS No. 57, S, W, & W held discussions with the company president, reviewed the prior year auditor's report, and used knowledge gained throughout the course of the audit. The following related parties were discovered:

Mary O'Reilly	CEO
Amelia Strong	Production Coordinator/CEO's daughter
John O'Reilly	Director of Trademarking/CEO's son
Magda Sullivan	CEO's mother

Corporate Real Estate, Ltd.: Affiliated Entity owned 98% by Amelia Strong and John O'Reilly; 2% by Mary O'Reilly

Figure 11.13

Sample Workpaper/Analytical Memo—*continued*

Omega, Inc.: Affiliated Entity owned 98% by Amelia Strong and John O'Reilly; 2% by Omega L.P.

Omega L.P.: Affiliated Parent Company of Omega, Inc., owned 100% by Madga Sullivan

RELATED-PARTY TRANSACTIONS

S, W, & W identified the following related-party transactions during 1999:

1. **Note Receivable from Omega, Inc.**

   In connection with a purchase of equipment by Omega, Inc., Country Crafters paid $100,000 on Omega's behalf to the equipment supplier. The note is noninterest bearing and will be paid in full by September 2000.

2. **Note Receivable from Corporate Real Estate, Ltd.**

   In connection with the purchase of a building by Corporate Real Estate, Ltd., Country Crafters paid $938,682 on Corporate's behalf for the purchase of and renovations to the building. Country Crafters will lease the building from Corporate Real Estate, Ltd., for its new corporate headquarters. This note is noninterest bearing and will be paid in full by June 2003.

3. **Stockholder/Officer Loan**

   Mary O'Reilly, CEO and 25% stockholder of Country Crafters, advanced $450,000 to the company. The loan is being administered by First National Bank. Annual principal payments are due on May 31 each year in the amount of $45,000 with interest payable monthly at 9%.

   Given the nature of the above-described loans, in our opinion, full and adequate disclosure of these related-party transactions has been made by the client in the notes to the financial statements.

---

prior years' workpapers for the names of known related parties, and identifying evidence of related-party transactions in various audit documents. Notice that the writer begins by establishing the authoritative source (SAS 45) she followed in conducting her audit procedures as well as the source (SFAS No. 57) on which she based her analysis.

After establishing the authorities for her investigation, the auditor summarizes the methods used to identify related parties ("held discussions with the company president, reviewed the prior year auditor's report, and used knowledge gained throughout the course of the audit") and identifies the transactions discovered. Because the audience for this workpaper is confined to experts—other auditors and possibly attorneys—the writer does not need to discuss in detail how SAS 45 and SFAS 57 apply to the facts of this audit situation. Other auditors—familiar with SAS 45 and with SFAS 57—will know what defines a "related party" and will quickly see that the writer used appropriate procedures to identify them in this case. Attorneys reviewing this workpaper in litigation would have to research the relevant authorities as part of the case preparation. Therefore, the writer can, without extensive explanation, draw the conclusion that "full and adequate disclosure" has been made.

The Audit Workpaper Review Process

In a typical accounting firm hierarchy, staff accountants' workpapers are subject to review by the audit senior. The writing of audit seniors is subject to review by the audit manager and often by the audit partner. To make your writing better able to stand up to a supervisor's scrutiny, here are a few suggestions:

- Familiarize yourself thoroughly with the style, structure, and conventions of your firm's workpapers and other documents. Studying these documents will give you an idea, in most cases, of what the firm considers to be model documents and what your supervisors expect of your writing.

As you review the documents, ask yourself the questions you learned in Chapter 2:

Who is/are the audience(s) of this document?
What is its primary purpose? Secondary purpose?
Have I adopted the appropriate tone for this audience and purpose?
Have I organized the material in the most effective way?

- Always allow time for revising and editing whatever you draft. Revising and editing are key steps in the writing process. Submitting unrevised drafts is a surefire way to stop your career advancement in its tracks.

Remember: Strong, clear writing reflects strong, clear thinking. Both will be noticed, appreciated, and rewarded.

MANAGEMENT COMMENTS AND THE MANAGEMENT COMMENT LETTER

During and after the audit fieldwork, staff auditors are expected to write *management comments,* or descriptions of *reportable conditions* that they observed during the audit. Reportable conditions are defined by the AICPA as "matters coming to the auditor's attention that, in his judgment, should be communicated to the audit committee because they represent significant deficiencies in the design or operation of the internal control structure, which could adversely affect the organization's ability to record, process, summarize, and report financial data consistent with the assertions of management in the financial statements."[6] A management comment letter to a client's audit committee or board of directors simply communicates any reportable conditions detected during the audit. However, auditors will often write directly to the company's management as well, including in this second version of the management comment letter suggestions for improvement to the client's internal control system and/or to business operating methods. We focus in this section on the type of letters written to a client's management because these letters present particular rhetorical challenges: They must point out the client's areas of weakness and at the same time motivate the client to make improvements. If these comments are written carelessly, they may offend the client and fail to achieve their purpose. Moreover, well-written management comments can create an opportunity for the audit firm to provide value-added services to the client and, possibly, to develop further business as a result. For all of these reasons, management comments should be drafted with great care.

Like audit interviews, management comments are communication tasks requiring sensitivity on the one hand and thoroughness on the other. Well-written management comments describe the problem accurately, but do so in a way that identifies solutions. They emphasize the positive effects that a solution will bring as well as the consequences that will ensue if the problem is ignored. They motivate management to initiate change by presenting the situation clearly and logically. They never use "finger-pointing" phrases or accusatory language. Obviously, writing effective management comments is a tricky business! With practice, however, you can master this important skill.

Here is an example of a poorly written management comment, along with a revised, improved version:

> **Poorly written comment:** *Finding:* Our investigation revealed that GeoCorp does not summarize customer return credits. The lack of a summary makes it difficult to monitor the propriety of credits issued or the existence of performance problems with a particular product line. Furthermore, an evaluation cannot be readily performed at the end of each period to ensure that sales and profits are not overstated due to significant returns in the following period.
>
> *Recommendation:* Monthly, or at a minimum, quarterly, GeoCorp should generate a report listing credits to assist management with monitoring sales returns. In addition, a review of credits issued should be performed quarterly to prevent overstatement of profits.
>
> **Improved comment:** *Observation:* GeoCorp processes customer return credits without summarizing them. Regular summaries of these credits would help the company make better decisions about issuing credits and monitor performance problems with particular product lines. In addition, regular summaries would allow the company to evaluate performance at the end of each period to ensure accurate statements of sales and profit.

Management action: Issuing a regular report (monthly or quarterly) listing credits issued would help management monitor sales returns. Conducting a quarterly review of credits issued would help ensure that sales and profits are accurately stated.

Let's compare the two versions to see why the revised comment is more effective than the original.

In the original comment, the writer uses the label *"Finding"* to introduce the item under discussion: This word suggests that the auditor had to ferret out the truth about the situation rather than simply learn about it from the client. In addition, the writer's language suggests that GeoCorp was trying to hide something from the audit team: *"Our investigation revealed that GeoCorp does not summarize customer credit returns."* In the revised comment, the label *"Observation,"* along with the straightforward statement of the problem *("Geo-Corp processes customer credit returns without summarizing them"),* avoids these negative implications.

The original comment relies on negative words and phrases to express the central idea: *"GeoCorp does not summarize customer credit returns. The lack of a summary . . . an evaluation cannot be readily performed at the end of each period to ensure that sales and profit are not overstated due to significant return in the following period."* Not only does this language increase the difficulty of the passage but it also produces a condemnatory tone. The revised comment is couched, for the most part, in positive language *("Regular summaries of these returns would help the company make better decisions about issuing credits and monitor performance problems with particular product lines. In addition, regular summaries would allow the company to evaluate performance at the end of each period to ensure accurate statements of sales and profit").*

The label *"Recommendation"* in the original version, along with the bossy language *("at a minimum, quarterly, . . . should generate a report . . . a review of credits issued should be performed quarterly"),* could well put the reader on the defensive. The phrase *"to prevent overstatement of profits"* might further antagonize the reader, suggesting as it does that the company may be deliberately trying to overstate profits.

In the revised version, the label *"Management action"* implies that management has already planned to correct the situation and fully intends to do so. The phrasing of the recommendation here sounds more like a gentle suggestion than an order: *Issuing a regular report (monthly or quarterly) listing credits issued would help management monitor sales returns. Conducting a quarterly review of credits issued would help ensure that sales and profits are accurately stated.*

The differences between these "before-and-after" comments may seem subtle, but they will result in real perceptual differences for the reader, differences that will make an impact on how the advice will be received.

When all the management comments are in, they are compiled and edited, usually by the audit senior, into the management comment letter, which formally notifies the client of reportable conditions found during the audit and offers suggestions for improving them. The letter is reviewed by the audit

Figure 11.14

Sample Management Comment Letter

LETTER

Smith, Williamson, & Walker, LLP
85 Industrial Park Drive
Cincinnati, OH 45210

March 21, 2000
Mr. Chris Adams, Controller
Country Crafters, Inc.
636 Apple Street
Glenside, OH 45214

Dear Mr. Adams:

In planning and performing our audit of the financial statements of Country Crafters, Inc. for the year ended December 31, 1999, we considered its internal control structure in order to determine our auditing procedures for the purpose of expressing our opinion on the financial statements and not to provide assurance on the internal control structure. However, we noted two matters involving internal control and its operation that we consider to be reportable conditions under the standards established by the American Institute of Certified Public Accountants. Reportable conditions involve significant deficiencies in the design or operation of internal control that, in our judgment, could adversely affect the company's ability to record, process, summarize, and report financial data consistent with the assertions of management in the financial statements.

I. Reportable Conditions

Segregation of Duties

A basic element of the internal control structure is adequate segregation of duties. However, given the size of Country Crafters, Inc., segregation of duties among authorization, recording, and custody of assets is not always possible. Currently, one employee is responsible for opening mail, posting receipts to customers' accounts, preparing deposit slips, and making deposits at the bank. The company could achieve the proper segregation of duties by reassigning job responsibilities among other team members. We will be pleased to discuss with you our ideas for how to resolve this problem efficiently and economically.

Figure 11.14

Sample Management Comment Letter—*continued*

Written Procedures for Disposal of Fixed Assets

No written procedures exist to inform employees of the necessary steps to be taken upon the disposal of a fixed asset. Disposals without the notification of accounting personnel could result in an overstatement of fixed assets and depreciation expense.

The company could achieve better control over fixed asset purchases and disposals, improved accountability, and more accurate financial record keeping by limiting authorization for disposals of fixed assets to supervisors. To implement a procedure for such limitation, the company could create a form to list the disposal date, asset description, area, and tag number; supervisors disposing of fixed assets could route the form to accounting, who, in turn, could remove the fixed asset and the related accumulated depreciation from the books.

II. Recommendations for Operational Improvement

The following comments are intended to improve your internal structure or to result in other operating efficiencies.

(1) Procedures Manual

The company does not have a formal procedures manual. By developing a written manual, you could ensure that transactions be treated in a standardized manner and that proper internal controls exist. A manual may also reduce the amount of training time necessary for new team members.

(2) Update of Computer Systems

Consider replacing your current computer system with a new general ledger package containing an integrated accounts receivable and payable module. In addition, we suggest keeping the customization of new software to a minimum. Custom software increases the cost of new-technology upgrades.

(3) Production Capacity

Your two current suppliers may not have the capacity to handle the increased volume you anticipate with the growth projected in your business plan. Moreover, the projected growth could create real

Figure 11.14

Sample Management Comment Letter—*continued*

problems if one or both of your plants should be unable to produce to meet demand. Contracting with a third mill could help you handle the increased volume that you anticipate.

This report is intended solely for the information and use of the board of directors and management within the company.

Sincerely,
Smith, Williamson, & Walker, LLP

manager and ultimately the audit partner before it is sent to the client; therefore, its writer is under much scrutiny from superiors.

Figure 11.14 provides a sample management comment letter. Notice that the letter begins with some rather formal language about "reportable conditions" (paragraph 1). Although management comment letters should be written in the most positive manner possible, such authoritative language should be included because it is required by SAS No. 60. Following the necessary opening, the writer has organized the letter by describing the reportable conditions (the items of greatest significance) first and by listing operational recommendations afterward, in a descending order of importance, as you learned in Chapter 5. Also notice that the writer of the letter incorporated strategies to make points gently and to avoid a critical tone. Tact and proper organization are the keys to writing a management comment letter that will get the points across while fostering positive client relations.

THE AUDIT REPORT

The audit concludes with an audit report, comprising the final set of documents produced by the audit team. The audit report contains, in addition to the audited financial statements themselves, an opinion letter stating whether or not the financial statements of the audited company fairly present the financial situation of the company. The language of the audit opinion letter is largely dictated by the AICPA and depends on what type of opinion the audit firm is rendering. Staff auditors usually do not participate in the writing of the opinion letter. Examples of a standard audit opinion letter and of the possible variations can be found in any auditing textbook. For your immediate information, Figure 11.15 illustrates a standard audit opinion letter.

Although the wording of the audit opinion letter is specified by the AICPA, these letters are nevertheless important as the primary means of communicating the auditors' opinion about the credibility of a client's financial statements.

Figure 11.15

A Standard Audit Opinion Letter

> ### LETTER
>
> **Smith, Williamson, & Walker, LLP**
> **85 Industrial Park Drive**
> **Cincinnati, OH 45210**
>
> To the Board of Directors of Country Crafters, Inc.:
>
> We have audited the accompanying balance sheet of Country Crafters, Inc., as of December 31, 1999, and the related statements of income, retained earnings, and cash flows for the year then ended. These financial statements are the responsibility of the company's management. Our responsibility is to express an opinion on these financial statements based on our audit.
>
> We conducted our audit in accordance with generally accepted auditing standards. Those standards require that we plan and perform the audit to obtain reasonable assurance about whether the financial statements are free of material misstatement. An audit includes examining, on a test basis, evidence supporting the amounts and disclosures in the financial statements. An audit also includes assessing the accounting principles used and significant estimates made by management, as well as evaluating the overall financial statement presentation. We believe that our audit provides a reasonable basis for our opinion.
>
> In our opinion, the financial statements referred to above present fairly, in all material respects, the financial position of Country Crafters, Inc., as of December 31, 1999, and the results of its operations and its cash flows for the year then ended in conformity with generally accepted accounting principles.
>
> Smith, Williamson, & Walker, LLP
> March 21, 2000

CONCLUSION

The communication events described in this chapter do not merely support the financial statement audit; they actually play a large part in *creating* it because it is the communications that generate the plan, solicit the information the auditors need, document the work performed, and formulate the conclusions. From beginning to end, from client interviews through workpaper documentation to the management comment letter, the communication skills of the audit team will determine the success of the audit.

NOTES

[1]William A. Nolen, "Reading People," *Internal Auditor* 52, no. 2 (April 1995): 50.

[2]A 1996 study on written communications at Big Six firms indicated overwhelmingly that working papers are the most common documents written by entry-level accountants. Susan M. Moncada, Sandra J. Nelson, and Douglas C. Smith, "Written Communication Frequently Composed by Entry-Level Accountants," *New Accountant* 12, no. 4 (January/February 1997): 26–28.

[3]American Institute of Certified Public Accountants, *Working Papers,* Statement on Auditing Standards No. 41, AU section 339 (New York: American Institute of Certified Public Accountants, 1982).

[4]American Institute of Certified Public Accountants, *Related Parties,* Statement on Auditing Standards No. 45, AU section 334 (New York: American Institute of Certified Public Accountants, 1983).

[5]Financial Accounting Standards Board, *Related Party Disclosures,* Statement of Financial Accounting Standards No. 57 (Stamford, CT: Financial Accounting Standards Board, 1982).

[6]American Institute of Certified Public Accountants, *Communication of Internal-Control-Structure-Related Matters Noted in an Audit,* Statement on Auditing Standards No. 60, AU section 325 (New York: American Institute of Certified Public Accountants, 1989).

EXERCISES

1. **Scenario:** Mark O'Brien, the audit senior on an upcoming assignment, has asked you to help develop an agenda for the audit planning meeting for Fleet Technologies, which will be held on May 5, 2000. He has left a few sketchy notes on your desk listing briefly the topics to be covered in the meeting as well the people who will be responsible for presenting the information.

   Meeting Participants
   Jim Avakean, partner
   Evan Roy, audit manager
   Mark O'Brien, audit senior
   Eileen Wood, staff accountant

   Topics to Be Addressed
   - Firm issues: increased competition, revenue growth risks, and new business areas
   - Audit issues: client industry, potential audit problems
   - Scheduling: interim, year-end, report date
   - Staffing: team work, assignments, expectations

- Client information: history, management personnel
- Miscellaneous: time budget, materiality.

Writing task
  a. Formalize the notes into a meeting agenda that will be sent to the audit staff, senior, and partner on the engagement.
  b. Write a memo to your supervisor, Mark O'Brien, justifying how you organized the agenda.

2. **Scenario:** Your firm has just accepted an audit engagement with a large publicly held company, which, for this assignment, you may choose. Obtain the most recent SEC 10-K filing for this publicly held company using the SEC's EDGAR database on the World Wide Web.
  Writing task: After reading the document carefully, prepare the "Client Background and Industry" portion of the planning memo for the working papers. Comment on any possible audit issues you discover in your research, including lawsuits, significant industry events, emerging technologies, economic factors, or other situations related to the company you have chosen.

3. **Scenario:** The following instructions are excerpts from an audit program that will be used by a first-year staff accountant to perform substantive tests of sales and accounts receivables balances.

- Confirm AR.
- Perform alternative procedures for confirmations not returned.
- Perform analytical procedures to test sales and AR.
- Trace the AR aging schedule to the ledgers.
- Perform a sales cutoff test.
- Verify mathematical accuracy of the AR aging schedule.

Writing task
  a. Write a memo to the audit team critiquing the audit program steps just listed.
  b. Revise the audit program steps by rewriting them, reordering them, and/or combining them, as needed. Make up any additional information you feel is necessary to make the explanations clear and understandable.

4. **Scenario:** You are a staff accountant auditing the books of a small, privately owned business. During the audit of the cash account, you examined the backs of several canceled checks and noticed some striking similarities in the handwriting of three different endorsers. In addition, you found several unexplained reconciling amounts on the bank reconciliation. You suspect there may be some fraudulent handling of cash in the company. After some discussion with the senior on the job, you have decided to speak to the client's controller about

the apparent discrepancies and have come up with the following list of questions.

■ Why is there an unexplained difference between the general ledger balance and the bank account balance?
■ Who routinely prepares the bank reconciliation?
■ Who handles cash disbursements?
■ Are all vendor invoices reviewed and approved prior to payment? By whom?
■ Are the reconciliations reviewed after they are prepared?
■ If reconciliations are reviewed, why were the unexplained differences not resolved properly?
■ Has anyone been fired from the company for stealing?
■ How many vendors have complained about incorrect balances in their accounts?

Writing task: Create a written plan for the interview that answers these questions:
a. What are the goals of the upcoming interview?
b. What risks are involved in the upcoming interview?
c. Which questions should not be asked or should be revised to be less inflammatory?
d. How could some of these questions be rephrased or grouped to streamline the interview and give the manager greater opportunity to respond?
e. Prepare a revised listing of questions in the order you would ask them. Include any additional comments or questions you would use to start and end the interview.
f. Explain the reasoning behind your choices in answering question (e).

5. Scenario: Linda Davis is a first-year staff auditor working on her first audit. Unfortunately, over the course of the first two weeks, she has managed to annoy the client's controller, Amy Walters, on more than one occasion. On Monday, Linda asked one of Amy's staff for help in obtaining some files. Proper procedure requires, however, that all requests be directed to the controller. As a result of Linda's unintentional gaffe, Amy barged into the conference room, where the entire audit team was working, to criticize Linda for her actions. The audit team sat in silence as Amy left the room and Linda attempted to continue functioning after the outburst.

Over the following days, Linda made every attempt to avoid contact with Amy. However, on Wednesday, Linda was given a list of follow-up questions by the engagement partner, Jim Fallen, who had reviewed her working papers. She was given until Monday morning of the following week to prepare write-ups for the outstanding issues. Despite this deadline, Linda has put off meeting with Amy, fearing another unpleasant confrontation. The following conversation took place between Linda and Amy at 4:45 p.m. on Friday afternoon.

Linda: [Arriving unexpectedly and entering without being asked] Hi, Amy. I know it's getting late, but I have a few questions to ask you.

Amy: [While straightening up her desk for the day] Oh. OK. I have a few minutes. What's up? *[Amy is shuffling papers and stuffing them into her briefcase.]*

Linda: Well, I tried to get here earlier but I got bogged down on this one account. Anyway, I'm a little unclear about the company's policies and procedures for issuing credit memos. Could you review them with me?

Amy: [Listening to her voice mail] Hmmm. Credit memos. Well, nothing's changed since last year. You should have something about that in your prior year's workpapers. *[Pauses while she listens to a message]*

Linda: Yes, well, I guess I could go back and look that up, but . . .

Amy: [Putting on her suit jacket, gathering her briefcase, and leading Linda to the door] Glad I could help. Stop by Monday if you have any other questions.

Linda: [Realizing that Amy is going to leave] Wait! These questions are really important and will only take a few minutes! *[Blocking the door with her body while riffling through a folder for the papers needed to ask the questions]* Hold on a minute. I have everything right here.

Amy: [Very annoyed and angry] I don't have time to answer questions that you should have been able to answer by looking in your own workpapers. You also need to learn some manners and how to follow procedures around here. Now, please get out of my way or I'll call security! You should also be aware that I plan to meet with Jim to discuss your unprofessional behavior and ask him to have someone else assigned to our engagement.

Linda steps aside and stands speechless as Amy quickly walks past her to the elevator.

Writing task: Write a letter to Linda explaining why the interview was unsuccessful and suggesting what she could have done to make the meeting productive.

6. **Scenario:** Steve, warehouse manager, and Tom, staff auditor, just met to discuss the upcoming physical inventory count and observation. Their conversation was as follows:

Tom: Hi, Steve. Thanks for taking the time to meet with me.

Steve: No problem. Where shall we start?

Tom: Why don't you start by telling me how you've planned the physical count?

Steve: Sure. We've broken down the plant staff into two teams, A and B. Within each team, workers will be paired and assigned specific sections of the warehouse to count the stock. We've done it this way for the past two years and it's been really successful. For example, Pair 1 from Team A counts the first row of the warehouse. Later, Pair 1 from Team B will recount it to make sure the first count is accurate. If the teams disagree on the count, we get a supervisor to count it again to make a final determination.

Tom: Where is the more valuable inventory located?

Steve: The premier line goods are in the southeast corner. We've rearranged the location of goods since last year to improve warehouse operations and reduce losses from spoilage.

Tom: Has spoilage been a problem? And for that matter, what's your experience with obsolescence and theft of merchandise?

Steve: Whoa! No need to get alarmed! It's just that given the climate control and security systems we use, this was a better arrangement. It reduced our insurance costs, pilferage, and improved the flow of goods. Wish we would have thought of it sooner.

Tom: Fine, fine. *[Mumbling more to himself than addressing this to Steve]* We'll have to be really careful about this issue; there could be problems with inventory valuation. Definitely an increased risk all around.

Steve: What's that? Did you ask me something?

Tom: No, no. Sounds like you have a good grasp of this area. Is there anything else I need to know?

Steve: Not really. But I have some other information you might find helpful. Here's a map of the warehouse, listing of the pairs by team, inventory costing sheet, and schedule for the inventory count.

Tom: Thanks a lot. This is a great help. I'll see you on the 31st.

Writing task: Write a memo to the workpapers summarizing Tom and Steve's meeting. Structure the memo like a report and include an introduction, background description, explanation, and conclusion. Also include your opinion on the adequacy of the client's plan for counting the inventory.

7. **Scenario:** The following is an excerpt from the audit workpapers for Bob's Auto Repair.

WORKPAPER

Bob's Auto Repair
Bank Reconciliation
December 31, 2000

Balance per bank	$17,851.76 a
Plus: deposit in transit	2,222.56 b
Less: outstanding checks	(5,465.25) c
Adjusted balance	$ 14,609.07 d
Balance per general ledger	$ 14,864.07 e
Less: bank service charges	(45.00) f
Less: ISF check returned	(210.00) g
Adjusted balance	$ 14,609.07 h

Tickmark Legend

a) Confirmed balance with bank; agrees with cutoff bank statement
b) Agrees with cutoff bank statement; traced to cash receipts journal; inspected copy of deposit slip
c) Traced to cash disbursements journal; examined checks returned with cutoff bank statement
d) Footed; agrees with general ledger
e) Agrees with general ledger balance
f) Agrees with December bank statement
g) Followed up on the disposition of this check
h) Footed; agrees with general ledger.

Writing task: Many of the tickmarks on this workpaper are incomplete, others are unclear, and some are duplicates. Revise the workpaper tickmarks and tickmark explanations for greater clarity and efficiency. Add information that you think is necessary to make the explanations clear.

8. **Scenario:** You are a first-year staff accountant assigned to Outlook Company's audit team. Your senior asked you to interview Outlook's treasurer, controller, and sales manager to obtain an understanding of their sales processing and credit approval procedures. Your goal was to understand this part of Outlook's accounting system clearly enough to be able to write the internal control narrative for these procedures for the audit workpapers. During your interviews you took the following notes.

Controller's Information

- Sales orders and invoices are prenumbered documents.
- If credit is approved, the billing department gets the sales order and the customer purchase order from the credit manager.
- Billing department prepares a sales invoice after it receives the sales order.
- Sales invoice is a four-part form; two copies are kept with the sales order and the customer PO and put into a temporary file, pending shipment.
- A third copy of the sales invoice goes to the shipping department and is filed in a temporary file until the goods are released from the warehouse.

Sales Manager's Information

- Salesclerks receive POs from customers from mailroom.
- Phone orders are also taken by salesclerks (keep phone log).
- After getting customer's order, salesclerks prepare a "sales order" that includes an estimate of the total price of the order.
- Sales order goes to credit manager for approval.
- Customers' POs (if received) are attached to the sales order by the salesclerks.

Treasurer's Information

- Credit approval based on a predetermined credit limit for each customer and current outstanding AR for that customer.
- Credit manager signs the sales order if credit is approved.

Writing task

a. Write the internal control narrative for Outlook's sales processing and credit approval procedures handling based on your notes. Supplement your text with a flowchart.

b. Write a memo to the senior summarizing any unanswered questions or areas that may require additional information.

9. Scenario: Jerry, the audit senior responsible for the Coffee-Time Company audit, has been given an emergency assignment and does not have time to write all of the management comment letter. Because you are the staff auditor with the most experience on the job, Jerry has asked you to draft the recommendations for operational improvement which, if implemented, will strengthen Coffee-Time's internal controls. The letter will be given directly to the partner in charge for her approval. Jerry has provided you with the following set of notes:

Information System Records

- All employees, including programmers, have access to computer programs and data files.

Capitalization of Plant and Equipment

- No formal policy for capitalization vs. expensing of acquisitions of PP&E; lots of inconsistencies—some acquisitions for $1,500 are expensed when they should be capitalized; others, purchased for as little as $300, are capitalized.

Bank Reconciliations

- Bank reconciliations are prepared by the same accounts payable clerk who prepares and signs checks; no review of reconciliations.

Writing task: For each of the three areas, draft comments suitable for inclusion in the management comment letter to Coffee-Time. Clearly describe what the company has been doing in each of these areas and what consequences will ensue if the problem is ignored. Also, explain the actions management could take to improve their system and the positive effects that your solution will bring.

10. **Scenario:** You are a staff auditor for Merck & Morgan, CPAs, and have just completed the year-end audit of Technology Unlimited, Inc. Doing business as Computers Unlimited, the company owns four stores in local strip malls and provides extensive customer service along with the computers and other high-tech equipment it sells. During the audit you discovered several weaknesses in the company's internal control and operations systems that are not material and do not constitute reportable conditions as defined by the AICPA, but nevertheless are situations that management might want to address to improve the company's operations and internal control structure.

- No management approval is required for a sales associate to override the system and give a percentage discount on merchandise that is not on sale.
- The accounting system does not distinguish between discounts for merchandise that is on sale (where the discount was approved by management) and discounts that are given by sales associates overriding the system.
- No password is required to gain access to the point-of-sale (POS) system (checkout computer and cash register).
- Although each sales associate is required to enter a unique ID into the POS system when ringing up a sale, the IDs are commonly known by everyone since they are printed on each receipt.
- When an employee is terminated, it may take several weeks for the human resources department to complete paperwork and remove the employee's ID from the system.

Communication task: Prepare a management comment letter for Technology Unlimited, Inc., that includes suggestions for improving the weaknesses described. Use the *Observation* and *Management Action* format discussed in the text. Be sure to explain why each weakness in the current system poses a problem and how your suggestion will strengthen the company's internal controls. Make up any additional facts you need to prepare a well-written letter.

Exercises 11 through 17 relate to the following audit scenario:

Wilco in Trouble*

Client Background

You are an audit senior at Andrews, Keller, and Baskin, a public accounting firm. You have been assigned to the audit of Wilco Corporation for the current year. Wilco Corporation is a publicly traded manufacturer of computer chips.

Wilco has been a good audit client of the firm for the past six years, paying bills on a time, employing cooperative management, and complying with authoritative accounting pronouncements. During those years, however, Wilco has been losing market share in an increasingly competitive global marketplace. Although Wilco's unit sales have been increasing each year, they drastically lag behind industry increases. Currently, stagnation in the computer chip and router markets is significantly reducing the market demand for Wilco's chips. Wilco's stock has declined in value from approximately $95 per share in 1994 to $48 per share in 2000.

Despite these downward trends, Wilco remains a widely recognized name in the computer chip market.

Planning Meeting

At the instruction of the engagement partner, you will hold a planning meeting with Samantha Strong, CEO, to discuss current year events and plan the strategy for the upcoming audit. In your meeting, Samantha indicates that Wilco is going to have a very good year, despite some difficulties in the recent past. The company's main difficulty has involved revocation of its line of credit: As a result of lower-than-expected sales volume last year, Wilco violated its bank debt covenants, and the bank refused to renew the line of credit. Samantha indicates, however, that a new discount policy, encouraging customers to pay on a more timely basis, has increased cash flow, and operations have not been hampered despite the lack of credit from the bank.

Samantha further indicates that in May of the current year, Jane Smith, CFO, resigned to pursue other opportunities. Jane was replaced as chief financial officer by Samantha's close personal friend, Jonathan White. Samantha praises Jonathan's mastery of accounting and reporting, commending his ability to record financial transactions in ways that more accurately reflect the operations of the business than Jane's methods had. Samantha feels that Jonathan's philosophy is more practical than Jane's "overly conservative" approach to accounting. "Jonathan's logical approach to recording transactions and his ability to record results that better reflect our performance is doing wonders for our business. Just knowing that we were doing things so wrong in the past has bothered me tremendously," Samantha states.

---

*The comprehensive audit engagement exercise "Wilco in Trouble" was prepared by Ryan R. Fox of Deloitte & Touche, LLP.

Samantha indicates that one of Wilco's major suppliers went on strike during June and July of the current year. During this strike, Wilco was forced to buy parts from another supplier at significantly higher costs. Nevertheless, Samantha explains, the bottom line did not suffer. The new CFO performed a study of the overhead application process and redistributed items that were incorrectly accounted for in the past. Due to the lower overhead costs, Samantha expects product cost to be significantly lower after the month of July than in prior years. She explains: "Despite the increase in product cost for those two months, we experienced no negative gross profit impact because Jonathan reworked the overhead formula to reflect overhead costs more accurately. In fact, our products are significantly cheaper than we thought. Now we can reduce sales prices and increase volume due to more competitive pricing."

Samantha says that no other significant events occurred this year. She mentions a few minor items, such as the purchase of a significant amount of fixed assets and a growth in the customer base as a result of a new credit granting policy.

While discussing your planning meeting with the audit partner, you note the following concerns and areas of risk:

- Management's integrity (specifically the CFO)—the drastic improvement in current year results
- Inventory Valuation—the new overhead application formula
- Propriety of Cost of Goods Sold—the new overhead application formula
- Possibility of a going concern issue—lack of bank funding
- Valuation of reserves and liabilities
- Potential risk of loss—new credit granting policy.

Audit Fieldwork

Sales/Cost of Sales

In performing your regression analysis of sales and cost of goods sold, you note that, according to prior year workpapers, gross profit rates have averaged between 38% and 41% over the past six years. The client provided the following data for the analysis:

Month	Sales	COGS	Gross Profit
January	14,534,672	8,867,134	38.99%
February	15,068,010	9,063,465	39.85%
March	14,835,456	8,968,979	39.54%
April	14,236,726	8,613,564	39.50%
May	15,255,664	8,974,685	41.17%
June	14,365,790	8,313,646	42.13%
July	15,489,454	9,016,465	41.79%
August	14,964,889	8,065,646	46.10%
September	15,032,469	8,074,656	46.29%
October	17,028,646	8,765,646	48.52%
November	18,900,644	9,564,698	49.39%
December	19,365,471	9,679,879	50.01%
TOTAL	$189,077,891	$105,968,463	

In reviewing the data provided by the client, you note that sales increased significantly in the last three months of the year. Additionally, you note that gross profit margins increased beginning in August and further increased beginning in October. Discussions with Richard Jones, accounting manager, indicate the following:

- Profit margins would have increased beginning in June, but the strike affected the cost of direct materials used in production.
- The cost-of-goods-sold formula was altered to exclude insurance, depreciation, and sales salaries. Richard indicated that such items were excluded from overhead because they are paid for and utilized by nonproduction departments.
- Overtime paid to production workers is now recorded in the Human Resources Department as a fringe benefit. Such cost has historically been tracked in the production department and included as a component of cost of goods sold. Jonathan, the CFO, changed this policy under the rationale that this overtime premium is given by the Human Resources Department as part of the new contract and should therefore be a Human Resources expense (recorded as administrative expense on the income statement), not includable as a component of cost of sales. This policy went into effect in October.
- A promotion went into effect in October whereby Wilco sold bulk quantities of computer chips to a significant number of customers. Wilco is trying to promote the use of its products by having them readily available in bulk to customers. Wilco shipped these additional quantities to customers in good faith along with their regular orders. In a letter to customers, Wilco said, "We want to be the supplier of choice for computer chips. Please accept these chips for use in your production needs. If you do not need or use them, you may return them within three months with no obligation." Wilco recorded the sale of goods and the related account receivable upon shipment.

Fixed Asset Additions and Disposals

Remembering Samantha's statement that considerable fixed assets were purchased this year, you ask Joseph Danna, fixed asset clerk, about the nature of these fixed assets. Joseph indicates that a significant portion of the fixed asset additions represent labor by company mechanics. Such labor was incurred during a routine two-week plant shutdown in which each machine was thoroughly cleaned and inspected by the maintenance department. Additionally, plant walkways and work areas were resurfaced. Joseph tells you that these costs were capitalized because they enhance the useful lives of the machinery and equipment. Additionally, all replacement parts bought during the year for these machines (nuts, bolts, compressors, arms, etc.) were capitalized because they become part of the fixed asset.

When you ask Joseph why these labor and replacement costs were treated as fixed assets, he replies that Jonathan, the CFO, ordered the change from the previous capitalization policy. Joseph assures you that the policy is correct because these items and labor costs are related to fixed assets and should be capitalized. Continuing your discussion of fixed assets, you ask whether any disposals occurred during the current year. Joseph is not aware of any; however, such disposals occur at the discretion of the plant managers and are not brought to the attention of the accounting department.

Credit Granting Policy

While talking to Richard Jones, accounting manager, you learn that Wilco is relaxing the guidelines by which credit is granted. In the past, only the credit manager could approve credit. Now, however, credit approvals have been decentralized: Each credit clerk is responsible for a region of the market, authorized to grant credit for that region, without credit manager approvals. Additionally, clerks are responsible for determining bad debt write-offs and recoveries for their own region based on whether or not, in their professional judgment, they feel that collection will be made. This policy change—decentralizing the credit granting function—was initiated to empower the employees and create a greater sense of participation in management.

Conclusion

When you complete your audit fieldwork, you report your progress to the engagement partner, Steve Smart. Although net income has increased significantly in the current year and outpaced the industry average, the audit partner is uneasy with this increase. Steve is concerned that the company's sales policy is too aggressive and its accounting for certain sales is possibly not in accordance with GAAP. Additionally, Steve is not sure whether the company's overhead policies follow procedures recommended under GAAP. Both you and Steve are uncertain about the entity's ability to continue as a going concern, and about Andrews, Keller, and Baskin's ability to issue an unqualified opinion without significant adjustment to the financial statements.

11. Write an audit-planning memorandum.

12. Write tickmark explanations describing the reasons for changes in gross profit percentages. Indicate whether or not the changes are justified with regard to overhead application.

13. Write a memo to the workpapers indicating whether you think Wilco's cost of goods sold policy is acceptable.

14. Write a memo to the workpapers indicating whether the client's sales policy is in accordance with the guidelines of FASB 48, Revenue Recognition.

15. Write a memo to the audit partner describing the client's new fixed asset additions policy and whether or not you feel that such policy is in accordance with GAAP.

16. Write a workpaper supporting your position about whether or not a going concern issue exists regarding Wilco.

17. Write a management comment letter to the board of directors of Wilco indicating any inefficiencies, weaknesses in internal control, or recommendations you may have to improve the accounting operations of Wilco.

CHAPTER 12

Communication and the Tax Engagement

Although tax is considered the most technical and number-intensive field in accounting, consensus is growing among tax accountants that communication skills are vital to successful practice. Increasingly, accounting firms are realizing that the more effectively tax accountants communicate with clients, the better service they can offer. Tax accountants who can explain complex issues clearly help their clients work better with the tax law and maximize their tax savings; those who know how to interview clients effectively—and listen actively to their answers—gain a better understanding of their clients' financial goals. Effective communications also heighten the perceived value of tax accountants' services because clients who understand the complexity of tax practice can more fully appreciate the tax services the accountants perform on their behalf.

Tax accountants have also become more aware in recent years of the role poor communications can play in exposing firms to costly litigation. According to a 1996 article in *The CPA Journal,* between 50% and 55% of all malpractice claims against public accounting firms involve tax engagements.[1] Although many of these cases arise from substantive errors by tax accountants, many others are occasioned by poor or inadequate documentation of communications such as discussions with clients involving tax decisions. For this reason, the tax accountant must know how to communicate clearly and must keep accurate records of all communications with clients, colleagues, and taxing authorities.

In CPA firms, tax practitioners communicate with corporate, partnership, estate, and individual clients in the course of preparing federal, state, and local tax forms, resolving problems with taxing authorities, and planning tax-saving strategies. Accountants also communicate regularly with their colleagues to solve tax problems and write to client files to document the results of research into authoritative sources such as the Internal Revenue Code, Treasury Department regulations, revenue rulings, and tax court decisions. And accountants communicate with taxing authorities such as the IRS and state and local government tax boards to act as advocates for their clients.

Tax professionals (usually CPAs and attorneys) are also often employed full time by large corporations to prepare their tax returns and plan tax strategies. In addition to regular communications with the company's accounting and legal departments, these professionals might also communicate with CPAs from accounting firms who have been retained to consult on specialized tax problems or simply to review the corporation's tax returns before they are filed.

The types of communications involved in tax practice are similar to those that occur during an audit. Like auditors, tax accountants gather information through interviews, write workpapers summarizing information and analyzing problems, and communicate orally and in writing with clients and taxing authorities. Like auditors, tax accountants participate in meetings and make oral presentations, both informal and formal, to clients and taxing authorities. And like auditors, tax accountants must take great care to document their work because some of their communications may be subject to future litigation.

The *rhetorical* relationship between tax accountant and client, however, is quite different from the one between client and auditor. Those being audited often perceive the auditor as a kind of police officer, someone who is out to discover mistakes and company wrongdoings. As we noted in Chapter 11, this client perception presents auditors with unique rhetorical challenges. Auditors must handle client interviews with special sensitivity to the feelings that may lie below the surface. They must take care to write workpapers in a neutral tone, one that does not personalize blame for problems. They must also take care to phrase management comments diplomatically, using a positive tone even if the message is negative.

During a tax engagement, clients are more likely to perceive the accountant as an ally, someone with expert knowledge who will save them money. Clients look to the tax accountant to lead them through the complexities of tax rules and forms, to remain up to date on the latest tax law changes, and to come up with sound ideas for future tax savings and financial planning. This trust on the clients' part makes communication in a tax engagement easier than in an audit. Because clients trust the accountant to reduce their tax liability as much as possible, they are likely to communicate candidly and offer as much information to the accountant as they can. They are also less likely than an audit client to have hidden agendas or buried sensitivities that may erupt during the course of the engagement.

The amount of written documentation in tax practice varies, depending on the size of the firm and the nature of its client base. The types of communication in which staff and senior accountants engage also vary considerably. At Big Five and other large firms that handle large corporate clients, staff and senior accountants may communicate with clients by telephone, in meetings, and occasionally in writing, although official written correspondence is almost always handled by partners. The bulk of written communication done by staff and seniors at such firms involves researching tax issues and writing tax memoranda (workpapers) to client files. In firms that have a tax client base consisting largely of smaller companies and individuals, a greater percentage of client communications takes place by phone or at face-to-face meetings, with staff and seniors participating more directly with clients than they do at larger firms.

COMMUNICATION EVENTS IN THE TAX ENGAGEMENT

In this chapter, we show you typical examples of communications from two tax engagements, emphasizing how the work of staff and senior accountants fits into the larger picture of the engagement as a whole. Our two client scenarios, one corporate and one individual, are modeled on tax engagements actually performed by CPA firms.

Here is an overview of the communication events that can *typically* occur before, during, and after tax engagements. The order in which these events are presented follows the general sequence in which they usually occur.

1. *Initial meeting.* When new tax clients are obtained (usually by referrals from business associates, bankers, attorneys, family members, or friends), the accountant will most likely have an **initial meeting with the client.** At a small firm, the partner usually conducts this meeting, whereas at a large firm, the partner or tax senior conducts the meeting. In either case, the staff accountant assigned to the engagement may be invited to attend as well. The purpose of the initial meeting is for the accountant and the client to get to know each other and for the accountant to gather preliminary information from the client. The accountant will often prepare a meeting **agenda** in advance and send it to the client. The agenda helps new clients begin to think about their information and to organize it appropriately for the accountant.

2. *Engagement letter.* When a tax engagement is an additional service to a client's financial statement audit, review, or compilation (as is the case with many corporate clients), or when the tax client is a returning one, the accounting firm may not need to schedule an initial meeting. In such cases, the firm will draw up the **engagement letter** based on information it already has. In the case of a new client, the firm writes the engagement letter after the initial meeting with the client. The engagement letter outlines the terms and conditions of the engagement, the services the firm will perform and the returns it will prepare, and the fees that will be charged. The engagement letter, whether adapted from a standard form or newly written, is always reviewed and signed by a partner.

3. *Requests for information.* With new clients, the accountant in charge of the engagement (either the tax engagement senior or the staff accountant assigned to the engagement) often writes a **letter requesting information.** This letter formalizes the requests for information made at the initial meeting, listing the documents and other information that the accountant needs to prepare the tax returns. In cases where the tax engagement follows or coincides with an audit, review, or compilation, the tax accountant will already have access to much of the information that she needs. But usually even more information is needed to complete the returns. In the case of returning individual clients, many CPA firms make their requests for information at the beginning of the tax season through tax information questionnaires. These questionnaires help clients organize their tax information by asking them to fill in the appropriate questionnaire line items.

4. *Follow-up phone calls and letters.* During tax engagements, questions inevitably arise from either the staff/senior accountant or the client, and communication takes place to resolve them. Questions can often be answered by **telephone call** during and after which the accountant should make written documentation of the conversation. In some cases (where issues are highly complex or detailed) the accountant may choose to ask or answer questions by writing a **letter to the client.**

5. *Tax research memoranda.* When unusual or complicated tax law issues arise for a client's return, staff/senior accountants perform research in the tax law and derive a solution to the problem. (In many cases, the accountant's solution will be reviewed by a partner.) Such work is documented in a **tax research memorandum** to the client's file so that other members of the firm will understand the accountant's treatment of the issue. This documentation may also serve as evidence of the accountant's rationale for his treatment of the tax item should the accounting firm ever have to help the client defend his position to the IRS or another taxing authority.

6. *Opinion letters.* Senior and, sometimes, staff accountants write **opinion letters** in which they take an official and legally liable stand on how a client's tax matter should be treated. Because opinion letters serve as legal documentation of tax research performed, they must contain all the facts of the tax event, language cited from the relevant tax law, and the firm's rationale for its interpretation of the law. The tax research memo (just described in paragraph 5), with some modification of language and added explanations, can serve as an opinion letter to a client. In almost every case, the partner in charge of the tax engagement reviews the opinion letter for correctness and completeness before approving it.

7. *Transmittal letter to accompany the tax returns.* When the tax returns have been completed, the staff/senior accountant prepares a **transmittal letter** to the client that contains instructions for filing the returns and, sometimes, a brief summary of the results of the tax return.

8. *Exit meeting.* In some instances, the staff accountant, senior, or partner holds a final **meeting with the client** after the returns have been prepared. Such meetings typically are held if the client requires an explanation of the tax returns, if the accountant feels it is necessary to discuss a particularly troublesome issue and how it was resolved, or if the client or accountant wishes to discuss tax planning ideas for the future. When tax planning or other additional services are discussed at the exit meeting, the accountant has an opportunity to market the firm's services.

9. *Tax planning report.* If tax planning is performed for a client, depending on the nature of the individual client and on the amount and complexity of information to be related to the client, the tax accountant may write a **tax planning report** for the client. Tax planning reports may contain ideas for minimizing tax liability as well as ideas for ways in which to take advantage of favorable provisions in the tax law. The partner or senior who conducted the planning engagement usually authors the report, but sometimes staff may be asked to furnish sections concerning issues that they may have researched.

10. *Corrective action letters to taxing authorities.* Throughout the course of the tax year, problems with the IRS or other taxing authorities can arise.

Typically, the client receives a notice or an assessment of additional tax from the taxing authority. Usually the problems involve **factual errors** made either by the client (or client's accountant) or by the taxing authority. Client/accountant factual errors might consist of an incorrectly transcribed dollar amount from a Form W-2 or 1099 or the omission from the return of an income item that had been reported to the taxing authority. Taxing authority factual errors might consist of allocating a client's tax payment to the wrong tax year or even losing a taxpayer's return. In these cases, the accountant may have to write to the authority on behalf of his client to straighten out the mistake and request corrective action. Letters of this type are fairly simple; the accountant simply explains the facts in question, provides any necessary documentation such as copies of W-2s or of the tax return itself, and requests that the correction be made.

11. *Tax protest letters to taxing authorities.* Disputes with taxing authorities can also involve **the interpretation of tax law** that the taxing authority or accountant has applied to the client's case. In these disputes, the accountant writes a letter to protest the authority's interpretation or to set forth his own. Protest letters are more challenging to write than letters requesting corrective action because they require the construction of a formal argument about applying the tax law to the client's case. To advocate successfully for the client in these circumstances, the accountant must ground the argument in the IRS Code and must cite all relevant sections carefully.[2] Some protest letters can be as long as 50 pages!

Although the communications just described represent those typical of most tax engagements, not all 11 types are necessarily present in every engagement (see Figure 12.1). What occurs in actual practice depends on the nature of the tax client and on the communication environment within the accounting firm.

A CORPORATE TAX ENGAGEMENT

Tax accountants working on corporate engagements usually find themselves communicating with others whose knowledge is similar to their own: accountants of the client company, the company controller, the chief financial officer, and members of the company's legal department. Because these audiences possess expert knowledge as well as experience in accounting and finance, the tax accountant can assume they share a basic understanding of accounting concepts, accounting rules, and tax law. In both oral and written communications with these audiences, therefore, the tax accountant can use technical language without extensive explanation.

This mutual understanding does not, however, allow the tax accountant to adopt a casual or informal attitude toward communications with the corporate client. Quite the contrary. The accountant must record information meticulously to show she understands all the facts of the client's tax situation as well as the client's goals for the engagement. She must document research thoroughly, citing relevant authorities fully and clearly explaining the reasoning that led to her opinions and recommendations. She

Figure 12.1

Communication Events During a Typical Tax Engagement

a. Initial Meeting with the Client

**Initiates Contact with the Client
and Gathers Information**

b. Engagement Letter

**Formalizes Contract Between Firm
and Client**

c. Requests for Information

**Formalizes Initial Meeting and
Requests and Asks for
Additional Information**

d. Follow-Up Phone Calls and Letters

**Gathers More Information;
Answers or Asks
Client Questions**

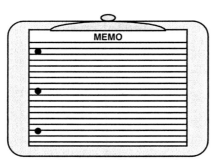

e. Tax Research Memorandum

**Documents Results of
Tax Research**

f. Opinion Letter

**Explains Tax Issue to Client
and Gives Opinion of
Proper Tax Treatment**

Figure 12.1

Communication Events During a Typical Tax Engagement—*continued*

g. Transmittal Letter to Accompany Tax Returns

Provides Instructions to Client for Filing Returns

h. Exit Meeting

Explains Returns and Discusses Tax Planning

i. Tax Planning Reports

Provides Ideas for Minimizing Client's Tax Liability

j. Corrective Action Letters to Taxing Authorities

Explains the Facts, Provides Documentation, and Requests Correction

k. Tax Protest Letters

Disputes Taxing Authority's Interpretation of the Law

must also provide explicit instructions to the client for the filing of returns even when she knows the client is aware of how to proceed. These practices are necessary because every document the tax accountant produces—letters to the client, memoranda to the files, and write-ups of meetings and interviews—creates an official record of the engagement, a record that may need to be defended should disputes arise later with the client or with taxing authorities.

Figures 12.2 through 12.9 illustrate documents from a sample corporate engagement that exemplify the communication practices just described. In this engagement, Ruth Nolan, senior tax accountant for a large international accounting firm, Johnson & London, LLP, is in charge of preparing the corporate tax returns for General Plastics, Inc., a manufacturing company. Johnson & London does the financial statement audit for General Plastics each year. As is the case with many audits, this one has led to an annual tax engagement as well because General Plastics' management is already confident about Johnson & London's integrity and the capability of its staff. In addition, because Johnson & London already has a strong understanding of General Plastics' business and accounting records, the firm can get the job done more efficiently and at a lower cost than could an accounting firm unfamiliar with General Plastics.

Because Johnson & London already has a working relationship with General Plastics, no introductory meeting is necessary, but Johnson & London will prepare an engagement letter, specifying what services will be performed and explaining how the work will be conducted. Like audit engagement letters, those for tax work often contain boilerplate legal language necessary to protect the firm. Because engagement letters create a contractual relationship between the firm and the client company, they are not written by entry-level accountants. We have nevertheless presented an example of one for your information (Figure 12.2).

Requests for Information

Fact gathering about the client's tax situation is the first step in the communication process; it is also the foundation for the engagement as a whole. The accountant needs a full picture of the client's tax situation to decide on how to handle that client's taxes. A complete set of facts creates the big picture, and any change in those facts can alter the accountant's recommendations about tax strategies. As one accountant puts it,

> The hardest part about getting anybody's return done correctly is not the [tax] law; it is the facts. But the reason that's hard is because the law has become so complicated, and there [are] so many different variations of facts and so many specific little details you have to know about each time in order to make sure you're complying with the law. . . . We struggle more with getting the facts than we do deciding what to do with the facts once we have them.[3]

In our sample engagement, the accountant uses both oral communications in meetings and phone calls and written requests for information to gather facts

Figure 12.2

Sample Engagement Letter—Corporate Tax Client

LETTER

Johnson & London, LLP
1825 Southwest Plaza Tower
Phoenix, AZ 85055

December 15, 1999
Ms. Lorraine Taylor, Controller
General Plastics, Inc.
27 Industrial Park Boulevard
Nogales, AZ 85625

Dear Ms. Taylor:

We intend that this letter serve as an estimate of our fees regarding the tax return preparation services for the year ended December 31, 1999 for General Plastics, Inc. The scope of our services will include the preparation of the company's federal, Arizona, Illinois, and North Dakota corporate income returns for the tax year ended December 31, 1999.

We base our fees on our best faith estimate of the actual hours we will need to prepare, review, and process the returns. In preparing the estimate of our fees, we are relying on the maximum assistance of your accounting personnel and your timely completion of our pre-preparation information requests. Our billings to the company for these services will range from $4,750 to $5,250. Expenses, which include computer processing, secretarial work, and overhead charges, are included in the fee estimate.

Our above estimate does not encompass any nonrecurring services that may be necessary as a result of the discovery of unusual issues or special consulting. These services would include responses to any federal or state tax notices due to late filing, preparation of registration forms, or any other tax matters not mentioned above. Should such services be required, we will bill you separately on the basis of time required by individuals assigned to perform the work. Such additional fees would be based on the degree of technical difficulty associated with the engagement and the specialization of the team members required to perform the work.

Additionally, we would like to set forth pertinent information about the scope and nature of our tax preparation services in order to ensure a complete understanding between us.

Figure 12.2

Sample Engagement Letter—Corporate Tax Client—*continued*

- We will prepare the above mentioned federal and state tax returns from information furnished to us. We will rely on the information that is supplied to be accurate and complete to the best of your and your management team's knowledge. Although we may need to ask you for clarification of some of the information, we will not audit the submitted data.

- Our work in connection with the preparation of the tax returns does not include any procedures designed to discover errors or other irregularities, should any exist, in the information provided to us. We will, as noted above, provide accounting assistance as we deem necessary for preparation of the returns.

- We will use our professional judgment in resolving questions where the tax law is unclear or where there may be conflicts between the taxing authorities' interpretations of the law and other supportable positions. Unless instructed otherwise by you, we will resolve such questions in your favor whenever possible.

- You and your management team have the final responsibility for the tax returns and you should review them carefully before you sign and file the returns.

- Your returns may be selected for review by the taxing authorities. Any proposed adjustments by the examining agent are subject to certain rights of appeal. In the event of a tax examination, we will be available to represent you and will render an additional fee statement for the time and expenses incurred.

- The maximum liability of Johnson & London, LLP, relating to services rendered under this letter regardless of form or claim whether in contract, statute, or tort—including without limitation, negligence or otherwise—shall be limited to the fees paid to J & L for the portion of J & L's services or work giving rise to the liability. In no event shall J & L be liable for lost profits or for any consequential, special, incidental, indirect, or punitive damages.

If the foregoing fairly sets forth your understanding, please sign the enclosed copy of this letter at the space indicated and return it to our office.

We want to express our appreciation for this opportunity to work with you.

Very truly yours,
Johnson & London, LLP
By Alexander P. Hunicutt, Partner

APPROVED:
By: _____ Date: _____

thoroughly. To get started on the client's tax return, Ruth Nolan meets with the audit team to get items that she needs from them, such as the year-end trial balance and a schedule of fixed assets. Although she is already familiar with the client's general tax situation (because her firm prepares the client's taxes each year), Ruth makes an initial written, formal request for detailed information (see Figure 12.3). By documenting her request in this way, she begins building a solid engagement file.

Because she is writing to a knowledgeable reader, Ruth can request information on such items as "fixed assets" and "accumulated depreciation." Were she writing to another type of client, she might have to define her terms. After her initial meeting with the General Plastics auditors, Ruth attends a joint meeting of the audit and tax teams for the company. In that meeting, she learns that GP's management is considering selling a parcel of land they own near their Illinois facility and that the controller is interested in the tax implications of the transaction. Ruth takes notes at the meeting and later summarizes her understanding of the situation in a letter to GP's controller (see Figure 12.4). Ruth's letter serves two purposes: It documents the conversation in which she learned of the controller's concerns, and it makes a formal request for the information needed to respond to those concerns.

Tax Research Memorandum

As the letter in Figure 12.4 suggests, Ruth will have to *interpret tax law* to respond to the controller's questions about the tax consequences of the land sale. She will have to do the following:

- study the facts
- identify the issues raised by those facts
- research the IRS Code sections that apply to those facts
- apply the provisions of the Code to the facts
- render an opinion based on her analysis of the facts in the light of the law.

This process of interpretation is the heart of tax practice. When clients seek the advice of tax accountants, they are, in effect, asking for an interpretation of tax law as it relates to their own unique financial situation. Clients pay top dollar for these interpretations, and they rely on their accountants to recommend the most cost-effective course of action under the law.

If the IRS disputes a client's tax liability, the accountant must be able to defend the interpretation of tax law used to calculate the liability amount. For this reason, tax accountants must be very careful to explain how they arrived at their calculations and to cite the authority they used to do so. The tax research memorandum is the document they use to create this explanation. Because it articulates the accountant's argument for the recommendation to the client, the tax research memo is the central and most important text in tax practice. It is the anchor for the engagement workpapers and the source for other written communications, such as the opinion letter and tax protest letters (described later).

Figure 12.3

Request for Information—Corporate Tax Client

LETTER

Johnson & London, LLP
1825 Southwest Plaza Tower
Phoenix, AZ 85055

February 1, 2000
Ms. Lorraine Taylor, Controller
General Plastics, Inc.
27 Industrial Park Boulevard
Nogales, AZ 85625

RE: Information request for 1999 tax returns

Dear Lorraine:

We will need the following information to complete the federal and state tax returns for General Plastics, Inc., for the year ended December 31, 1999. Please note that this list is only a preliminary one. We may find that we need additional information as we proceed with the preparation of the returns.

1. Detail of intercompany transactions including loan balances, interest paid on loans, and inventory purchases.
2. A detailed report of sales by state.
3. A breakdown of salary expense by state.
4. A breakdown of inventory value by state.
5. A breakdown of property and equipment value by state (cost and accumulated depreciation).
6. A list of officers of the company including compensation and any benefits received.

We have obtained your 12/31/99 trial balance and schedule of fixed assets directly from your Johnson & London auditors. If you have any questions concerning the above information, please call me.

Sincerely,
Johnson & London, LLP
Ruth Nolan, CPA
Tax Engagement Senior

Figure 12.4

Summary/Request for Information—Corporate Tax Client

LETTER

Johnson & London, LLP
1825 Southwest Plaza Tower
Phoenix, AZ 85055

February 5, 2000
Ms. Lorraine Taylor, Controller
General Plastics, Inc.
27 Industrial Park Boulevard
Nogales, AZ 85625

Dear Lorraine:

Our audit manager, Harry Jones, has told me that at a recent audit meeting you mentioned that GP management is considering selling a parcel of land to a nonprofit hospital in Chicago. Harry has relayed to me your request for information about the likely tax consequences of such a sale.

Allow me to summarize for you the potential tax effects and to ask you for some relevant information that I will need to determine the exact consequence of the transaction, should GP decide to undertake it during this year.

- If GP sells its property to the hospital, the capital gain it enjoys will be taxed at the company's tax rate (approximately 35%). The capital gain can be used to offset any capital losses that the company has carried over from prior years.
- If the property is sold at an amount less than the property's fair market value (FMV), the difference between the FMV and GP's cost basis in the property will be considered a potentially deductible contribution to charity.
- The tax law allows corporations to deduct charitable contributions of capital gains property for any given year up to an amount equal to 10% of the company's taxable income before certain deductions.

Figure 12.4

Summary/Request for Information—Corporate Tax Client—*continued*

To calculate the amount of your potential capital gain and charitable contribution, I will need the following information from you:

- The original price GP paid for the land
- The costs of any major improvements GP made to the land
- The fair market value of the land (as assessed by a licensed appraiser)
- The selling price to the hospital
- Any major changes expected in GP's 2000 taxable income (best estimate)

I look forward to assisting you further in this matter.

Sincerely,
Johnson & London, LLP
Ruth Nolan, CPA
Senior Tax Accountant

As the tax memo is written "to the file," its writer assumes a knowledgeable audience—other tax accountants who will refer to it during and after the engagement. The writer of this important memo must clearly explain, however, the context from which the memo arises, the issues it will discuss, the answers to those issues, and the analysis that led to those answers. The sample in Figure 12.5 illustrates these elements in proper format.

In our model engagement, the tax senior conducts the research and writes the memorandum when she has received the information she needs from her client's controller. But she might just as likely have asked a staff accountant to do the research and preliminary drafting. In almost all tax practices, entry-level accountants spend a great deal of their time working on tax research memos so they learn early how to perform this crucial function.

Examine Ruth's tax research memo in Figure 12.5. Notice that she has organized the memo according to the method suggested in Chapter 4. Ruth provides *context* by briefly summarizing the situation in question. She indicates the memo's *purpose* by articulating the issues to be discussed. She *forecasts* the memo's structure and content in her answers to those issues. She discusses *one idea per paragraph* and organizes her analysis from *most to least important*.

Notice also how Ruth has cited the appropriate part of the Internal Revenue Code in each section of her analysis. In many cases, the Code is the final authority for any interpretation of federal tax law an accountant makes. Each issue and fact in the memo must be discussed, therefore, in light of the Code, and each point of discussion must be correctly cited.

Figure 12.5

Tax Research Memorandum

MEMO

TAX RESEARCH MEMORANDUM

To: General Plastics Tax File, Tax Year 2000
From: Ruth Nolan, Senior Tax Accountant
Date: February 11, 2000
Subject: Bargain Sale as Charitable Contribution

The Situation:

General Plastics owns a piece of land that it intends to sell to a non-profit hospital. The appraised value of the property is $500,000, its adjusted basis is $235,000, and the hospital intends to pay $475,000.

The Issues:

Under IR Code Section 170,

1. What would be the capital gain on the property?
2. What would be the allowable charitable deduction?

The Conclusions:

1. Under IRC Section 170(e)(2), which calls for a reduction in the property's adjusted basis for purposes of calculating gain, General Plastics would realize a capital gain of $251,750 on the bargain sale of its land to charity (calculated below).
2. Under IRC Section 170 (e)(1), which allows a charitable contribution deduction for the "bargain element" of a sale of property to a charity, General Plastics would be able to take a deduction. Section 170(e)(1) states that the deduction will be equal to the difference between the fair market value of the property at the time of the sale and the actual price at which the property is sold to the charity ($25,000 in the case of General Plastics' transaction). Also, the $25,000 deduction allowed in tax year 2000 will be subject to a 10%-of-adjusted-taxable-income limitation that likely will prevent GP from taking all of the deduction in 2000. Any amount not taken in 2000 may be carried forward and used in the five years to follow. [Section 170(d)]

413

Figure 12.5

Tax Research Memorandum—*continued*

1. Application of Internal Revenue Code:

Section 170(a), "Charitable Contributions and Gifts": A taxpayer may sell property to a charity and receive less than the property's fair market value, intending the bargain element as a contribution to the charity. Under Section 170(e)(2), however, the adjusted basis of the property must be reduced to a proportion of the selling price calculated as follows:

(Original Adjusted Basis./.FMV of the Property) $\times$ Selling Price

Therefore, the reduced basis for General Plastics' land would be $233,250:

$$(\$235,000 \div \$500,000) \times \$475,000 = \$223,250$$

and General Plastics' capital gain would be $251,750:

Selling Price	−	Reduced Basis	=	Capital Gain
$475,000	−	$223,250	=	$251,750

2. Application of Internal Revenue Code:

Section 170(e)(1) indicates that the amount deductible for a charitable contribution of property other than money is the fair value of the property at the time of the contribution (less any sale proceeds received), so long as the property is not ordinary income property, tangible personal property, or property contributed to a private foundation.

GP's potential maximum charitable contribution deduction would be $25,000 calculated as follows:

FMV	−	Selling Price	=	Charitable Contribution
$500,000	−	$475,000	=	$25,000

Another capital gain property rule under IRC Section 170(b)(1)(C) states that the deduction for the total amount of contributions of capital gain property made during the year is limited to 10% of the company's taxable income before deductions for the dividends received deduction, NOL carrybacks, and capital loss carrybacks. Therefore, if GP has taxable income (before the above mentioned deductions) of less than $250,000 this year, it will not be able to take all of the $25,000 as a charitable deduction in 2000. However, any amount by which the contribution exceeds the 10% of taxable income limitation can be carried forward and deducted in any of the five succeeding years. [Section 170(d)]

Note: Further research will have to be done to determine the effects of the transaction on GP's Illinois (and possibly Arizona) state corporate income taxes.

Citing the IR Code   To cite a given statutory provision, it is helpful to understand the organizational structure of the law. The Internal Revenue Code of 1986, the statutory federal tax law, consists of divisions organized in the following order: title, subtitle, chapter, subchapter, part, section, subsection, paragraph, subparagraph, and sub-subparagraph. Of particular importance to the tax researcher are the divisions called "sections" because these are uniquely numbered in a consecutive manner throughout the Internal Revenue Code. Because each section number is used only once in the Code, one can use, for example, the simple citation, "IRC, Section 8," and not have to list the title, subtitle, chapter, subchapter, and part in each citation.

In specific code citations, sections are broken down into subdivisions as shown here. Section 170(e)(1)(B) serves as our example:

SS Abbreviation for "Section"
170 Section number
(e) Subsection designation
(1) Paragraph designation
(B) Subparagraph designation

These guidelines apply to the citation system for the Internal Revenue Code. Other authoritative tax law sources, such as treasury regulations, tax court cases, and state tax law, follow their own system and style of citation. Consult your tax textbook for more details on citing tax law.

Opinion Letter

After showing the memo to Alex Hunicutt (partner) and getting his approval of the contents, Ruth writes an opinion letter to the controller at General Plastics summarizing the information in lay terms but being sure to include the authoritative details of the tax law research that she did. Writing an opinion letter allows Ruth to explain all the details to her client and to create a written record for both herself and the client to refer to next year when the tax return is prepared (and the details perhaps forgotten). In addition, the opinion letter is crucial to the firm's legal defense if the client or a taxing authority should ever question the handling of the tax issue. With this purpose in mind, Ruth cites the Internal Revenue Code specifically and frequently, although she does so in footnotes to the letter so the client may read the document easily.

Because her client has a certain amount of accounting and general tax expertise, Ruth writes the opinion letter, seen in Figure 12.6, using technical terms, although she places her Code citations at the end to create a letter that flows smoothly. But whether writing a tax research memo or an opinion letter, accountants must be sure to provide a legally defensible body of relevant information that includes a thorough identification of the situation and issues and a complete, well-organized analysis of the client's case, including citations from the tax law sources.

Figure 12.6

Opinion Letter

LETTER

Johnson & London, LLP
1825 Southwest Plaza Tower
Phoenix, AZ 85055

February 12, 2000
Ms. Lorraine Taylor, Controller
General Plastics, Inc.
27 Industrial Park Boulevard
Nogales, AZ 85625

Dear Lorraine:

After reviewing the relevant tax law, I have determined that a "bargain sale" of land to St. Mary's Charitable Hospital would have two effects on GP's 2000 federal income tax return:

1. GP would report a capital gain of $251,750* on the sale, which could be used to offset any capital losses that it might incur during 2000. Any remaining capital gain will be taxable at the company's predicted tax rate of approximately 35%.

2. GP would be able to deduct as a charitable contribution the $25,000 "bargain" element of the transaction (the difference between the appraisal value on the property of $500,000 and the selling price of $475,000).** However, the $25,000 may not be fully deductible in 2000 if the company sees taxable in-

---

*Under Internal Revenue Code Section 170, "Charitable Contributions and Gifts," when a taxpayer sells property to a charity and receives less than the property's fair market value, the "bargain element" of the sale is considered a contribution to the charity. Under Section 170(e)(2), however, the adjusted basis of the property must be reduced to a proportion of the selling price calculated as follows:
(Original Adjusted Basis ÷ FMV of the Property) × Selling Price
Therefore, the reduced basis for General Plastics' land would be $233,250
($235,000 ÷ $500,000) × $475,000 = $223,250
and General Plastics' capital gain would be $251,750.
Selling Price − Reduced Basis = Capital Gain
  $475,000 − $223,250 = $251,750

**Internal Revenue Code Section 170(e)(1)

Figure 12.6

Opinion Letter—*continued*

> come (before certain deductions) of less than $250,000 because corporations are limited to deducting a maximum of 10% of their taxable income (before certain deductions) for charitable contributions. If GP cannot take the full deduction in tax year 2000, and that seems likely, it will be able to carry the deduction forward for the following five years.***
>
> 2000 seems to be a good year for this transaction to take place because the losses you expect on your other capital asset sales this year could be used to reduce the capital gain, on which you will have to pay tax.
>
> Please let me know whether or not GP intends to proceed with the sale. If it does, I should make adjustments to the federal and state estimates for the year 2000. If you have any questions, please call me.
>
> Sincerely,
> Johnson & London, LLP
> Ruth Nolan, CPA
> Senior Tax Accountant
>
> ———
> ***Internal Revenue Code Section 170(d)

Transmitting the Completed Tax Returns

Transmittal Letter   When the tax returns have been completed, the accountant prepares a transmittal letter giving instructions to the client for filing the returns. Even when the accountant knows the client is familiar with filing procedures, written instructions must be provided. Such instructions provide documentation that the client was properly informed about filing deadlines and procedures. In cases where a detailed explanation of the return is warranted (i.e., there are matters of great complexity that the client or the accountant wants to discuss), the accountant may set up a meeting with the client. Because the General Plastics' tax engagement is relatively straightforward, Ruth Nolan deems such a meeting unnecessary, and she prepares the transmittal letter and delivers the returns to General Plastics (see Figure 12.7).

Letters to Taxing Authorities   On occasion, a client may receive notification from the IRS or other taxing authority of a problem with a tax return or payment. Part of the tax accountant's job is to troubleshoot such problems for

Figure 12.7

Transmittal Letter to Client

LETTER

Johnson & London, LLP
1825 Southwest Plaza Tower
Phoenix, AZ 85055

March 5, 2000
Howard Michaels, Acting Controller
General Plastics, Inc.
27 Industrial Park Boulevard
Nogales, AZ 85625

Dear Howard:

Enclosed are the filing copies of your federal and state corporate income tax returns, which we have prepared for the tax year 1999. If upon review of the returns you have any questions, please call me.

FILING INSTRUCTIONS

U.S. Income Tax Return for a Corporation:

- Should be signed and dated by an officer on page 1
- Should include a check to **Internal Revenue Service** in the amount of $15,000
- Should be mailed to the **Internal Revenue Service Center, Denver, CO 80221**
- On or before March 15, 2000.

Arizona Income Tax Return for a Corporation:

- Should be signed and dated by an officer on page 2
- Should include a check to **AZ Department of Revenue** in the amount of $8,000
- Should be mailed to the **Arizona Department of Revenue, Phoenix, AZ 85010**
- On or before March 15, 2000.

Figure 12.7

Transmittal Letter to Client—*continued*

Illinois Income Tax Return for a Corporation:

- Should be signed and dated by an officer on page 1
- Should be mailed to the **Illinois Department of Revenue and Taxation, Chicago, IL 60605**
- On or before March 15, 2000.

North Dakota Income Tax Return for a Corporation:

- Should be signed and dated by an officer on page 2
- Should be mailed to the **North Dakota Tax Board, Fargo, ND 58105**
- On or before March 15, 2000.

To create a record of timely filing, we strongly recommend that you send the returns by certified mail, return receipt requested. Your receipt must be postmarked at the post office.

Thank you, and we look forward to serving you again in the future.

Johnson & London, LLP

the client. Often the troubleshooting simply involves a written request to have factual errors corrected, as in Figure 12.8.

Here is some background on the situation: Ruth and the tax partner, Alex Hunicutt, recently finished assisting General Plastics with an IRS audit of its 1996 corporate income tax return. The audit resulted in an increase in taxable income on which additional taxes and interest were due. After the IRS audit, Ruth properly amended the 1996 Arizona state income tax return, which was affected by the findings of the federal audit. General Plastics paid the additional state taxes due, and approximately three weeks later, as expected, received a letter from the state showing the state's calculations of interest owed on the additional taxes.

When the interest assessment letter arrived from the state, Ruth reviewed it and found that the state had incorrectly calculated the interest to be paid because it had used the wrong date in its calculation. Ruth wrote the letter in Figure 12.8 to the Arizona Department of Revenue on behalf of General Plastics.

In the case of the letter in Figure 12.8, the matter will probably be resolved by the single correspondence, and General Plastics will receive a letter of closure/resolution from the state taxing authority.

General Plastics has another kind of problem to resolve, however, that calls for a more elaborate persuasive effort. At the end of February 2000, Lorraine Taylor, the company's controller, resigned her position. During the subsequent

Figure 12.8

Corrective Action Letter to a Taxing Authority

LETTER

Johnson & London, LLP
1825 Southwest Plaza Tower
Phoenix, AZ 85055

June 1, 2000
State of Arizona
Department of Revenue
Office of Corporate Taxes
Phoenix, AZ 85055
RE: General Plastics, Inc.

To whom it may concern:

This letter is in response to your interest settlement notice dated May 30, 2000 for General Plastics, Inc. General Plastics incurred additional Arizona state taxes as the result of a recent IRS audit and paid those taxes on May 9, 1998. At that time, General Plastics requested that you calculate the interest due on the additional taxes. Your calculations of that interest appear to be incorrect, however. We request a correction of the interest charged, based on the facts below.

The applicable Arizona Department of Revenue policy for back taxes due as a result of an IRS audit is to begin charging interest from the date of the IRS final assessment. In General Plastics' case, this date was April 14, 2000. It appears, however, that the state mistakenly used the date of the IRS auditor's preliminary report (March 30, 2000).

Although the audit report does indeed bear the date of March 30, the auditor on that date had not yet reviewed General Plastics' proposed adjustments. The auditor subsequently reviewed the adjustments and required General Plastics to accept the report only on April 14, 2000, the date of the auditor's final assessment.

As soon as the IRS audit was finalized, we prepared the Arizona amended returns, and General Plastics sent them to you on May 10, 2000, well within the required 30 days from the April 14 conclusion of the audit.

Figure 12.8

Corrective Action Letter to a Taxing Authority—*continued*

We have enclosed copies of the following information, originally sent to you by General Plastics, Inc.:

1. Signed and dated IRS 1996 examination reports;
2. Signed and dated Arizona corporate income tax return for 1996 revised for IRS audit changes;
3. Copies of Form 1120 for 1996 revised for IRS audit changes.

Please call me if you have any further questions. Thank you for your help in this matter.

Sincerely,

Johnson & London, LLP
Ruth Nolan, CPA
Senior Tax Accountant

period, as the company was searching for a new controller, the inexperienced assistant controller, Howard Michaels, inadvertently failed to file the corporation's tax return on the March 15 deadline. (He thought the deadline was April 15, as it is for individual taxpayers.) General Plastics now faces late filing and late deposit penalties. The new controller has asked Ruth Nolan to handle the situation in hopes of having the penalties abated. Ruth writes the tax protest letter in Figure 12.9 on behalf of her client to the IRS.

Even though the letters in Figures 12.8 and 12.9 concern problems of different magnitudes, they both are organized in a manner that should be familiar to you by now: Ruth summarizes the situation up front, indicates her purpose by requesting a certain corrective action or application of a law, and communicates her analysis by stating the facts and showing how the appropriate rules apply to her case. The major difference between the two types of letters is that the first *asks for action in correcting a factual error* and the second *argues that the IRS should apply a particular rule of law* in a way favorable to the client. In the former, a clearly defined mistake needs to and will be rectified; in the latter, the outcome is much less certain and will depend on the strength and clarity of the accountant's argument.

AN INDIVIDUAL TAX ENGAGEMENT

The rhetorical situations that arise from corporate tax engagements are often quite different from those involving individual clients. Whereas corporate

Figure 12.9

Protest Letter to a Taxing Authority

> ### LETTER
>
> **Johnson & London, LLP**
> **1825 Southwest Plaza Tower**
> **Phoenix, AZ 85055**
>
> June 18, 2000
> Department of the Treasury
> Internal Revenue Service
> Attn: Penalty Coordinator
> Denver, CO 80221
>
> **Subject:** Formal Request to Abate Penalty
> **Taxpayer:** General Plastics, Inc.
> **Form:** 1120
> **ID Number:** 89-356999
> **Tax Period:** December 31, 1999
>
> To whom it may concern:
>
> This letter is a formal request to abate the Section 6651(a)(1) late filing and Section 6651(a)(2) late deposit penalties of $9,500.05 you charged on the attached notice dated June 9, 2000. I believe there is **reasonable cause** for the removal of these penalties.
>
> Section 301.6651-1(c) provides guidance in determining reasonable cause as it relates to late filing and payment penalties. The penalty for the failure to timely file a tax return and pay a tax liability does not apply if it is shown that the failure is due to reasonable cause and not willful neglect. In United States v. Bishop, 123 Fed 2d 1996, the Supreme Court defined willful to mean a voluntary, intentional violation of a known legal duty. Furthermore, a taxpayer is considered to have acted reasonably if it exercised ordinary business care and prudence in meeting its filing and payment requirements.
>
> The employee who was acting as temporary controller of General Plastics, Inc. inadvertently confused the date for the filing of corporate tax returns with the date for filing of individual tax returns. General Plastics never willfully intended to be delinquent in its tax obligations. Rather, it believed that it was meeting its requirements by remitting its Form 1120 and the balance of its tax liability by April 15, the date on

Figure 12.9

Protest Letter to a Taxing Authority—*continued*

which it mistakenly believed payment was due. Moreover, General Plastics, Inc. acted responsibly by depositing its estimated payments for the tax year 1999 either before or on their due dates and is current with its estimated payments for the tax year 2000.

Based on General Plastics' past history as a timely filer and its clear intent to meet its filing requirements for the 1999 tax year, I respectfully request that you abate the late filing and deposit penalties.

In the event that you do not agree with our position, I request that this matter be referred to the regional director of appeals.

Thank you for your consideration in this matter. Should you have any questions or require additional information, please contact me at (111) 555-3377.

Sincerely,
Johnson & London, LLP
Ruth Nolan, CPA
Senior Tax Accountant

engagements usually involve accountants in communications with experienced financial professionals, the accountant's audience in individual tax work can vary widely. At one end of the spectrum are clients with broad knowledge of financial planning, tax shelters, allowable deductions, and general provisions of the tax code. At the other are clients who know next to nothing about finances or tax.

Financially savvy taxpayers often come to the tax accountant with complete and well-organized information as well as clear ideas of their financial goals. In meetings and written correspondence with these clients, the accountant can rely on a shared body of knowledge and can expect questions and discussions based on that knowledge. Although the accountant may have to explain the finer points of tax law or define complex issues in some detail, he can assume these knowledgeable clients understand the broad outlines of his advice. He can also use some technical vocabulary without explaining every term.

With naïve or inexperienced clients, however, the tax accountant must function as a kind of educator, explaining basic principles, defining fundamental terms, helping these clients understand how one aspect of the financial situation affects other aspects. Clients with limited knowledge of tax rarely come to meetings with complete information because they do not know what records the accountant needs. And the accountant cannot simply ask such clients for their financial records; instead, he must explain to them what categories of information he is seeking and what kinds of documentation they need to provide.

Although tax accountants must be able to communicate appropriately and effectively with this entire range of audiences, most clients fall somewhere between these two extremes. The individual tax engagement described here is based on such taxpayers: reasonably well-informed businesspeople without special expertise in tax and finance.

In this engagement, taxpayers Jack and Suzanne Bennett have been referred by their local banker to Connor, Lafferty, and Sonoma, CPAs, a medium-sized regional accounting firm. Jack is a corporate executive with General Plastics and Suzanne is an interior designer. Jack and Suzanne recently moved to Arizona when Jack was transferred from the General Plastics Illinois facility to the company headquarters in Nogales. As the result of a phone call from Suzanne, an initial meeting is scheduled during which the tax partner, Eliza Sonoma, accompanied by staff accountant, Art Jackson, will acquaint the Bennetts with the firm, discuss the tax engagement, and offer other firm services to the Bennetts.

Eliza is aware that initial meetings with new clients are always important to the success of engagements because it is at such meetings that clients form their first impressions of the firm's competence and integrity. Although the Bennetts have already decided to engage C,L,&S based on their banker's recommendation, Eliza plans her communications with these new clients carefully.

Initial Meeting with the Client

Eliza has asked Art to prepare an agenda to be sent out prior to the meeting with a cover letter of introduction (see Figure 12.10). Both documents will be subject to Eliza's review before they are sent out. Receiving the agenda in advance will help the Bennetts begin to organize their tax information and gather preliminary documents for the accountants. Because the agenda specifies what the meeting will cover, it can also help the Bennetts formulate questions about material not included for discussion. Notice the informal, friendly tone of the cover letter.

The initial meeting gives the accountant the chance to do more than simply discuss services that she can provide and begin gathering preliminary information. The meeting also allows the accountant to create a rapport with the new client. Clients are often sensitive about exposing their private financial information to strangers, so the accountant must take care to present herself as not just intelligent and knowledgeable but as personable and trustworthy as well.

To create this positive impression, the accountant must use effective interviewing techniques and active listening skills. She should begin by breaking the ice with the client to establish a relaxed, conversational atmosphere. If she senses the client has questions about her competence or knowledge, the accountant should discuss experience and credentials; if the client seems to need a more personal connection, she can bring personal elements to the conversation such as sports she enjoys, children or grandchildren, or upcoming

Figure 12.10

Cover Letter and Initial Meeting Agenda

> ## LETTER
>
> **Connor, Lafferty, and Sonoma, CPAs**
> **1823 Drywood Road**
> **Nogales, AZ 85621**
>
> January 20, 2000
> Mr. and Mrs. Jack Bennett
> 20050 Meteor Lane
> Nogales, AZ 85623
>
> Dear Jack and Suzanne:
>
> Thank you for choosing Connor, Lafferty, and Sonoma, CPAs to be your tax preparation professionals.
>
> We would like to confirm our meeting date for Monday, January 27, 2000, at 10 A.M. Our office is located in the office complex north of Nogales Mall. Simply turn right from the mall road onto Drywood Road.
>
> Please bring along last year's federal tax return, if you have found it among all your moving boxes!
>
> I look forward to meeting you both.
>
> Sincerely,
> Eliza Sonoma, Partner
> Connor, Lafferty, and Sonoma, CPAs

---

holiday or vacation plans. Putting the new client at ease helps the accountant obtain the information she needs to maximize the client's tax savings.

As we mentioned earlier, Eliza, the tax partner, has invited Art Jackson, a staff accountant, to attend the meeting. Not only will Art be working directly with the Bennetts and preparing their tax returns, but Eliza also wants him to see how the meeting is run so Art will be better trained to conduct such a meeting himself someday. Eliza introduces herself and Art to the Bennetts, and she begins the meeting (following the agenda) by collecting basic information such as home and business addresses, phone numbers, and so on. She breaks the ice by asking the Bennetts how they like Arizona and their

Figure 12.10

Cover Letter and Initial Meeting Agenda—*continued*

AGENDA

Meeting Agenda
Jack and Suzanne Bennett
January 27, 2000

1. Introduction of the professional team
   - Eliza Sonoma, partner
   - Art Jackson, staff accountant
2. Collection/verification of addresses, phone and fax numbers, e-mail addresses, etc.
3. Client personal information:
   - Marital status
   - Dependents
   - Child-care expenses
4. Employment and/or other sources of earned income:
   - Jack's job with General Plastics
   - Unreimbursed business expenses
   - Suzanne's interior design business
   - Use of auto
   - Use of home as office
5. Sources of unearned income:
   - Bank accounts
   - Other interest-bearing investments
   - Broker accounts
   - Dividend-bearing investments
   - Interests in partnerships or S-corporations
6. Purchases or sales of property items:
   - Sale of residence in Chicago
   - Purchase of residence in Nogales
   - Investment activity
7. Deduction items:
   - Moving expenses
   - Contributions to charity
8. Client concerns/questions:
   - Timetable for return preparation
   - C,L,&S fees
   - Interest in tax planning

new neighborhood. Eliza mentions the golf course she plays on near their house, and the Bennetts enthusiastically discuss their passion for golf.

During the discussion of the next agenda topic, Eliza learns that in addition to the Bennetts' two younger children who live at home, Jack has a 2-year-old granddaughter for whom he paid extensive medical expenses during 1999. Jack asks Eliza whether he can deduct these expenses from his current return. Eliza then questions him to determine whether the necessary dependency tests have been met (The Internal Revenue Code's five tests for dependency status are the gross income test; the support test; the relationship test; the joint return test; and the citizenship or residency test.)

Jack: My grown daughter and her husband live in Chicago, and, unfortunately, last year, their daughter needed an operation. Pete, the father, was out of work and they got caught without health insurance, so I paid $60,000 in medical bills for them. Can I get some kind of tax break for that?

Eliza: Possibly, yes. May I ask you a few questions about the situation?

Jack: Sure.

Eliza: Is your granddaughter a U.S. citizen?

Jack: Yes.

Eliza: Did she have any income of her own for the year?

Jack: No, I don't think so.

Eliza: Would you say that your daughter and her husband spend less than, let's say, $100,000 per year to run their household? I mean for rent, food, utilities, and all that sort of thing?

Jack: Absolutely less. Ann doesn't work, and Pete couldn't be making more than $40,000 a year.

Eliza: (Figuring that the five dependency tests have probably been satisfied) Well, then, based on what you've told me, your granddaughter could qualify as a dependent for you to take on your tax return *and* the $60,000 could qualify as deductible medical expenses, provided you are able to take the medical expense deduction. That deduction, you see, depends on your income for the year, and I don't know what that is yet.

Jack: This is great!

Eliza: I must tell you, however, that all of this will depend on one other important factor: Your daughter and her husband will have to agree *not* to claim their daughter as a dependent on their own return this year. You see, only one party can claim the child in a given tax year.

Jack: Well, I guess I'll have to talk this over with Ann and Pete.

Eliza: I'd be happy to explain the matter to your daughter and her husband or to their tax preparer if you would like me to.

Jack: OK. Let me call Ann and tell her about this first. And then maybe I will ask you to call her. Thanks!

As you can see, during this part of the meeting, Eliza had the opportunity to demonstrate her knowledge of the tax law and to build the Bennetts' confidence in her as their new tax accountant. Also, by offering to explain the situation to Jack's daughter in Chicago, she has shown how helpful she can be to the new clients.

The Engagement Letter

After the meeting with the Bennetts takes place, the firm sends out an engagement letter to confirm the arrangements. Like an audit engagement letter, it serves as a contract between the firm and the client and outlines the responsibilities of each party. An engagement letter is usually prepared following established firm guidelines, or even copied from a model, because the language it contains must cover specific legal areas of potential liability. For an example of an engagement letter, refer to Figure 12.2.

Written Request for Information   Although Eliza and Art collected quite a bit of information orally from the Bennetts at the initial meeting, they did not receive much of the supporting documentation (Forms W-2 and 1099 that the Bennetts had not yet received from the issuing parties, Suzanne's business accounting records, which she had not remembered to bring to the meeting, etc.) that they need to prepare the returns. Art (who will be preparing the Bennetts' returns under Eliza's supervision) writes a follow-up letter to the Bennetts to request the documents he needs (see Figure 12.11). (For returning clients, the firm simply sends out a set of computer-generated checklists that ask the client for their tax information and documentation.)

Notice that Art's letter is written in February, shortly after the initial meeting and over two months before the April 15 filing deadline. Not only is it important for accountants to request client information well ahead of filing deadlines, they must create a written record of having done so. Such records protect the accountant and the firm if clients do not supply necessary data in a timely fashion.

After Art receives the clients' information and begins to prepare their tax returns, he discovers that he needs to clarify a piece of information with the client. He calls Suzanne to get the clarification he needs, and he makes a written record of her response (see Figure 12.12). This written record, which becomes part of the client's file, will help Art remember the details of the event when he conducts his research. The record will also provide the firm with documentation of the client's description of the event if the IRS should ever question the matter.

Note that the writing style of this phone record is quite informal because it was literally written from notes Art took while conducting the phone call. Nevertheless, the memo is still coherent and complete enough to provide a record of the information. This record will allow Art to conduct his research on the issue properly.

Figure 12.11

Letter to Client Requesting Initial Tax Information

LETTER

Connor, Lafferty, and Sonoma, CPAs
1823 Drywood Road
Nogales, AZ 85621

February 3, 2000
Mr. and Mrs. Jack Bennett
20050 Meteor Lane
Nogales, AZ 85623

Dear Jack and Suzanne:

Eliza and I enjoyed meeting you last week, and I am looking forward to preparing your tax returns.

To help me complete your 1999 income tax returns as early as possible, please gather and bring in or send to me the following information:

1. Jack's Form W-2 from General Plastics, Inc.
2. All Forms 1099 for interest and/or dividends received.
3. Year-end statements that you received from your investment broker.
4. Year-end total for day-care costs for your two children.
5. A summary of Jack's unreimbursed business expenses (broken down into the categories we discussed at the meeting: auto mileage, other travel costs, meals and entertainment).
6. Suzanne's interior design business records:
   - year-end trial balance generated by your accounting software
   - an inventory list of decorator items you had on hand at 12/31/99
   - a list of your office equipment and furniture, along with any cost/depreciation records from your previous accountant.
7. Settlement sheets from both the sale of your Chicago home and purchase of your Nogales home.
8. Moving expenses incurred for which you were not reimbursed.
9. 1099s for mortgage interest paid on each home during 1999.

Figure 12.11

Letter to Client Requesting Initial Tax Information—*continued*

I foresee no delays in getting your returns prepared by March 1, as you requested, if I receive your information by February 15. Please call me if you have any questions.

Sincerely,
Connor, Lafferty, and Sonoma, CPAs
Art Jackson, CPA
Senior Tax Accountant

Figure 12.12

Written Record of Phone Conversation

MEMO

Record of Oral Communication
Date: 2/17/00
Client Name: Jack & Suzanne Bennett
File Number: 80545
C,L,&S Contact: Art Jackson
Client Contact: Suzanne Bennett
Phone Number: 555-1234
Subject: Employer-paid travel for spouse

Conversation Summary: I noticed that Jack's employer (General Plastics) had put $850 of income on Jack's W-2 for payment of spouse's travel expenses. I asked Suzanne to explain the nature of the trip she and Jack had taken in 1999. She told me that General Plastics had decided to send Jack to the North Dakota plant for five days in September. When he complained that their twentieth wedding anniversary fell during the time planned for the trip, GP offered to pay Suzanne's airfare, incremental charge for the hotel room, and meals, so she could accompany Jack on the trip. She said that GP never mentioned to Jack that the $850 would be taxable income, and she and Jack had forgotten about it.

Tax Research Memorandum   After learning the details of the travel reimbursement, Art researches the subject and writes his analysis of the situation in a memo to the clients' file (see Figure 12.13). Notice that he cites the relevant section of the tax law and applies it to the situation at hand.

Transmitting the Completed Tax Returns

The Transmittal Letter   As we noted earlier, a transmittal letter with explicit filing instructions should always accompany the completed tax return (see Figure 12.14). Accordingly, Art has prepared one for the Bennetts, although he will be meeting with them to go over the returns.

The Exit Meeting   Occasionally, clients want to meet with their tax accountant to go over their tax returns before filing. Sometimes a complex issue appears on the return, and the client wants clarification of how the item was treated. Other times, clients may simply want the accountant to explain their returns to them. In the Bennett engagement, Suzanne is curious about how her interior design business fared in 1999, and she wants Art to walk her through the Schedule C (which reports profits and losses for sole proprietorship businesses). Suzanne meets with Art at the office, and during the course of the meeting, Suzanne questions the *gross fees earned* figure.

Suzanne: I see here that my fees earned for last year were $90,000. When I tallied them up I only got $85,000.

Art: Well, let's look at the supporting documents I have for sales. You had 20 small decorating jobs that totaled $60,000. And then you had three big jobs: Mane Events Hair Salon came in at $15,000, Elite Boutique's contract was for $10,000, and then the Covington Jewelers contract for $5,000.

Suzanne: But I haven't collected any money from Covington yet. So that wouldn't be fees earned, right?

Art: I see that the contract is dated November 1 of last year. When did you finish the job?

Suzanne: Right before Christmas. But Mr. Covington said that he wouldn't be able to pay me until he collected on his Christmas sales. I let him know that I was moving to Arizona, but I haven't received anything from him yet.

Art: Yes, I know that *seems* like money you haven't earned. But under the rules of accrual-based accounting, which is the method your business uses, we record all your revenues as you perform your services. We also record all the expenses that you incur while doing the jobs. By accounting this way, we match the expenses that you incur with the income you are going to receive.

Suzanne: I see. But what if I never get paid for that job? Then I will have paid tax on money I never received.

Figure 12.13

Tax Research Memo to the Client's File

MEMO

To: File of Jack & Suzanne Bennett, #80545
From: Art Jackson, Tax Engagement Senior
Date: February 17, 2000
Subject: Employer-paid travel for spouse

The Situation

Jack Bennett took a business trip to North Dakota in September 1999, and Suzanne Bennett accompanied him for nonbusiness reasons. In addition to paying for all of Jack's expenses, his employer (General Plastics) paid for Suzanne's expenses (incremental hotel charge, airfare, meals, and entertainment). On Jack's 1999 W-2, General Plastics reported $850 of additional compensation, the total expenses for Suzanne's travel, and so on.

The Issue: Does the $850 Jack received in additional compensation represent taxable income under IRC Section 274?

The Conclusion: According to IRC 274(x)(C), the $850 represents taxable compensation by an employer for expenses incurred with respect to a spouse on business travel.

The Rule

Code Section 274 states that monies received by an employee for travel, meals, and entertainment expenses incurred with respect to a spouse, dependent, or other individual accompanying the taxpayer on business travel, represents taxable compensation to the employee, unless the spouse, etc., is an employee of the taxpayer, the spouse's travel is for a bona fide business purpose, *and* the expenses would otherwise be deductible by the spouse.

The Analysis and Tax Treatment

In the case of the Bennetts, $850 in travel expenses for Suzanne were paid for by Jack's employer. Suzanne is *not* employed by Jack, her travel was *not* for a bona fide business purpose, and her expenses would *not* otherwise be deductible by Jack. The $850 was rightly included on Jack's 1999 W-2 as taxable compensation, and I included the amount on Line 7 of the Form 1040.

Figure 12.14

Transmittal Letter to Client

LETTER

Connor, Lafferty, and Sonoma, CPAs
1823 Drywood Road
Nogales, AZ 85621

February 28, 2000
Mr. and Mrs. Jack Bennett
20050 Meteor Lane
Nogales, AZ 85623

Dear Jack and Suzanne:

Your completed 1999 federal and Illinois income tax returns are enclosed. The returns should be signed and dated by each of you and mailed on or before April 15, 2000. We recommend that you mail them both "Certified Return Receipt" and that you retain your return receipt with your copies of the returns.

Mail your federal income tax return to:
Internal Revenue Service
Denver, CO 80221

No payment is required, as you are due a refund in the amount of $1,459.

Mail your Illinois income tax return to:
Illinois Department of Revenue and Taxation
Chicago, IL 60605

Enclose your check for $180 made payable to "IDRT." On the check, write your Social Security number, daytime phone number, and "1999 Form IL-V."

Your copies of the returns are enclosed for your files. We suggest that you retain these copies indefinitely.

Yours sincerely,
Connor, Lafferty, and Sonoma, CPAs

Figure 12.15

Tax Planning Report

LETTER

Connor, Lafferty, and Sonoma, CPAs
1823 Drywood Road
Nogales, AZ 85621

Ms. Suzanne Bennett
Suzanne Bennett Interiors
20050 Meteor Lane
Nogales, AZ 85623

Introduction

This report addresses the advisability and tax implications of adding your daughter, Lucy, to the company payroll.

The intent of this report is to give timely answers to your specific questions and does not represent a fully comprehensive study of your company.

1. Your Situation and the Issue

Your 12-year-old daughter, Lucy, has begun to work approximately ten hours per week in your office, helping with bookkeeping and other paperwork as well as doing research for your business on the Internet. You expect to pay her approximately $2,500 this year. You want to know whether or not you should put Lucy on the company payroll.

2. Our Recommendation

We recommend that you sign Lucy onto your payroll as soon as possible, paying her the minimum wage and maintaining viable employee records for her. As you have no other employees, we suggest you consult us for instructions on establishing your payroll procedures.

3. Rationale for Our Recommendation

Employing the minor child in the family business can be very beneficial for several tax reasons. If the child is currently being paid out of your own pocket, those payments are not tax deductible, but if she is

Figure 12.15

Tax Planning Report—*continued*

paid wages as an employee, you may deduct the payments as a business expense. Lucy will pick up the wages as income, but her standard deduction will more than cancel that income to zero, and she will pay no tax. In other words, if Lucy is on the payroll, her $2,500 is deductible to you and tax free to her. Assuming your average tax rate of 30%, you will save $750 in 2000.

To put Lucy on the payroll, it must be evident that she is performing valuable services and receiving a reasonable amount of pay for the work performed. Be careful to handle all the paperwork for her just as you would do for an unrelated employee. The IRS has been inclined to look unfavorably on arrangements that are undertaken merely to obtain tax advantages. In at least one situation, a wage arrangement was voided and treated as nondeductible where substantial services were rendered, but no actual payment was ever made to the child. Instead, funds were deposited directly to bank accounts. Connor, Lafferty, and Sonoma can assist you in setting up the proper employee paperwork.

As for the amount she is to be paid, the payments should be comparable to those paid to other persons who would perform similar services. Your suggested amount of the current minimum hourly wage would be acceptable. Social Security taxes are not required with respect to the compensation of an owner's employee-child under 18 years old.

Another benefit for a child with earned income is the opportunity to set aside and deduct up to $2,000 for an IRA. This deduction would serve no purpose for this year, but in the future, if Lucy is earning beyond $4,000 per year, then an IRA deduction would be useful for avoiding any tax liability on her earnings. And, as you know, an IRA is a great way to save money and reap the rewards of compounded growth on a tax-free basis. Since there is a delay in the payment of income taxes until funds are withdrawn, the IRA's growth rate far outperforms that of taxable savings accounts.

Please let us know of your decision and we will be more than glad to assist you with making all the necessary arrangements.

Connor, Lafferty, and Sonoma, CPAs
Art Jackson, CPA
Senior Tax Accountant

Art: If you don't get paid for the job, and you're sure you'll never get the money, then we'll take a bad debt expense on this year's tax return.

Suzanne: You mean we'll deduct the $5,000 from my income in 2000?

Art: Yes, that's right.

Suzanne: Oh, OK then.

Art effectively explains the accounting concept to Suzanne without overloading her with too much detail. He uses terms that Suzanne is familiar with and, in the end, Suzanne seems to have understood.

Tax Planning Report The exit meeting gives tax accountants excellent opportunities to market further services to clients. Based on the knowledge obtained in the engagement, the tax accountant can frequently recommend strategies for future tax savings. Increasingly, accountants are combining tax return presentations with discussions of services such as tax planning, financial planning, and estate planning. In many cases, recommendation reports or proposals for additional services result from such discussions.

At the exit meeting in the Bennett engagement, the conversation turns to Suzanne's business concerns after Art has explained the returns. Suzanne is thinking about putting her 12-year-old daughter on the company payroll. She has recently begun letting the child help her in the business, and she wants to know whether such a change is legal and whether it is a good idea.

To answer this question, Art agrees to conduct some research into the matter and to prepare a small report in which he outlines the tax implications of the decision and makes a recommendation for Suzanne to consider (see Figure 12.15).

Art was careful to document the authoritative sources he used during his research for Suzanne, but notice that he did not include those sources in the tax planning report. When working with individual clients, and particularly when giving advice on relatively routine, uncomplicated tax matters, accountants sometimes forgo providing all of the legalese details so their clients will feel comfortable reading the reports. So long as the firm maintains its own records of the basis in law for its recommendations, legal defense can be made if necessary. The primary goal of the tax planning report is, after all, not to overload nonexpert clients with complex detail, but rather to communicate recommendations and the reasons for them in a clear and comprehensible manner.

CONCLUSION

As you have seen, the types of communication events that take place during tax engagements can vary widely—from informal and brief (like a written record of a telephone conversation) to formal and relatively lengthy (like a complicated tax memorandum or an engagement letter). But one overriding principle applies to all tax engagements: The higher the quality of the communication that takes place, the better the preparation for handling tax engagements and for resolving questions and disputes that may arise in the future. Here is a checklist of proper communication procedures in taxation practice[4]:

1. Prepare for client meetings by carefully studying all available documents.
2. Prepare agendas for meetings, when practical, and distribute them to all those who are to attend.
3. Document all client meetings and phone calls.
4. Request client information by letter well ahead of deadline. If the information is late, write another letter to clients, warning them of the deadline.
5. Document research conclusions completely and accurately in tax research memoranda and opinion letters. Cite your authoritative sources in both documents, but do not allow them to be too obtrusive in opinion letters to clients.
6. Obtain appropriate supervisory approval of your work. Provide clear written instructions to clients on filing procedures and deadlines.
7. Conduct exit meetings with clients, when practical, to ensure that they understand their returns and to market other firm services.
8. In tax planning meetings or reports, encourage clients to stay in contact so the maximum benefit can be derived from the accountant's recommendations.
9. Write letters to taxing authorities clearly and with a professional tone. Organize the letters according to the method suggested in Chapter 4, and cite your authoritative sources completely and frequently.

NOTES

[1]William F. Yancey, "Managing a Tax Practice to Avoid Malpractice Claims," *The CPA Journal* 66, no. 2 (February 1996): 12.

[2]Amy J. Devitt, "Intertextuality in Tax Accounting: Generic, Referential, and Functional," in *Textual Dynamics of the Professions: Historical and Contemporary Studies of Writing in Professional Communications,* eds. Charles Bazerman and James Paradis (Madison: University of Wisconsin Press, 1991): 351.

[3]Quoted in ibid.

[4]Adapted from Yancey, "Managing a Tax Practice," p. 18.

EXERCISES

1. **Scenario:** Assume you are a tax consultant for Able & Associates, CPAs. Jeanette Boyer, an accounting intern, has drafted the following agenda for the initial meeting with one of your new tax clients, Robert and Mary Wald.

AGENDA

Meeting Agenda
Robert and Mary Wald
February 3, 2000

1. Provide information about Able & Associates: audit, tax, and management consulting services.
2. Introduce the tax team at Able & Associates.
3. Discuss the fee for this return.
4. Discuss possible deductions:
   - Medical expenses
   - Taxes
   - Job expenses
   - Other deductions.
5. Discuss sources of income:
   - Employment
   - Business interests
   - Interest
   - Dividends
   - Gains and losses on sales of investments
   - Rental properties, partnerships, etc.
   - Other income.
6. Obtain other information:
   - IRAs, Keoghs, SEPs, etc.
   - Moving expenses.
7. Obtain client background information:
   - Full names
   - Address
   - Phone numbers (work, home, fax)
   - E-mail addresses.
8. Discuss other possible deductions:
   - Interest
   - Contributions
   - Casualty and theft losses.
9. Obtain personal information:
   - Marital status
   - Dependents
   - Child-care expenses.
10. Provide names of other satisfied tax clients of Able & Associates, CPAs.

Writing task:
  a. Write a memo to the intern critiquing the agenda. Identify its strengths and weaknesses and explain what effect these elements would have on the meeting.
  b. Prepare a revised agenda, organizing topics to be discussed in a logical manner. Be sure to remove any irrelevant topics and add any you feel may have been omitted.

2. Scenario: Due to the sudden illness of Joan Clemens, a partner at Clemens & Jones, CPAs, Joe Smith, a staff accountant, was unexpectedly asked to meet with a new client, Donna Lightcap, who would be arriving within the next few minutes. Joe was told to make her feel comfortable, tell her a little about the firm, and to verify basic information, such as full name, address, phone, fax, and e-mail addresses. He was also told that Joan would follow up with the client within the next day or two to get the remainder of the information she needs to complete the tax return.

When Donna arrived the following conversation took place:

Joe: (Shaking Donna's hand.) Hello, how are you? I'm Joe Smith. Welcome to Clemens & Jones, CPAs.

Donna: (Smiling and returning Joe's handshake.) Hello. I'm just fine. How are you?

Joe: (Leading her toward the conference room.) Well, unfortunately Joan Clemens, who you were going to speak with, just went home sick with the flu a little while ago. Wow, was she ever sick! I'll be fine if I don't get those germs! Anyway, you'll have to talk with me today, and I never did this before, so I really don't know what I'm doing, but I guess we'll manage to get through.

Donna: I can easily reschedule my meeting with Joan for a time when she's feeling better. That would be no problem.

Joe: (As they enter the conference room.) Oh, no! We wouldn't want to inconvenience you like that. In fact, let's not waste any of your time. Why don't you sit down and tell me about the kinds of earned and unearned income you have this year.

Donna: Earned income? Unearned income? What exactly do you mean?

Joe: Why, you know—earned, like from a job. Unearned, like interest.

Donna: But my bank statement says "interest earned this year." Are there two kinds of interest? I don't understand. And what about my commissions from sales? That's why I really decided to come to a CPA firm this year—because my income has increased a lot due to commissions on the sales I make.

Joe: Did you do your own tax return in the past?

Donna: (Nods) Yes, I did.

Joe: Well, then, you really should understand the difference between earned and unearned income. That's pretty basic.

Donna: I think I'll eventually be able to figure it out, but what about my commissions?

Writing task: Write a letter to Joe critiquing the dialogue just described. Give him suggestions for "breaking the ice" more effectively; for creating a relaxed, conversational atmosphere; for making Donna feel the firm is competent to handle her concerns and tax issues; for explaining accounting concepts clearly; and for accomplishing the objectives of his meeting with her. Then give him some suggestions he can use the next time he interviews a client.

Exercises 3, 4, and 5 are based on the following information:

Scenario: On April 20, 2000, you receive a phone call from one of your established clients, Eric Dilworth, who is the sole proprietor of Ulti-Climate, a heating and air-conditioning contracting firm. You jot down the following notes during your phone conversation.

- built an addition onto home
- new rec room, guest bedroom/bath, and separate office for Ulti-Climate
- Ulti-Climate's office now in home office (former facilities were rented)
- Eric and secretary/bookkeeper work in office daily; no other office employees
- only other facility is a combined garage/warehouse for trucks and inventory (at separate location)
- usually meets with customers at customers' home/business; sometimes at Ulti-Climate's office; never at garage
- last year's gross income from Ulti-Climate was approx. $100,000
- will he be able to deduct expenses related to this home office? (principal place of business?)
- what specific types of expenses will he be able to deduct related to the office?
- his phone: (999) 555-7878.

3. **Writing task:** Based on the information just given, prepare a written record for the file of your phone conversation with Eric Dilworth, using the format illustrated in Figure 12.12.

4. **Writing task:** Prepare a tax research memorandum for the Dilworths' tax file. Research the subject of tax considerations for home office expenses. Can the Dilworths deduct expenses related to the business use of their home? If so, what types of expenses can be deducted? Are there any limitations on these deductions? Be sure to cite relevant sections of the Internal Revenue Code and apply them to this situation.

5. **Writing task:** Based on the results of your research into business use of a home and deductibility of expenses, prepare an opinion letter for Eric Dilworth. Include in your report all the known facts of this situation, specific language from the tax law, and your rationale for your interpretation of the law.

6. **Scenario:** Assume you are having an exit interview with Ralph and Sue Intel. During your preparation of their tax return, you realize they have significantly underpaid their estimated taxes because of income from rental properties. As a result, they owe approximately $2,000 in taxes on their 1999 return, plus interest and penalties. You have prepared a 1040-ES, estimate of individual taxes for 2000, so they can make estimated payments on a quarterly basis, as required by the tax code. When Ralph and Sue see they will have to pay out more than $2,500 by April 15, they respond with disbelief—how can they possibly be expected to make an estimated payment when they already owe so much for last year's taxes?

   Communication task:
   a. To prepare for your meeting with Ralph and Sue, write a paragraph or two in clear, simple terms explaining (1) the tax concept of "pay-as-you-go," and (2) why making estimated payments is to the benefit of your client. Because you will use this paragraph to help focus your comments to Ralph and Sue, make your paragraph conversational, yet professional.
   b. Role play: Take the role of the accountant working with Ralph and Sue and have a classmate play the role of an intern or trainee. Explain to the intern/trainee how discussing tax concepts with clients is different from explaining them to another accountant and why it is important to know something about clients' background and experience before talking with them about tax-related matters.

7. **Scenario:** You have been asked by one of the partners in your firm to prepare a tax planning report for Johnson & Martin, Architects. Currently Johnson & Martin is organized as a partnership, but they have come to your firm asking advice about whether or not they should consider incorporating the firm.

   Writing task: Prepare a tax planning report that explains the differences between organizing a business as a partnership and a corporation, including the advantages and disadvantages of each, tax implications to the owners, and possible tax savings strategies. Also discuss briefly any other forms of business that might be an option for Johnson & Martin. Try to communicate information in your report in a way that will lead to future tax, financial planning, or other business opportunities for your CPA firm.

The following information is used for Exercises 8 and 9.

Scenario: Your client, Bivens Manufacturing Company, has come to you with a problem related to its tax payments to the State Department of Revenue.

Somehow, the Department of Revenue has no record of one of Bivens's 1999 estimated income tax payments, which was made on December 10, 1999. As a result of the 1999 payment not being recorded, Bivens's first estimated payment for the 2000 tax year, made on April 8, 2000, was recorded by the state as a payment on the 1999 return. Bivens also received notice that it will be assessed interest and penalties on the 1999 tax because its payment was supposedly late. Bivens actually made all payments by check on time and should not be assessed any interest or penalties.

8. **Writing task:** Write a letter to Bivens requesting the additional details and documents you need to write a letter to tax authorities requesting corrective action.

9. **Writing task:** Write a letter to the State Department of Revenue explaining the situation and asking for corrective action. Be sure to mention any supporting documents you have enclosed to prove the facts you have described. (Make up the information you would have received from Bivens in response to the letter you wrote in Exercise 8.)

10. **Scenario:** The IRS has notified one of your clients, Smith Jewelers, that its handling of payments to James Thomas, registered appraiser, is incorrect. Smith Jewelers has been using James Thomas as a appraiser on a irregular basis. Thomas has his own part-time appraisal business, with a number of other clients, but he receives a significant amount of the income from his appraisal services for Smith Jewelers. The IRS contends that Smith should treat Thomas as an employee rather than a self-employed private contractor; thus Smith will be required to withhold taxes from Thomas's earnings and pay payroll taxes (FICA and unemployment taxes) on his earnings. Smith contends that Thomas is actually an independent contractor and their agreement is such that Thomas's work is not controlled by Smith.

    Writing task: Draft a letter to the IRS protesting their classification of Thomas as an employee. Summarize the situation at the beginning of the letter, indicate the purpose for your letter, state the facts of the case, and analyze how the appropriate rules apply to this case. Be sure to ground all of your arguments in the tax law, and cite all relevant sections of the IRS Code in your letter. The strength and clarity of your argument will have a significant impact on the outcome of this situation.

Exercises 11 through 15 are based on the following scenario and may be completed either individually or as a team (for advice on working in teams, consult Chapter 8).

Scenario: You are a tax senior with a public accounting firm, and your engagement manager has just given you the file of a new client, for whom you will prepare the federal income tax return on Form 1040. Your client, Stanley Johnson (Social Security number 189-45-6444), has been divorced for three years. He lives with his only son, Peter (Social Security number 196-45-6845), who earned $9,500 this past year. Stan provided over half the support of Peter. Other information in the file consists of Stan's W-2, 1098s, 1099s, and a K-1, and notes taken by the engagement manager during a recent phone call with Stan:

- Stan's salary: $100,000
- Stan's investment portfolio activity during the year:
  1/31: Sold 35 shares IBM @ $89/sh
  4/5: Sold 45 shares PP&L @ 45/sh
  9/15: Bought 2,000 shares of Toys-R-Us
- Dividends received during the year:
  General Foods $460
  General Motors $200
  General Electric $850
- Interest received during the year:
  Center Valley National Bank $370
  Center Valley Municipal Bonds $235
  Center Valley Savings and Loan $875
- Received a state tax refund during the tax year for taxes overpaid during the prior year. The amount of the refund was $290. (Stan itemized last year.)
- Paid alimony to ex-wife: $15,000
- Stan and Peter's medical expenses:
  Prescription drugs $1,400
  Dentist visits $300
  Doctor visits $200
  Over-the-counter medications $435
- State and local income taxes withheld: $4,322
- Mortgage interest paid: $12,540
- Charitable contributions:
  Clothing donated to Salvation Army $50
- Cash contributions:

Harvard University	$500
Boy Scouts	$100
March of Dimes	$200
Clothing donated to a needy family in the client's neighborhood	$75
Authentic Civil War saber with sheath donated to the Save the Whales Foundation: Appraisal Value:	$15,000
The foundation immediately sold the saber and sheath to a Civil War museum for	$15,000.

Communication tasks:

11. Letter to your client asking for missing information: To produce this letter, prepare a list of questions you have about the client and

phrase them in language a client could easily understand. You may either make up the answers to your letter or send the letter to your instructor, who will provide you with answers.

12. Memos to the client file: Describe (a) the answers to your letter that you receive from your client; (b) the research you perform in the Internal Revenue Code and other tax rule sources about the tax issues raised by your client's situation; (c) the strategies for minimizing the client's taxes, based on the issues raised and on your research.

13. Write a tax research memorandum to the client's file concerning the deductibility of the donation of the Civil War saber.

14. Write a short report (one or two pages) containing recommendations to your client for reducing taxes in the next tax year.

15. Write an oral presentation to the client laying out your recommendations and highlighting information on the Form 1040 that you have prepared. Create appropriate visual aids and handouts, and deliver the presentation to the class as if the students were your clients.

A. Grammar Reference Guide

How well you observe the conventions of standard English usage contributes significantly to the professional image you present to employers, co-workers, and clients. In every document you prepare, every conversation you conduct, every presentation you deliver, your handling of the language influences your credibility with your audience. Mistakes in grammar can seriously undermine that credibility, both for you as an individual and for the firm you represent.

SENTENCE PROBLEMS

Sentences are the basic units in writing because sentences express complete thoughts. As we saw in Chapter 3, accomplished writers know how to build sentences and control them to achieve the effects they desire. Because building effective sentences is a key to effective writing, we begin by focusing on the basic principles that govern sentence construction.

Clauses

Clauses, groups of words containing both a **subject** and a **verb,** are the basic units from whch sentences are built. The subject names who or what the sentence is about, and the verb says something about the subject.

Subjects establish the focus of the clause:

Susan . . .

Clients . . .

Arriving late for work too often . . .

Each of these subjects announces a topic. Each subject is incomplete, however, without a verb to make an assertion about it.

The verb completes the thought of the clause:

Susan *received a substantial promotion.*

Clients *complained about the rate hike.*

Arriving late for work too often *can result in dismissal.*

Clause Patterns   The most common clause patterns in English consist of the following:

- a subject + a verb [S-V]
- a subject + a verb + an object [S-V-O]
- a subject + a verb + a complement [S-V-C]

Consider these examples:

       S   **V**
The computer crashed.

    S   **V**   **O**
Susan received a substantial promotion.

           S   **V**   **C**
What seemed like the most serious problem was staff morale.

These patterns constitute by far the majority of sentences in written texts. One study found that professional writers use these three patterns 75.5% of the time. Another 23% of the time, the study found, sentences opened with some kind of modifier linking an S-V-O construction with the sentence that preceded it.[1] In other words, this study found that the S-V-O, S-V, and S-V-C patterns accounted for over 98% of the sentences in most professional texts.

These patterns represent the three categories into which verbs can fall: transitive, intransitive, and linking.

Transitive verbs need a direct object to complete their meaning. The word *transitive* implies an action that moves directly from the subject *across* ("trans-") the verb to a receiver or object. Transitive verbs create the S-V-O pattern:

    S   **V**   **O**
Susan received a substantial promotion.

    S   **V**   **O**
We conducted the audit.

Intransitive verbs do not need an object to complete their meaning. They are complete in themselves, although they often have modifiers:

       S   **V**
The computer crashed.

   S   **V**   **modifier**
Clients complained about the rate hike.

Linking verbs, a special type of intransitive verb, *link* the subject to a word or words following the verb, known as the **complement.** When the complement is a noun or pronoun, it refers to the person or thing in the subject:

      S   **V**   **C**
A partnership is a business owned by two or more individuals.

           S   **V**   **C**
Many small businesses are sole proprietorships.

---

[1]Frances Christensen, *Notes Toward a New Rhetoric* (New York: Harper & Row, 1967), pp. 41–51. Cited in Louise Johnson Rew, *Introduction to Technical Writing* (New York: St. Martin's Press, 1989), pp. 180–181.

When the complement is an adjective, it modifies the subject:

       S   **V**   **C**
Most nonbusiness entities are organized for a purpose other than to make a profit.

      S   **V**   **C**
The CPA exam is rigorous.

The most common linking verbs are forms of the verb "to be":

am	are	is	was
were	be	being	been

Other linking verbs include the following:

look	feel	smell	become
appear	taste	sound	remain

Tense is the property of verbs that indicates time distinctions. The three simple tenses in English are **present, past,** and **future.** The three perfect tenses are **present perfect, past perfect,** and **future perfect.** The simple tenses indicate simple time relationships. The perfect tenses indicate action that was or will be completed before another action in time. They are formed with *have* plus the *past participle* (the *-ed* form of the verb).

The simple present indicates action occurring at the moment or action that occurs regularly. The present perfect indicates an action that has occurred in the past and is continuing into the present:

> **Simple present:** I *work* at Johnson, Smith, and Berrigan, Ltd.

> **Present perfect:** I *have worked* at Johnson, Smith, and Berrigan, Ltd. since 1991.

The simple past denotes action already completed. The past perfect describes action completed before another past event:

> **Simple past:** Abco *purchased* a 200-acre parcel of land on which to build a new plant.

> **Past perfect:** After Abco *had purchased* the land, they began construction on the new plant.

The simple future describes action that will occur in the future. The future perfect indicates an action that will be completed before another future action. The future perfect is formed by adding the helping verbs *will* or *shall* to the past participle:

> **Simple future:** The company *will benefit* from these changes in future years.

> **Future perfect:** By next year, the benefits of these changes *will have begun* to make an impact.

Each of these six tenses also has a progressive form that shows ongoing action. The progressive forms are created by combining a form of the verb *to be* with the *present participle* (the *-ing* form):

Present progressive: I *am working* for Johnson, Smith, and Berrigan, Ltd.

Present perfect progressive: I *have been working* for Johnson, Smith, and Berrigan, Ltd. since 1991.

Past progressive: I *was working* for Johnson, Smith, and Berrigan, Ltd. last year.

Past perfect progressive: I *had been working* for Johnson, Smith, and Berrigan, Ltd. when I moved to St. Thomas.

Future progressive: I *will be working* for Entergy Corporation next year.

Future perfect progressive: By April, I *will have been working* for Entergy Corporation for seven months.

Types of Clauses   Clauses can be of two types: **independent** and **dependent.** Independent clauses can stand alone as **complete sentences.**

   S   V   O   **Prep Phrase**
Hal filed his tax return on April 15.

When two independent clauses are closely related, they can be linked together with a **coordinating conjunction** in a **compound sentence:**

  S   V   O   S   V
Max explained the 401K plan, and Mr. Blackwell immediately decided to participate.

Coordinating Conjunctions

and	for	or	yet
but	nor	so	

Although an independent clause may be part of a larger sentence, it can always stand alone as complete in itself.

  Prep Phrase **Prep Phrase**   S   V   O
After his meeting with Max, Mr. Blackwell explored several options.

Dependent clauses cannot stand alone; they connect with independent clauses to form **complex sentences.**

Although Max explained the 401K plan clearly, Mr. Blackwell chose not to participate.

Although Max explained the 401K plan clearly is a dependent clause functioning as a sentence "opener"; it modifies the independent clause *Mr. Blackwell chose not to participate.*

An independent clause is rendered dependent by means of a **subordinating conjunction,** a **conjunctive adverb,** or a **relative pronoun:**

Subordinating Conjunction

Ann opened a supplemental retirement account *because* she was concerned about future income.

Conjunctive Adverb

Three firms made attractive bids; *therefore,* the decision was difficult.

Relative Pronoun

Jake was the partner *who* made the final decision.

Subordinating Conjunctions	Conjunctive Adverbs	Relative Pronouns
although	consequently	who
after	furthermore	whoever
because	hence	whom
if	however	whomever
where	instead	whose
than	moreover	what
since	nevertheless	whatever
as	nonetheless	which
unless	otherwise	whichever
before	therefore	that
that	thus	
though		
when		
whereas		

Sentence Types

Sentences fall into three basic types: simple, compound, and complex. Each type is appropriate for a different purpose.

Simple sentences keep your ideas straightforward and clear:

Stockholders' equity represents the owners' claims on the assets of the business. [independent clause]

Compound sentences relate ideas of equal importance:

On the balance sheet, contributed capital appears in the form of capital stock, [independent clause] and earned capital takes the form of retained earnings. [independent clause]

Complex sentences relate ideas of unequal importance. The more important of the two ideas is expressed in the independent clause:

Because it is an absolute dollar amount [dependent clause], working capital is limited in its informational value. [independent clause]

Functions of Dependent Clauses   Dependent clauses can function as nouns, adjectives, or adverbs. As **nouns,** dependent clauses may serve as **subjects, objects,** or **complements:**

What is most important in accounting systems is documentation. [noun clause as subject]

Whoever transacts a cash sale should retain the register receipt. [noun clause as subject]

The cost principle requires *that we record an asset at its acquisition cost.* [noun clause as object]

The difference between these transactions is *that in the first case, cash was received.* [noun clause as complement]

When dependent clauses function as adjectives and adverbs, they are called modifiers.

Modifiers   **Modifiers** are words, phrases, or other clauses that describe elements in the clause.

Adjective modifiers describe nouns by pointing out attributes or properties of things. Adjectives can be single words:

The *left* side of any account records debits.

A *standard* format is used for recording entries.

Max conducted the *company's* audit.

Phrases and clauses can also serve as adjective modifiers:

Acting on behalf of management, accountants are responsible for providing accurate financial information. [adjective phrase modifying *accountants*]

The accountant, *who had been working overtime for two weeks,* completed the audit. [adjective clause modifying *accountant*]

The accountant completed the audit, *which had been unusually complex.* [adjective clause modifying *audit*]

Notice that the pronouns "who" and "which"—discussed later—serve as subjects for these adjective clauses.

Frequently, **prepositional phrases** serve as adjective modifiers. Prepositional phrases begin with a relational word and usually end with a noun or pronoun (object of the preposition):

With a sigh of relief, Scott closed the books. [prepositional phrase modifying *Scott*]

Adverb modifiers describe verbs, adjectives, or other adverbs. Adverbs tell *where, when, how,* and *how much:*

Max *carefully* reviewed the records. [how]

Max reviewed the records *yesterday.* [when]

Claire sent the message *forward.* [where]

Claire reviewed the *nearly* completed report. [adverb modifying adjective]

Claire's efforts on behalf of her client were *extremely* thorough. [adverb modifying adjective]

Joel studied the balance sheet *very thoughtfully.* [adverb modifying adverb]

Prepositional phrases also frequently serve as adverb modifiers:

In the perpetual system, the inventory account is updated [adverb/prepositional phrase modifying verb phrase] every time goods are purchased.

In the periodic system, the inventory account is updated *at the end of the period.* [adverb/prepositional phrase modifying verb phrase; adverb/prepositional phrase modifying adverb/prepositional phrase]

Dependent clauses can also serve the function of adverbs:

Before the goods can be released, the department must issue a requisition form. [adverb clause modifying verb]

When he came to the room where the records were kept, Max called his assistant. [adverb clause modifying adverb clause and verb]

A special type of modifier, called an **absolute,** can be thought of as modifying the sentence as a whole. Absolute modifiers are phrases that contain a subject and an *incomplete verb.* You can create an absolute modifier by eliminating forms of the verb "to be" from a sentence:

Sentence: The accounts were closed, and remaining balances were divided among creditors.

Absolute: *The balances were divided among creditors.*

New sentence: *The balances divided among creditors,* the accounts were closed.

Absolutes are always set off by commas and have no words connecting them to the sentence.

Summary: Sentence Structure

We have seen thus far that sentence structure is a function of relationships—relationships among subjects, verbs, objects, and complements; coordinate relationships between equal elements, subordinate relationships between unequal elements; and relationships among sentence elements and other elements that modify them. The next section explains how to correct problems that arise as a result of faulty relationships and improper usage.

GRAMMAR PROBLEMS

To feel confident about writing on the job, you need to be able to recognize and correct the common problems described here.

Sentence Fragments

A **fragment** is a group of words punctuated as a sentence that cannot stand alone. A fragment often lacks an essential element (a subject or a verb):

He is a terrific guy. *Like my brother.*

Here the fragment is an *afterthought,* carelessly added after the complete sentence. Sentence fragments are often **dependent clauses** punctuated as complete sentences:

When the net method is used. Sales are recorded net of the discount.

The new vice president got the resources he needed. *Because the division he took over was in crisis.*

Still other fragments result from **verbals,** forms of the verb that cannot function as a main verb in a sentence. Verbals (**infinitives, gerunds,** and **participles**) look like verbs but actually serve as other sentence elements: as subjects, objects, and modifiers:

Fragment: *Interpreting business data.* Is the major part of the accountant's job.

Corrected: Interpreting business data is the major part of the accountant's job. [verbal = gerund serving as subject]

Fragment: *Scanning* the balance sheet quickly. Cal spotted the mistake.

Corrected: Scanning the balance sheet quickly, Cal spotted the mistake. [verbal = present participle modifying *Cal*]

Fragment: There was no question about their goal. *To show* a profit in the first year.

Corrected: There was no question about their goal: to show a profit in the first year. [verbal = infinitive restating "goal"]

The following examples illustrate the most common types of fragments:

Wrong: *Because the cost of goods sold was understated.* The gross margin for the year was overstated. [dependent clause standing alone]

Corrected: Because the cost of goods sold was understated, the gross margin for the year was overstated.

Wrong: *Having considered the options for costing the inventory.* They decided on the weighted average method. [participial phrase]

Corrected: Having considered the options for costing the inventory, they decided on the weighted average method.

Wrong: Promissory notes are negotiable. *Which means that they can be endorsed and given to someone else for collection.* [relative clause]

Corrected: Promissory notes are negotiable, which means that they can be endorsed and given to someone else for collection.

Wrong: They had only one thing in mind. *Increasing the bottom line.* [appositive]

Corrected: They had only one thing in mind: increasing the bottom line.

On rare occasions, you may correctly use a fragment to create an effect.

To emphasize: Given what we know about the costs, is it economical for us to make this purchase? *Or prudent?*

Checking for Fragments

1. Does the sentence have a subject?

Fragment: Ramon moved to another firm. *And boosted his salary in the process.* (The lack of a subject creates a fragment.)

Corrected: Ramon moved to another firm and boosted his salary in the process.

2. Does the sentence have a verb that can stand alone?

Fragment: The committee *expecting* to hire him. (The verbal here cannot serve as a main verb.)

Corrected: The committee is expecting to hire him.

3. Does the sentence begin with a subordinating word? If so, does it contain a second, independent, clause?

Fragment: *Because* interest rates have gone up. Mortgages are more expensive than they were last year. (The subordinating conjunction here renders the clause dependent.)

Corrected: *Because* interest rates have gone up, mortgages are more expensive than they were last year.

For rules on correcting fragments, review pages A-8 and A-9.

To answer a rhetorical question: Can they afford to undercut our bid? *No.* Will they do it anyway? *Probably.*

To make a transition: We made tremendous progress last quarter. *So much for the past.* We need to focus on plans for the future.

Run-On Sentences and Comma Splices

A **run-on sentence** fuses two independent clauses without punctuation:

The new medical plan was comprehensive the employees were pleased.

A **comma splice** occurs when two (or more) independent clauses are joined by a comma:

Current assets are important to a company's short-term liquidity, operating assets are essential to its long-term future.

Here are four ways to correct run-ons and comma splices:

1. Join the clauses with a **semicolon.**

Current assets are important to a company's short-term liquidity; operating assets are essential to its long-term future.

2. Join the clauses with a **comma + coordinating conjunction.**

Current assets are important to a company's short-term liquidity, **and** operating assets are essential to its long-term future.

3. Join the clauses with a **semicolon + conjunctive adverb.**

Current assets are important to a company's short-term liquidity; **however,** operating assets are essential to its long-term future.

4. Subordinate one clause to the other.

Whereas current assets are important to a company's short-term liquidity, operating assets are essential to its long-term future.

Mixed Constructions

A mixed construction is a sentence whose parts do not function properly together: Either the subject and verb do not belong together or the clauses are not logically linked:

Mixed: One *skill* accountants need *is balance sheets.* (The subject and verb, *skill* and *is,* require an action or ability to complete the thought logically.)

Corrected: One *skill* accountants need *is the ability to read balance sheets.*

Checking for Run-Ons and Comma Splices

1. Are there two or more independent clauses in the sentence?

Run-on: *We had to pay capital gains tax* when we sold our stock *it had gained substantially in value.* (Although the independent clauses are separated by a dependent clause, the sentence is a run-on.)

Corrected: We had to pay capital gains tax when we sold our stock because it had gained substantially in value.

2. Are the clauses joined by a conjunctive adverb?

Run-on: *Jones cashed in his IRA, therefore he had to pay a stiff penalty.* (Always use a semicolon with a conjunctive adverb when joining independent clauses.)

Corrected: Jones cashed in his IRA; therefore, he had to pay a stiff penalty.

3. Are the clauses joined by a comma?

Comma splice: *Jones cashed in his IRA, he had to pay a stiff penalty.* (Substitute a comma + conjunction, a semicolon alone, or a semicolon + conjunctive adverb to eliminate the comma splice.)

Corrected: Jones cashed in his IRA, but he had to pay a stiff penalty.

Corrected: Jones cashed in his IRA; he had to pay a stiff penalty.

Corrected: Jones cashed in his IRA; therefore, he had to pay a stiff penalty.

For rules on correcting run-ons and comma splices, review page A-10. For further discussion of commas, see Punctuation Reference Guide.

Mixed: *When the boss consistently offers negative criticism causes* low staff morale. (The opening phrase *when the boss* cannot stand as the subject of the sentence; therefore, it cannot *cause* something.)

Corrected: Consistent negative *criticism* by the boss *causes* low staff morale.

Some mixed constructions forge illogical comparisons:

Wrong: The *cost* of a computer is greater than a *calculator.*

Corrected: The *cost* of a computer is greater than the *cost* of a calculator.

Wrong: The *food* here is better than any other *restaurant* in town.

Corrected: The *food* here is better than *that of* any other restaurant in town.

A special kind of mixed construction occurs with the combinations *is when/is where* and *the reason is because:*

Wrong: Depreciation *is where* you allocate acquisition costs over the useful life of an asset.

Corrected: Depreciation is the allocation of acquisition costs over the useful life of an asset.

Wrong: Straight-line depreciation *is when* you assume that the decline in usefulness occurs evenly over time.

Corrected: Straight-line depreciation assumes that the decline in usefulness occurs evenly over time.

Wrong: *The reason* straight-line depreciation is so popular *is because* it is simple.

Corrected: The reason straight-line depreciation is so popular is because it is simple.

These constructions are grammatically incorrect. A noun may not be linked by the verb *to be* with an adverb or adverb clause; linking verbs must join nouns to other nouns, pronouns, or adjectives.

Incomplete Constructions

The omission of essential words can render a construction incomplete:

Wrong: He *was unaware and undisturbed by* the noise around him.

Corrected: He was *unaware of and undisturbed by* the noise around him.

A special kind of incomplete construction is the **faulty comparison:**

Wrong: Inflation in Haiti is *as high if not higher than* Peru.

Corrected: Inflation in Haiti is *as high as if not higher than* inflation in Peru.

Wrong: They worry more *about their profit* than *their employees.*

Corrected: They worry more *about their profit* than *they do about their employees.*

EXERCISES

Revise the sentences to eliminate fragments, run-ons, comma splices, and mixed constructions.

1. Common stock and preferred stock are called equity securities, bonds issued by corporations and governmental bodies are called debt securities.

2. Although the FICA tax is assessed on both the employer and employee. The employee's portion of that does not represent an expense to the employer.

3. If the Dow Jones takes another dive will increase investment in money markets.

4. Officers of the corporation sit on the board of directors, however, the board also includes directors whom the corporation does not employ.

5. The report is due in the morning we need to work on it this evening.

6. An operating lease is where the lessee obtains the right to use an asset for a limited period.

7. They did not receive the invoice, accordingly they did not cut a check.

8. The loss to the stockholders is less than the corporation.

9. We look forward to working with you, if you have any questions please call me.

10. The cost of materials is up, therefore, we need to recalculate our projections.

SUBJECT-VERB AGREEMENT PROBLEMS

Subjects must agree with their verbs in person and number. Most subject-verb agreement errors occur in the following situations.

1. *Subjects and verbs separated by phrases and clauses.* Be careful not to make the verb agree with the noun immediately before it if the noun is not its subject. This mistake is especially common when a plural noun intervenes between a singular subject and verb:

> **Wrong:** *One* of the balance sheets *were* incorrect.

> **Corrected:** *One* of the balance sheets *was* incorrect. (The subject of the verb is *one*, not *balance sheets*.)

> **Wrong:** *Processing* of clients' tax returns *are* time consuming.

> **Corrected:** *Processing* of clients' tax returns *is* time consuming. (The subject of the verb is *processing*, not *tax returns*.)

2. *Collective nouns as subjects.* A collective subject takes a singular verb if the group is functioning as a unit:

> The *Financial Accounting Standards Board* has the authority to set accounting standards in the United States.

A collective subject requires a plural verb when members of the group are acting as individuals:

> Because the *FASB members were divided* on the issue, they were unable to reach a decision. (Because the sentence focuses on the different opinions of individual members, the collective subject requires a plural verb.)

3. *Parenthetical expressions following subjects.* Such expressions do not become part of the subject, nor do they change its number:

> **Wrong:** *Marie,* along with her assistants, *are planning* to go.

> **Corrected:** *Marie,* along with her assistants, *is planning* to go. (Marie, the subject, requires a singular verb. The phrase *along with her assistants* is not part of the subject, nor does it make the subject plural.)

4. *Indefinite pronouns as subjects.* Indefinite pronouns are those that do not stand for a particular person or thing. Although some of these pronouns *sound* plural, they are always singular and always take a singular verb. They include *anybody, anyone, anything, each, either, neither, everybody, everyone, everything, no one, somebody, someone,* and *something.*

> **Wrong:** *Each* of the partners *are* going to the meeting.

> **Corrected:** *Each* of the partners *is* going to the meeting.

> **Wrong:** *Neither* of the arguments advanced by the client *have affected* the IRS ruling.

> **Corrected:** *Neither* of the arguments advanced by the client *has affected the* IRS ruling.

Note: When they are used with the **correlative conjunctions** *or* and *nor, either* and *neither* are not subjects. They are modifiers in two parts of a compound subject. In this case, the verb then agrees with the part of the subject closer to the verb:

> **Wrong:** Either the *partner* or the *associates has made* an error.

> **Corrected:** Either the *partner* or the *associates have made* an error. (The verb is plural because it must agree with the part of the subject that is closer to the verb—*associates.*)

When the pronouns *some* and *most* are subjects, the verbs agree with the object of the prepositional phrase following the pronoun:

> Some of the funds were spent irresponsibly. (*Some* is plural because *funds* is plural.)

> *Most* of the money *was* spent irresponsibly. (*Most* is singular because *money* is singular.)

Checking for Subject-Verb Agreement Errors

1. Does a phrase or clause separate subject and verb?

Faulty subject-verb agreement: The inventory of computer supplies are in the file.

Corrected: The *inventory* of computer supplies *is* in the file. (The verb must agree with the subject, *inventory,* not with the noun immediately before it, *supplies.*)

2. Is the subject a collective noun?

Faulty subject-verb agreement: The board want to consider additional applicants before filling the position.

Corrected: The *board wants* to consider additional applicants before filling the position. (The members of the board are acting as a single unit here; therefore, the verb is singular.)

3. Does a parenthetical phrase separate subject and verb?

Faulty subject-verb agreement: The CEO, in conference with the board of directors, have decided to take early retirement.

Corrected: *The CEO,* in conference with the board of directors, *has decided* to take early retirement. (The parenthetical phrase is not part of the subject and has no effect on the number of the verb.)

4. Is the subject an indefinite pronoun?

Faulty subject-verb agreement: Either of those locations are suitable for our staff retreat.

Corrected: *Either* of those locations *is* suitable for our staff retreat. (Indefinite pronouns are singular and take singular verbs.)

For rules on correcting subject-verb agreement errors, review pages A-13 to A-15.

PRONOUN PROBLEMS

Pronouns must refer clearly to their antecedents and agree with them in person, number, and gender; in addition, they must be in the proper case. The **antecedent** is the noun for which a pronoun substitutes.

Three cases exist in English: the *subjective* (for subjects of clauses), the *objective* (for direct objects, indirect objects, and objects of the preposition), and the *possessive* (for possessive modifiers). Early in the history of the English language, both nouns and pronouns changed their forms to indicate the case in which they were used. Today, only pronouns change their forms in English. The table lists the case forms of the personal and relative pronouns.

Personal Pronouns: Subjective Case

	Singular			Plural		
	Masculine	Feminine	Neuter	Masculine	Feminine	Neuter
1st person	I	I		We	We	
2nd person	You	You		You	You	
3rd person	He	She	It	They	They	They

Personal Pronouns: Objective Case

	Singular			Plural		
	Masculine	Feminine	Neuter	Masculine	Feminine	Neuter
1st person	Me	Me		Us	Us	
2nd person	You	You		You	You	
3rd person	Him	Her	It	Them	Them	Them

Personal Pronouns: Possessive Case

	Singular			Plural		
	Masculine	Feminine	Neuter	Masculine	Feminine	Neuter
1st person	My	My	My	Our(s)	Our(s)	
2nd person	Your(s)	Your(s)		Your(s)	Your(s)	
3rd person	His	Hers	Its	Their(s)	Their(s)	Their(s)

Relative Pronouns

Subjective	Objective	Possessive
Who	Whom	Whose
Whoever	Whomever	
Which, That, Whichever	Which, That, Whichever	Whose

Errors in Case

Personal Pronouns with Linking Verbs   Pronouns should be in the subjective case (i.e., *I, you, he, she, it, we, they*) when the antecedent is the subject of a clause. The subjective case is correct when the pronoun follows a linking verb:

Wrong: The *people* you saw could not have been *them*.

Corrected: The *people* you saw could not have been *they*.

The verb here is a present perfect form of the verb "to be," which is always a linking verb; therefore, the pronoun is subjective.

Personal Pronouns as Objects   Pronouns should be in the objective case (i.e., *me, you, him, her, it, us, them*) when they receive the action of a verb or when they follow a preposition:

> **Wrong:** This is a private matter between *he* and *I*.

> **Corrected:** This is a private matter between *him* and *me*.

Personal Pronouns with Gerunds   Pronouns (and nouns) should be in the possessive case (i.e., *my, your, his, her, its, our, their*) immediately before a **gerund.** A gerund is the *-ing* form of the verb used as a noun. Like nouns, gerunds are commonly preceded by possessive nouns and pronouns:

> **Wrong:** He disapproved of *them* investing in the little known company.

> **Corrected:** He disapproved of *their* investing in the little known company.

Investing is a gerund serving as the object of the preposition *of.* Because it is serving as a noun, the pronoun that precedes it serves an adjectival function and so must be possessive.

Personal Pronouns with *As* or *Than*   To decide the case of pronouns following *as* or *than*, mentally supply the words left out:

> **Wrong:** Peter does not have as much experience as *her*.

> **Corrected:** Peter does not have as much experience as *she (has experience)*.

> **Wrong:** Blanca has worked at the firm much longer than *me*.

> **Corrected:** Blanca has worked at the firm much longer than *I (have worked)*.

Relative Pronouns   Determining the proper case of *who, whom, whoever,* and *whomever* is especially tricky because these pronouns are frequently used in questions and in relative clauses:

> **Wrong:** *Who did* the members *elect?*

> **Corrected:** *Whom did* the members *elect?*

Turning the question around (*The members [did elect = elected] whom*) will usually make the syntactical relationships clear. Here, it is obvious that the pronoun is a direct object, which must be in the objective case.

To determine the proper case of such pronouns in relative clauses, follow these steps:

1. Separate the parts of the sentence:

> **Example:** We wondered *(who, whom)* the competitors could be.

Independent clause: We wondered

Relative clause: *(who, whom)* the competitors could be.

2. If necessary, rearrange the words of the subordinate clause so that they follow normal word order: S + V + object or complement.

Normal word order: *the competitors could be (who, whom)*

3. Determine whether a subject form or an object form is needed in the position of *who/whom*. (Sometimes it is helpful to substitute other pronouns to check: *he, she, they* for *who, whoever; him, her, them* for *whom, whomever.*)

Substitute personal pronouns: the competitors could be *they.*

Because the verb in the clause is a linking verb, the pronoun must be in the subjective case.

4. Sometimes, you will need to make additional substitutions:

Example: Give the review materials to (*whoever/whomever*) needs them.

Independent clause: Give the review materials to (someone).

Relative clause: (Someone) needs them.

Substitute personal pronouns: (He/She) needs them.

Substitute relative pronouns: (Whoever) needs them.

Because the pronoun serves as subject of the clause, it must be in the subjective case. The entire clause, *whoever needs them,* is the object of the preposition *to.*

Example: I don't know *(who/whom)* the CEO appointed.

Independent clause: I don't know (someone).

Relative clause: The CEO appointed (someone).

Substitute personal pronouns: The CEO appointed (him/her).

Substitute relative pronouns: The CEO appointed (whom).

The entire clause *whom the CEO appointed* is the object of the verb *know. Whom* is the object of *appointed: the CEO appointed whom.*

Shifts in Person

Avoid shifts among first person *(I, we),* second person *(you),* and third person *(he, she, it, they).*

Wrong: *Employees* have to keep *your* own records of the vacation time *you* take.

Corrected: *Employees* have to keep *their* own records of the vacation time *they* take.

Corrected: *You* have to keep *your* own records of the vacation time *you* take.

Errors in Gender

In English, we must specify gender when we choose personal pronouns:

Carlos was wearing *his* new suit, hoping to make a favorable impression at the interview.

Angie could hardly control *her* anger during the staff meeting.

When gender is unspecified in the antecedent and the antecedent is singular, use both the masculine and feminine pronouns to ensure that gender references are inclusive:

Everyone is responsible for *his* or *her* own luggage on the trip.

If this construction seems awkward, change the antecedent to a plural so you can use *they* (or *them* or *their*):

All *travelers* are responsible for *their* own luggage on the trip.

Errors in Number

When the antecedent is singular, use a singular pronoun to refer to it. (*Remember:* Indefinite pronouns are always singular!)

Wrong: *Each* of the participants *were* carrying *their* conference materials in the tote bag provided.

Here we have both a subject-verb agreement error and pronoun-antecedent agreement error. Because the subject *(each)* is singular, both the verb and the pronoun must be singular. As we just noted, there are a couple of options for correcting this error:

Corrected: *Each* of the participants *was* carrying *his or her* conference materials in the tote bag provided.

Corrected: *All of the participants were* carrying *their* conference materials in the tote bag provided.

Pronouns that refer to compound antecedents (joined by *or* or *nor*) are singular if both elements are singular and plural if both are plural:

Neither *the policyholders* nor the *insurance companies* were interested in settling *their* cases.

Either *Henry* or *Isabel* should share *his* or *her* experiences at the new staff orientation.

When one of the antecedents is singular and one plural, the pronoun agrees with the one closer to it:

> Either the *owner* or the *employees* will have to give up *their* positions in this dispute.

Broad Reference

A broad pronoun reference, one that refers to the previous sentence or clause, may confuse your reader. The most common form of broad reference occurs in the use of *this* at the beginning of a sentence. To correct the problem, always use *this* with a noun:

> **Wrong:** The firm has decided to open a suburban branch office next spring. *This* will help it increase profits and build its client base.

> **Corrected:** The firm has decided to open a suburban branch office next spring. *This expansion* will help it increase profits and build its client base.

Another form of broad reference involves the relative pronouns *(who, that, which):*

> **Wrong:** The flights run every hour and cost little, which makes the commute easy.

> **Corrected:** The commute is easy because the low-cost flights run every hour. (See p. B-5 for further discussion of the uses of *that* and *which.*)

Ambiguous Reference

An ambiguous pronoun reference is one that can be interpreted in more than one way. When a pronoun may refer to either of two antecedents, revise the sentence to remove the ambiguity:

> **Wrong:** Tom discussed with Michael his concerns that his work was suffering as a result of personal problems.

> **Corrected:** Tom, worried that personal problems were interfering with Michael's work, discussed his concerns with Michael.

EXERCISES

Revise the following sentences to correct problems with subject-verb agreement, pronoun-antecedent agreement, pronoun reference, and pronoun case.

1. Each of the applicants had their résumés ready for the committee.
2. No one conducts interviews more thoroughly than her.
3. Ask whomever arrives first if they know how to install the new software.

4. Neither the manager nor the accountants know what caused the error.
5. Any communication with clients, including phone calls, letters, and presentations, are important for the firm's image.
6. This is a private matter between he and I.
7. Randall knows more about their accounting system than me.
8. One of the errors in the financial statements were corrected yesterday.
9. After John explained the procedures to Bruce, he prepared notes for the meeting.
10. The board of directors were unanimous in approving the revised budget.

MODIFIER PROBLEMS

Words, phrases, and clauses that function as modifiers should be placed as close as possible to the words they modify. **Ambiguous modifiers** are those placed so that they could modify either of two words:

Ambiguous: We decided *immediately* to withdraw the offer.

Corrected: We *immediately* decided to withdraw the offer.

Corrected: We decided to withdraw the offer *immediately*.

Ambiguous: We agreed *on the next day* to make adjustments.

Corrected: We agreed to make adjustments *on the next day*.

Corrected: *On the next day we agreed* to make the adjustments.

Misplaced modifiers are those that are placed too far away from the words they are intended to modify.

Misplaced: They gave a watch to the retiree *plated with gold*.

Corrected: They gave a watch *plated with gold* to the retiree.

Dangling modifiers are those with no clear word or phrase to modify. Dangling modifiers are usually verbals (*-ed, -ing,* and *to + verb* forms of the verb) and are often found at the beginning of sentences. To correct dangling modifiers, add the appropriate noun or pronoun for the phrase to modify:

Dangling: Keeping busy, the afternoon passed swiftly.

Corrected: Keeping busy, *Burt* felt the afternoon pass swiftly.

Dangling: After finishing the research, the job was easy.

Corrected: After finishing the research, *we* found the job to be easy.

Dangling: To improve computer skills, practice is needed.

Corrected: To improve computer skills, *you* must practice.

You can also correct dangling modifiers by making the phrase a clause:

> **Dangling:** When ten years old, his father started the company.
>
> **Corrected:** When *Dennis was* ten years old, his father started the company.
>
> **Dangling:** While waiting at the airport, his wife arrived home by taxi.
>
> **Corrected:** While Bob was waiting at the airport, his wife arrived home by taxi.

EXERCISES

Revise the following sentences to correct misplaced and dangling modifiers.

1. Students who study continually achieve top grades.
2. While reviewing the financial statements, his computer crashed.
3. When only ten years old, Andy's father founded the company.
4. Sam bought a fax machine at the outlet store which cost very little.
5. The revenues fell short of estimates, pointing to problems in the sales division.
6. To function properly, you must service the machines on a regular schedule.
7. Writing under pressure, the report was completed by the team.
8. Alex and Jeanne only worked together for three months.
9. Two weeks after passing the CPA exam, his son was born.
10. Confronted with escalating debt, the accountant discussed bankruptcy with the business owner.

Many of these sentences contain errors: fragments, run-ons, comma splices, mixed and incomplete constructions; subject-verb agreement problems; pronoun problems; modifier problems. Rewrite them as needed to correct these errors and be able to explain why you made the changes you did.

1. He reported that the cost of long-distance calls were getting out of hand.
2. To evacuate the building, the alarm should be sounded.
3. The income statement reports the excess of revenue over expense, that is, net income. Or in the event of an excess of expense over revenue, net loss.
4. Five minutes later, Bill went back to his office, leaving Stephanie and I in the board room.
5. Everyone in the investment group were pleased with the stock's performance, it gained steadily from the date of purchase.
6. The depreciation of a long-term asset is not a cash item, nevertheless it must be presented on the statement of cash flows.
7. The reason is because it was deducted from earnings in calculating the net figure.

8. Using the double-declining balance method of depreciation, the tax savings was calculated.
9. Either of the methods are appropriate for costing the goods sold.
10. Either the accountant or the clients is wrong.
11. Ellis is handling that account, therefore, it's him that you need to consult.
12. Neither of the returns have been analyzed.
13. While reviewing the balance sheet, an annoying fly buzzed around her head.
14. We sent out the RFP to potential bidders that included specifications for the job.
15. The error was detected while calculating the capital expenditures.
16. The engagement will be awarded to whomever offers the lowest bid.
17. We thought this incentive alone would change their minds.
18. After discovering areas where they could develop new markets, the campaign was launched.
19. This is a confidential matter between Abco and I.
20. The reason this document needs to be edited is because it's full of grammatical errors.

B. Usage Reference Guide

WORD-CHOICE PROBLEMS

Many words in English sound alike although they are spelled differently. Such words are called *homonyms,* and it is easy to confuse their meanings. Other words, although not technically homonyms, sound enough alike to be confusing as well. Still others have similar meanings but are properly used in different contexts. The list here covers the most commonly confused word pairs.

adverse/averse *Adverse* means *hostile. Averse* means *reluctant* or *disinclined.*

> Constructive feedback motivates employees better than *adverse* criticism does.
>
> Philip is hard to work with because he's sometimes *averse* to hearing the truth.

advice/advise *Advice* is a noun meaning *guidance; advise* is a verb meaning *to recommend* or *counsel.*

> Hanneman gave you excellent *advice* when he *advised* you to take the promotion.

affect/effect *Affect* is a verb meaning *to influence.*

> Mr. Takagashi's speech *affected* his colleagues deeply.

Effect is most frequently used as a noun meaning the *consequences* or *results.*

> His decision had far-reaching *effects.*

Effect is also a verb meaning *to bring about.*

> Mr. Takagashi's speech *affected* his colleagues so deeply that they *effected* an immediate resolution to change the bylaws.

aggravate/irritate *Aggravate* is a verb meaning *to make worse. Irritate* is a verb meaning *to annoy.*

> Rachel's hostility *aggravated* the already tense situation.
>
> Howie was so *irritated* by Sarah's complaints that he left the meeting early.

all ready/already *All ready,* an adjective, means *completely prepared.*

> I am *all ready* to accept the transfer to Portland.

Already is an adverb meaning *before* or *previously.*

> Have you finished that job *already?*

all together/altogether *All together* means *in a group; altogether* means *entirely.*

> The litigants were assembled *all together* in the judge's chambers.
>
> They were *altogether* ready to settle the case.

allude/elude *Allude* is a verb meaning *to refer to; elude* is a verb meaning *to evade.*

> Sal *alluded* to the criminal proceedings against the company.
>
> The controller has been fired and is now trying to *elude* the IRS.

amount/number *Amount* refers to items in bulk. *Number* is for items that can be counted.

> We netted a smaller *amount of money* this year because we served a smaller *number of clients.*

between/among *Between* is used to refer to two; *among* is used for more than two.

> The settlement negotiated *between the two* parties is binding.
>
> Please circulate this announcement *among all* partners.

brake/break *Brake* is a noun meaning *a device for stopping. Break* is a noun meaning *a period of relaxation* and a verb meaning *to tear* or *crack.*

> If the *brakes* don't work, you may collide with another car.
>
> If your head hits the windshield in such a collision, you may *break* the glass.
>
> After six hours at your desk, you need a *break!*

capital/capitol *Capital* is a noun meaning *resources* or *seat of government. Capitol* means *a building where a legislature meets.*

> Renfrew and Smith seem to have adequate *capital* to establish their electronics business.
>
> Baton Rouge is the *capital* of Louisiana, where Huey Long is remembered for the building of the *capitol.*

cite/site *Cite* is a verb meaning *to document. Site* is a noun meaning *a location.*

> It is important to *cite* the proper section of the tax code in your memorandum.
>
> Our office was the *site* of a historic meeting yesterday.

complement/compliment *Complement* means *to complete something else.* *Compliment* means *to give praise.*

> The rich bordeaux was the perfect *complement* to the steak au poivre.
>
> The chef deserved the *compliments* he received on that special meal.

disinterested/uninterested *Disinterested* means *impartial.* Use *uninterested* to mean *not interested.*

> A *disinterested* third party is needed to arbitrate between management and labor.
>
> Despite the teacher's best efforts, the students remained *uninterested* in the topic.

farther/further *Farther* refers to distance, *further* to time.

> Janet's office is *farther* down the hall than Leo's.
>
> O'Casey indicated that he wanted to discuss the numbers *further.*

fewer/less *Fewer* refers to items that can be counted; *less* refers to mass amounts.

> *Fewer clients* now means *less profit* at year's end.

foreword/forward A *foreword* is the *opening section to a book. Forward* is an adverb meaning *toward the front or future.*

> The authors explained their approach to the subject in the *foreword.*
>
> The best advice I know for success is to keep looking *forward* to your next accomplishment.

imply/infer *Imply* is a verb meaning *to suggest; infer* is a verb meaning *to draw a conclusion.*

> Her tone of voice *implied* disapproval.
>
> Can we *infer* from these data that bankruptcy is the only option?

its/it's *Its* is the possessive form of the neuter pronoun. *It's* is the contraction meaning *it is.*

> I cannot understand that company's success; *its* products are mediocre, and *its* service is slow.
>
> *It's* not easy to lose your prime account.

lead/led *Lead* is a metal. *Led* is the past tense of the verb *to lead.*

> Many children become ill each year from *lead* poisoning.
>
> Technology stocks *led* the bull market for a couple of years during the 1990s.

Usage Reference

lie/lay *Lie* is an intransitive verb meaning *to recline. Lay* is a transitive verb meaning *to put* or *place*. These verbs are frequently confused because the past tense of one is the same as the present tense of the other.

	Lie	**Lay**
Present	I *lie* down.	I *lay* the book down.
Past	I *lay* down.	I *laid* the book down.
Past Participle	I *have lain* down.	I *have laid* the book down.

like/as *Like* is a preposition and should be followed by a noun or noun phrase. *As* is a subordinating conjunction and should be used before a subject and verb (clause).

This looks *like* the right software.

As we were arriving at work, the police surrounded the building.

pair/pare *Pair* is a noun meaning *a set of two. Pare* is a verb meaning *to trim.*

For Greg's birthday, his staff gave him a *pair* of marble bookends.

John decided his company had to *pare* costs.

passed/past *Passed* is the past tense of the verb *to pass. Past* means *of a former time.*

Eileen's vacation days *passed* too quickly.

To complete the audit, they had to review every transaction of the *past* year.

precede/proceed *Precede* means *to go before. Proceed* means *to go onward.*

The final will *preceded* his death by only three weeks.

Proceed to your workstations as soon as possible.

principal/principle *Principal* is an adjective meaning *first in importance.* It is also a noun meaning *the head of a school* or *a sum of money. Principle* is a noun meaning *rule* or *basic truth.*

The *principal* told the students, "Your *principal* responsibility here is to study hard and learn."

The financial planner took what steps he could to protect Morgan's *principal.*

Everyone needs a set of core *principles* by which to live life.

stationary/stationery *Stationary* is an adjective meaning *immobile. Stationery* is a noun meaning *writing paper.*

When Gwen was promoted to partner, the firm *stationery* had to be reprinted to include her name.

While MacKenzie reprimanded her, Consuelo stood *stationary* in front of his desk.

that/which *That* introduces restrictive clauses. *Which* is used to introduce nonrestrictive clauses. Nonrestrictive clauses, which are set off with double commas, provide additional information, information that is not essential to the meaning of the sentence.

The clients will select the firm that provides the best service.

The clients selected Compunet, which provided the best service.

In the first sentence, the restrictive clause *that provides the best service* provides information essential to the sentence. It specifies the firm to be chosen. In the second sentence, the clause *which provided the best service* is nonrestrictive because the meaning of the sentence is complete without it.

Although *which* is frequently used to introduce both restrictive and nonrestrictive clauses, careful professional writers should observe the distinction.

their/there/they're *Their* is the third person plural possessive pronoun. *There* is an adverb meaning *at that place.* *They're* is a contraction meaning *they are.*

They're spending the summer at *their* place in Maine.

They always have a relaxing time *there.*

to/too/two *To* is a preposition meaning *toward.* *Too* is a conjunction meaning *also* and an adverb meaning *excessively.* *Two* is a number.

To seek advice *too* often may make a person seem insecure.

The *two* of them were ready to help.

weather/whether *Weather* is a noun meaning *atmospheric conditions.* *Whether* is a conditional meaning *if.*

Jan wondered *whether* the *weather* over the weekend would be nice enough for sailing.

who/which/that Use *who* or (in informal discourse) *that* to refer to persons. Never use *which* to refer to persons.

Charles is the banker *who* handled my loan.

First City is the bank *that* granted my loan.

who's/whose *Who's* is a contraction meaning *who is.* *Whose* is a *possessive pronoun.*

Whose password do we need to get into this database?

Who's your best player?

your/you're *Your* is a *possessive pronoun*. *You're* is a contraction meaning *you are.*

You're the most successful of all *your* brothers and sisters.

CAPITALIZATION

1. Capitalize proper nouns (names of specific persons, places, or things) and the adjectives derived from them. All other nouns are common nouns, which are not capitalized.

Proper Nouns	Common Nouns
President (preceding name)	the company's president
God (used as name)	the gods
the West (as region)	a western city
the Constitution (of the United States)	a constitution was drawn up
the University of Texas	a major university
Shakespeare, Shakespearean	the great playwright

Here are some categories of words usually capitalized.

**Place Names, Nationalities,
Languages, Ethnic Groups**

Berlin	Canadian
Russian	Lincoln Center
Chippewa	Orange County
Indian Ocean	Grand Canyon

**Business Names, Trade Names,
Abbreviations for
Government Agencies and
Political Organizations**

Westinghouse	Toyota Corolla
FDA	Nike
Donna Karan	NATO

**Months, Days of the Week,
Holidays**

April	Christmas
Wednesday	Memorial Day

Note, however, that names of the seasons are not capitalized.

summer	spring
autumn	winter

Historical Eras, Events, and Documents

the Renaissance	the Battle of the Bulge
the Gettysburg Address	the Roaring Twenties

Religions and Religious Terms

Buddhism	Allah
the Torah	Catholic
African Methodist Episcopal Church	

2. Capitalize all major words in titles and subtitles of books, articles, magazines, and other works. Do not capitalize articles *(a, an, the)*, prepositions, or coordinating conjunctions unless they are the first or last words of the title or subtitle.

Tax Planning for Professionals: A Guidebook

The Journal of Accounting Education

Note: These rules are not absolute and may vary according to the style conventions in a particular discipline or type of publication.

GENDER BIAS

Readers may be offended by language that seems to be a casual perpetuation of gender bias. Here are some ways to eliminate such bias from your writing:

1. Replace biased words with neutral ones:

Biased	Neutral
businessman	businessperson, manager
chairman	chair, chairperson
fireman	firefighter
foreman	supervisor
landlord/landlady	owner
mailman	mail carrier
mankind	humanity
manmade	synthetic
manpower	effort, power
men	human beings, people
policeman	police officer
stewardess	flight attendant

2. Do not use masculine pronouns to refer to a group that includes both men and women. Change *Every worker must submit his travel expenses by Monday* in one of the following ways.

Make the subject of your sentence plural and thus neutral:

Workers must submit their travel expenses by Monday.

Use *his or her* instead of *his:*

Every worker must submit his or her travel expenses by Monday.

Reword the sentences using the passive voice:

All travel expenses must be submitted by Monday.

NUMERALS VERSUS WORDS

Write the following as words:

- Numbers from one through nine (with exceptions as listed later)
- The smaller of two numbers together: two 6-hour classes
- Numbers beginning a sentence: seventy-eight transactions
- Ordinal numbers in text: the third meeting

Write the following as numerals:

- Numbers above ten: 11, 37, 675
- Dates and times: September 5, 9:30 A.M.
- Numbers before a percent sign: 75%
- Measurements: 3 feet, 17 pounds, 6 decibels

EXERCISES

Correct any usage errors in these sentences.

1. The presenter had 2 strikes against him: defective equipment and a disinterested audience.
2. During the performance appraisal meeting, Jan's comments inferred her appreciation of Alan's hard work.
3. The Y2K problem has effected all aspects of the company's operations.
4. The Chairman announced that the new office would be set up twenty miles further from the city than originally had been planned.
5. The system logged seventy-three % less customer inquiries than we had at this time last year. To increase our customer base, we will have to increase our manpower.
6. Because Chad attended an outstanding University and made excellent grades, he had many job offers.
7. To resolve this matter, I'd like to call a meeting between Jenkins, Holloway, Rippner, and McDonald.

8. Hopefully, the chairman will be able to explain the shortfall.
9. Before we take on the engagement, I want to meet with president Sanders and vice president Walker.
10. Some elderly clients are adverse to dealing with the realities involved in prudent estate planning.
11. The firm had new stationary printed to reflect the expansion of the partnership.
12. The Forest Park store closed for three days to complete its Summer inventory.
13. Cheryl felt badly because she had become aggravated during the meeting, and she had shown it.
14. Please condense these reports into 2 three-page summaries.
15. Martha paid Randy a nice complement on the job he had done.

C. Punctuation Reference Guide

Proper punctuation helps your reader understand your writing because punctuation underscores the relationships among elements in your sentences. This section explains the correct uses of the most common punctuation marks: the comma, the semicolon, the colon, the period, the apostrophe, the dash, the hyphen, parentheses, quotation marks, and ellipsis. It also discusses the proper use of italic type.

THE COMMA

The comma is the most frequently used punctuation mark. It links elements and separates elements in the following ways.

Five Ways to Use the Comma

1. *To set off introductory elements.* Introductory words, phrases, and clauses are followed by a comma:

Normally, gaining control of a company requires acquisition of more than 50% of that company's stock.

In general, long-term liabilities are obligations that will not be satisfied within one year.

Because he did not anticipate the recent economic downturn, our client must request an extension.

Working long into the night, Kate rushed to meet the deadline.

2. *To set off interrupters.* Interrupters include parenthetical elements and nonrestrictive phrases and clauses:

They did, *however,* insist on meeting before the end of the week. [parenthetical element]

Kate, *working long into the night,* rushed to meet the deadline. [nonrestrictive participial phrase]

Our new Denver office, which will open in January, will employ 35 people. [nonrestrictive relative clause]

3. *To separate items in a series.* Although the comma before the last item is considered optional, use it consistently to help prevent ambiguity. Consider the following sentence:

To complete your return, we will need your W2 forms, your 1099s, and your statements of expenses, interest and capital gains. (Are *interest* and *capital gains* considered one unit? How is the client to know? You can remove ambiguity by using the final comma: *statements of expenses, interest, and capital gains.*)

Use a comma to separate adjectives modifying the same noun. (If the adjectives can be separated by *and,* you need a comma.)

Hubbell is a talented, conscientious, imaginative member of the team.

Sandy sorted through the stack of dusty, yellowing documents.

4. *To link two sentences with a coordinating conjunction.* A conjunction alone is insufficient to link two independent clauses. A comma must precede the conjunction.

Accounts payable usually do not require the payment of interest, *but* terms may be given to encourage early payment.

The power surged, *and* the computer crashed.

5. *To separate the parts of dates, addresses, and numbers.*

Dates. "House style" varies on the arrangement of dates. Here are the proper ways to punctuate different versions. Use a comma to separate numerical elements:

July 22, 2001

Omit the comma when the day is omitted:

July 2001

Omit the comma when the date is set military style:

22 July 2001

When the complete date appears in a sentence, enclose the year in commas as well:

On July 22, 2001, Mary celebrated finishing the project.

When only part of the date appears, do not use a comma:

In July 2001 Mary celebrated finishing the project.

Addresses. Use a comma to separate parts of an address (except the zip code) within a sentence:

Ann Randolph, 1432 Webster Street, New Orleans, LA 70118

Numbers. Use a comma to separate the digits of long numbers into groups of three:

2,785,670

The comma in four-digit numbers is optional:

3540 or 3,540

Common Comma Errors

1. The *comma splice* (joining two sentences with a comma)

Wrong: Accounting is the universal language of business, accountants are in demand all over the world.

Corrected: Accounting is the universal language of business; therefore, accountants are in demand all over the world. [semicolon + conjunctive adverb]

Corrected: Because accounting is the universal language of business, accountants are in demand all over the world. [one clause subordinated to the other]

Corrected: Accounting is the universal language of business, and accountants are in demand all over the world. [comma + coordinating conjunction]

See page A-10 for more on comma splices.

2. *Unnecessary commas*

Do not separate subject and verb with a single comma:

Wrong: Volatile market conditions at home and abroad, make planning next year's budget difficult.

Note: Between a subject and verb you will either have *two* commas (to enclose a parenthetical or nonrestrictive element) or *no* commas.

Corrected: Volatile market conditions at home and abroad, of course, make planning next year's budget difficult.

Corrected: Volatile market conditions at home and abroad make planning next year's budget difficult.

Note: Do not separate the elements of a compound subject or predicate with a comma:

Wrong: The chairman of the board, and the president prepared for the news conference.

Corrected: The chairman of the board and the president prepared for the news conference.

THE SEMICOLON

Use the semicolon, as illustrated earlier, to join two closely related independent clauses.

Use the semicolon to separate items in a series that are long and contain other punctuation.

Wrong: Among those present were Ralph Thompson, senior partner at PricewaterhouseCoopers, Miami, and Chris Robinson, tax accountant, Hank Ledbetter, president of ABC Corporation, and Cal Mitchell, district manager of Compunet.

Corrected: Among those present were Ralph Thompson, senior partner at PricewaterhouseCoopers, Miami, and Chris Robinson, tax accountant; Hank Ledbetter, president of ABC Corporation; and Cal Mitchell, district manager of Compunet.

THE COLON

Use the colon to introduce a list:

We need three forms from you: your 1040, your W2, and your 1099-INT.

Use a colon *only* after an independent clause:

Wrong: The most important skills for advancement are: technical knowledge, writing skills, and oral communication skills.

Wrong: I would like to be transferred to: Tucson, Boston, or New York.

THE PERIOD

Use a period to indicate the end of a declarative sentence:

The supplies you ordered are in the top drawer.

Use a period to indicate abbreviations:

Ransom and Barker, Inc.

THE APOSTROPHE

Apostrophes are used to show possession and to indicate the omission of letters in contractions. To show possession, add *'s* to singular words:

Jack*'s* computer

a week*'s* vacation

Doris*'s* briefcase

Note: Although singular nouns ending in *s* may form the possessive either by an apostrophe alone or by *'s,* the latter is preferred. When a singular word ends in *z* sounds or multiple *s* sounds, an apostrophe alone is sufficient:

> Judy Moses' secretary is out sick.
>
> New Orleans' restaurants are internationally acclaimed.

Add *'s* to plurals not ending in *s:*

> the women's center
>
> the children's room

Add *s'* to plural words ending in *s:*

> ten years' experience
>
> the tax accountants' association

To show joint possession with pairs of nouns, make the latter noun possessive:

> Hal and Linda's spreadsheet was a work of art.

To show individual possession with pairs of nouns, make both nouns possessive:

> Hal's and Linda's spreadsheets were works of art.

To make plurals of letters and numbers, add *'s* to the letter or numeral:

> How many *s*'s are there in *Mississippi?*
>
> How many *0*'s are there in one billion?

To form contractions, use an apostrophe to show where letters have been left out:

> I *can't* go because *it's* raining.

THE DASH

Many word processing programs have a long dash, usually command- or control-shift-hyphen; if this option isn't available to you, create a dash by combining two hyphens (--). Do not put spaces before or after the dash. Use a dash in these three situations:

1. To indicate a sudden shift:

> We need all the help they can give us—*but we probably won't get it.*

2. To set off lists that introduce the sentence:

Brains, technical skill, and motivation—these are the qualities we're looking for in new associates.

3. To set off supplemental material:

Working downtown—*with its traffic jams, parking costs, and surging crowds*—is more stressful than working in the suburbs.

THE HYPHEN

Hyphens are used to divide words at the end of lines or to connect words in compound expressions. Use hyphens for the following three situations:

1. To connect words that serve as adjectives *preceding nouns:*

Hyphen: *Nineteenth-century* laws restricted the rights of women.
No hyphen: Women's rights were restricted in the *nineteenth century.*
Hyphen: Louis Baker is a *well-known* philanthropist in this town.
No hyphen: Louis Baker is *well known* for his generous philanthropy.

Do not, however, use a hyphen to connect *very* and *-ly* adverbs to words they modify:

No hyphen: The *clearly bewildered* student stared at the exam.
No hyphen: The *very generous* bequest allowed him to buy a new car.

2. To form compound nouns:

life-form
head-hunter

3. To form compound numbers and fractions:

Fifty-eight
Three-quarters
Twenty-three thousand

PARENTHESES

Use parentheses for the following:

1. To set off supplemental material from the main part of the sentence and minimize its importance:

She drove the Honda *(their older car)* to work every day.

2. To enclose numbers or letters in a list:

This package contains several items: (1) the parts for your new computer, (2) an operating manual, and (3) a one-year limited warranty.

QUOTATION MARKS

Use quotation marks for the following:

1. To enclose words spoken or written by others:

"Mrs. Jefferson is on the line," said Michael. "Shall I take a message?"

2. To indicate the titles of essays, articles, book chapters, and other short works. Note that the titles of long works—books, magazines, journals, films—are italicized.

An article entitled "Communication Skills: What You Need to Succeed" appeared in the January/February 1997 issue of *New Accountant.*

3. To enclose a word or phrase you are defining:

"Taxable income" is defined as gross income less all allowable deductions.

4. To draw attention to a word or phrase being used in a special way:

Congress has enacted two "umbrella" provisions in the code that provide deductions for various expenditures.

Punctuation with Quotation Marks

1. In American usage—unlike that of most other English-speaking countries—periods and commas are always placed *inside* quotation marks:

To determine gross receipts, you may deduct "returns and allowances."

Punctuation Reference

2. Semicolons and colons are placed *outside* quotation marks:

Deductions for individual taxpayers are classified as deductions "*for* adjusted gross income" and "*from* adjusted gross income"; sometimes these deductions are referred to as "above the line" deductions and "below the line" deductions.

3. Question marks, dashes, and exclamation points are placed inside the quotation marks when they are part of the quotation:

Arriving late to the meeting, Jeanne asked, "What did I miss so far?"

4. Question marks, dashes, and exclamation points are placed outside the quotation marks when they refer to the whole sentence:

How does the IRS define "net income"?

THE ELLIPSIS

The ellipsis (three spaced periods) is used to indicate that material has been omitted from a quotation. When the omitted material comes at the end of a sentence, the ellipsis follows the period:

According to Ben & Jerry's 1992 Annual Report, "Net sales in 1992 increased 36% . . . due to the national introduction of frozen yogurt pints . . . as well as to a new flavor (Chocolate Chip Cookie Dough) introduced in March 1991. . . ."

ITALICS

Italic type is used for titles of books, magazines, journals, newspapers, films, musical works, plays, television programs, and art works:

The Accountant's Guide to Professional Communication

Newsweek

the *Journal of Financial Accounting*

the *Wall Street Journal*

Star Wars

Professor Longhair: The London Concert

Phantom of the Opera

Hamlet

Seinfeld

Mona Lisa

EXERCISES

Correct any punctuation errors you find in these sentences.

1. When an investor reads a balance sheet he or she wants to distinguish between current debt, and long- term debt.
2. All travelers, who have not submitted expense statements, should do so by February 15 2000.
3. Because bond maturities are as long as 30 years the secondary market in bonds, the market for bonds already issued, is a critical factor in a companys ability to raise money.
4. Alice ran the numbers again; fearing that she had made a mistake.
5. Late twentieth century technology increased the ease and speed of communications.
6. One stockbroker describes her work; "I help clients save for their kids college educations, plan for retirement and evaluate the investments that they already have".
7. Two important factor's should be kept in mind in evaluating any financial statement ratio. They are: 1. how does this years ratio differ from that of prior years? 2. how does the ratio compare with industry norms?
8. The article on software in the CPA Journal helped Wanda make her decision.
9. An existing business is bought for $150000 on March 20 1999, the values assigned are $25000 for the land, $75000 for the supplies, and equipment, and $50,000 for the buildings.
10. Landing a job is easy, keeping it is the challenge.
11. Our priorities for 2001 are: broadening our client base, training staff in new computer systems and cutting our expenses.
12. In a stock acquisition two companies combine; however, after the combination both entities maintain their legal identities.
13. When Gerry and Barbara left the firm we lost Holsum Grains our biggest client.
14. Eighty two percent of our trainees reported that the seminar was useful.
15. I stayed here until 10:30 last night to finish Drews taxes.
16. The policies, that I relied on in making my recommendation, were issued only three weeks ago.
17. Capital lease assets, must be depreciated by the lessee over the life of the lease agreement capital lease payments must be separated into interest expense and reduction of principal, using the effective interest method.
18. The partner group was really impressed with Phoebe's and Ben's report which clearly explained the companys position vis a vis the competition.
19. "Don't look now", Sam said "but I think someones following us!"
20. Decision making skills are essential for promotion to partner.

Supply the punctuation missing from the following paragraphs.*

The popularity of mergers and acquisitions peaked in this country in 1988. In that year alone the value of announced domestic mergers and acquisitions M&A was approximately $350 billion. After 1988 the number of merger and acquisitions decreased primarily because the engine of 1980s style deal making the highly leveraged transaction in which large amounts of debt were used went out of favor. The market for junk bonds dried up with the demise of Drexel Burnham Lambert the infamous investment firm that controlled that market.

After a few years the M&A business gradually came back to life this time with much less debt and much more strategic rationale. The Wall Street Journal reported on October 14 1993 that the "merger bandwagon is rolling again" The story was in the aftermath of the announcement of a planned acquisition of Tele Communications Inc. a cable TV company by Bell Atlantic Corp. a regional phone company.

---

*Adapted from Gary A. Porter and Curtis L. Norton, *Financial Accounting: The Impact on Decision Makers* (Fort Worth, TX: The Dryden Press, 1995), p. 688.

D. Formats Reference Guide

MEMOS

Memo format varies from company to company. In some organizations, memos are produced on company letterhead; in others, templates or preprinted forms are used to generate consistent formatting. Regardless of minor differences, however, all memos begin with a heading, which distinguishes memos from other types of correspondence. The heading usually begins with the word *Memorandum* or *Memo;* it always specifies the sender, the receiver, the date, and the subject of the memo (see Figure D.1).

Parts of the Heading

Names of Sender and Receiver   First and last names of both sender and receiver should be included in the heading. When the writer and reader are closely acquainted, the writer may choose to use shortened names or nicknames, as in Figure D.1. When the memo is communicating with more than one reader, the writer has two options: either to list the names of all recipients on the "TO" line or to list the primary reader in the heading and the secondary readers at the bottom of the document after the letter "C," an abbreviation for "copy."

Titles of Sender and Receiver   It is important to supply the titles of both the sender and receiver in addition to their names because memos often document the history of a project occurring over time and may be read by people who were not even at the company when the memos were written and filed. Position titles help clarify routes of communication for readers unacquainted with the sender or the receiver. The position titles in Figure D.1, for example, allow any reader familiar with the firm's organizational chart to recognize that the memo was sent from a staff accountant to a supervisor and thus to understand the information flow.

Figure D.1

Sample Memo Heading

Formats
Reference

MEMO
TO: Andy Thibodeaux, Auditor in Charge FROM: Carol Pratt, Staff Accountant DATE: November 5, 2000 SUBJECT: Completion of Accounts Receivable Work Papers for Delta Pipe Audit

Subject Information   The subject line in the heading should alert the reader to the content of the memo. By supplying a subject line, the writer helps the reader see the general context of the memo without the need to read the whole document. This contextualizing allows the reader to categorize the communication quickly and assign it proper priority. In Figure D.1, the subject line lets the reader know precisely what aspect of an audit is being referenced.

In some companies, other information, such as phone numbers, fax numbers, or e-mail addresses, is included in the heading. Be sure to follow the standard format for your organization.

Memo Text

Set the body of the memo flush left, single spaced, and double-space between paragraphs. In place of signatures, most memos display the initials of the writer next to the typed name. If the memo will be distributed to other readers, indicate their names at the bottom (see Figure D.2).

Figure D.2

Sample Memo Text

MEMO

TO: Jim Debit
FROM: Joe Baxter
SUBJECT: Status/Big Apple Insurance Company
DATE: August 27, 2000

This memo is in response to your question about Big Apple Insurance.

Big Apple is a wholly owned subsidiary of Holliwell International Group. As of 2000, Big Apple has ceased assuming, ceding, and writing new business. However, it still maintains the necessary licenses to operate as a property and casualty insurance company.

The attached financial statements, which will give you the information you need, were prepared in conformity with the statutory accounting practices of the National Association of Insurance Commissioners.

If you need more detailed information, please call me.

C: B. Morgan

LETTERS

All business letters have six parts (see Figure D.3):

1. Heading
2. Inside address

Elements of a Business Letter

	LETTER
Heading	*Hoffman McCormack* *Certified Public Accountants* *Suite 3500* *1753 Lincoln Avenue* *Albuquerque, NM 87108*
Inside Address	March 3, 2000 Mr. Stephen Hallowell Vice President, Client Services Citibank 111 Wall Street 14th Floor New York, NY 10043
Salutation	Dear Mr. Hallowell:
Body	In connection with our audit of the Minerals Exploration Employee Stock Ownership Plan for the year ended December 31, 1999, would you please provide an account summary for the Plan Year ended December 31, 1999? The report should detail the transactions that occurred during the year, including the transfer of assets to the successor trustee. Please send the report to my attention. Thank you for your help.
Complimentary Close	Sincerely,
Signature	*William F. O'Reilly* William F. O'Reilly Phone 000.863.4000 Fax 000.863.4125

Formats Reference

   3. Salutation
   4. Body
   5. Complimentary close
   6. Signature

Elements of a Business Letter

Heading   The heading tells the reader the source of the letter. It states the writer's address (company name, street, suite number, city, state, and zip code) and the date. Most frequently, the heading is printed on company stationery; all the writer must add is the date, at least two—and for short letters as many as eight—lines below the printed address.

In the absence of letterhead, place the heading at the top of the front page and position it to be consistent with the format you are using (see "Business Letter Formats" later). Write out all words—including those such as *Street, Avenue, First, South,* and the name of the month—with the exception of the state name, which may be abbreviated with the standard U.S. Postal Service abbreviation. When creating your own heading, place the date immediately below the last line of the address:

226 Carondelet Street
New Orleans, LA 70130
August 11, 1999

Inside Address   The inside address includes the name, title, organization, and full address of the recipient. If the recipient has a professional title *(Dr., Honorable),* use it. If not, use the courtesy titles *Mr.* or *Ms.* If the recipient's title fits reasonably on the same line as the name, place it there after a comma. If not, place it on the line below.

Ms. Lelia Armstrong
Director of Executive Education
School of Business Administration
City University
Atlanta, GA 30307

If you do not know the recipient's name, use an *attention line:*

The School of Business Administration
City University
Atlanta, GA 30307
Attention: Director of Executive Education

Begin the inside address flush with the left margin (always *at least* one inch wide) and place it two spaces below the heading.

Salutation   Place the salutation (greeting) two spaces below the inside address. The traditional salutation is *Dear* followed by the reader's title and last name. The salutation is followed by a colon:

Dear Mr. Tinsley:

Dear Dr. Gunderson:

If you are on a first-name basis with the reader, include full name and title in the inside address and use only the first name in the salutation:

Dear Frank:

If you are unacquainted with the reader and the name could be either masculine or feminine, use the full name in the salutation:

Dear Chris Wood:

Dear Pat Trevor:

If you do not have a name for the reader, use a title appropriate to the context:

Dear Client Services Manager:

Dear Marketing Director:

Or, somewhat more formally, use

Dear Sir or Madam:

Body   The body of the letter usually consists of at least three paragraphs: an opening paragraph, a concluding paragraph, and one or more body paragraphs. Begin the body of the letter two spaces below the salutation. Single-space within paragraphs and double-space between paragraphs.

Complimentary Close   The complimentary close consists of one of the following phrases:

Sincerely,

Yours truly,

Sincerely yours,

Very truly yours,

Cordially,

Regards,

Note that the complimentary close is followed by a comma, and only the first word is capitalized. Place the complimentary close two spaces beneath the last sentence of the body.

Formats Reference

Signature   Type your full name four spaces below the complimentary close. Most organizations prefer that you include your title as well, one line below your typed name. Sign the letter in the space between the complimentary close and your typed name.

Optional Elements   Sometimes further notations are needed on business letters.

Typist's Initials   In some organizations, the initials of the person who typed the letter are included two spaces below the signature. The standard method for this notation is to type the initials of the writer in capital letters followed by a slash and the initials of the word processor in lowercase. On a letter from Sarah Ann Kinney typed by Todd G. Markham, for example, the notation would read as follows:

SAK/tgm

Enclosure Line   If additional documents will accompany the letter, it is customary to make a notation of it at the bottom of the page. For a single enclosure, use this format:

Enclosure *or* Enc.

For multiple enclosures, use this format:

Enclosures (2) *or* Encs.

In some cases, enclosures are described:

Enclosures: 1999 Tax Return
              Expense Records

Even with a notation line, however, mention the enclosure in the body of the letter.

Copy Line   If copies of the letter will be sent to additional readers, list the name(s) below the enclosure line as follows:

c: Martin Engstrom

copies: Martin Engstrom
         Jose Murrillo

If you do not want your reader to know about the other readers, use the abbreviation *bc* (blind copy) *on the copies only,* not the original.

Place optional elements two spaces below the signature. When all three optional elements are needed, arrange them as follows:

SAK/tgm
Enclosure
c: Martin Engstrom

Business Letter Formats

To format business letters, use one of the three styles pictured on the following pages. Consult the files to see which is the preferred format at your firm or company.

The *full block style* begins every line flush with the left margin. This format is the easiest to type, although it may appear lopsided (see Figure D.4).

In the *modified block style,* the return address (if not on letterhead), the date, the complimentary close, and the signature are aligned immediately to the right of center. Everything else begins flush with the left margin (see Figure D.5).

The *semiblock style* is identical to the modified block with the exception that the first line of each paragraph is indented five spaces (see Figure D.6).

Figure D.4

Full Block Format

LETTER

Bergeron, Stallworth, D'Aquilla & Dane
3687 North Causeway Boulevard
Metairie, Louisiana 70002
(504) 837-2254
Fax (504) 837-2389

March 28, 2000

Ms. Jacqueline Stoddard
1287 Napoleon Avenue
New Orleans, LA 70115

Dear Ms. Stoddard:

Enclosed are your 1999 federal income tax returns and 2000 estimated tax vouchers. Please review the returns for completeness and accuracy. You will need to sign and date the returns and send them to the Internal Revenue Service on or before April 15, 2000.

Enclose a check for $3,626 with your federal return. To make your first estimated tax payment for 2000, enclose a check for $900 with voucher 1 of Form 1040-ES. Make both checks payable to the Internal Revenue Service, and be sure to include on the checks your Social Security number, daytime phone number, and the words "1999 Form 1040/ 2000 Form 1040-ES," respectively.

We are enclosing the documents you gave us to assist in the preparation of the returns. Please preserve these records as documentation for your return.

Thank you for the opportunity once again to meet your tax service needs.

Sincerely,

Myra F. Bluestone
Certified Public Accountant

MFB/bke
Enclosures

Figure D.5

Modified Block Format

LETTER

Bergeron, Stallworth, D'Aquilla & Dane
3687 North Causeway Boulevard
Metairie, Louisiana 70002
(504) 837-2254
Fax (504) 837-2389

March 28, 2000

Ms. Jacqueline Stoddard
1287 Napoleon Avenue
New Orleans, LA 70115

Dear Ms. Stoddard:

Enclosed are your 1999 federal income tax returns and 2000 estimated tax vouchers. Please review the returns for completeness and accuracy. You will need to sign and date the returns and send them to the Internal Revenue Service on or before April 15, 2000.

Enclose a check for $3,626 with your federal return. To make your first estimated tax payment for 2000, enclose a check for $900 with voucher 1 of Form 1040-ES. Make both checks payable to the Internal Revenue Service, and be sure to include on the checks your Social Security number, daytime phone number, and the words "1999 Form 1040/ 2000 Form 1040-ES," respectively.

We are enclosing the documents you gave us to assist in the preparation of the returns. Please preserve these records as documentation for your return.

Thank you for the opportunity once again to meet your tax service needs.

Sincerely,

Myra F. Bluestone
Certified Public Accountant

MFB/bke
Enclosures

Semiblock Format

LETTER

Bergeron, Stallworth, D'Aquilla & Dane
3687 North Causeway Boulevard
Metairie, Louisiana 70002
(504) 837-2254
Fax (504) 837-2389

March 28, 2000

Ms. Jacqueline Stoddard
1287 Napoleon Avenue
New Orleans, LA 70115

Dear Ms. Stoddard:

Enclosed are your 1999 federal income tax returns and 2000 estimated tax vouchers. Please review the returns for completeness and accuracy. You will need to sign and date the returns and send them to the Internal Revenue Service on or before April 15, 2000.

Enclose a check for $3,626 with your federal return. To make your first estimated tax payment for 2000, enclose a check for $900 with voucher 1 of Form 1040-ES. Make both checks payable to the Internal Revenue Service, and be sure to include on the checks your Social Security number, daytime phone number, and the words "1999 Form 1040/ 2000 Form 1040-ES," respectively.

We are enclosing the documents you gave us to assist in the preparation of the returns. Please preserve these records as documentation for your return.

Thank you for the opportunity once again to meet your tax service needs.

Sincerely,

Myra F. Bluestone
Certified Public Accountant

MFB/bke
Enclosures

Acknowledgments

2 "Technology Trends and You," by Gregory H. Toman reprinted by permission from The Ohio Society of CPAs, *The Ohio CPA Journal,* December 1996.

6 Monster.com material reprinted by permission of Monster.com. More information about Monster.com is available at www. monster.com, or by calling 800-MONSTER.

7 Rutgers Accounting Research Center material reprinted by permission of Rutgers Accounting Research Center.

26 Questions from Interviewing with KPMG: Interviewing Tips, www.kpmgcampus.com, July 7, 1998 reprinted by permission of Bernard Milano, KPMG. "Internships," by Bernard Milano from www.kpmgcampus.com/bernie7, July 15, 1998. Reprinted by permission.

97 Material from "Author! Author!" by Gale Ruby Cohen, in *CA Magazine,* March 1993. Reproduced with permission from *CA Magazine,* published by the Canadian Institute of Chartered Accountants, Toronto, Canada.

206, 236 CPA Web Trust material reprinted with permission. ©American Institute of Certified Public Accountants, Inc.

282–284 Guess?, Inc. material reprinted courtesy of Guess?, Inc.

288–303 Gap Inc. material reprinted by permission of Gap Inc.

Index

Abrupt phrasing, 104
Absolute modifiers, A-7
Acceptance letter, 28, 29
Active listening, 167, 168
Active voice, 74
Adjective modifiers, A-6
Adverb modifiers, A-7
adverse, averse, B-1
advice, advise, B-1
affect, effect, B-1
Agenda, 183–185, 352, 353
aggravate, irritate, B-1
all ready, already, B-1
all together, altogether, B-2
allude, elude, B-2
Ambiguous modifiers, A-21
Ambiguous pronoun
    reference, A-20
among, between, B-2
amount, number, B-2
Analysis and evaluation, 138
Analytical memo (workpapers),
    373, 377–379
Annual reports, 279–311
   auditor's report, 303
   financial review section, 291–299
   financial statements, 299–303
   forward-looking statements,
      281–285
   hypertext version, 305
   introductory overview, 286–291
   management's discussion and
      analysis (MD&A), 294–299
   notes to financial statements, 303
   plain English guidelines, 285
   production cycle, 303–305
   10-K reports, 280–285
   users, 301
Antecedent, A-15
Apostrophe, C-4, C-5
as, like, B-4
Asynchronous conferences, 260
Audit engagement, 345–398
   agenda (planning meeting),
      352, 353

audit program, 357, 358
audit report (opinion letter),
    384, 385
client interviews, 358–366
communication events, 346–350
engagement letter, 350–352
management comments,
    379–384
planning meeting, 350–353
planning memo, 354–357
proposal, 350
relationship with client, 400
reportable conditions, 379, 380
workpapers, 366–379. *See also*
    Workpapers
Audit opinion letter, 384, 385
Audit program, 357, 358
Audit report, 303, 384, 385
Audit workpapers, 366–379. *See*
    also Workpapers
averse, adverse, B-1

Bar graphs, 214–218
between, among, B-2
Body movements, 165
Brainstorming, 253
brake, break, B-2
Briefings, 180
Broad pronoun reference, A-20
Budgeting, 315, 316
Business correspondence, 99–118
   bad-news messages, 116
   closing a letter or memo,
      113–116
   multipoint message, 111, 112
   organization, 107–116. *See also*
      Organization
   positive tone, 103–106
   requests to skeptical readers,
      116–118
   simple message/single point, 109
   "*you* attitude," 99–103
Business development
    meetings, 181
Business letters. *See* Letters

Capital expenditure
    planning, 315
    postaudits, 316
    proposal, 329–336
capital, capitol, B-2
Capitalization, B-6, B-7
Case (pronouns), A-16 to A-18
Chartjunk, 218, 219
Charts, 212–227
cite, site, B-2
Clarity, 78–81
Clause patterns, A-1, A-2
Clauses, A-1 to A-7
Clean opinion, 303, 345
Clichés, 71, 72
Client interviews, 358–366
Closed questions, 170, 171
Collaborative communication,
        245–277
    advantages, 247, 248
    analyze individual strengths, 257
    appoint group leader, 255, 256
    asynchronous conferences, 260
    computer conferences, 259
    conflict, 253, 254
    create a schedule, 260
    define task/problem, 256
    divide/delegate tasks, 259
    establish procedures, 259, 260
    examples, 246, 247, 261–273
    generating ideas, 253
    group communication
        technologies, 245
    group structure, 252, 253
    multiauthor collaboration,
        248, 249
    nominal groups, 253
    phone conferences, 259
    planning the project, 255–260
    primary-author collaboration,
        248, 249
College placement office, 3, 4
Colon, C-4
Comma, C-1 to C-3
Comma splice, A-10, A-11
Communication events
    audit engagement, 346–350
    tax engagement, 401–405

Communication technologies, 1, 2
Complement, A-2
complement, compliment, B-3
Complimentary close, D-5
Compound sentences, A-4, A-5
Computer conferences, 259
Concise writing, 69–73
Conjunctive adverb, A-5
Context statement, 107–109
Control function, 316
Cooperative education programs, 4
Coordinating conjunction, A-4
Copy line, D-6
Cornell split-page format, 176
Corporate planning, 314–316
Cost accountants, 315
Cover letters, 19–25
Critical evaluator, 255
Cross-cultural factors, 167, 168

Dangling modifiers, 80, A-21, A-22
Dash, C-5, C-6
Data sifting, 45
Data worksheet, 46
Deadwood, 70, 71
Defining unfamiliar terms, 43
Delayed verbs, 77
Delphi technique, 255
Dependent clause, A-4, A-6, A-7
Descending order of
        importance, 109
Devil's advocate, 255
disinterested, uninterested, B-3
Dovetailing, 53, 54
Drafting, 46–48

E-mail, 98, 99. *See also* Business
        correspondence
E-mail privacy, 98
Editing, 57, 84, 85
Editing checklist, 86
effect, affect, B-1
Electronic brainstorming, 253
Electronic résumé templates, 18
Ellipses, C-8
elude, allude, B-2
Emphatics, 104
Enclosure line, D-6

Engagement letter
   audit engagement, 350–352
   tax engagement, 401, 407,
      408, 428
Engagement proposals, 127–134
Ernst & Young, 198
Executive summary, 136
External proposals, 128

Fact-finding interviews, 168–179
   closed questions, 170, 171
   concluding the interview, 176,
      177
   conducting the interview,
      173–179
   documenting the interview,
      177–179
   note-taking, 175, 176
   open questions, 170
   planning, 169
   probing questions, 171, 172
farther, further, B-3
Faulty comparison, A-12
fewer, less, B-3
Financial accountants, 314, 315
Financial analysts, 315
Financial reporting. *See* Annual
   reports, 10-K reports
Financial statements, 299–303
Finger-pointing phrases, 104
Flowchart to illustrate narrative,
   374, 375
Flowcharts, 226–230
Forecasting statement, 111
foreword, forward, B-3
Formal definition, 43
Formal vs. informal style, 67, 68
Formats
   letters, D-3 to D-10
   memos, D-1, D-2
Formatting, 54, 55
Formulaic expressions, 71, 72
Forward-looking statements,
   281–285
Fragments, A-8 to A-10
Full block style, D-7, D-8
further, farther, B-3
Future perfect progressive tense, A-4

Future perfect tense, A-3
Future progressive tense, A-4
Future tense, A-3

Gender bias, B-7, B-8
Generally accepted auditing
   standards (GAAS), 345
Generating ideas, 253
Grammar
   clauses, A-1 to A-7
   comma splices, A-10, A-11
   grammar problems, A-8 to A-13
   incomplete constructions, A-12
   mixed constructions, A-10
      to A-12
   modifier problems, A-21 to A-23
   pronoun problems, A-15 to A-21
   run-on sentences, A-10 to A-11
   sentence problems, A-1 to A-10
   subject-verb agreement
      problems, A-13 to A-15
Graphics. *See* Visual aids
Graphs, 212–225
Group communication
   technologies, 245
Group decision-support systems
   (GDSS), 255
Group procedures worksheet,
   261, 264
Group structure, 252, 253
Group work. *See* Collaborative
   communication
Grouped bar graph, 215
Groupthink, 254, 255

Handouts, 235, 236
Homonyms, B-1 to B-9
Hostile tone, 104, 105
Hyphen, C-6

imply, infer, B-3
Incomplete constructions, A-12
Independent clause, A-4, A-5
Informal vs. formal style, 67, 68
Inside address, D-4
Instructions, 357, 358
Interactive groups, 252
Internal proposals, 127–130

Internal Revenue Code, 415
Internet
    general searches, 5
    job-search Web sites, 5–7, 20
    Web sites of accounting firms, 5
Internships, 4
Interviews
    client, 358–366
    fact-gathering, 168–179. *See also*
        Fact-finding interviews
    job, 25–28
Intranets, 98
Intransitive verbs, A-2
irritate, aggravate, B-1
it is, 72
Italics, C-8
its, it's, B-3

Job fairs, 4
Job interviews, 25–28
Job search, 3
    cover letters, 19–25
    follow up, 28–30
    interviews, 25–28
    reference sheet, 18, 19
    researching the market, 3–7
    résumés, 8–18. *See also* Résumés

Key words/phrases, 50
Kinesics, 165, 166

Latin countries, 167
lay, lie, B-4
lead, led, B-3
Learning by imitation, 67
less, fewer, B-3
Letter of acceptance, 28, 29
Letters, 96. *See also* Business
        Correspondence
    body, D-5
    complimentary close, D-5
    copy line, D-6
    enclosure line, D-6
    full block style, D-7, D-8
    heading, D-4
    inside address, D-4
    modified block style, D-7, D-9
    optional elements, D-6, D-7

salutation, D-5
semiblock style, D-7, D-10
signature, D-6
typist's initials, D-6
lie, lay, B-4
like, as, B-4
Line graphs, 218–225
Linking verbs, A-2
Listening, 167, 168
Lost signal, 176

Management comments, 379–384
Management's discussion and
        analysis (MD&A), 294–299
Managerial accounting, 313–343
    capital expenditure planning,
        and, 316, 317
    capital expenditure proposal,
        329–336
    collecting the data, 319–321
    corporate planning, and,
        314–316
    example, 317–336
    presentation to executive
        committee, 324–332
    summarizing/organizing data for
        presentation, 321–323
Meetings, 179–190. *See also* Oral
        presentations
    agenda, 183–185
    closing/following up, 189
    leading the meeting, 185–187
    notifying participants, 183
    preparing to lead, 182
    preparing to participate,
        181, 182
    preparing to present
        information, 182
    preparing your notes, 185
    sample meeting, 187, 188
    types, 179–181
Memos, 96, 97, D-1, D-2. *See also*
        Business correspondence
Misplaced modifiers, 79, A-1
Mixed constructions, 80, 81, A-10
        to A-12
Modified block style, D-7, D-9
Modified option, 303

Modifiers, A-6
    absolute, A-7
    adjective, A-6
    adverb, A-7
    ambiguous, A-21
    dangling, 80, A-21, A-22
    misplaced, 79, A-21
Monster.com, 6
Multiauthor collaboration, 249–252
Multiple choice voting, 255

Narration, 135, 136
Narratives (workpapers), 368–373
Negative statements, 78
Negative words/phrases, 103, 104
Nominal groups, 253
Nominalization, 74
Nonverbal behavior, 165–167
Note-taking, 175, 176
Notes to financial statements, 303
number, amount, B-2
Numerals vs. words, B-8

Objective case, A-16
Oft-confused words, B-1 to B-6
Open questions, 170
Oral communication, 163–243
    active listening, 167, 168
    cross-cultural factors, 167, 168
    feedback, 164, 165
    interviews, 168–179. *See also*
        Fact-finding interviews
    meetings, 179–190. *See also*
        Meetings
    nonverbal behavior, 165–167
    presentations. *See* Oral
        presentations
Oral presentations, 197–243
    analyzing audience/purpose,
        199, 200
    catching the listener's attention,
        201
    concrete examples, 204
    context/purpose of remarks,
        202, 203
    credibility, 201, 202
    delivery, 237, 238
    handouts, 235, 236

informative vs. persuasive
        presentations, 200
    introduction, 200–203
    limiting your points, 203
    organizing the information, 200
    rehearsing, 235, 237
    repeat key words/phrases, 204
    rhetorical techniques, 203–205
    stage fright, 199
    visual aids. *See* Visual aids
Organization of correspondence
    close with summaries/ask for
        action, 113–116
    create context, 107, 108
    descending order of
        importance, 109
    one idea per paragraph, 109–113
    state your purpose, 108, 109

pair, pare, B-4
Parallel structure, 52, 53
Parentheses, C-7
passed, past, B-4
Passive voice, 74, 76
Past participle, A-3
Past perfect progressive tense, A-4
Past perfect tense, A-3
Past progressive tense, A-4
Past tense, A-3
Period, C-4
Phone conferences, 259
Pie charts, 226, 227
Plain English Handbook, 81, 285
Planning, 314
Planning meeting (audit
        engagement), 350–353
Planning meetings, 181
Planning memo (audit
        engagement), 354–357
Positive tone, 103–106
Positive words/phrases, 103, 104
Possessive case, A-16
Postaudit, 316
PowerPoint, 206, 231–235
precede, proceed, B-4
Preference ranking, 255
Prepositional phrases, 72, 77,
        A-6, A-7

Present participle, A-4

Present perfect progressive tense, A-4

Present perfect tense, A-3

Present progressive tense, A-4

Present tense, A-3

Presentation to executive committee, 324–332

Presentations. *See* Oral presentations

Prewriting, 40–46

Primary-author collaboration, 248, 249

principal, principle, B-4

Private Securities Litigation Reform Act, 281

Probing questions, 171, 172

Problem-solving meetings, 180

proceed, precede, B-4

Professional communication style, 67–93

 active vs. passive voice, 73, 74

 clarity, 78–81

 concise writing, 69–73

 editing, 84, 85

 editing checklist, 86

 formal vs. informal style, 67, 68

 learning by imitation, 67

 mixed sentence constructions, 80, 81

 official language of accountancy, 68, 81–83

 SEC guidelines, 81, 285

 sentence structure, 76–78

 smothered verbs, 74–76

 unclear modifiers, 79, 80

 vague pronoun reference, 79

Pronouns, A-15 to A-20

 ambiguous reference, A-20

 broad reference, A-20

 errors in case, A-16 to A-18

 errors in gender, A-19

 errors in number, A-19

 relative, A-16, A-17

 shifts in person, A-18

 vague reference, 79

Proposals, 127–134

Proxemics, 166

Punctuation

 apostrophe, C-4, C-5

 colon, C-4

 comma, C-1 to C-3

 dash, C-5, C-6

 ellipses, C-8

 hyphen, C-6

 italics, C-8

 parentheses, C-7

 period, C-4

 quotation marks, C-7, C-8

 semicolon, C-3, C-4

Purpose statement, 108, 109

Quotation marks, C-7, C-8

Reader profile worksheet, 44

Record of phone conversation, 430

Redundant expressions, 71

Reference guides

 format, D-1 to D-10

 grammar, A-1 to A-23

 punctuation, C-1 to C-10

 usage, B-1 to B-9

Reference sheet, 18, 19

Referendum voting, 255

Reframing, 168

Relative pronouns, A-16, A-17

Reports, 131–148

 analysis and evaluation, 138

 background section, 141

 body, 142

 conclusion, 142

 instruction, 141

 narration, 135, 136

 summary, 136, 137

 visual support, 138–141. *See also* Visual aids

Requests for information (tax engagement), 401, 406–412, 428–430

Requests for proposals (RFPs), 127, 128

Requests to skeptical readers, 116–118

Restatement, 167, 168

Résumés
  activities, 15, 17
  career objective statement, 12, 14
  education, 14
  experience, 14, 15
  heading, 12
  proofreading/editing, 17, 18
  revising, 17
  samples, 13, 16
  scannable, 18
  self-assessment, 8–11
  skills, 17
Resumix, 20
Revising, 48–57
  conclusion, 55
  dovetailing, 53, 54
  formatting, 54, 55
  introduction, 49
  key words/phrases, 50
  parallel structure, 52, 53
  topic sentences, 49, 50
  transitions, 50–52
Rhetorical situation, 37–39
Run-on sentences, A-10, A-11

Salutation, D-5
Scannable résumés, 18
Second-chance meeting, 255
Securities and Exchange
    Commission (SEC), 81,
    279, 285
Self-analysis worksheet, 258
Semiblock style, D-7, D-10
Semicolon, C-3, C-4
Sentence fragments, A-8 to A-10
Sentence length, 73
Sentence structure, 76–78
Sentence types, A-5
Simple future tense, A-3
Simple past tense, A-3
Simple present tense, A-3
Simple sentences, A-5
site, cite, B-2
Skeptical readers, 116–118
Slide shows, 230–235
Smothered verbs, 74–76
Speaking, 164
Stage fright, 199

stationary, stationery, B-4
Strategic planning, 315
Stub, 208
Subject-verb agreement, A-13
    to A-15
Subjective case, A-16
Subordinating conjunction, A-5
Summaries, 136, 137
Summaries (workpapers), 373,
    376, 377
Superfluous words/phrases, 71

Tables, 207–212
Task-statement worksheet, 256, 263
Tax engagement, 399–444
  communication events, 401–405
  corporate tax engagement,
      403–421
  engagement letter, 401, 407,
      408, 428
  exit meeting, 402, 431, 436
  individual tax engagement,
      421–436
  initial meeting, 401, 424–428
  Internal Revenue Code, 415
  letters to taxing authorities, 402,
      403, 417–423
  opinion letter, 402, 415, 416
  relationship with client, 400, 403
  requests for information, 401,
      406–412, 428–430
  tax planning report, 434–436
  tax research memorandum, 402,
      409–415, 432
  transmittal letter to client,
      417–419, 433
  written record of phone
      conversation, 430
Tax planning report, 434–436
Tax research memorandum, 402,
    409–415, 432
10-K reports, 280–285. *See also*
    Annual reports
Tense, A-3, A-4
Thank-you note, 28, 29
that, which, B-5
that, who, which, B-5
their, there, they're, B-5

there are, 72
there is, 72
Tickmark descriptions, 367–371
Tickmarks, 367
Time line worksheet, 262, 265
to, too, two, B-5
Topic sentences, 49, 50, 109
Transitions, 50–52
Transitive verbs, A-2
Transmittal letter to client (tax
    engagement), 417–419, 433
Tufte, Edward R., 207
two, to, too, B-5

Unclear modifiers, 79, 80
uninterested, disinterested, B-3
Unique selling proposition
    (USP), 205
Unqualified option, 303, 345
Update meetings, 180
Usage
    capitalization, B-6, B-7
    gender bias, B-7, B-8
    numerals vs. words, B-8
    word choice problems, B-1
        to B-6

Vague pronoun reference, 79
Variance analysis, 316
Verb tenses, A-3, A-4
Verbals, A-8
Verbs
    delayed, 79
    intransitive, A-2
    linking, A-2
    smothered, 74–76
    transitive, A-2
Videoconferences, 198
Visual aids, 138–141, 205–236
    bar graphs, 214–218
    chartjunk, 218, 219
    distortion, 217, 218, 220, 222–225
    flowcharts, 226–230
    graphs, 212–225
    guidelines, 207, 230
    handouts, 235, 236
    line graphs, 218–225

pie charts, 226, 227
    slide shows, 230–235
    tables, 207–212
Visual anchor, 205
*Visual Display of Quantitative
    Information, The*
    (Tufte), 207
Vocalics, 166
Voice, 73, 74

weather, whether, B-5
which, that, B-5
who, which, that, B-5
who's, whose, B-5
Word choice problems, B-1 to
    B-6
Workpaper review process, 379
Workpapers
    analyses of work performed, 373,
        377–379
    flowchart to illustrate narrative,
        374, 375
    narratives, 368–373
    review, 379
    summaries, 373, 376, 377
    tickmark descriptions, 367–371
World Wide Web. *See* Internet
Writing process, 40–57
    drafting, 46–48
    editing, 57
    prewriting, 40–46
    revising, 48–57. *See also* Revising
Writing self-assessment statement,
    266, 267
Written communication
    letters, 96. *See also* Business
        correspondence
    memos, 96, 97. *See also* Business
        correspondence
    proposals, 127–134
    reports, 131–148. *See also* Reports
Written record of phone
    conversation, 430

"You attitude," 99–103
your, you're, B-6